Best Wishes and Go Big Red!

Diary of a Husker

David 74 Kolowski 1998-2002

by

David Kolowski

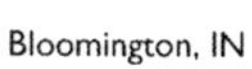
Bloomington, IN

Milton Keynes, UK

AuthorHouse™
1663 Liberty Drive, Suite 200
Bloomington, IN 47403
www.authorhouse.com
Phone: 1-800-839-8640

AuthorHouse™ UK Ltd.
500 Avebury Boulevard
Central Milton Keynes, MK9 2BE
www.authorhouse.co.uk
Phone: 08001974150

First published by AuthorHouse 12/26/2006

ISBN: 1-4259-6242-4 (sc)

Library of Congress Control Number: 2006909110

Printed in the United States of America
Bloomington, Indiana

This book is printed on acid-free paper.

To my wife Lauren, my parents Rick and Bonnie, my brother Jason and his wife Stacy Markus, and all the other friends, family, players, and coaches that gave me so much to write about.

Table of Contents

Preface

This journal was written during the five years that I was a part of the Nebraska Cornhuskers football team. I wrote what I experienced, as things happened and as much as I knew about them. This is the story of my life for five years on one of the best college football teams in the nation during one of their most tumultuous eras in recent memory.

Before I joined the Huskers, they had been a team that was synonymous with success. Legendary head coaches like Bob Devaney and Tom Osborne had lengthy careers at the top of the college football world. For several decades, Nebraska was one of the most well-known teams in the world. In the 1990's, Nebraska seemed to always be in the national championship spotlight. The Huskers were in four national championship games that decade, winning three of them. They were also in three Big XII conference championships, winning two of them. "Husker Power" was felt across the nation, led by a strong running game that ate up the clock and wore down defenses. This is where my story picks up.

Foreword from Eric Crouch

When I came to the University of Nebraska, I had very high expectations for my time on the football field. I just came from a very successful high school football program at Millard North (in Omaha) and I was entering a very important part of my life as a student and an athlete. After accepting the offer to play for the Huskers, I was very excited about my future at the University of Nebraska, but I still didn't know what exactly to expect.

I remember being called to Head Coach Tom Osborne's office after my first training camp in 1997. He told me that it was in the best interest of the team and my career if I took a medical red shirt year. I was floored to hear this news, but I knew he was right. I took Coach Osborne's advice and was placed on a medical red shirt. There were two reasons I was placed on the medical red shirt list. The first was that I needed two operations. The second reason was that I wasn't going to see any playing time anyway. Scott Frost was the starter at the time and Frankie London and Bobby Newcombe were also in the picture at quarterback.

Being injured and out for the year was difficult for me to handle. I was morbidly depressed and home sick during this time. I honestly felt that I would never be the same. I still remember the day that I left the hospital in a wheelchair with a cast on each leg. What a hit to my ego! It was very painful, although it wasn't that serious in hindsight. I basically had to stay off my legs for two weeks straight. I could barely get off of the bed to reach my crutches. My ankle felt like it had a compound fracture and I remember other players telling me it looked like I was attacked by a shark when they saw the scar behind my left knee.

Towards the end of the season I had the opportunity to play on the scout team. I got to know a lot of the other players during that time. Athletes that were on the scout team were mainly new guys and there was a mix of scholarship and walk-on players. This mixture of teammates gave me the opportunity to get to know and build relationships with most of new players on the team. It was a very important time for most of us because it allowed us to bond with one another.

This bonding is what people in the sports industry always talk about. When a football team has great camaraderie and chemistry, they have a better chance for success. Camaraderie and chemistry are formed by taking small steps. The first step was to build a solid relationship with your teammates. However, I definitely sensed that there was an abnormal amount of animosity on the scout team. I felt that every player was not content with being on the scout team. Most players felt they were not getting a fair chance or that they were better than the guy ahead of them on the depth chart. To be honest, you had to have that feeling. That feeling meant that you wanted more, you wanted to compete and you wanted to be the best. You needed to have that feeling about yourself or you probably didn't deserve to be there. Similarly, if you were content to be on the scout team, it was unlikely you would ever play.

Most of the teammates were very cool, and in return I

was cool to them. I never felt like there was anyone on the team that I didn't get along with. I can remember sitting next to all the quarterbacks in the locker room and having a special bond between us. It was like we always had each other's back even though we were competing against each other for a job. I know this sounds weird, but it's true. I think this was the reason we had so much success. It didn't matter what position we were or our place on the depth chart. What mattered is that we came together for one common goal. That goal was to win the game on Saturday.

Among the quarterbacks, we discovered that we had something in common between our personal and professional goals; we all wanted to be successful in whatever we did. We worked hard to build this success and in the process became leaders on and off the field. Our teammates looked up to us to make the decisions. It was a lot of pressure, but our success as a team depended on the quarterbacks taking control.

Imagine spending eight hours a day thinking about football; in meetings, on the practice field, you name it. With so much effort put into it, you have to start believing in something. As a quarterback you have to make people believe in you. Your friends and family start relying on you to make quick and efficient decisions. I felt like I had a special bond with not only the quarterbacks, but every player on the team. This feeling took some time to develop. I had this feeling after my medical red shirt year in 1998. I knew I was not going to be the starting quarterback that year, but I ended up starting 8 games and playing in 11.

I had a strong will to succeed, and believed that I could lead the Huskers to success. I had the silent confidence that was necessary and I also had deep motivation from many sources. Most of my motivation stemmed from outside factors. Growing up, I was always told that I was too small, too short, too slow or whatever. Believe me, that was enough motivation for me. This same motivation now pushed me to compete for the starting quarterback job.

The process I went through to be the first string quarterback in 1999 was a character builder for me. I competed with Bobby Newcombe and Frankie London all spring, summer and fall camp for the starting job. Yet, at the beginning of the season I was not the starting quarterback. I was very shocked that I didn't get to start and almost quit playing football at that point in my career. Instead, I told head coach Frank Solich that I would do anything to get on the field to help the team win. I just wanted to play. I was told that I would get that opportunity as a receiver, so I changed positions. I was also told that I would still be used at quarterback at some point in the game.

The first game of the 1999 season was a road game against the University of Iowa. At the beginning of the game, I was told by coach Solich and quarterbacks coach Turner Gill that I could see some game-time in the second quarter. We were struggling in the second quarter when my number was called. I came into the game and we ended up routing Iowa 42 to 7.

This may have been a good starting point for my college career, but I believe it was actually the next game against the University of California at Berkley. I replaced Bobby again in the second quarter of the game and had a touchdown running, throwing and catching. The next day, the Lincoln Journal Star was comparing me to the 1972 Heisman Trophy Winner Johnny Rogers. I was named the new starter that next week against Southern Mississippi. From then on, I was the starting quarterback for the 1999, 2000, and 2001 seasons.

During my career at Nebraska I was fortunate enough to make many friends on the football team. I had the opportunity to get to know many of the walk-on players. I felt that walk-ons were a very important part of the success at Nebraska. They were definitely a much bigger part of the success than they were credited for. I remember that the walk-on program allowed for our team to have around 185 athletes. We were able to practice with three teams getting reps at each practice. That meant that our first, second and third team players were all getting prepared for the upcoming game. Most universities could only prepare the first and second team depth charts because they did not have the number of players that Nebraska had. Thanks to this depth, if we had an injury during the game, we had another player that could come in and perform like nothing ever happened.

The walk-on athletes had things a bit different than the scholarship athletes. There were the obvious things like having to pay for books, tuition and other college needs. For several guys, this meant possibly having another job on the side. I really had a great amount of respect for walk-ons. I felt like they really wanted to be a part of the program like anyone else, but I also felt like they had to try harder to get there. Since they didn't have the security of the scholarship, they had to impress the coaches more often and be able to do more on the field.

There have been several walk-ons that have become starters at Nebraska and went on to have great professional careers, but for the majority that does not happen. The walk-ons were against all odds and I respected them for that reason. For many walk-ons, I guess it came down to being a part of the team at Nebraska, because I know that I would not have been able to do what many walk-ons did. They were able to stick it out when they knew they were not going to play.

There were some players that never got to play at Nebraska in their four or five years on the team. They practiced everyday, went through training camp every year, but never got one snap in a game. That didn't happen very often because most players got some sort of playing time during our huge wins, but it did happen to a few. I know that I would have had trouble with that, and that is why I have so much respect for what they did and how they did it.

I would like to thank the walk-ons for what they did. If it wasn't for them, I don't know that I would have had the success that I did at Nebraska. As matter of fact, I know that I would not have had the success I did. The diary that follows, written by fellow teammate David Kolowski, is the complete story of the life of a walk-on at the University of Nebraska.

Eric Crouch
August, 2006

1998 Summer

Here I am in the summer after high school graduation getting ready to be a part of one of the biggest college football programs in the country. The Huskers are fresh off of winning the National Championship this last year, not to mention three of the past four years, so I know I definitely have my work cut out for me.

As a high school freshman, I would not have believed it if someone had told me I would play for the Huskers one day. It's every Nebraska boy's dream to play for the Huskers. Born and raised in Omaha, we were an hour away from Memorial Stadium, which becomes Nebraska's third largest city on game days and I saw several games there when I was growing up. But, in high school I was undersized; 5'11" and 175 pounds, the second-string center for the *B* team, without much muscle or any real chances of playing. I remember testing out before the season started, where the coaches make you run, jump and do all sorts of things so they can narrow you down for which team they want you on. I stepped up to the line for the 40 yard dash for the first time in my life and took off, noticing the look of amazement on the faces as I flew past. At least that was what I thought until I got my time. Seven seconds flat. Pathetically slow.

It took me a while to develop the necessary skills to be a good player. My dad taught me how to long snap (snapping the ball for punts and field goals), and this has been one of those skills that really helped me get noticed. My dad was also a big influence on me being a lineman, teaching me what he knew after being a standout lineman for Lake Forrest College and then being drafted by the Kansas City Chiefs.

By my senior year I was 6'4", 245 pounds. My offensive line coach, Mr. Joe Vojtech, kept encouraging me about my potential and I started to see it, too. My frame was coming into shape and that was one of the things recruiters looked for. If I had been unable to get bigger and had a body that could not support a lot of muscle, the Huskers would have never considered me.

I was not highly recruited as a high school senior. Most of my recruiting letters came from Division 3 colleges in Nebraska and the Midwest. My first letter from the Huskers was a simple form letter telling the basics of the program. I dismissed it as a formality because I had attended the Husker summer clinic for the previous three years, but I quickly realized they were serious. I was invited to the last three home games and each time had a student escort (always a very beautiful one—apparently they want to make these recruiting visits as pleasant as possible). We had a buffet lunch, met the coaches, and Coach Tom Osborne gave us a little speech before he went to the locker room. For these types of recruiting visits, the NCAA allows the team to provide three free tickets for myself and my parents. They were pretty nice seats, right on the 30-yard line and up about 15 rows. Before taking our seats we watched from the sidelines as the team warmed up. Parents had to leave the field and then the recruits got to see the team run onto the field. This was the biggest thrill to watch—the sensation of the loud, pulsing music making everyone in the stadium clap in unison and then hearing the roar of the crowd as the players charged onto the field was overwhelming.

In mid-November I was informed that the Huskers wanted me to walk-on. This meant they wanted me on the team, but didn't want me enough to waste a scholarship on me. This was a big gamble on their part because they were relying solely on potential. I was not one of the best, but I guess they felt I would develop to the best of my ability under the walk-on program. It also was a gamble on my part. I needed to decide if I wanted to go to a school where I was not guaranteed a position. I hoped that my long-snapping skills would allow me to play a small role in a huge organization but it was possible that I would never play. My decision was further complicated when legendary Head Coach Tom Osborne retired a short time later. Unsure of the future, I took the chance to be on the best team in the nation and hoped to prove myself on the field.

I'm so nervous leading up to the first day of workouts in Lincoln that I almost got in a car accident that would have been entirely my fault. I'm not sure what's ahead of me, but I can guess it's going to be a lot of hard work.

> Later on, I learned that my invitation to walk-on was not as valuable as I thought. The program was overflowing with walk-ons. Offers were made to guys all across the country to walk on and who wouldn't want to be on this team after the four years they just had with three National Championships? Their gamble on me as well as many other guys was backed by the fact that they'd have a live blocking dummy for five years. My freshman year we had more than 180 guys on the team. Only about 40 guys play in a single game, leaving 140 others to do

nothing but practice.

All of the fellow walk-ons had all done fairly well in high school football, so to come to college and find up to six guys ahead of you on the depth chart was very discouraging. With the coaches struggling just to learn everyone's name, the possibility of impressing them seemed very limited. Instead of a close-knit group of athletes working hard to make each other better, we slowly turned into divided positional groups with a lot of fighting and backstabbing to try to get a starting spot.

As time wore on, many guys had mentally given up and were just sticking around for the benefits. Their example was followed by the next round of new guys who saw that hard work will only get a person nowhere unless you're on scholarship or a coach's favorite. Apathy abounded. Intensity decreased. We knew we wouldn't play but knew how much to do to not get cut, and we didn't care anymore. The inevitable decline of the team will become clearer later on. I'll do my best to foreshadow what is necessary throughout the rest of this book.

1998 Summer Conditioning

The off-season program starts soon after the last game is played. After a couple of weeks off for rest and rehabilitation, the workouts begin and continue through the winter and summer straight into fall. Some guys even graduate from high school midway through their senior year and start up with the team in January. This gives them the opportunity to go through spring practices and really have a leg up on the other guys coming in. The rest of us show up for summer conditioning (if we're close enough to Lincoln) and this is where it all starts.

The workout program for the summer conditioning lasts about 10 weeks on average. With only weekends and Wednesdays off, the workouts keep you busy. This first summer, we did our running workout right before the lifting workout in the evening. In later years we would split that up so we would lift in the morning and run in the evening. Either way, a lot of time and energy went into these sessions.

Monday, June 8, 1998

Today was the first time I entered Memorial Stadium as a Husker. I arrived at the South Stadium complex (a building tucked neatly under the south end of the stadium that houses the football offices, training room, and locker room) at 5:00 this evening to start my workouts with the team. Another major structure under the west side of the stadium houses the cafeteria, academic center, and weight room as well as a mini hall of fame museum. I found the cafeteria and joined the rest of the team for a meeting. We were given information about eligibility and rules, and our new head coach Frank Solich talked about Louisiana Tech, our first opponent. He read a whole list of accomplishments, records, and national rankings that have been posted by Tech and told us to start thinking about them now. The freshmen had to introduce themselves by standing up and saying their name and high school, and I actually got tongue tied just trying to do that! I guess the excitement of being in a place that is so sacred to all of Nebraska was getting to me. I then went to the training room to take a small physical and sign a waiver that said the university is legally covered for me to use the weight room. I finally made it to the weight room and met up with Chad and Luke Smith, brothers who also are walking on, and one of the weight room staff. We had a fairly simple workout but I became surprisingly sore later. After lifting, I filled up my squirt bottle with some recovery mix and headed back to Omaha. I think I'm going to like it here.

> Connected to the weight room was a small room with some cardio equipment but also some offices for the sports nutritionist who regulates our meals and makes suggestions to certain guys about their weight. This room also had drink dispensers with a Gatorade-type energy mix drink and a thick, high calorie meal supplement drink called recovery mix. The nutrition staff also was responsible for getting us our creatine before and after workouts.

Later, the NCAA barred schools from supplying any supplements.

Tuesday, June 9, 1998

I arrived slightly late, even though I didn't realize it. Nobody spread the word to me that I was supposed to be there for earlier offensive-line drills in the Pit. *(The Pit is the old fieldhouse at the north end of the stadium that has since been destroyed in the name of progress).* I'll need to be here on time every day to make a good impression, even though the coaches aren't allowed to be a part of this. The NCAA forbids the coaching staff (excluding strength coaches) from interacting with the athletes in any coaching capacity except during specified times like spring practices and the regular season.

The strength coaches so far have picked apart many of my lifts to help me do them better. In particular, squat was one of the lifts that needed a lot of work and I ended up having to back the weight down quite a bit. It's become pretty apparent that most of the guys who come out of high school who say they can squat over 400 pounds actually were using terrible form and had to be broken down to a very light weight for their own good.

Thursday, June 11, 1998

We were warned about being late to the Offensive Line workouts, but it had to happen for someone. Incoming freshman Wes Cody showed up late and was bound to pay for it later, valid excuse or not. We started practice with light warm-up and stretching, and then we started some drills on a sled loaded with blocking dummies.

We spent about a half hour on the sled work, then the fun began. We all went out onto the field to watch Wes Cody run steps as punishment for being late, and of course the freshmen had to join in, too. The south part of the stadium has about 100 rows of seats and the stairs get steeper the higher you go. All five of the freshmen, including me, staggered ourselves along the steps and cheered Wes on by singing the great Village People song, "YMCA," while doing the actions, of course. Then we all had to run stairs while singing "Macho Man." I was lightheaded when I was doing the sled, but now I felt like I was going to die. When we finished, my legs were quivering, my shirt was soaked, and my mouth was parched, but I knew I had to stick it out.

I made my way to the weight room taking short, slow steps. My legs were too tired to support me so I tried not to bend them. After a short rest, I started my lifting routine and lifted with some new guys. It's a good thing this was an easy lifting day because I was worn out.

I'm amazed at how friendly everyone is here. You can't pass another player without saying 'hi' and the older players introduce themselves to me before I even know they're there. I guess the mentality of the team is that we are all some of the best athletes in the state and everyone is unified by the desire to be the best and do the best. Here, you aren't just playing for your team or your school; you're playing for your state.

Monday, June 15, 1998

Today was a pretty good day. We worked on learning some of the offensive line plays and with the help of the older guys, I think we're progressing pretty quickly.

Another guy showed up late to practice and earned himself four sets of steps. As before, freshmen spread out along the steps and this time we had to take our shirts off and do a hula dance (Dominic Raiola was the reason for this. He's from Hawaii and wore an ugly pair of Hawaiian shorts to practice. His punishment was to stand at the top of the stairs and sing the University of Hawaii's theme song while doing the hula). Luckily, we didn't have to run a set.

In the weight room Jason Schwab (starting tackle and former walk-on) called me over and told me that he liked my hustle today. It's a big compliment to hear this from one of the veteran upperclassmen and it basically made my day.

The nutritionist, Dave Ellis, checked our body fat percentage today. They keep a running total of all the guys here and I started out at 17%, weighing 275. This is a pretty good report for a lineman, even though Ellis thought that I need to fill out my shoulders a lot more. Hopefully my late-developing body will allow this to happen.

Thursday, June 18, 1998

I was way too close to being late today. The trains near the stadium cut me off, but I sped the rest of the way and ran into the Pit with one minute to spare. We had a relatively easy workout, which really surprised me, and we didn't have to run stairs.

I had a good, quick lifting workout and then a couple other freshmen and I went back to the fieldhouse to work on the O-line drills to improve on our overall footwork and timing with the sled. I think it really helped.

Monday, June 22, 1998

We started agility drills today. After an incredibly long warm-up period, we started on the jump ropes. This one got to me. We did a lot of work with different shuffle steps, crossovers and other footwork all while jumping the rope and moving 15 yards as quickly as possible. I need a lot of work on this. We then ran some cones and bags courses, and I thought I did pretty well. Then we did low ropes (basically a rope ladder laid on the ground with two columns of 10 squares) which I had a little trouble with at the start but finished fairly strong. We're supposed to run over the ropes, stepping in each square either once or twice as fast as we can and then sprint out at the end. We then went to the northwest fieldhouse and worked on some pass protection with the defense.

After all the O-line stuff, Jason Schwab, Adam Julch (the other starting tackle), Justin Valencia (another new walk-on) and I went out to the field and worked on some more pass protection. Jason has proven to be one of the nicest guys I've met. He seems genuine in his desire to help me along the way. I guess he remembers how overwhelming it was his freshman year. I think he sees some potential in me and I know he's right. I'm going to give this my all to become the best I can be, but I know it won't happen overnight and will take a lot of patience on my part to put up with disappointment here and there.

Thursday, June 25, 1998

Today I got a taste of how hot it can get for the summer workouts. It was 95 degrees today (about 110 degrees on the field) and I was already tired from being at new student enrollment all day. I started off strong in the drills but in the transition from the low ropes to the jump ropes, I got sidetracked by having to do push-ups so I had to run the jump ropes without much of a break. I had just enough time to get my mouth wet at the fountain and that had to last me. I made it to the jump rope station and did much better this time, thanks to a little overtime we put in the other day. With the sun beating down, my shoes felt like ovens and I could feel with every step that I was getting blisters. My feet were on fire, my head was light, my legs were shaking, and my lungs felt like they were going to implode but I knew I had to remain strong. I managed to finish, using up all my energy to show the guys I won't do anything halfway.

After a good break in the drink room, I did my complete lifting workout and went home entirely exhausted.

Thursday, July 2, 1998

I showed up late to the practice, apparently they moved the stretching and warm-up session to 5:15 and nobody told us. That didn't matter, luckily, and I jumped right into the stretching. We started on the low ropes and I've improved a lot. Many of the players noticed this and complimented me. John Archer, the head strength coach who also works with the O-line, told me I looked a lot better and that my footwork is really looking good. I also did some long snaps to Schwab and Russ Hochstein (sophomore guard) and they were impressed with that also. I think I'm beginning to be accepted into the Huskers.

There is lifting at 6:00 tomorrow morning but I will be on my way to Illinois to see family for the Fourth of July. There was talk today about a punishment for those who miss lifting but how am I to get around it? I guess I'll just take what they give me and have to live with it.

Monday, July 13, 1998

In our drills today Archer and Heskew complimented me on almost everything we did. On the other hand, I started the jump rope circuit with a rope that was too short and had trouble with many of the drills. I later changed ropes and did much better.

It was blistering hot and humid today and the heat took its toll on all of us. During the pass pro drills with the defense, one excessive block turned into a potential brawl between the offense and defense. Luckily, most of us still had cool heads and stopped it immediately. The veterans told us that this happens a lot so we should stick together and fight as a group. I think this is just stupid. We are some of the best players in the nation brought together to play as a team. If we begin to divide into separate gangs where we need to watch out for each other, we've lost our unity. Somebody is bound to mess up or have a disagreement with another player but the solution should not be a fight.

Monday, July 27, 1998

I heard today was a pretty hard practice. I wouldn't know because I spent some time with the police and a tow truck after falling asleep at the wheel and driving my mom's Buick straight into a median. I was really tired after spending the last week at the Shrine Bowl camp and as well as working all day today (the Shrine Bowl is like a high school all-star game and included some of the hottest practices I've ever been through. I played as back-up center in the game and helped come away with the win). I walked away without injury but the car was totaled. When I got home my missed workout was replaced with carrying 45 railroad ties with my dad from the driveway to the backyard. That oughta do it.

Tuesday, July 28, 1998

I was set up with a job by the Huskers at a computer company called Inacom here in Omaha. I won't move to Lincoln until school starts in the fall, so I have to drive an hour each way to get to the afternoon workouts. Today, I left work after two hours and went home to sleep until the workout. I would do this every day if it wouldn't get me fired. It looks like I won't have a vehicle at all for my freshman year after wrecking my mom's.

The workout was a little more intense today but I did just fine. I think the Shrine Bowl helped me get into better shape. After the lifting I was ready to go home and crash but this time I made it home and crashed on the living room floor and not in my car.

Friday, July 31, 1998

With two-a-day practices starting Monday, this is the

last day the upperclassmen have complete control over the freshmen and they lived it up. They made us do sit-ups and push-ups, with a couple of extra sets just for fun. Then Adam Julch and Jason Schwab made us run steps in the north end zone. We did enough steps to make us all incredibly worn out (probably 10 or more sets—I lost track). After a long rest break, we crawled into the weight room and did a perfunctory lifting job.

I won't be involved in the two-a-day practices this year (also known as Fall Camp), because there's an NCAA rule that only 105 players can go through the practices. The scholarship freshmen are the only freshmen required to participate. Once school is in session, I'll be able to join the team for practices.

Tuesday, August 4, 1998

I picked up Justin Valencia and headed in for a voluntary workout. The two of us doubled the number of people in the weight room. We did a good, quick workout and left. I don't really mind not going to two-a-days but I know I'm missing out on a lot of important stuff that will put the scholarship freshman further ahead of me. I guess that means I'll just have to work that much harder.

Thursday, August 6, 1998

Today was probably the hardest and most intense conditioning practice we've had. We had a group of 18 freshmen and did a variety of speed and agility drills, which left all of us entirely exhausted. It's still better than two-a-days.

Monday, August 17, 1998

Last Saturday, I went to a funeral. It was for a good friend and all-around great guy named Jared Russell. He was involved in a car accident while driving on a beer run at very high speeds. This shows how quickly and how strangely things can happen. I don't know if he had been drinking, but in Jared's memory I am making a pledge to myself to not drink in college. Truthfully, I have drank before so I know what it's like and I wasn't all that thrilled with it anyways. I don't think that it is very fun to willfully limit control of your motor skills. I also had an alcoholic grandfather who took his own life before I ever met him, which makes my pledge even more personal. I know that this will be a very difficult pledge to keep but I need to stay strong and not get caught up in the peer pressure and the college culture.

> Sadly, this was one promise I didn't keep. I underestimated what I was getting into; the friends I would make, the atmosphere of peer pressure, and sometimes just the simple desire to take the night off mentally and escape to a drunken stupor. As you'll continue to see, when football takes more control of my life, sometimes it was the only sure way to get away, if only temporarily. Looking back, I'm disappointed that I let myself do that, that I did that to my body, and that I wasted so much time and money in this stupid pursuit. What's even worse is that I was not the only one who came in with such a plan and ended up failing.

Saturday, August 22, 1998

All the new guys were tested today, which included taking numerous measurements and doing 10- and 40-yard dashes, vertical jump, and agility running. Two 300-yard shuttle runs were the incentive to reach a certain level but I fell short. The shuttle is 25 yards, down and back until you've covered 300 yards total in less than an average of 64 seconds for linemen, and you have a five-minute break before doing it again. If you fail it, you'll run it again another day until you get it. I missed the right composite time by just a few seconds so I will have to do it again later. My body fat decreased 2% to 15% since the first test in the summer, which is really good. I had a little stomach flu before the test and my weight dropped from 285 pounds after dinner last night to 271 this morning. (My parents took me out for Mexican food last night and I had a case of diarrhea today. Actually, I thought I just had gas and then discovered quite by accident that it was diarrhea while I was on my way to testing. With no spare clothes to change into, I did the best I could in the bathroom and went on with the testing. I don't think anyone really noticed, except for the poor guy who was testing my leg flexibility by stretching me out while I was on my back.)

After testing I got my equipment fitted and they gave me two pairs of shorts, my jersey (number 53), shoes which fit like a dream, and a media guide. We put our jerseys and red shorts on and then went out for Photo Day. I got my mug shot for the program taken along with an action shot, a team photo in the bleachers, and a team panoramic photo on the field. After that, 8,000 people streamed into the stadium to get autographs. The freshmen didn't have seats on the field so we sat in the stadium seats, which turned out to be better because we were out of the sun. Even though we were pretty far up, people still lined up for our signatures. I signed my name at least 100 times on posters, footballs, t-shirts, notebooks, and whatever else the fans brought in with them. We had a team meeting after Photo Day, and on the way out I borrowed some food laying out in the varsity locker room and headed back to the dorm for the rest of the day.

1998 Season

The regular practice day goes something like this. Classes in the morning and done by 2:00 in the afternoon at the latest. The team meeting starts promptly at 2:00 and we go over any important issues or news about the upcoming game. The team then breaks up into positions and each group goes to their coach's office to analyze game and practice film. Scout team guys are dismissed to go lift, get taped, relax, or do whatever they need to do before practice starts.

At 3:30, the practice whistle blows and we get going. Warming up and stretching is done with your position; those coaches have you for about 45 minutes to go over specifics. Then everyone gathers on the main field and we start running plays as a scout offense into the first- and second-string defense and vice versa with a scout defense. The scout teams mimic what our opponent will most likely do, so we do our best but most often we just get demolished. The intensity quickly grows through the rest of practice, broken only by a short session during which we practice special teams, and culminates with intense play. Monday and Wednesday we run two gassers (sprinting sideline to sideline twice), and other days vary in intensity depending on when the game is. The day immediately before a game is always just a half-hour walk-through in sweats. The two to three days before that (usually Tuesday and Wednesday) are very intense.

One interesting thing that I noticed this first year as well as the following years is that the scout teams tend to mature very quickly. We start out as a bunch of guys who don't know each other and have never played with each other, but when we are facing the top defense and prodded by the coaches to perform, it's amazing how quickly we develop into a group that is 10 times as good than where we were at the start of the week.

After practice many of the guys finish their lifting, shower, and go eat at the training table. Then, for freshmen, study hall is held from 7:00 to 9:00 in the evening. It all makes for a long day.

Monday, August 24, 1998

The first day of classes was okay, then came the moment we've all been waiting for: the first practice. I got to the locker room early and got my new equipment—a pair of grass shoes (which I hear don't feel too good), a t-shirt, jock, helmet, and later I got my practice jersey. After a team meeting I got my ankles taped and had a little time to relax before heading out to the field for punt snaps.

I thought I did pretty well with my snaps. I didn't have any wild ones like some of the other guys. When practice began I joined the O-line in the Pit and stretched out. I went with the centers and we did some basic blocks on each other, focusing on footwork and hand placement. I was then used as a body in the defense while the first string ran plays against us.

We then went to the field and broke into two scout teams. I switched with both the run and the pass teams because they needed a center to rotate. After a couple of plays in which we literally got blown away, I realized we were going against the number one and two defenses. Most of the guys on the scout team were new today so many of us had a tough time adjusting. It has been a while since most of us practiced in full pads.

The defense got mad at us a couple of times because of miscommunication and minor mistakes that accompany the first day of practice. One of the biggest problems was the center-quarterback exchange while snapping the ball. I know how to do this but one of the quarterbacks just couldn't take a snap if his life depended on it. The quarterbacks started just holding the ball from the start and the plays went a lot smoother and quicker. We then did some punt team against the first-team defense and I alternated the center job with Wes Cody (a scholarship lineman in my class). Coach Solich talked a little bit at the end and then we ran gassers. We did two of them in less than 40 seconds each, and we cheated a lot by stopping about five yards away from the opposite sideline, which shortened the running greatly. We also took off right when Coach raised the whistle, which gave us an extra second. I made those easily and then we circled up, stretched, and did three sets of 25 sit-ups.

We then lifted, which I was really too tired to do but I did it anyway. Then I showered, ate, and sat through a study hall orientation until 9:30. Then I was free.

The practice was easier than I expected, which surprised me. It was very intense, however; they don't like you going half-speed for much of anything. It was all very quick and precisely planned to the minute.

Wednesday, August 26, 1998

It was a rainy afternoon so we worked out in Cook Pavilion, an indoor field located just to the east of the grass fields and connected to the Campus Recreation Building. We were in shorts and jerseys, and the hitting was toned down a little but sometimes not enough. Even though I'm just on the scout team, I'm working as hard as I can. If I don't give a good effort, the guys I'm going against won't get a good look at what's coming Saturday. Even though I'm not as good as the guys they will play against, I need to give it all I've got to help our guys be the best they can be.

I snapped most of the punts during the scout punt team and Nelson Barnes, the rush-end coach, pulled me aside to make sure Coach Dan Young knew I could long snap. (Young is an assistant offensive line coach and kicking coach). I think this is a good sign that the coaches are noticing me and realizing what I can do, even if it's only long snapping for now.

So far I've gotten a new pair of shoes every day. Now I have shoes for dry turf, wet turf, and grass.

Thursday, August 27, 1998

This is a typical day for me:

Wake up at 8:00 and shower if I have the energy

Eat breakfast at the dorm

Go to classes (three on Monday and Tuesday, two the rest of the week)

Eat lunch at the Hewit Center

Go to the locker room and get taped and dressed

2:00 team meeting in the auditorium, usually about 15 minutes

Return to locker room (only linemen who will play go to the group meeting in offensive line coach Milt Tenopir's office)

Lift and/or relax until 3:15 (watch TV, take a nap, finish getting dressed)

3:20 snap to punters

3:30 start practice, warm up within groups and do basic work with those guys

4:15 scout team runs plays against defense

5:00 special teams practice

5:30 practice ends, start conditioning (two gassers on Monday and Wednesday)

Stretching with O-line, sit-ups

Finish lifting

Shower

Eat dinner at Hewit Center

Study hall (7:45-10:00, Monday-Thursday)

Go home to finish up any work and then go to bed

Jim Tansey, a junior tackle, has been an enormous help to me so far. He's probably the easiest to talk to of all the older guys on the team and I've learned a lot about the program from him. He has even shared some privileged information about stuff that I hope never happens to me. I'm not sure how much of it is true but supposedly in the past few years, the older guys have kidnapped the younger linemen from their dorms late at night, taken them to some secluded location and then done something disgusting to humiliate them. The story we heard was that the freshmen were all stripped naked and forced to watch porn. The first one to show any sign of arousal got beat up.

Friday, August 28, 1998

The day before a game is supposed to be light, and this one lived up to it. All I did was stretch and re-do the 300-yard shuttle run, which I made under the required 64 seconds. After that I was dead tired. I had done most of my lifts before practice so all I had to do was heavy squat, which I kept light, doing 275 x 10 for the final set. Then I was officially worn out. I went to the locker room and relaxed for a while, and then went to a barbecue for athletes out on the track. I was free the rest of the night.

Saturday, August 29, 1998

Nebraska 56 – Louisiana Tech 27

Today was the first time I watched a game as a Husker. It felt different from other Husker games that I've attended because I knew what went on to get here. I know the difficulties the team has had. I could better picture myself playing out there, like my dad always told me to do, because I actually went up against most of these guys. The game seemed kind of slow but it was still a win.

As a player, I'm allotted four tickets that I can sign over to anyone, in addition to the free ticket for me to sit in the student section. During the week of the game I have to go to the ticket office and designate who will get my tickets. Those people then have to show identification on game day to receive their tickets. It probably would be fairly easy to just sign someone up and then sell the tickets but the coaches have warned us against doing that, saying there are stiff penalties for such actions.

There were a lot of parties after the game. We kept the police busy as we hopped from house to house looking for a party that hadn't been busted up yet.

Monday, August 31, 1998

Today was the new "typical Monday" where we practice with only shoulder pads and helmets. The first half of practice I just stood around in the defensive formations for the offensive line to read. The second half I was on the scout team running University of Alabama-Birmingham plays against the number one's and number two's. I have a long way to go if I want to be an effective member of the O-line. My strength is increasing, thanks to the proper nutrition I get from the training table combined with the workouts, which are intentionally harder for freshmen redshirts.

Tuesday, September 1, 1998

The temperature outside today was hot and so were the tempers. On one play, rush end Chris Kelsay knocked down Nate Kolterman, a freshman scholarship tackle who is quickly becoming known for his love of fighting. Kolterman then pushed Kelsay as he was walking back to the huddle and a little shoving match took place. Chad Kelsay, Chris' brother and fellow rush end, finally stepped in and stopped the fight before it got out of hand. In another battle, a defensive end and a running back got into a full-out wrestling match and the defensive guy ended up sitting on top of the running back, punching him in the head. Other players quickly pulled him off and he was thrown out by the refs who are there for our practices. I think this is only the beginning.

Coach Tenopir made a joke at my expense today. I was acting as a linebacker standing in the defensive formation and Coach was talking about how the backer would shoot the gap between our linemen, making a motion for me to go there. I walked quickly to the spot and he said, "That's about as fast as you ran the 40." I didn't laugh but some of the guys found it funny.

My blocking has gotten better and I'm noticing a considerable difference in my body and strength. My weight hasn't increased much; I'm still hovering around 280 pounds.

Wednesday, September 2, 1998

We practiced on the grass again today. I appreciate the free stuff we get, especially the clothes and shoes, but the grass spikes we were given are probably the worst pair of spikes I've ever owned. They kill your feet when you walk on solid ground, there is minimal cushioning, and the overall design is cramped in the toe area. I guess I'll have to live with them for now but if I have any say in what type of shoe we get next year, I will request a change.

The scout team showed great improvement today. We made some big plays against the defense but they had their fair share as well. It goes to show that you get better when you play with the best.

Thursday, September 3, 1998

I really like practicing only two days a week in full pads compared to how it was in high school. Today we ran in just helmets and the whole thing was pretty easy except for the heat. The team is ready for the game against the University of Alabama but the pressure isn't there that was there last week. I think they're very confident and able to get ready without all the stress. Tomorrow will be another half-hour practice where we do next to nothing.

Saturday, September 5, 1998

Nebraska 38 – University of Alabama-Birmingham 7

Eric Crouch started at quarterback for the first time in his career today and did really well. He definitely was the leader out there on the field. The offense and the defense really played a complete game.

Tuesday, September 8, 1998

We practiced on the grass yesterday and today, Monday in half pads and today in full pads. A lot of fights broke out on the other scout team. Nate Kolterman caused most of them and is developing an interesting reputation so far. I don't know how he can get away with picking fights with the number one defense. I would think those guys would beat him to a bloody pulp but instead he just gets a lot of talk.

Monday was Labor Day so there were no classes. On days that we practice and there is no school, we usually get money for meals. This time we received around $80.

> Anytime we're required to do anything football related on a non-school day, the administration has a choice of whether they want to provide a meal (or meals) to us or just give us the money that meal(s) would have cost. Most of the players in charge of making this decision choose to get the money, which usually turns out to be a lot more then the average meal would cost. They assume we're going to a nice steak house to eat just like at the training table when most of the guys usually just order a pizza. Fortunately for us, this program has pretty deep pockets to be able to do this. There are many colleges and universities who aren't as fortunate, but most of their players never know they're missing out on anything.

Wednesday, September 9, 1998

Today was the first time in the three weeks of practice that the scout team actually got some coaching. Coach Charlie McBride took the offense and laid down a couple of rules for effort and explained some of the blocking techniques that we see everyday on the cards. We needed this little bit of coaching. It's hard to know what to do when you're just thrown in the line of fire and expected to figure it out.

This was probably one of my worst practices yet. I was tired and had a miserable time trying to block anybody.

We each received a CD that Jack Stark, the team sports psychologist, made. It has tracks that help with relaxation, focus, and better sleep. I'm going to use it tonight to help me rest up for tomorrow. We also received a warm up suit that the guys on the travel squad are required to wear when they are traveling. I'll never be on the travel roster this year, but it's nice to get the same treatment.

Thursday, September 10, 1998

I had to buy a new pair of gray workout shorts today because the pair I got from the team was stolen last week. They cost $30; I also saw the jogging suit they gave us and it was $100.

I went to the team doctor today and got a prescription for my allergies, which I later found out wasn't allergies but a head cold. We are one of only a handful of athletic departments with a full-time doctor and on-campus pharmacy where we can get medicine for free. Just another benefit from one of the best programs in the nation.

Practice was good. Sam Gutz, one of the scout team quarterbacks, and I worked on the snap before practice. Coach Solich gave us a pretty heated and emotional speech during the meeting today, making a strong turn from the casual two-minute meetings we usually have. He talked about being mentally prepared for the game, ignoring the media, and making practices intense. The team leaves for California tomorrow at noon so we don't have a practice, only lifting.

Saturday, September 12, 1998

Nebraska 24 – California 3

Eric Crouch set them up and Monte Christo knocked 'em down. Steady performances by both of our quarterbacks paved the way. We were also carried by the strong running of our fullback Joel Makovicka and I-back Correll Buckhalter. The defense had a solid game as well with several sacks.

Monday, September 14, 1998

After the win in California, Coach Solich called off practice to give us a day to get healed up and rested; he told everybody to just lift. During lifting I was doing rack cleans and was on my last set of five. I asked Archer if I could put a little more weight on for the last one. I got the first one pretty easily but I failed on the next three. I was frustrated and Archer told me to quit. I said, "one more," and got the next one and ended up finishing the entire set. I was really pumped after that but I also was very sore with a sudden headache. Archer then used me as a motivational example to get the other guys going harder.

After lifting, the redshirts had position meetings for the first time. Coach Young went over some of the most basic and fundamental aspects of the offense such as similar plays and a couple of line calls, and how to block some of the most common defenses. This was very helpful because now we'll have a clue about what the older guys are doing in practice when they use us as blocking dummies.

Tuesday, September 15, 1998

We received a new pair of shoes today. I got a different style (and a better one, I think) than everyone else because I have size 16 feet, a size in which the other shoes are not produced. These are apparently given to us as "travel shoes" to go with our "travel warm-ups."

Wednesday, September 16, 1998

Today was probably one of the hardest practices yet. It was in full pads on the turf and went just over two hours. The scout team got a lot of work done. We continued to improve and beat the defense on more plays. I finally began to move people.

I received an e-mail from my dad today saying he talked

to graduate assistant Chad Stanley, who helped out with my recruiting, and he said I've caught the coaches' eyes with my long snapping, hard work in the weight room, and my overall development. This boosted my spirits even more. My hard work is beginning to pay off and the coaches actually do notice the freshmen. It's impossible to tell if the coaches notice you in practice because they're more concerned about the older guys and getting them ready for the games. I'm feeling a lot better about my situation now.

Friday, September 18, 1998

After the meeting yesterday, the freshmen O-line guys talked about coming in Friday morning to do squats. I was under the impression that we could either go in the morning or we could lift after practice like we always do. Apparently when I was over snapping to the punters, they made it mandatory for the morning and I never heard about it. Today when I ran into one of the other freshmen he immediately pointed out that I wasn't at lifting and said I was going to be punished. I heard many different stories from then on: I'd have to run stadium steps, we would get red bellies. (I wasn't alone in the punishment—Justin Valencia and Andy Gwennap also missed lifting.)

After an intense practice, we ran two gassers and then after the stretching and the breakdown, the entire O-line lined up to give us red bellies. I was pinned to the ground but I didn't resist because there was no point to even try, and took a full-force slap on my bare belly from every guy. Jason Schwab squirted water on me to heighten the effect and Dominic Raiola did a flying drop-slap on me. Eight hours later, I'm still sore and I can pick out definite handprints in the bruises on my stomach.

Saturday, September 19, 1998

We had an early practice today but I was unable to go because of a workshop for my education class. Not only did I miss out on practice, I couldn't get the money for the weekend either. I missed out on about $60.

Monday, September 21, 1998

Today I found out what it's like to be between a rock and a hard place. During the scout team punt station where I was working as the long snapper, Coach McBride told me to just go 20 yards, not the whole way to the ball after it's kicked. I did this about three times, just jogging 20 yards and walking back. Coach McBride apparently was dissatisfied with my performance and then chewed me out like I've never been yelled at before. To paraphrase, he said, "63, what are you doing, taking a walk?!" I replied, "Well, what did you tell me to do?" which, I quickly learned, was an improper tone and possibly the worst thing to say to this man. This set him off. He said, "Don't you ever talk to me like that, you *&#@! You don't even deserve to be on that line, you *&#@! I could fit your guts into a thimble!" and so on for a good two minutes, without saying the same demeaning insult twice. It really was a masterpiece of ass chewing. This got me pretty steamed up and made me determined to show him what I can do. A few plays later, one of the coaches called a couple positions to go live and I was included. I busted down the field as fast as I could and pretty much made the tackle. Then Coach Craig Bohl said, "63, where did you come from?" I said I was the center and he said, "You're not supposed to run that fast, the center is supposed to be slow." Now I was getting yelled at for doing what another coach told me to do. I later talked to Coach McBride about the misunderstanding. He said it was okay and added, "you'll be fine here."

Other players and assistants got a kick out of the coach yelling at me, saying it was one of the funniest cursings they had ever heard. I didn't laugh about it but I do think it was kind of funny to be in that situation. This kind of miscommunication happens to me a lot.

> Different coaches inspire their players in different ways. Coach Charlie McBride was definitely one of the coaches that led through fear and intimidation. However, if you were lucky enough to earn a spot on his good side, he was very loyal to you. As the defensive coordinator, his bloodlust attitude was easily picked up by his players and the blackshirts played great football because of him.
>
> Coach Frank Solich led through example as best he could. He knows the game, he knows the techniques and if he has to he'll get in there and show you how it's done. Solich always seemed to carry himself with a certain air of power, but at the same time never seemed entirely comfortable in his role. I sincerely believe he should be remembered as one of the greatest assistant coaches ever for the Huskers; however, he failed as a head coach because he lacked certain qualities. I feel he didn't have the organizational abilities to look at the big picture and then lead his troops efficiently at the same time. I wish I could have had Tom Osborne as a coach. I can't help but think I missed out on something great.
>
> Coach Milt Tenopir led by reputation. His offensive lines had been some of the best in the nation for several years and he was well aware of it. For a new guy coming in, he either liked you from the start or he didn't and there was little you could do for the next couple years to change that. He either

saw you as a contributor or a dummy and it was up to you to prove him wrong. Tenopir's glory years had just passed as I came in. His ability to go out and recruit as well as his ability to demonstrate technique was severely hampered by terrible ankle pain that required him to have his ankles fused. We had some very good recruits during my time, but we also had some catastrophic injuries happen to most of them. He worked as hard as any other coach and couldn't see himself doing anything other than coaching until the end of his career.

Coach Dan Young (assistant offensive line and kicking coach) was the most imitated coach on the team. His gravelly, congested drawl could be heard being copied by players and younger coaches alike. His glory days were long gone before I showed up. A withered old man with a disposition to match, he was Tenopir's Ed McMahon (that works on so many levels). His excessive drinking was rumored and legendary. His comb-over was also a thing of beauty. Apparently, no one had the nerve to tell him it looked like a small animal died on his head. The best was when he would take his hat off during practice, run his fingers through it, and put his hat back on with a wild clump of eight-inch long hairs sticking out (standing behind him on a few occasions, out of his range of vision, I would flick this outcropping, drawing several suppressed laughs from the other guys). It seemed as though he had a very limited quota of positive things to say throughout the day and he would save them carefully. The best you could hope for was to hear nothing back from him. If you ever did receive a compliment from him, you knew you really did something incredible.

Coach Ron Brown was a coach who gave a strong foundation for many athletes, not just his receivers. As the spiritual backbone of the team, he led many things, including Fellowship of Christian Athletes as well as post-game prayers in the middle of the field. He is a man of strong character and devotion and was a great coach. One time, one of his receivers was dancing on Wednesday nights at a club that had an amateur night with prize money, which this player won frequently. Coach Brown told him to stop or he'd be off the team. The receiver needed the money more than the position and he got cut.

Quarterbacks coach Turner Gill seemed to everyone the obvious choice to follow Osborne's footsteps and you can't help but wonder what would have happened. A great athlete in his own right and a tremendous competitor, he brought a high level of energy and ability to the coaching staff. He should have succeeded Solich as well, but again was turned down.

Nelson Barnes, the defensive ends coach, could have done his job without even showing up. That's according to his players who said he never imparted many gems of wisdom to them. But what he lacked in ability, he made up for with energy.

Craig Bohl, linebackers coach, was more of a distraction to the coaches than an assistant. Personal relationship issues overflowed into his work more than once and in the end it was just getting too hard to keep covering his tracks.

I know I'm leaving out a few coaches, but I just didn't have enough interaction with them to really know them.

Saturday, September 26, 1998

Nebraska 55 – Washington 7

It warmed up through the week and Saturday was another hot game day. The Huskers burned up the field with the best show of the year. We finally had all of the starters healthy and we looked like a different team than the one that played the past three games. This could be the turnaround point that makes us more deserving of a national championship bid.

Even with the hot weather, many of the freshmen who didn't suit up chose to show their affiliation the hard way; by wearing their warm-up outfit. Apparently some were so concerned that they be seen as a football player that they would brave a heat stroke just for some (female) recognition.

Wednesday, September 30, 1998

This week has been pretty easy compared to the rest. I think the guys and the coaches are taking it kind of easy after the big game last Saturday because they have the team they want and they don't want to wear anybody out.

The coaches and the older players tend not to focus on the freshmen. When the scout team does a good job and breaks a play for long yardage, the coaches yell at the defense and usually make us do it again, but they never compliment us. The graduate assistants working with the scout team give us pats on the back but they have no real authority with the other coaches.

Coach Solich is in a strange position right now. I have no doubt that he can be a good coach, and I know he's a great man. His control of the team shows that he has amassed an amazing amount of respect, most of which was passed on from being an assistant coach for 19 years and also being the play caller during the games. However, there's one thing I've noticed about Coach Solich that hurts his image, and that's the way he talks to the team. He uses way too many verbal pauses ("ummm," "ahhh," etc.). Most of the time they happen when he's just reading through stuff like stats and other info to the team. I think when he's reading through stuff or saying things from memory, he loses much of his meaning due to these pauses. But when he's talking about things from the heart he hardly uses any pauses and sounds like an entirely different person. I think the media is picking up on this, but for now there is too much respect for the program to start this kind of childish finger pointing.

I think in three to four years, we'll have the best offensive line that Nebraska has ever seen. The freshmen class of linemen is one of the biggest to date and holds more potential than any other spot on the field. I can't wait to be a part of it.

> Solich never turned out to be a stirring speaker. At best he seemed like a relayer of information, devoid of any original insight or motivation. When he tried his best to motivate, it sometimes caused laughter. His broken speech clouded many of his statements and made some of them truly incomprehensible. Words seemed to trip out of his mouth, falling over one another, sprinkled with a few common phrases so frequently used that every new speech sounded like the last.

Saturday, October 3, 1998

Nebraska 24 – Oklahoma State 17

We had some of the worst showings all year in this game. As Coach Solich put it, the game was won because we had no turnovers, broke a few big plays including a punt return, and lost very few yards to penalties compared to 59 yards of penalties by Okie State. We lost the game statistically but we won by the score. Basically, we played a really good team and came out ahead in the end.

Monday, October 5, 1998

Today we practiced in helmets and sweats. Coach Solich said this time of the year the Monday practices are usually just in helmets. The practice was mostly mental, running through a lot of plays and making sure everyone knows where they're supposed to go.

In the Monday meetings we always evaluate the previous game by reviewing the stats and seeing how many goals we met. Someone on the staff set up a computer program that lists our goals for offense, defense, and special teams. In the column for each of the opponents, that stat is displayed in green if we achieved it and in red if we did not. These are displayed on the video screen at the front of the auditorium and Coach Solich goes through each goal individually, making sure to note when we did better or worse than previous weeks. This is a fairly effective way to get across that we are playing as a team and need to think as a team. It's obvious that the more goals we reach, the better the outcome of the game.

Tuesday, October 6, 1998

Nate Kolterman got into another fight today (hard to believe). I was in the other scout team offensive group so I didn't get to be a part of it, but I saw the last half of it when someone threw a helmet and hit Nate hard enough to cut his eye and break a bone in his face. Later in the breakdown the older O-line guys made the rule that if there is a fight, anyone who is not in there throwing punches and raising hell will get a red belly. So much for my pacifist attitude.

Wednesday, October 7, 1998

I like Wednesdays. When Wednesday rolls around, the week is over for me. It's the last full-pads practice of the week, there's no lifting, and my classes are incredibly easy (I actually skipped calculus this morning so I could sleep until 10:00.). I would have gotten up in time for class but every night after we return from study hall there's always something going on here on our dorm floor. I can't get to bed before midnight because everyone else is having fun and I don't want to miss out. I think I'll like it a lot better when I have my own apartment where I can study when I need to and get to bed as early as I want. But for now, the goal is to have as much fun as possible.

Thursday, October 8, 1998

We received a grade slip for most of our classes today. They were in our lockers, which amazes me because this would take a lot of effort. A grade slip has to get to every teacher for every athlete, the teacher has to figure out the student's grade, get it back to the football office, and then someone distributes them to all of the players after reviewing them. If someone is getting below a *C* in a class, they get a note and are told that their parents will be notified about the grade. I think this is a great way to keep the players in check and it was a wake-up call for me because two of the three slips I got were *C*'s, the other one was an *A*. I never got a *C* in high school so this was kind of a surprise for me. I think I'll get a tutor for calculus but I don't foresee any real problems with the others. Tutors are available free for all athletes and for any class, and can be assigned very quickly. This is just another perk and also a reason why Nebraska is one of the highest-rated student-athlete institutions.

I expect I'll do pretty well in my classes, as I have always done in the past, but it's a whole new world here in college.

I really have to be careful to make time to study and get my stuff done, otherwise all the other activities like football and dorm life will easily get in the way. The lure of slacking off a little bit is just so tempting. Also, with all the time and energy commitments that football has required so far, it's very hard to find time to do all the work outside of class. It's even harder to stay awake while in class. My body is in a constant recovery phase jumping from lifting to practice and every chance I get to sit quietly and do nothing is a chance for my body to finally shut down. I'm sure my professors hate looking out in the crowd and seeing a student fast asleep, but I can't help it. It seems to be a theme with me. My senior year in high school I was voted "Most Likely to Sleep Through Graduation."

The team seems ready to take on Texas A&M. The defense got yelled at quite a bit this week and there seems to be problems between some of them. For example, Jason Wiltz and Mike Rucker, starting defensive lineman and rush end respectively, got into a little pushing match the other day. I hope they keep their heads clear and focus on the game and show the nation what Nebraska football can do.

Saturday, October 10, 1998

Nebraska 21 – Texas A&M 28

This was a very disappointing loss to Texas A&M, our first loss in 20 games. The whole state is in shock but it was inevitable. No one can be on top forever, and furthermore, we were in a mindset that this was going to be a cakewalk. We figured that the reputation of Nebraska football would make us good and we just coasted through everything. This served as a wake-up call for us.

We were ranked second in the nation before this game. There's no doubt that we will drop a few notches after losing to the Aggies, the number 18 team in the nation.

Monday, October 12, 1998

The players were all very quiet in meetings today, sitting in shame while Coach Solich went through the pitiful summary of goals that we didn't come close to achieving in our loss to Texas A&M. His tone was much more concerned, angry, and disappointed. He spoke surprisingly fluently and explained how we need to change our overall attitude. He explained again that when teams play us, it is their big game of the season. Everyone wants a piece of the guys on the top so we have all become marked men. We have to think that every game is a big game but we also have to take one game at a time. Every game matters when the national championship is on the line.

There is still a chance we could go to the championship game. Ohio State has no more ranked teams on its schedule so if no upsets occur, they will be in the game. Every other team below us plays at least one ranked team and we play up to five more ranked teams. To be in contention we have to buckle down and dominate every team. It would also be necessary for a couple of teams below us to lose one or two games, which gives us a pretty low chance to pull this off. It would also help if we could have a rematch with Texas A&M in the Big 12 championship.

Coach Solich later talked to the offense as a whole, including the freshmen. He explained how we ran the option way too much in the game and how in practice, instead of doing an option drill, we will now do an inside run drill. We then went to Coach Tenopir's office and he just asked us who would be practicing and who was hurt. My fellow freshmen quickly and quietly left the somber office area and hurriedly pressed for the elevator to take us away from this scene of anguish and down to our locker room. From all the way around the lobby, we could hear Coach Tenopir yelling at the older guys with the most intensity that I have ever heard from him. Once the doors closed, no one really knew what to say on the ride down.

Everyone was much more reserved in practice. No one talked or joked around. Everyone listened intently to the coaches and we basically punished ourselves by working harder and quicker than we usually do. No one likes to lose, especially when you are part of a team that's known for winning. The practice was intense but it also seemed very short. That's probably because we were working so hard that we lost track of time.

A highlight of the practice was that I got to play I-back when the scout team linemen showed the defensive line the Kansas formations and blocking styles. I actually got to run a little bit, too, and didn't do too badly. It helped that the defense was supposed to go half-speed but I still found the holes and ran it pretty well.

I think this will be the turning point for the program. We found out that our reputation can't win games. We have to step up and play our best every Saturday. Every game is a big game.

Tuesday, October 13, 1998

Today was a good day for the defense. They had the momentum from the beginning of practice and kept it up until the end. They got over feeling sorry for themselves, and stepped it up and finally dominated the scout team. The players were much more vocal today and they hyped each other up and talked trash to us whenever they could. The coaches seemed pleased with this practice. They know we need a big win this weekend and they are ready to produce.

Wednesday, October 14, 1998

Today's practice was one of the most intense practices we've had in a couple of weeks. Luckily, we went in a good rotation so I was able to take breaks now and then. The varsity offense had a bad day from what I heard. There were a lot of mistakes and the guys seemed disappointed but they know what they have to do. They need to post some huge yards this Saturday if they want to keep up the tradition of being the best offensive line in the nation.

Coach Solich has been very focused in meetings this week. He has changed his tone dramatically and tells us exactly what he expects. He's obviously disappointed by the loss but he still gives us speeches assuring us there's a chance to be the best. He stays positive and that helps keep us positive. Now that he is taking more control of this program, what he says has more legitimacy. I can tell the older guys respect Coach Solich but a couple of them apparently still have their hearts with Coach Osborne.

Thursday, October 15, 1998

After another pretty brisk practice, this week turned out to be the most physical yet. I am more bruised now than I've been in a while. I now have more confidence in this team than ever before. I feel this week's game will be the best so far. There will be a walk-through at 7:30 tomorrow night so the team can get used to playing under the lights.

Saturday, October 17, 1998

Nebraska 41 – Kansas 0

We got $72 after the game to cover food for the weekend since there will be no school next Monday or Tuesday. To get the money, we had to go through the tunnel that the players walk out of at the beginning of the game, which also leads to the varsity locker room where a table was set up outside the training room. There were hundreds of fans outside the tunnel waiting for players they knew. Being dressed in Husker apparel and also being as big as we are, I'm sure a couple of fans wondered who we were. Even this was pretty exciting but it's only the tip of the iceberg.

Monday, October 19, 1998

Today we had a practice on the turf in half-pads (helmet and shoulder pads). We are about midway through the season but it really doesn't feel that way to me. I guess it's because I don't have to build myself up mentally for the games and because of that, I have no sense of time. All I do is practice. This is very hard to cope with because I put in as much effort as any other guy on the team but on game days I'm forced to sit in the stands and watch. I realize that I'll get my chance later but for now it seems too repetitive. The redshirt program allows people like me to grow physically and mentally, which will give me an advantage in the future. It's something that most of the players here go through and I guess it helps to break in the younger players faster.

The redshirt and walk-on programs have had a major impact in the history of Nebraska football. Many great players started out just like me, walking on and redshirting their first year. One walk-on who is playing this season is Joel Makovika. He has developed into one of the finest fullbacks Nebraska has ever had, on the field and off. As a great student, co-captain, and a speaker at many functions, Joel has proven that the walk-on program is a valuable resource.

I'm basically a commodity. The coaches see someone who has the potential to be a player and they get him as a walk-on. If the gamble pays off, he will develop into a superb athlete and thrive in the college football world. If not, he will fade into the footnotes of Nebraska football history as a practice dummy. Most of the freshmen offensive linemen are walk-ons, roughly three-fifths of the freshmen class is made up of walk-ons.

Tuesday, October 20, 1998

Joe Freeman, a fellow walk-on, became the first freshman lineman to quit the team today. He missed being in Omaha and plans to transfer to the University of Nebraska-Omaha next semester but I don't know if he'll play football there.

His departure is sad but it's the harsh reality. Take this year for instance. We have about 14 freshman offensive linemen and there are only three senior linemen. That shows the kind of dedication needed to stay with a program like this. Some guys have what it takes to succeed here but they don't have the patience to wait for their turn. Other guys are continuously trying to improve and when they get their shot, it's well deserved. I'm patient, now I must continue to improve. Joe will be missed. He was finally getting comfortable with the other guys and we found out he has a great sense of humor. I hope he doesn't look back on this and ask "what if..."

Wednesday, October 21, 1998

Even though we didn't lift today, I ended up more sore and bruised than I have ever been. This week has been really intense and I've paid the price. My arms are bruised all over, my knees are sore, my neck hurts, my brain is fried, my hands are cut and bruised, and today I was too tired to even go to class. But besides these things, I'm perfectly fine.

Thursday, October 22, 1998

Today we had our first random drug test. At the end of practice, Coach told the O-line to go to the north locker room and take the test. We were not the first to be tested, I think the receivers or backs took one about a week ago. I know I'll pass because I've never done any drugs and I hope for the team's sake that everyone else can say the same.

It's somewhat interesting how these tests are conducted.

The guys come into the visiting team locker room and grab a cup and then basically huddle around a lined trash can, under the watchful eye of an athletic trainer to make sure we're actually getting our own urine into the cups. Then we'll put a lid on it, get the temperature read, initial a couple things which double check that we have our cup listed correctly and sealed securely and then we're done.

Friday, October 23, 1998

As usual on a Friday morning, the O-line was up before the sun and at the weight room by 6:30. We were all ready to go but we had one small problem—we couldn't get into the weight room. John Archer usually is there at 6:20 to let us in but today he slept in. We waited around until 6:45 and then we all decided to go back to bed. Then I did the same thing as Archer and slept right through my first class. I woke up just in time to run to my 11:30 class.

I can get in trouble with the team for skipping class. If we do something that's against team rules, we receive a point. When you have three points you have to go before the Unity Council and try to get some of them taken away.

The Unity Council is a relatively new organization composed of players from each position, mostly the older guys, who discuss matters relating to the team and any issues of the day. Jack Stark, the sports psychologist, leads this group. Everything that's discussed is brought before Coach Solich and he then acts on the comments or suggestions as he sees fit. This council has proven to be a very comfortable place to bring issues out that may be too uncomfortable to tell the coaches directly. I'm going to try to never get a point while I'm here, that's another one of my goals and I have no idea how tough this one will be.

Saturday October 24, 1998

Nebraska 20 – Missouri 13

The game was at 11:30 this morning, the earliest of the season, and throughout the week Coach Solich stressed how important it would be to be ready to go early. I think the guys were ready but a few key mistakes early in the game hurt the outlook. In the end, we won in one of the most exciting home games in a long time. This was a good test for the team and shows us that we can hang with anybody even though we are a young team.

Monday, October 26, 1998

During meetings we saw how the game looked from the statistical side. The defense had a superb game with most of their goals being reached. The offense on the other hand met only a few of their goals.

The practice today was the most physical one yet, and we were just in half pads! For the first half, all I did was stand around but the second half was full force, full-steam action and we ran those plays as fast as humanly possible. In my opinion, today was one of my best practices because I was really giving some good drive blocks and keeping my guys out of the play.

The scout team offense, which I'm a part of, runs plays that are drawn up on a card, similar to what the coaches believe the opposing team may run in the game. This gives the defense a look at what they should expect during the game. Many of the running plays have the center chip off of the nose guard or the tackle and go for the middle linebacker, and on a couple occasions I totally missed him. Damion Peter, brother of legendary Huskers Jason and Christian and supposedly the best football player of the three, is coaching the scout team and constantly cursed at me when I missed the block. The stuff that he said would not be acceptable for this book but it got me mad enough to try my best on every play. At the end, I was doing the block pretty well, but Damion never said anything.

I got a tutor for calculus today. I haven't been very focused on my schoolwork the past two weeks and now I'm behind in two of my classes. I think I got behind because I wasn't studying very well in study hall and I never do homework in the dorm because there's always something more exciting to do. Tonight I stayed at the Hewit Center studying and catching up on my math until midnight, two hours longer than what's required. This is what I have to do to catch up.

I can see now why it's so hard to be a good student athlete in a Division 1 school. The team GPA last year was around 2.85 while I'm used to receiving a 3.8 in high school. Football takes so much time and energy that when practice and lifting are done, I just want to relax. If I weren't in football, I could do very well in all of my classes. Now I'm dragging myself through assignments, fighting sleep, and constantly being interrupted by other events.

Tuesday, October 27, 1998

Today was very similar to yesterday. The only exception is that Damion Peter actually complimented me on a block that I put on Jay Foreman. It's not very often that you hear something like that from him but I took it for what it's worth and worked even harder in the hopes of getting another one. I was extremely tired today since I stayed at study hall so late last night. Somehow I got through practice and made the best of it, and even stayed at study hall until midnight again. I'm a stupid man working hard to be smart.

Wednesday, October 28, 1998

A group of the seniors started off the meeting with only the players in the room. This has happened a few times now, but this meeting was destined to be different. Josh Heskew, Jay Foreman, Lance Brown, Chad Kelsay, and Sheldon Jackson all talked about the shape of the team and the present conditions. They said we're all spoiled brats, and that having won three national championships in the past four years has given us a comfort level that makes us think everything will happen by itself. They also talked about how every Saturday we wait until the third or fourth quarter to finally start playing. One main point was that the defense is saving the day while the offense is horrible, especially the line. The speech was full of swearing and heated talk, especially from Lance Brown who was most mad because he's had to watch all of this from the sideline every week. Lance also said that when he was on the scout team he never left a practice without getting the living hell beat out of him. Now, everyone is too nice and the scout team players even talk back to the number ones, something that was unheard of just two or three years ago.

They said we put too much effort and time into this program between fall, winter, spring and summer workouts to come out and not give 100% only 14 times a year on game days. I think this meeting, which lasted about 45 minutes, will have a dramatic effect on the team as a whole. The older guys have to keep up the traditions that they learned when they were young and these traditions will keep the team strong.

Friday, October 30, 1998

We finally received some more free stuff today. It's a long-sleeved white shirt with a high collar and has the Husker *N* on the chest.

Practice today was short and mostly pointless for redshirts like me. We ran a couple of plays against the defenses and then sat on the benches and waited for the special teams to finish their run-throughs.

Tonight was the first time I had a Friday dinner at the Hewit Center. The team always has dinner on Friday night but I never knew we could be there too. The meal was pretty much the same good food we always have but tonight the main course was a choice between crab legs and huge slices of inside round. I chose the crab legs and they were great. When I got back to my room the guy next door said the dorm dinner was horrible. He thinks the Hewit Center got all of the funding for dinner on Friday nights, which forces the other places to serve bad leftovers. As long as we get good food, I don't care what everyone else gets. If the quality of our food fell to the level of the dorms, I'm sure that would cause a huge problem.

Saturday, October 31, 1998

Nebraska 16 – Texas 20

Mike Brown and Eric Crouch had outstanding personal efforts, but that couldn't stop Texas from slowly dissecting us all game long. Our 47 home game win streak has officially come to an end. So it goes.

Monday, November 2, 1998

After the shocking and disappointing loss to Texas, the locker room was deathly quiet. No one said a word and looks of disbelief and frustration were on many faces.

The goals we went over in meetings reflected the game. Neither the offense nor the defense met even one-third of the 12 goals. We still have a chance to go to the Big 12 championship game but Kansas State will have to lose to Missouri and we will, of course, have to win the rest of our games. The meeting wasn't as solemn as the last time we lost. I think most of the players have accepted that certain factors, including injuries, lack of depth, and young players, add up to us being just a good team trying to play up to exceptional standards. We know we won't go to the national championship game this year, and we don't deserve to. Our offense is "the worst offense in the last five years," according to Lance Brown, and we have not played a full game on any given Saturday.

I got my body fat tested today for the third time since I've been here. The results showed that since the last test, which was at the beginning of the season, I've lost four pounds of fat and gained nine pounds of muscle. Since last summer I've lost nine pounds of fat and gained 11 pounds of muscle. Dave Ellis, the nutrition expert and body fat tester, said I'm in a really good position right now. I'm at a very acceptable 14 percent body fat and with 10 more pounds of muscle, I would be ready to play. I guess that means my ideal weight is around 290 pounds.

I know I'm not done growing. I'm still not fully developed in my shoulders or upper body but I'm not so far behind that I'm struggling to catch up. I'm on the lower half of the freshmen O-line when it comes to strength but I expect that to change through the hard work and lifting that will go on the rest of the season and in winter workouts. I also really need to start gaining some good weight. This has been my biggest problem. I eat very well; one of the people in charge of the training table saw my plate one day and said I should teach everyone else how to eat. I think my problem comes from not eating breakfast all of the time. I always wake up late and rush to my first class, usually choking down a breakfast bar along the way. I picked up a big canister of the high-calorie recovery drink mix from Dave Ellis and I hope that will help.

Today was one of those days you hate to play a game in. I guess the coaches thought it would be a great day for practice, though. We went out on the grass and the weather was in the high '30s with light drizzle the whole time. We slipped around on the field for the entire practice and by the end I was covered in mud. It's hard to have a good practice when you have no footing. The practice seemed very short for a Monday, especially when Coach gave us the day off from gassers. I was still ready to go and actually wanted to run gassers. Something must be wrong with me.

Tuesday, November 3, 1998

Today was not my best practice. In fact, it probably was my worst. My focus wasn't there today because of many factors, including test anxiety. I found myself on the ground many times and was yelled at a couple times by Damion. I just need to put this day behind me and get over it.

I've stayed at study hall past midnight the past couple of nights studying hard for upcoming tests. It's my fault I have to cram so hard. I have discovered that it truly is harder to catch up than to keep up. I'm trying to catch up now and it's hurting me, especially the lack of sleep. I was expecting to get a 4.0 GPA this semester but that's now in question. One problem is that there are so few graded assignments in college classes that it's almost impossible to bring your grade up after a bad start.

Wednesday, November 4, 1998

Through some huge change, today was one of my best days of practice. I was more focused and didn't let anything affect me. Every time I stepped up to the ball I said to myself, "I'm the best lineman on the field, I can block anybody." Jim Tansey, junior tackle and my new mentor, introduced me to this technique. This really worked and I gave some of the best blocks I've given all season, especially drive blocks. One way I know I did a good job today was that Damion didn't yell at me once. Also, the defensive coaches yelled at guys I blocked for not playing well, so that in turn means that I was playing good.

Jim Tansey has been a great mentor. He has helped me adjust to college and also is someone I can share my personal problems with. He's always been good for advice on any subject and he is the best friend I have on the team right now. I guess he remembers what it was like to be a freshman and how tough it is to go through all of these changes.

Thursday, November 5, 1998

Today was an abnormally long Thursday practice. Practice usually doesn't last long when we're just in helmets but today was a totally different story. We must have run at least 100 plays at the defense and I never took a break. I usually don't take breaks and because of that I've become very well conditioned. I guess the coaches and the players realize they need a big game this weekend against Iowa State because we didn't stop until we went through every possible play and did each one perfectly.

For some reason, Thursday is always a tough day to lift. No matter how much rest I get or the amount of energy I have at the time, lifting on Thursdays is always tough. For years, Nebraska has been able to claim that it has the best weight program in the nation. I believe it now because I'm living it. I know what they expect, I know how much emphasis they put on proper lifting, and I know that they tie lifting in with football, nutrition and total body control. Boyd Epley and his staff probably know more about sports-related lifting than anyone in the country. They've done the research and put it to work in the weight room, and the results speak for themselves in the history of the program.

Saturday, November 7, 1998

Nebraska 42 – Iowa State 7

I-Back Dan Alexander carried us to victory over the Cyclones today. The 1997 Lifter of the Year showed us what a little muscle can do if you use it correctly. Dan is really an amazing individual. Actually, freak of nature is more like it. He has an uncanny ability to seemingly grow muscle at will. His freshman year, he put on so much muscle and improved so much in strength and performance that it was no contest for him to win Lifter of the Year. Now, the strength coaches realize something isn't normal with him and restricted his lifting to just one or two lifts a day…and he's still gaining muscle! Apparently he's not alone. I heard he has a sister who runs track for a different university and her calf muscles got so big so fast that they were starting to tear the skin.

Monday, November 9, 1998

The future of this season looks much brighter after this past weekend. We had a huge game against Iowa State and finally played a complete game. The defense had one of the best games of the year, meeting 10 of its 12 goals, and the offense was incredibly close on the goals it didn't reach, so if you scale them a little bit, we played the best game of the year so far. Ohio State lost to Michigan State Saturday, knocking them off the top of the polls and putting Kansas State first. This means that if we can pull off a major victory over K-State and if Missouri can also, we have a good chance of going to the Big 12 championship game and possibly going to a good bowl after that. I'm still sure that the national championship is out of the question but stranger things have happened.

In meetings today, there was an atmosphere of good feelings about the game. Coach Solich must have realized this so his attitude was very focused on the task at hand, which is the K-State game. He remained very serious the entire meeting and laid down the law about this week of practice, saying that we need a great week with lots of progress on both sides of the ball. He knows that if we get comfortable with a big win, we'll take it easy and think it will happen naturally the next Saturday. He made it plain, as he has before, that we must take one game at a time and remain focused. If we look too far ahead, we might miss what is right in front of our face.

Today's practice was a little different for a Monday. I did the regular punt snap thing at the beginning and then went with the scout team to Cook Pavilion to practice against the defense. It was warmer in the Cook than it was outside, so I liked being in there. For the first two-thirds of the practice we stood around and watched Coach Darlington coach the defensive line. Then for the last third we ran a bunch of pass-and-run plays at the defense like we usually do.

We didn't run as many plays as before—I guess the coaches want to make sure the players know all of their assignments perfectly. This will be the biggest game of the season for us and we wouldn't want something as simple as a broken assignment to ruin it. I believe this will be one of our hardest played games this year, not because of all of the press hype but because it will show the nation that we just had a couple of off games and we're still the dominating football team everyone knows and expects. This could make or break all chances of a Big 12 championship or a good bowl game.

We received a stocking cap today. Perfect timing after I just bought a pair of stocking caps to get ready for the cold weather. Everything that the team supplies us with is perfectly legal in the eyes of the NCAA as long as it serves a purpose related to football or a situation we might encounter because of our sport. Warm-ups, socks, shoes, hats, shorts, t-shirts and anything else that can be useful in this dynamic sport. I feel sorry for some of the other athletes here like the swimmers. They're supplies are much more limited. Sure, they would get travel clothes and coats, but they wouldn't get the haul like we get.

Tuesday, November 10, 1998

Sleep. I know that word, but it has no meaning anymore.

It's funny how 10 years ago I would have begged to stay up a little longer than my bedtime. Now, I'm fighting just to stay awake in my classes and study hall and wishing that I could go to sleep at 8:00pm. Practice and lifting have drained my body, studying is draining my mind. I'm not sure what's worse.

Wednesday, November 11, 1998

One of the main things I worked on today was to translate the Jammer from the weight room to the practice field. The Jammer is a lift you stand in—it sort of looks like a weird cage—and you push up two arms with weights on them. This lift is great for gaining strength to push into someone and drive them back. I used this lift today right when I fired off of the ball and made contact with the defender. This really worked! I was finally getting some really good drive blocks and making some good holes for the running backs to go through.

As we gear up for the K-State game, the varsity guys appear more confident than ever. This confidence was evident as they totally dominated the scout teams. The defense shut down the offensive scout team and we hardly ever broke a long play. We usually break about one of every five plays for more than five yards, but not this week. Everyone on the defense seems very comfortable in their positions and the defense as a unit has come together as a strong group. The leadership of Jay Foreman, Chad Kelsay and a few others has had a huge effect on the spirit of the defense. Foreman, for example, is one of the most talkative members on the team. He's out there calling the defensive plays and fixing mistakes immediately. He seems to be one of the few guys on the defense who knows everything about the Nebraska defensive schemes. He's also the best linebacker that I've gone up against. Other linebackers on the team can hit hard, some can read the offense well, and others have great aggressiveness, but Jay is the only one who has all of these abilities.

Thursday, November 12, 1998

If one word could describe this week leading up to Kansas State, it would be "focus." The coaches this week were very focused in their efforts to prepare the team for K-State. Before, they would yell at the players about their mistakes and tell them to not do it again. This week, we ran plays over and over again until the defense did their job perfectly. I think this game will not be as close as everyone thinks it will be. The defense will shut down the K-State offense, giving the ball to our offense so they can punch it in for touchdown after touchdown. I think the final score of this game will be at least a two-touchdown difference but it will probably be close up until the third quarter when we'll take over and conquer. Only time will tell.

Saturday, November 14, 1998

Nebraska 30 – Kansas State 40

Well, I was right in my prediction of a close, two-touchdown game. Unfortunately it wasn't in our favor. I could argue for hours about how there were bad calls in the game, most notably the blatant facemasking of Eric Crouch on our final drive just as Matt Davison was wide open (there was a picture printed in the paper showing Eric's helmet being spun a full 180 degrees around by a K-State player).

It was a disappointing loss, especially because it marks the first loss to K-State in 30 years. I guess a good way to look at it is that losing once every three decades isn't too bad.

Overall, it was an exciting game. There were several lead changes, lots of fumbles and special teams plays, and a few nail-biting scenarios as well. What really kept us in this game was a lot of luck with some big plays. This game won't go down in history as an all-time best, but it was fun.

Monday, November 16, 1998

In the meetings today the goals reflected the game fairly well. The offense and defense met a combined total of three goals out of 24. This is, to say the least, pathetic. The game would have been a complete blowout if it weren't for a few key errors made by K-State, including five turnovers. We showed sparks here and there but they were short-lived and usually were followed by a failure. That's the way it has been most of the season. We'll wake up for a moment and play like the other team isn't even there, displaying the true colors of Nebraska football. But this kind of momentum rarely lasts long. I guess we get too comfortable and figure it will happen by itself or that someone else on the team will be at their best so the others can take it easy. This is not the Nebraska football we all know in which the other team leaves the field beaten and bewildered, a game where we play a full four quarters and totally dominate.

Many people talked before this season about how we would not be as good as teams of recent years. They were right. We are a team with a majority of non-senior starters and that has hurt team leadership. The players who are starters don't seem ready to assume a leadership role. This could be good for the team in the future. As they gain experience I hope they will be great leaders in the years to come. And, with the team's youth, the future of Nebraska football is incredibly bright.

This last game sealed our fate and we will not go to the Big 12 championship game. If we beat Colorado (which shouldn't be much of an "if"), it looks like we'll go to the Holiday Bowl in San Diego. The game is on December 30, which means we'll be gone for Christmas but will be back by New Year's.

My progress is continuing. Over the past two weeks, since I got back on creatine (a nutritional supplement for muscle growth), people have commented on how much more filled out I look. I can also tell a difference, mostly in my chest and neck. I now have greater strength which is proportionate to my new physique. I haven't gained much weight lately like I wish I would, however. I've paid close attention to my diet over the past week and I can't figure it out. Maybe my metabolism is too high. If this is the case, I need to have food in me at all times so I don't get any muscle atrophy. If I'm ever to gain weight, one thing I need to do is eat breakfast everyday. I did today, and because of that I didn't show the normal weight loss that usually accompanies the weekends. I was a strong 280 pounds today when I usually weigh in at 277 on Mondays.

We started on hang cleans today. It was a little difficult after doing rack cleans for so long but in the end I was doing weights that were previously impossible for me. Last year a good hang clean max for me was around 215 pounds. Today, for the first time in a long time, I did my last set of five at 242 pounds. Just another good sign that the weight program here can really do wonders.

Tuesday, November 17, 1998

I saw the team doctor today to get some medicine for a little congestion. He also gave me the number of an optometrist where I can get contacts for free. The athletic department picks up the bill because I play with them in.

This week is an off-week before we play Colorado for our last regular season game. The general sentiment of the varsity guys (especially the seniors) is that we have to go out winners. The guys know this season was not the best, and their dreams of another national championship ended a long time ago. Now is the time to play for pride and go out with two last wins to make it a 10-3 season.

Wednesday, November 18, 1998

Matt Shook, a scholarship freshman offensive lineman, got into a fight with one of the defensive guys today. It didn't last long but it was enough to get Coach McBride's attention. Coach asked Matt if he was fighting and Matt tried to defend himself but was asked abruptly again if he had been fighting. He said, "Yes, Coach," and McBride sent him to the locker room.

I asked Jim Tansey if that kind of consequence was the norm in previous years and he said the person fighting usually would have to run steps. The change was probably because NFL scouts are here this week and the coaches don't want anything to happen that could hurt their players' chances of going pro. The pro scouts have been sifting through loads of game film, watching practices, observing lifting and inquiring about all of the players. This week is a little more tense because of the scouts, but it makes the older guys work harder to get their attention and, in turn, they get better. Maybe we should have pro scouts around all the time.

Thursday, November 19, 1998

Today was full pads again and left me even more tired than I already was. Our normal routine is off because we don't have a game this week and next week the game is on Friday. My mind has been screwed up and I have to struggle to think what day it is. It doesn't help that this is one of the busiest weeks I've had for a while. Every night this week I've something to do that takes me past midnight to finish. It really pays to have a good calendar book to manage your time. Being organized has saved me a lot of stress.

Today was supposed to be light day for hang cleans. I finished doing hang cleans with the same weight that I finished with on Monday, the heavy day. When we started doing rack shrugs and then rack cleans, Archer said when we go back to hang cleans we'd be able to do a lot more weight. He was right. For my last set I handled 20 more pounds than my max was less than six months ago. For a compound lift like hang clean, that's impressive

Dinner tonight was a nice change. They moved the food bars out into the eating area and it was set up like it is for recruiting visits. We had our Thanksgiving meal tonight and it was one of the best meals I've had here. Everything was delicious, with turkey and all the trimmings, and I topped it off with a slice of cheesecake.

Friday, November 20, 1998

This morning's lifting was mandatory for all redshirts. The O-line didn't care but many of the other guys whined a whole lot about having to get up so early just to lift. I was one of the first people there at 6:20 and we sat around until 6:40 waiting for everyone to show up. About 10 guys showed up after 6:40 and had to run three sets of South Stadium steps. This would be horrible to do right before heavy squats but that's what they get for not doing as they were told.

We still don't know where we'll go for a bowl game but I guess we should first worry about getting a nine-win season.

Colorado shouldn't be a tough game but that was also said about OSU and we barely came out of that. This next week will be nice because we only have school on Monday and Tuesday, and then just practice on Wednesday. Then I can go home for Thanksgiving break. I'm not sure what it will be like to be away from my family for Christmas. Instead, I'll be with the Huskers, probably practicing on Christmas day and not doing all those traditional things that make Christmas special.

Monday, November 23, 1998

We're doing our best to get ready for Colorado without thinking too much about our bowl game. We were in full pads, which always makes us focus a little more, and ran through tons of plays. It was a pretty good day overall.

I'm finally starting to gain some solid weight now. I've gained about two pounds a week the past two weeks, and am now at 283 pounds. It's all due to getting up early enough and eating breakfast every morning.

Tuesday, November 24, 1998

We were in half pads today, which surprised everybody. I assumed we would be in full pads to get our typical two days of full pads per week. Coach also told us it would be a split practice—defense in the Cook and the offense on the main field. He also said it would be shorter than yesterday and that we wouldn't do team work at the end. This all combined to make a pretty easy practice but we still ran a lot of plays and worked hard.

Tomorrow night, I can go home after practice and spend Thanksgiving break with my family since I won't be suiting up for the game. I heard that if we wanted to, we could practice with the team on Thursday and then suit up on Friday for the game. I think that would be awesome to be out on the field for a game, but I just don't feel it would be right. I'm putting my time in on scout team now so I can be out there on game day ready to play. I'll suit up when I know I've earned it.

Friday, November 27, 1998

Nebraska 16 – Colorado 14

We barely beat Colorado. The game was saved by the defense and the kicking. The offense was highly unproductive and didn't score one touchdown despite being inside the 30-yard line six times. Not a good way to play a game but at least Coach Solich preserved the nine-game win streak for another year. Now the seniors have one more game to go out winners.

Tuesday, December 1, 1998

Our regular season is over now. We won't be going to the Big 12 championship game this year, and our bowl game future is still undetermined. Today was one of the first weekdays since school started that I didn't have to lift or practice. The only football-related thing I did was go to a team meeting. Coach Solich said he still doesn't know who we will play or even where. We're hoping for the Holiday Bowl but there is still the possibility of going to the Cotton Bowl. We're required to get in four days of lifting this week and I'm taking today off because I need the entire day to study.

Wednesday, December 2, 1998

We had our first practice today after our nice little break. It was different because only coaches Solich, McBride and Tenopir were there. The others were out on recruiting trips. We found out that we will play in the Culligan Holiday Bowl in San Diego. The field there is grass, so our practice was on the grass today. The weather is unbelievably beautiful for Nebraska this time of year. It must be in the mid-60s in December!

It was tough to get going again and it took a long time to find my groove and play as well as I did before the break. Since we don't know who we'll play yet, we ran a wide variety of offenses at the defense. The practice was relatively short and we ran four half-gassers afterward, just down and back the width of the field in under 20 seconds.

Monday, December 7, 1998

We had another short, half-pads practice that ended in four half gassers. It was a productive practice and I did a good job. On one play Jason Wiltz swam right over me and made the play (Jason is one of the biggest and strongest men I have ever gone up against and he routinely gives me a challenge). We had to "bingo" it, the call the coaches yell when they want us to redo the play, and that time I got straight in front of him and stopped him cold. When the play was over he looked at me and said, "You were ready for me that time." I was, and I didn't want to look bad two plays in a row.

Coach Solich talked about the bowl game today. We will play Arizona, and most of us will leave on December 22; the rest will fly out on the 28th. The players who go early are those needed for practice, including the redshirts, I hope. The guys who come later are those who are injured or aren't needed for practice, like the extra kickers and some of the redshirts. We also saw what we will receive from the bowl: a faux-leather travel bag, a nice collared shirt, a hat, a jacket, a watch and a camera. I also hear that we get roughly $500 for food and expenses if we go with the early group. I don't care when I go. I wouldn't really mind missing Christmas with my family; I just want to go. I want to be a part of it and witness all of the inside stuff that goes on. I can't wait, but first I've got to get through finals.

Wednesday, December 9, 1998

I had a great day at practice today. It all started when we were working with the defense in one-on-one pass blocking drills. Scout team coach Damion Peter was in charge and I was going up against Jason Wiltz. We went at it and I put up a pretty good block. When we were done, Jason said he wanted a rematch and that time I stopped him cold. Damion Peter said, "Yeah, stuff his ass!" so I know I got his attention. My blocks were great the rest of the practice. I think it's mostly due to my overall development. I'm getting stronger in my shoulders and arms, and my squat is feeling much better now.

I found out today that I will go to San Diego with the first group. All but one of the freshman linemen are going down early. The majority of the freshmen aren't going, mostly because the varsity guys have enough depth in those spots that they don't need them. That means the scout team will have a lot of older guys on it to make up for the loss. Our next practice is on Saturday, which makes this week very nice. I will have plenty of time to study for finals. I'm not too worried about them; I just need to get to work.

Saturday, December 12, 1998

We usually have more good practices than bad ones. However, today's was bad. To start off with, there was no breakfast because the Hewit Center can't serve us on a weekend when school is still in session. Instead, there was a table of Nutri-Grain bars and fruit. This tided me over for only about 30 minutes.

The practice started at 10:00 in the Cook. I was going pretty hard and gave a full effort on scout punt team by sprinting down to the ball every kick. This effort, combined with the absence of breakfast, caught up to me later. At 11:30 we were doing inside running plays at the defense. As usual, I didn't have a person to alternate with and my energy level was falling fast. I got light-headed and about fainted. Jim Tansey hopped in for me for a couple plays and then I had to go back in and finish out the practice. Coach McBride must have noticed we were all getting tired because a few minutes before the final whistle he told us to take a knee and rest. We finished the day with two full gassers. I found out after practice that they also can't serve us lunch or pay us for practicing on the weekend since the University was still in session on Saturdays. I wasn't in the best mood. I took a nap in the locker room, got some fast food for lunch and headed home for a long weekend of studying.

I later read an e-mail from my dad saying that before I signed with the Huskers, my high school O-line coach, Joe Vojtech, talked to the Nebraska coaches and told them I had unbelievable potential. He said I had a great frame, great feet and the possibility to be one of the best players he ever coached. This is a great statement because he coached Outland Trophy winner Zach Wiegert just a few years ago. This brightened my day a lot.

Monday, December 14, 1998

The beautiful weather just keeps on coming. We practiced in half-pads on the grass, and it was a relatively short and easy practice. I was very tempted to say I had a final so I could skip practice and get some rest, but decided against it because it would break my almost-perfect streak. I've only missed one practice this whole year. Luckily, I haven't been injured seriously this year and have been a lead player at center on the scout team.

The practice ended with gassers and then I went to the

locker room and relaxed instead of lifting. I've been studying for finals like a madman. My schedule is turned around right now, staying up late into the night and sleeping during the day. This doesn't work well with football because I have to be ready to go at the normal time everyday.

Thursday, December 17, 1998

Kenny Walker, an ex-Husker all-star rush end who is deaf, is now working in the weight room as an assistant. He really knows his stuff and put me through one of the hardest workouts yet. I was doing some shoulder lifts by myself and he came over and made me keep going and going on about six different lifts until my shoulders and arms were completely dead. He told me I need to do a lot of shoulder work because that is one of the weakest parts of my body. To be on the offensive line, you have to have a big shoulders and a big chest. I'm not there yet. I hope after doing this workout many times, I'll catch up with the other guys and start looking like a real Husker.

Friday, December 18, 1998

Short practice today in sweats. We received $105 for the weekend before we leave for the bowl trip. We also received a bag of Adidas stuff—a black sweatshirt, a gray hooded sweatshirt, a black golf shirt, a red golf shirt, a navy blue golf shirt, a black hooded heavy jacket, a black hat, an Adidas shoulder bag, and a pair of Adidas sunglasses. I also was able to sell my books back to the bookstore and got another $100. This break is starting off pretty good so far!

Instead of going home for a short weekend, I'm staying with Jim Tansey at his apartment until we leave. The dorms are closed now, so everyone had to move out for winter break. The team can put guys up in a hotel for free, but the team is allowed to give us more money for the weekend if we found other accommodations.

Tuesday, December 22, 1998

We arrived at the airport at 6:30 this morning just as winter is finally starting to show itself with -3 degree weather. We got another $211 to start us off on the trip. The plane was delayed an hour, so I had a nice nap and more than doubled the amount of sleep I got last night. We finally got on the plane and arrived in San Diego at 10:30. Our first stop was the hotel, the Hyatt Regency, which is the crown hotel in all of San Diego, and checked into our rooms. The third floor of the hotel has several meeting rooms of different sizes and we took over all of them for various reasons. Some are meeting rooms for different positions, others are administrative rooms like the coaches meeting room, a room for all the video equipment, a training room, and the player's lounge. We had a few minutes to get settled, some guys got their ankles taped and then we were off to practice.

We practiced at the University of California at San Diego. The grass smelled like moss and felt incredibly spongy. It was a typical practice, and when it was over everyone showered and ate lunch in a big tent outside the locker room. We then were bussed back to the hotel in large Coach busses with big soft seats and huge windows. We had a team meeting at the hotel, and all of the rules and expectations for the trip were laid out. Coach Solich complimented us on not having any off-field incidents this year and said he hopes to keep it that way. I then checked out the players' lounge, which I think will be my home for the next couple of days. In it are about a dozen different arcade games, all set up to play for free. There's also a wall-long table full of snack food like granola bars, Pop Tarts, fruit, and many other healthy snacks. Next to those are four big glass-doored refrigerators with water, juice, iced tea, pop, milk, yogurt, pudding, applesauce, and more. One nice thing about being sponsored by Culligan is that we get as much bottled water as we could ever want. At 10:00 every night there will be a hot snack like nachos, pizza, tacos, and hamburgers. We also get free shuttle vans to take us anywhere we want to go in the city. Jim and I went to a huge outdoor mall called the Horton Plaza and walked around for a while. We were tired after this long day and called it a night by 11:30.

Wednesday, December 23, 1998

We had our first and only scrimmage of the trip today. There were a surprising number of fights on all sides of the ball. While I was standing on the sidelines on a break, I overheard one guy say, "We are no more than a really good high school team." Jim Tansey said there are too many egos on the team.

Later in the day I was talking with Sheldon Jackson, starting tight end, and he said some of these guys think that once they get that *N* on the helmet, all of the opposition will just roll over. The scrimmage lasted forever and at the end, all of the guys who were caught fighting had to run extra gassers. Lunch was at the practice site again and then I went back to the hotel for a quick swim with some other linemen. In the pool, I learned just how hard it is to play 'chicken' and carry a fellow 300 pounder on your back, even if it is in the water. Later, we had dinner in the hotel ballroom; it was all gourmet food and was incredibly delicious.

I went out to see the city again tonight. Jim and I went into a jazz bar to see some live music and enjoyed seeing some of the nightlife in a city outside of Nebraska. At first it didn't look like I'd get in, since I'm only 19 and you have to be 21 or over. Luckily for us, the doorman was bored, the night was slow and we were able to talk football long enough with him until he finally said "go ahead, have fun." My pledge to not drink during college lasted a full semester.

Everywhere we've gone so far has been pretty deserted. Some people in one of the shopping centers said it's because most of the locals either don't do much during the Holidays or they are out of town, some of them going to the mountains east of here to ski. We're hoping that the city livens up a little bit, it's pretty boring right now.

There is one amusing thing about this city. The temperature is getting down into the 50's in the evenings and the locals are in shock. They are bundled up in their heaviest jackets and those poor souls who run the kiosks in the outdoor mall are having to buy space heaters just to stay warm. All of us players are just fine in shorts, t-shirts and sandals, which causes the locals to look at us like we're trying to create a scene. Apparently they forgot that the rest of the country actually has seasons.

Thursday, December 24, 1998

I went to meetings at 10:00 this morning and then went back to bed until 2:00 in the afternoon. This is the only day the team gets off for the whole trip. A bus went to Tijuana at noon but we didn't make it.

Jim and I went to Hooters for lunch and we each got a Christmas gift from our waitress, Renee. It was only a card and a little chocolate bar but it was the thought that counts, and she said she felt bad for us being away from home on Christmas. We were very grateful for the cards so we had a dozen roses delivered to her while she was still working. She later called to thank us and said she was baking cookies for the whole team. These cookies turned out to be pretty bad, but once again it was the thought that counts.

We then did some shopping and went to some dance clubs and saw a bunch of other players there. We ended up having dinner at Denny's and later ordered a half-pound hamburger and soup from room service at 12:30 in the morning. Merry Christmas.

When you put a couple hundred bucks in the hands of young men in a new city, give them free transportation, no curfew and very little surveillance, they are bound to do anything. The drivers of the shuttle buses were given some guidelines about where they're allowed to take us (more of a general radius boundary) and we relied on their opinions to pick the next hot spot. There are a few under 21 strip clubs in San Diego and I think we hit them all by the end of the week. Jim Tansey taught me the etiquette of a strip club; how to act (calm, collected, outgoing), how to tip (again, you can either be a jerk or a gentleman. Gentlemen get remembered, jerks get tossed out).

We were standing outside one of the clubs, waiting for a shuttle bus with about a dozen players huddled together. One of the girls must have finished her shift and came walking out, covered up tight in the chilly night air. One of the older guys, a little cockier and more boisterous than most, started talking to her nicely but then quickly proposed that she come back to the hotel with him and his buddies. She said she could do private parties, but he'd have to officially book it. He quickly corrected her, saying how it wasn't dancing he was looking for. She walked away quickly while he and his buddies broke out laughing. Several of the guys around me were as amazed as I was by his behavior and I heard a few of them whisper, "what a jerk."

On later bowl trips, I grew increasingly tired of going out and instead saved my money and my energy. Even though San Diego was very fun for a bowl trip, I had just as much fun during later trips when I hardly went out at all.

Friday, December 25, 1998

It's Christmas. Instead of waking up and opening presents, we go to meetings and practice. Today is the last day of the season that we will be in full pads. Hallelujah!!! Again, it was a very long practice. Coach Solich stopped practice halfway through to talk to us. He told us to stop all of the fighting and scuffling because it wastes energy and is unproductive. After practice, the guys who dress for the game had to lift while the redshirts just showered up and ate lunch. Coach Solich also let the scout team players out of doing gassers. The scout team won't lift this whole trip because we could only bring a certain amount of weights and the older guys need to get through their workouts fast.

After lunch, about 20 of us took the bus to La Jolla beach. We walked around and saw seals on the beach. I was very surprised to see so many people at the beach on Christmas day. We then went back to the hotel and had another great banquet. We got our Christmas gifts from the Culligan Holiday Bowl at dinner. Inside of a nice leather bag was a nice thick jacket (which was incredibly small), a white golf shirt, a hat, a Vivitar 35mm camera and a Pulsar watch with the Holiday Bowl logo and the date on the face. I guess this Christmas wasn't too bad.

Saturday, December 26, 1998

Another early wake-up and practice. We went half-pads; this is the last practice in any kinds of pads. It was a rough practice but fellow redshirt o-lineman Scott Koethe and I were in a good rotation so I got some rest. Once again, the scouts got out of gassers. The lunch today was baby back ribs, which were very meaty and really tasty. We then were taken to Sea World. The team captains got into the Shamu act and did a little show with the Arizona guys. Shamu was trained to make us look like fools and did a good job. Shamu would do what the Arizona guys wanted him to do, but when our guys tried the same trick, Shamu pulled a trick on them and splashed the audience instead. Along with the free admission, we got free food from one of the many eateries in the park.

We then went back to the hotel and I took a long nap. My legs are very sore from all of the running in practice and walking around the city. I went to the players lounge and finally made it for the hot snack. I usually get back to the hotel too late. Tonight's snack was pizza and breadsticks. This also is the first night with a curfew and an 11:30 bed check.

Sunday, December 27, 1998

We had a 7:00 wake-up but as usual we slept until 7:50 and ran to meetings. After meetings, I went back to sleep until 9:20 before the busses left at 9:30. We got $166 before meetings. We practiced in sweats for about two hours. Lunch was at the site and then we were bussed to the San Diego Zoo. My parents and brother are in town for the game and we met at the zoo, and again later in the evening for some food. Another lazy, boring night with an 11:00 bed check.

Monday, December 28, 1998

This was my last practice of the year today and it was in sweats. Always a great way to finish.

The rest of the freshmen and the injured players arrived today. We had meetings and then took the busses to the naval yards and boarded the U.S.S. Peleliu. After a good lunch and a short program, we got a full tour of the ship. A couple of helicopters were on display and there also were a couple of Hummers with 50-calibre guns on them. Arizona brought their mascot dressed in their big-headed outfit onto the ship. I didn't see it happen, but the girl inside the suit couldn't see where the edge of the deck was and fell overboard. The only thing that saved her from breaking her skull on another ship was that big, overstuffed head.

The city finally came alive tonight with all of the fans who came for the game. Before now, the city has been eerily barren. I guess you shouldn't expect the holidays to be very exciting, even in a big city. This was probably the most exciting night yet.

Tuesday, December 29, 1998

My second day this trip without practice. We had 8:30 meetings this morning and later had a luncheon at the convention center where the guest speaker was Lou Holtz. Coach Holtz was an amazing speaker and it was easy to see how great of a motivator he is.

After lunch I did a little shopping in a seaside village behind the hotel and then went back for the 3:00 meetings. The guys who will suit up for the game went to Qualcomm Stadium. My brother and I took a trip to Tijuana. We only spent an hour walking around Revolucion Avenue and saw all of Mexico that we would ever want to. I bought some blankets and some other knock-off items. As soon as it was getting dark, we were out of there. Perhaps the only amusing thing that we saw while we were there was a sign on one of the businesses that said "Sorry, We're Open." I made the mistake of pointing it out to my brother and laughing, which drew the attention of a couple guys who were apparently part of the business and tried very hard to get us to come inside. If the stories of some of the guys who were here a couple days ago are true, I'm glad we didn't go in. Donkey shows, mother/daughter duos, you name it. That's all I've got to say about that.

After getting back through customs, we then went to Hooters and saw firsthand how busy the city is really getting. Thousands of people are pouring in and filling the downtown area. I spent most of tonight with my family.

Wednesday, December 30, 1998

Nebraska 20 – Arizona 23

We picked up $65 at breakfast as the last of the money we'll get for the trip, for a grand total of $547. With a team of 180 guys, that adds up to a lot of money.

At 2:30 we had a police escort to the stadium. I found my parents at a big tailgate party and sat with them at the game. The game was great for the defense besides a few key errors but the opposite was true for the offense. The inferno of Nebraska football that lit the whole country a few short months ago has now been reduced to a campfire with sparks of greatness jumping here and there. There is a lot of fresh wood in the fire and it will only take time before they catch and add to the whole. The potential for our team is immeasurable; we need to work hard and stay healthy. We lost the bowl game 20-23 and I felt responsible at the end even though I wasn't playing. Maybe I could have worked harder and played better in practice so the defense would have a challenge everyday. Maybe the defense shouldn't go against the scout team so much because in the game they won't be playing against freshmen. They want a good look and a good effort from us, but if we could block them the way they should be, we would all be playing in the game and not redshirting. I think a lot needs to change if next season has any chance of getting off the ground.

After the game, most of the players were looking for something to do with their free night, even if it was just to quietly pout about the loss in their room. One of the guys apparently had an exciting night when he and his roommate polished off a couple bottles of liquor and he mistakenly went through the wrong door when he got up to use the bathroom later on. He found himself out in the hallway in nothing but his boxers and a t-shirt. After stumbling around for a little bit trying to figure out why he couldn't find the toilet, he realized his mistake. Unfortunately, the lack of his glasses combined with the excessive alcohol in his system and made it impossible to read any of the door numbers. This still didn't change the fact that he really needed a bathroom. Unable to locate a restroom on the floor, he finally had to make use of the trash cans by the elevators.

He wasn't sure if he was on the right floor to begin with, so he hopped in the elevator and hit the button for his floor. Nothing happened. Undaunted, he hit the button for the floor with the players lounge. From there, he would try to regroup and get his bearings. Making it back up to his floor, he carefully went room to room, reading the numbers slowly and putting the puzzle together. He finally found his room, but at this point needed a restroom again. Not having a key on him, he began knocking in hopes that his roommate would get up. No luck. He knocked for a solid 15 minutes, resting only long enough to urinate in the trash can set outside his neighbor's door. His roommate finally opened the door after his alarm went off, did a double-take and watched him fall wearily onto his bed. He said the flight home a few hours later was not the most pleasant.

End of the Year Summary

The year started off with a sort of country club atmosphere. Everyone was happy living in a bubble of predestined victory. The bubble burst many times during this 9-4 season. One reason, which everyone noticed, was the lack of strong leadership. We had our leaders but they were never vocal enough or in-your-face enough when you made a mistake. It was too laid back. Another reason this season failed was the false belief that when you have that *N* on your helmet, you will automatically decimate the other team. Other reasons include the list of injuries to some of our top players, the overall youth of the team, and the weakness of the O-line. The attitude now is very much down to business.

For me personally, this first year was a huge transition. I was forced to dive right into football, college, and all that college life entails. It took me a little while to adjust but now I have a lot more confidence and am looking forward to my future here. In short, I got my butt kicked over and over every day and it seemed like the only time I ever did anything well was when the other guys were letting up a lot. I've got a long way to go.

1999 Winter Conditioning

Friday, January 15, 1999

School started again on the 11th and we have had all this time off from football. We're not required to go lift but I did anyway, just to keep my strength where it should be and also keep me in shape.

We had our first team meeting of the year today. Coach Solich recapped the year and gave us hope for next year. In his typical style, he didn't tell us anything that wasn't painfully obvious. After this meeting, all of the O-line guys met in Coach Tenopir's office. He talked about the need for unity within our group and also how we all need to get huge and show how to dominate again. Coach Tenopir then left and the seniors talked to us. They said one of the first things we're going to do this year is build unity. One way we're going to do that is by having everybody lift at the same time. If we're not there by 7:00 in the morning and we don't have an excuse, we get three sets of stairs. Every unexcused absence after that adds one stair to that number. If you are excused with a legitimate reason, you have one stair just because you missed a workout and you have to make your workout up somehow. We will lift in the morning four days a week, and we will have running and other activities in the afternoon.

This year, there will be a rebirth of Nebraska football and it will start with the O-line.

I had my body fat tested today and it wasn't anything good to report. I guess the winter break wasn't very good for me because, according to the test, I lost a little muscle and gained some fat. I'm now up to 16% body fat, the same as when I started. I know this isn't good and I also know it's temporary. Once I get going in the full swing of the program, I will see a whole new Dave Kolowski.

Wednesday, January 20, 1999

We had testing today and nothing has really changed. I gained a half-inch on the vertical jump and was slower by a couple hundreths of a second in the 40-yard run and the agility run. It wasn't really too bad if you consider that I'm 10 pounds heavier since the last time we tested. I hope that will factor in, making my score for each test better than the previous one.

This testing session is also an open tryout for any student who wants to be on the team. They go through every test just like we do, but in the end it is very hard for any of them to get noticed by the coaches. Rarely, someone will test well enough to be asked to join the team for winter conditioning and spring practices, but it's very hard to actually make the official roster or ever see playing time.

Thursday, January 21, 1999

Today was the first official day of lifting and it started early. The O-line met at the weight room at 6:50; anyone later than 7:00 had to run. I was there at 6:30 because my car pool leaves at 7:30 to go to my class in which I observe the teacher at an elementary school. I don't know if I will be able to make all of the Tuesday and Thursday lifts; I think it's pointless to just do two lifts and get sweaty so I will have to go back and shower and run. I also don't know if I can push myself to get there a half hour before everybody else on those days. I finished my lifting later at 4:00.

We have a few more additions to the O-line. I don't know all of their names yet but the ones that I got are Aaron Patch and Dan Swantek.

Friday, January 22, 1999

We lifted at 7:00 again. I got more done today because my first class is at 8:30. The weight room staff is much more critical about our form and weight than they have been for a while. They know of our goals as a unit and they're doing their part to make sure everything happens like it should.

Monday, January 25, 1999

Tonight we had a dinner meeting with Dave Ellis, the team nutritionist, about what to eat and how to eat. Basically, he wants the O-line to become the biggest and strongest position on the team, and that will come with the combination of proper eating and weightlifting. He said that on workout days we need to eat a lot of carbohydrates. We also need to eat healthier by selecting the best-choice carbs and protein. The best-choice foods are labeled on the bars so it's easy to figure out what to eat. These items are usually the foods that have the most nutrients and fewest fats and sugars. On off days (days without practice or lifting), we should eat about half as many carbs. As for fruit and vegetables, we can have as many as we can stuff down our throats.

Tuesday, January 26, 1999

We lost a few more linemen recently. Justin Valencia, my friend from the summer who I thought would do well, stopped working out for unknown reasons. Kyle Eisenhauer, who posted the fastest 40-yard time for linemen, and Steve

Ziemba, who now is devoting himself to throwing shot-put, also are gone.

Thursday January 28, 1999

Yesterday was our only off day during the week. It was very nice because we had nothing to do—no lifting, no running, and to top it off, no study hall. It was a beautiful day.

Jim Tansey was late to lifting last Thursday by about an hour and a half, and the punishment for that was three sets of stairs for him and one set of stairs for us. Right at 7:00, we all went out to the South Stadium bleachers and lined up for the stairs while Jim had to watch. I had to run them in jeans and a t-shirt (I was smart and also brought my coat while most guys were just in shorts and t-shirts). We got through the stairs pretty easily and then Jim counted off 20 push-ups while the rest of us did them. After that I was very awake and ready to go to my class, right after breakfast.

Tuesday, February 2, 1999

The linemen met in the Pit this afternoon and we had a guest coach. Aaron Graham, former Husker and currently in the pros, showed us some of the pass-blocking drills they do at the professional level. He had a lot of good tips and ran us through some of the drills.

I got to the weight room at 5:00, later than I should have and had to rush through the workout. At the end, Sean, one of the weight room staff who works with the O-line, put me through an abdominal workout that left me crawling on the floor. It was a new workout for me and I expect to keep doing it until I get it perfect.

Monday, February 8, 1999

We did an actual running circuit today for the first time. Now, along with the morning lifting, we meet in the afternoon to run. Our group started out on the low ropes and the bags. I felt a little rusty running through them but I never really messed up. We did jump rope drills after this and that was a whole other story. I did better at them than most people but I was still pretty rusty. Sean, who is leading us through these drills, complimented me a lot on my feet and my overall work. I think my main reason for having trouble is that the ropes are too short. All of the offensive linemen are over 6 feet tall and the ropes are made for people around 5'10" to 6'. I got through it all and then finished up my lifts and called it a day.

Tuesday, February 9, 1999

I continued to improve my strength by raising my rack clean by six more pounds. My weight is up to about 285 pounds and I'm pretty confident it is mostly muscle. I always try my best to eat healthy, especially at the training table when all of the best food is labeled for your convenience.

Thursday, February 11, 1999

The weather is actually acting like it should now and dropped 60 degrees in one night to a -2 degrees wind chill. I hate Nebraska weather because it's never the same for more than two or three days.

At 3:30 this afternoon we ran in the Cook. My group started on the jump ropes and this time we were penalized 10 push-ups for every mistake we made. I probably messed up on jump ropes six or seven times. I think it really sucks to have that kind of punishment, especially when the ropes are too short. I didn't mess up on the low ropes or the bags so I was happy about that. Coach Tenopir and Coach Young were there to watch us and I didn't hear anything bad about what I was doing so that was very positive for me. We had to run a half-gasser as punishment for Andy Gwennap being late to morning lifting. After it was all over, my legs were tired and I still had to do heavy squats.

I did some mediocre long snaps to Josh Brown, a freshman place-kicker, and then went in to the locker room for a quick rest before doing squats. I got to the weight room at about 4:30 and went to work. I surprised myself again by raising the weight another 10 pounds to 325 on my last set of 10. I let out a yell as I got the bar up and that helped me get the adrenaline flowing, and I finished the whole thing pretty strong. Sean said I could have gone 335 pounds and I think so, too. So far, I've raised my squat weight 40 pounds in three weeks. Next week we start doing sets of five and I plan to give myself a good challenge with that.

Friday, February 12, 1999

We played racquetball today for our running workout. I played freshman tackle Scott Koethe and beat him two out of three games. I took some lessons from Danny Cork, another freshman, and have really improved my game.

I went around and interviewed Dennis Leblanc, Boyd Epley and Dave Ellis today for a speech I plan to give about a side of Nebraska football that most people don't see—academics, training and nutrition. Boyd Epley told me about his plans to build a huge, all-in-one training facility at the north end of the stadium. It would have a bigger weight room with state-of-the-art equipment and a complete testing facility with two whole football fields of Astroturf. It will cost $50 million and he hopes to start building it in five to seven years.

The stadium is currently getting a facelift by adding a new press box and skyboxes. It's supposed to be pretty amazing and is, at my best guess, about halfway done. A third of it has windows up and the rest of it is mostly naked steel beams. The outside is almost complete and looks really good. They just finished tearing down the old press box about a week ago.

Tuesday, February 16, 1999

Today was the first day since I've been here that I couldn't complete my lifts due to injury. I have a shoulder strain and it caused me to break my seven-month streak. I went to the trainers and they didn't really diagnose it; they just iced it and told me not to do anything with a lot of arm movement. Thanks anyways.

John Archer, our head strength coach, wasn't too happy with this. He's the type who wants you to do your lifts no matter what and go as hard as you can each day. We've become so accustomed to hearing him turn down requests for a reprieve that it's become an inside joke. "Archer, I'm pretty sure I broke my back. I can't feel my legs. I don't think I can squat today." "Nonsense, just add 10 pounds to your last set and you'll be fine."

Wednesday, February 17, 1999

I had my body fat tested today and the results were very good. I not only weighed in at a record 285 pounds, I lost three pounds of fat and gained eight pounds of muscle. Dave Ellis said I could have one of the best reports of the winter if I keep up that kind of progress. He also said I have the frame to be a real man out there on the field. I think he is on to something.

Thursday, February 18, 1999

My shoulder still hurt today and I was unable to do all of my lifts. I did all of the squat, 365 pounds for my last set of five, but I had a little trouble with it. I don't think Sean believes I can make it to 405 for my last set in two weeks but that is my goal. Dan Morrison, a fellow redshirt from

Council Bluffs, Iowa, just quit. It wasn't his choice, he has a strange medical condition where his spine shrinks. He said his brother had it and he is starting to show the signs of it. This just adds to the list of players who aren't coming back. Steve Ziemba is much happier throwing for track than he was with football. One of the guys who was a year ahead of me, Lonnie Fulton, also recently quit for medical reasons. I hope this is the last of the attrition but I know it won't be. Some guys will get hurt, others will have to quit for academic reasons, others will have something happen to them that can't be put in the papers. All we can do is keep looking to tomorrow with a positive attitude.

Monday, February 22, 1999

This was a rough day. I didn't get much sleep last night and really didn't do anything or eat much over the weekend. That all caught up to me today.

I only messed up three times at practice—once on the bags, which is unheard of for me, and twice on the jump ropes. After running was over, I was totally dead. I took about a half-hour to recover and then finished lifting. Afterward fellow freshman lineman Aaron Patch wanted to play some racquetball and I ended up beating him soundly.

The bright point of the day was that study hall was called off for the night due to the snowstorm that rolled in this morning. It started snowing at 7:00 and it didn't stop until 11:00 tonight. Everything is icy and covered in snow, and I had to catch myself from falling many times. I hope my morning class is called off tomorrow, then I can lift in the morning and use the rest of the day to get some work done.

Tuesday, February 23, 1999

I was finally able to do hang clean today. I did 264 pounds for my last set of five and didn't have too much trouble except that my shoulder was slightly affected by it. We did pass-protection drills with Aaron Graham again, and I'm getting better. We did some different drills today like punching up while holding a 45-pound weight out and popping a heavy ball back to the thrower, both done in a good stance and with proper form.

I received my first email from the elementary school class that I'm a pen pal with through H.E.L.P. (Husker Email Literacy Program). The first email is just basically an introduction and sharing of vital statistics. I think this will be kind of fun to do.

Thursday, February 25, 1999

Billy Diekmann hurt his knee today while running shuttles. He planted wrong and the sounds that came from his knee and his mouth would have made you believe he totally blew it out. Later I heard from Doak Ostergard, the head trainer, that Bill just strained his knee. He really got lucky.

> Something that sort of makes this scene funny was that we had a guest coach from Japan here today and he had a video camera to tape what we were doing. Somewhere in Japan right now is a video of a bunch of us working out, with the audio portion filled with some of the loudest swearing I've ever heard.

I was able to get Archer to switch today's workout with Friday's because I really didn't have the energy to do heavy squat after all the running. I also played Dominic Raiola in racquetball before lifting; he beat me 15-10 in a very fast-paced and tough game.

Friday, February 26, 1999

Brian Nelson, a good friend from high school, came down today and made an unofficial/official visit. He has been asked to walk-on next year and I'm pretty sure he will accept it. He came down at 2:30 and we went over to the stadium. He watched us do our pass-pro stuff and after that Jim Tansey took him to the training room and talked to him while I was lifting. We ate dinner with Aaron and Jimi, and talked all about football and everything else we could think of. Later we took him to a huge party at Ralph Brown's (starting defensive back) house. It was busted around 11:30 so we went to a truck stop and got some good old greasy food and then called it a night. I think he enjoyed his visit and now will be able to make a stronger decision about coming here.

Tuesday, March 2, 1999

We're having a racquetball tournament now and I am staying alive in it so far. Today I beat Dave Volk and Russ Hochstein and am in the semi-finals. We should have a winner by Friday. Russ has become quite the media darling in the past few weeks. We have had a photographer come to the weight room and take pictures of him and he has been interviewed about all sorts of topics. We only have two more days of lifting in the mornings and I can't wait to get over with it.

Thursday, March 4, 1999

This was the last day of the winter conditioning running program. Before we ran, Archer told us it would be an easier workout today. We cut out one of the jump rope drills, one of the low ropes drills and a lot of the bag drills. When it was over, I beat Scott Koethe in racquetball to make it to the quarterfinals. I then did my Friday workout and called it a day.

I spent the night in my room doing homework instead of going to study hall. It's very easy to get out of study hall—all you have to do is fill out a form saying you're going to be at a study group for one of your classes and give it to your counselor. I've only truly skipped study hall twice. I don't think this one actually counts as skipping because I was still doing homework in my room.

Some of the older guys have to attend study hall too, but in a different way. If their grades are bad enough, they are required to spend a certain amount of time per week in the academic support center. To keep track of this, they sign in on a computer and sign out when they're done. Jim Tansey has to do this, but most of the time I'll sign him in and out so he doesn't even have to show up.

Friday, March 5, 1999

We finished up the racquetball tournament today and I ended up third. I was beat by Jon Rutherford, and Kyle Kollmorgan won the whole thing. I flew through the workout and did some extra stuff just for kicks, and then rejoiced when the day was over. Winter conditioning is finally over. I no longer have to get up at 6:00 in the morning to lift; I no longer have to worry about running stairs and getting a red belly for being late; and I no longer have to do any of those damn drills, at least until spring ball is over.

Dave Volk had a party at his house tonight. All of the O-line was there. Various people, including most of the seniors and John Archer, gave speeches about the hard work we all had just put in and how proud all of us were of each other. In his speech, Archer said Coach Tenopir told all the other coaches that this O-line is the best group he's had in a while. He has never had a group that has been this unified or a group that was so dedicated to getting their work done and done well. We all knew this, yet it was nice to hear it from someone like Archer.

The best part of this night was getting our strength coach to do a keg stand. Priceless.

Tuesday, March 9, 1999

I had my body fat tested today and the results continue to improve. I'm now at 13.3% body fat with about 37 pounds of fat. Dave Ellis said that's one of the best reports of the winter, and I'm about 10 pounds of muscle away from being a force on the O-line.

Wednesday, March 10, 1999

We tested out today and the improvements keep coming. I had to test early because I had a career-interest survey class at 3:00 so I went with the seniors who were being looked at by the pro scouts. I have a problem running by myself though, I always seem to mess up or do things wrong. I run best when I'm competing with someone. I forget about getting myself to move as fast as I can and just focus on beating the guy. I improved on all four tests: 10- and 40-yard runs, vertical jump, and pro agility. I'm running a 5.84-second 40-yard dash, which is still slow as hell. My speed definitely needs to improve.

I also did the 300-yard shuttle run today and, thanks to winter conditioning, I was able to pass it, barely. I ran the first shuttle in 62.7 seconds. After the five-minute break, I ran the second one and totally lost my strength about halfway through. James Sherman and Jason Schwab were encouraging me, yelling at me and asking if I wanted to do this again. I didn't want to do it again, and ran the last 100 yards as fast as I could. I finished the second one at 67 seconds flat. The average of the two times has to be below 64.99 and I was 64.85, just a click of the button away from having to do it over again. After I was done running that, I could barely walk and arrived late to the career-interest thing. Now, all I have to do for the rest of the week is go to class and look forward to spring break. I swear that I will sleep for two days straight once I get home.

1999 Spring Ball

Spring Ball is a great excuse to have a mini in-season during the off-season. I'm sure this is great for the coaches since they are very limited in their ability to interact with their players outside of the regular season. However, for the players it causes a few mixed feelings. Some are looking for a chance to show how far they've come since last fall and are looking to earn some respect. Others are just plain tired and need a break after winter conditioning. I was a mix of the two. I had nowhere to go but up, but I also would have loved some time off.

Monday, March 22, 1999

Today was the first practice of spring ball. We started out with meetings and Coach Solich and other coaches gave us an overview of the spring program. Basically, we will have four weeks of Monday/Wednesday/Friday practices with scrimmages on Saturday. The NCAA only allows 15 official practices, so the last Friday will be a free day before the final scrimmage.

We then had the first of many O-line meetings in Coach Tenopir's office. He started at the bottom and explained some rudimentary parts of the running and passing games.

It went pretty quickly and he went over a lot of plays. My head was spinning afterward. I really couldn't tell you what to do for a certain play based on the meeting but I had my head full of the terminology and that got me started.

I joined the kickers and other snappers in the Cook for the specialty period and was filmed for the evening news doing a long snap. I then went to the Pit and went through some drills with the O-line. We divided into our groups—I'm on the fourth team offense—and learned some of the most basic plays. We learned some of the pass plays and some of the outside zone running plays as well. Then we all went to the Cook and ran the plays against the defense. I thought I did fairly well and picked up the center's job pretty quickly. I had a fair share of mistakes but for practicing for the first time without looking off of cards, I think I did pretty well.

After study hall tonight, one of the defensive starters was lurking outside the stadium doors, waiting for one of the freshmen inside. Apparently, this freshman, Justin Smith, said that this senior standout was gay. Judging from the look of Justin's face the next day, I'd say he took great offense to this.

> However, it seems this defensive star was just covering up for his image. One of my former girlfriends was friends with a very outgoing gay guy named "Martin." He met another man in an online chat room one night and they arranged to meet. This football player showed up and "Martin" didn't really know who he was nor did he care. The football player said that he requires total discretion about this activity, which he implied he'd done before several times. He kept asking "Martin" if he was sure he never heard of him, which he hadn't, and this must have been a turn off for the football player who left a short while later.

This is nothing new. You can't expect a group of 180 guys to all be straight. Statistically, there's a very slim chance of that happening. Football has long been satirized with homosexual jokes. But so what? As long as it's not a disruptive nuisance to the team or to the individual, it shouldn't matter if someone is gay or not.

Tuesday, March 23, 1999

At 2:00 a small group of younger players met in Coach Tenopir's office and we went over the tape from yesterday's practice. Starting tackle Adam Julch led the session and it amazed me how well he knew the offense. I was able to watch myself run the plays. Some I did right, others I did horribly wrong but I learned from all of it. There are so many plays to know that it's easy to get mixed up. Tomorrow we learn more plays and I'll need to study all of these really hard if I'm to do any good.

They have the testing results posted in the weight room going from the highest total points to the lowest. It really surprised me to find that I was second to last on point totals. I was right above my friend Aaron Patch, who is now cut for academic reasons. I have nowhere to go but up, and I know I will be one of the best.

Today I received my "Survivor" sweatshirt for making it to all of the winter workouts. I put in a lot of hard work during those six weeks and it's nice to get something out of it. It's just a gray sweatshirt with a special "Survivor" logo on the left breast.

Wednesday, March 24, 1999

Today's practice was in sweats again and I think it went a lot better than Monday. We added another six plays today and it's getting easier to memorize them because they all fit into certain categories that are blocked the same way. The only hard part is remembering which play is in which category. I'm fairly good compared to the rest of the guys.

Thursday, March 25, 1999

I found out from Adam Julch today that I was wrong on my blocking a lot more than I thought. Apparently, there was a whole series of blocks where I went the wrong way and it really stood out on the film. I don't know what I was thinking but I was consistent in blocking the wrong way, so all I have to do is switch what I was thinking and I should be good.

Friday, March 26, 1999

Today was the first day of full pads since Christmas day. All the O-line was in the Pit to begin with, as usual, and we stayed there for a good part of the practice going over plays and making sure that we (especially the freshmen) knew what we were doing. We then went up to the field and ran through the stations with the defense and ended up doing pretty well. I had to ask what to do from the guards or the coaches about half of the time, which didn't look too good, but it was a lot better than making a fool out of myself and messing up the play entirely. With everything combined, I think this was a pretty good practice, especially with all that I had to know.

Saturday, March 27, 1999

Today does not feel like a Saturday. This week has been incredibly long. Spring break was a curse in disguise.

We had our first unofficial scrimmage today. Most of the practice was just like yesterday but today we added a 15-minute scrimmage drill at the end. Each group had 15 minutes to scrimmage and we were the last to go. I felt like

I had a really good day compared to yesterday. I hardly ever had to ask what to do and did the right things about 90% of the time. During the scrimmage, we scored once on a drive from the 40-yard line and really didn't do much else.

We still have a long way to go for our offense to gel, and no one should expect us to be perfect within a week. I worked with the punt team today and did a live punt where I got creamed on a hit that could be heard around the state. I was setting up to take on a guy coming from the right and had my weight off balance enough that when I was hit by another guy from the left, it blew me up and I actually blacked out for a second. Luckily, I was able to get up as soon as I hit the ground and just continued running even though I didn't know exactly what I was doing. It must have been a good hit due to all the laughing and fingers pointed at me from the sideline.

Tuesday, March 30, 1999

Another easy day of lifting. I like these off days because it gives me time, if I need it, to get extra work done in the weight room or with homework. We're only going to practice on Monday, Wednesday, Friday, and Saturday during the four weeks of spring ball. Tuesday and Thursday are the days we're supposed to lift.

There was an unofficial meeting for all of the players today. We had a speaker—I think his name was Don Johnson—and he talked to us about how to treat women. He's a former professional football player and now runs the M.V.P. program, which stands for Men for Violence Prevention. He talked about how we are all marked men; if we screw up with even something as small as a speeding ticket, it could turn into national news. He also talked about how to treat women and the stereotypes around both genders, especially with football players. It was a short speech but we had a lot of crowd interaction and I thought it was a very good program.

Thursday, April 1, 1999

My dad sent me the program from the Outland Trophy dinner, where he saw the winner, Kris Farris, speak about his football career. Farris said that when he was a freshman, he was pretty bad. At one point, he went to his coach and said, "Well, I guess you heard how bad I am." This is pretty much how I feel; now I hope I can turn out to be an Outland Trophy winner. Another thing he talked about was that he focused on fixing one thing each day until his whole package as a lineman was excellent. I have many things I need to fix, but I have found one thing in particular that I need to work on. On the film today I noticed that on almost every running play, my first step goes backward about three inches instead of forward like Coach Tenopir says it should. After my workout I worked on making my first steps forward and powerful. This is the kind of work that is going to make me the best I can be.

Coach Tenopir told me I made a lot of mistakes in the scrimmage on Wednesday. I saw this, too, when I watched the film and I know that my grade for that scrimmage won't be very high.

> Footwork is something that is very important for a lineman. Your feet determine where your weight is distributed and you need to be centered when you take on a big guy so they don't just toss you to one side or slip by you when you're off balance. You need to be low and you need to be firm in your position, yet ready to move quickly. It may look easy on TV, like we just get a bunch of sumo wrestlers in pads and let them run into each other,

but there's an amazing amount of skill and technique involved as well as brute force.

For all the finesse that is required, of which I'm quite capable, I never agreed with this first step principle. As a lineman, you don't want to signal where you're going by how your stance looks. For instance, if you are going to pull to the left, you don't want to appear to lean to the left to give it away to the defense. A smart defense can pick up on these subtle clues and figure out what a play is before the ball is even snapped. Instead, you want to have a neutral stance so that you can move forward, backwards, and side to side quickly and easily.

Most coaches say that when in a three-point stance (one hand on the ground), your hand should have a little weight on it, but not so much that you would fall over if you picked it up. This gives you a little forward momentum, but not a lot. Taking your first step forward almost completely negates that initial momentum. Plus, being a center, I can't hardly have any weight on my hand because it has to snap the ball to the quarterback. To further compound the situation, the guards and tackles give themselves about a 6-inch cushion behind the line of scrimmage to build up some steam but I'm right there with a guy inches away from my face ready to bulldoze me. It just seems natural to take that first step backwards to press for some forward force. Other centers before me have done perfectly fine with the technique; I guess that could have been one reason why I was never great. Perhaps I just never had the physiological structure to be a great center, but I tried anyways.

Saturday, April 3, 1999

Scrimmage today. We all got $30 for the weekend. I took 17 snaps and I think I did pretty well on them. We scored once on a 71-yard run from Paul Kastl, a freshman fullback from Lincoln. My offensive group still isn't very effective at moving the ball, and we have a ways to go before we gel into a working offense. The number ones and twos had a good practice. The defense pretty much dominated but the offense had their share of good plays.

Rush end Kyle Vanden Bosch was voted Lifter of the Year. This is a very prestigious honor because it shows that he stood out amongst everyone as having the most positive work ethic and determination over the past year. This is even more special because the players vote on it. I don't know if I could ever win this. It would take a lot of work and leadership, something that wouldn't be too hard for me, but I would also have to win over everyone on the team, which is very hard to do.

Tuesday, April 6, 1999

I discovered that I am developing an eye infection right now. My eye was irritated last night but I thought it was just from my contact. Apparently, I touched my eye with a contaminated finger during practice and now I'm paying for it. I saw the team doctor, Dr. Lonnie Albers, and he gave me some eye drops.

Wednesday, April 7, 1999

Today was not a good day for practice. My right eye is swollen to the point where I can barely open it, and bending down all the time caused blood rushes that made it swell even more. My peripheral vision is cut in half and that didn't help my blocking. One time, Coach Young told me, "Your guy made the tackle, didn't you see him?" I wanted to laugh at the irony but I held it back.

I went to the training room after practice to get my eye examined and I had to wait while Randy Stella, a sophomore linebacker, got his back sewed up. Somehow he got a gash in his back about five inches long. Also, Jim Tansey broke his foot in a pile during one of the first plays. He has to have surgery and will be out for about three months.

Injuries plagued us last season and was the hidden cause of our bad season and the number of injuries keeps rising. Some of the most desperate positions are the running backs and quarterbacks. All the papers are commenting on the problem and the future doesn't look too bright. Somehow, we became cursed.

Thursday, April 8, 1999

My eye was pretty much the same today; it was swollen and leaked a lot. Dr. Albers washed it out thoroughly and gave me some new drops. After that, I went to lunch and experienced some of the worst pain I have felt in a while because the numbing drops had worn off and the medicine was starting to work. I thought I was having an allergic reaction to the medication, but Dr. Albers reassured me that I wasn't. He said I shouldn't lift today and sent me home to take a nap and let the medicine work. I hope I'll be able to practice tomorrow and also lift after practice. It will be up to Dr. Albers to make that decision.

Friday, April 9, 1999

This day was a waste of 24 hours. My eye has gotten a lot better since yesterday. I can open it almost all the way and it's hard to tell that it is still swollen. I went to Dr. Albers about my eye and he said it was 50% better than yesterday, but I shouldn't practice because I might contaminate the team and the timing would not be good before the Spring Game. I couldn't even lift because Boyd Epley said I should get better before I touch any weights. I'm not sure if I will scrimmage tomorrow. All I did at practice today was stand around and watch the third team run plays. Today was also the start of the Coaches Clinic and I had to be held out while hundreds of high school coaches from around the country were watching.

Saturday, April 10, 1999

Today was the last scrimmage before the Spring Game. I tried to see Dr. Albers today before practice, but he wasn't there. I finally gave up and gave myself permission to play; I hope he doesn't mind, but I had to do it. I had 21 snaps in today's scrimmage and thought we did reasonably well. The number one offense had an incredibly tough time moving the ball against the number one defense. The twos had a much better scrimmage, but they didn't score a single touchdown either. The third team defense had a great day against the third team offense and we produced the only touchdown of the day.

I practiced without my contacts, so everyone I blocked just appeared as a fuzzy body. It was impossible to distinguish faces and I could barely make out numbers. I worried most about blocking the right fuzzy body and blocking him well. We also got $30 today but it didn't seem like enough for the time we spent today. We started meetings at 9:30 and we got home at 5:30.

Sunday, April 11, 1999

Funny story time! A couple of months ago, one of the guys on my floor thought it would be funny to order *Playgirl* for me from one of those "bill me later" ads. This guy, Adam, told Mike Wilford, a fellow walk-on lineman who lives on my floor, that he did it. I got the first magazine about a month ago and have been plotting my revenge ever since. Last night, when I knew he wouldn't be here, I acted. At around 3:30 in the morning, I told the student assistant from another floor that I was locked out of my room, giving him Adam's room number. He let me into his room without checking my ID. I ripped the magazine in half and taped pages all around the room—on walls, on his dressers, on his TV and his stereos, on his fridge, and on the ceiling. I also put pictures in his clothes drawers, clothes pockets, school books, folders, in his CD case, under cushions, under his bed, in his sheets, and just about any place I could think of. On the front of his door I put a picture of a bare-chested guy and wrote on it "Welcome home, Adam, we've been waiting."

Today when he returned and saw the door he laughed because that's a pretty typical prank in a guys' dorm. But when he opened the door and was greeted by dozens of pictures of naked men, he flipped out. I could hear him screaming and raving halfway down the hall.

Leif Sidwell, my roommate and fellow lineman, and Mike saw Adam carrying a huge handful of crumpled pictures to the trash can. Mike started laughing at the situation and a small fight broke out between the two but was over quickly.

Adam told Mark, our floor student assistant, that he wanted whoever did this punished. He even threatened to call the police and press charges. As Mark went from room to room to get any information, I confessed that I had done it. I told him the whole story, and then the residence director told me Adam really wanted an apology.

So I apologized. He accepted the apology and then went on a little lecture about how he didn't pay all this money to have a single room in the dorm and not be safe (I'm leaving out his colorful adjectives). I think I might get kicked out of the dorm, but there are only three weeks of school left and any kind of action will take a while to go through, so I'm not too worried about it.

Monday, April 12, 1999

Today was the last day of practice in full pads and it showed. Everyone had very low energy and I don't think I heard anyone screaming and shouting for their group to step it up. I focused a lot on getting my hands where they should be on the blocks. I had a lot of good blocks today and don't think I messed up too badly on anything. All in all, it was a good day and I'm glad to see it end.

Wednesday, April 14, 1999

Today was probably one of the worst days of my life. The past couple of weeks have been really stressful. I'm having a hell of a time getting all of my classes taken care of in proper fashion, I'm probably going to get in trouble for the prank I did to Adam, my best friend just got back from the Marines and I haven't even been able to talk to him on the phone, I don't have any free time to just relax, and my social life is in a coma. Today's practice just topped it off nicely. For starters, I went without my contacts because I'm still recovering from pink eye. I couldn't see when coaches were talking to me or telling me where to go with motions.

During Coach Tenopir's station, I must have messed up more than half of the time and he noticed everything. My brain stopped working and I had a nice view of my colon. After that, my practice was over. I just didn't care.

For the first time since I've been here, I've begun to question whether I should stay here or try another school. These thoughts didn't bother me like I thought they would. I just have to remember that this is a rough, stressful time and a lot of things will seem silly later on. I hope this is one of those things.

Saturday, April 17, 1999

It has been 10 months since I played in the Nebraska Shrine Bowl football game. That was the last game I played in Memorial Stadium and not much has changed. In the Shrine Bowl, I only had two series of plays and took all of the long snaps. In today's Spring Game, it was only slightly different. I had most of the long snaps for the White team, but I played in no series of plays in the whole game. I don't know if that was just an oversight by Coach Tenopir, but it made me kind of mad. Everyone I talked to had at least two or three series and I had none. One reason for this oversight could have been that we had two teams of offense on the Whites and I was the third center. At one point during the game, Coach Tenopir told us that the second team would be going in. I was standing by Matt Shook, the other center, when Coach told him to take the first series. I thought I would get the next series, but they ended up fumbling and Shook went out there again to make up his time. After that, the number ones stayed in and tried to win the game. I never got my chance.

I wanted to talk to Coach during the game and ask him when I would go in, but I don't like to do that. It makes me seem impatient and egotistical and I don't want him to have a bad opinion of me. I'll talk to him about it next week and hope to get a lot of things straightened out then. The Whites lost to the Reds 12-27. We got another $30 today. Nate Kolterman tore his ACL, a major ligament in the knee, during the game. He will be out for a long time, possibly until November.

> This turned out to be a career ending injury for Nate. He appeared to be rehabbing forever. He played sparingly in several games, but never made much of an impact. These sort of seemingly tempo-

rary injuries that eventually cost people their athletic careers appeared to be a common theme with dozens of guys that I played with.

Tuesday, April 20, 1999

I talked to Coach Tenopir today. He wondered how I didn't get any offensive plays in the Spring Game and told me he had wanted me to have a couple of series. He said my snaps for the punts and the field goal were all pretty good, and that my long-snapping skill is a plus (I hope he means that I won't be cut since I have a valuable skill). He told me I need to improve my speed, size, and strength. That also goes for most of the young O-linemen. We all have many areas to improve on. Leif Sidwell has a chance to be second team next year and that would mean he would get a full scholarship. He's going in for shoulder surgery this Thursday.

I finally got a car. I went through the majority of my freshman year without a vehicle and that waiting has finally paid off. I now have an '89 Chevy S10 Blazer 4x4 with all the features and no rust. The only bad thing is that it is Colorado's colors, black and gold.

Since we're officially done with football for the next month, I have the most freedom that I've had this whole year. Archer told us he doesn't even want to see us this week. I've been playing racquetball and running a little, just to keep in shape, but I haven't done anything monumental. From now until May 17 we're in a period of "active rest," which means we're not required to do anything, but it would look good if we did. I really enjoy having all this time to myself, but have found that I waste most of it. I guess without football placing solid constraints on my time, I don't have the pressure to get my work done.

I got a certificate from the Big 12 conference saying I made the Commissioner's Honor Roll. I knew I would get this and hope there are many more to come. All that's needed to receive this honor is to keep a 3.0 GPA or better throughout a single semester.

This is the time of year when the team doctors love to have surgeries done. We have plenty of time before the season starts and the athlete can be allowed to fully rest and recover while school is not in session for the summer. Three offensive tackles had surgery: Jim Tansey had surgery for his broken foot, Leif Sidwell had shoulder surgery, and Nate Kolterman had surgery on his knee, along with guard Chris Saalfeld, and many more people who will be out for a long time.

This is also a time, near the end of a school year, when a lot of guys make bold decisions for their next year. One of my neighbors and freshman scholarship wing back Shawn McGann is transferring to Notre Dame. That means that we will be playing against him in two years.

Tuesday, May 4, 1999

I met with Coach Solich today. He wanted to meet with each player before school got out. The whole point of the meeting was to touch base before the summer, answer questions, and get some confidence and goals for the summer. He asked me what I think I need to work on and I said the same things I did in my meeting with Coach Tenopir: speed and strength. He was pleased with that assessment.

There wasn't much room for small talk, even though there could have been. Frank and my dad played football together for the Omaha Mustangs, a short-lived semi-pro team back in the late 1960's. My dad has been able to keep up with Frank off and on over the years, as well as a couple other people within the Husker organization. No time for talking about that here I guess.

1999 Summer Conditioning

Monday, May 17, 1999

Today was the first day of our official summer conditioning workouts. For the next couple of weeks, we'll do our base lifting program to get everyone strong again after the long break. After that, we'll start running and doing all of that fun stuff. Also, we have to be there at 5:30 in the evening every day (except Wednesdays and weekends) or else we have to run stairs for being late.

Friday, May 28, 1999

After two weeks of summer workouts, I'm starting to feel a lot more positive about my whole situation. My weight has been consistent around 280 pounds and I feel as trim as I ever have in my life (I realize the irony, thank you). I can really tell a difference in my overall strength, especially in my upper body, and am filling out with a lot of muscle in my shoulders and arms. I'm finally starting to grow into my body and it couldn't have happened any later. Other people are starting to notice the size change as well and I'm really feeling comfortable with it.

I started working at the Royal Grove nightclub about a month ago. Last Wednesday night, after the dancing stopped, I was helping clean up and tried to hop up on the stage like I've done many times, but this time my foot slipped and I cut my shin on the metal edge of the stage, creating a gash about an inch in diameter. I went home and slept with it elevated all night to stop the bleeding. This didn't help. It continued to bleed all night and the next morning. I saw Jason Schwab as I was walking to class and he insisted I go see our team doctor about it. I did and he sewed me up with four stitches. I guess it was worse than I thought.

Monday, June 7, 1999

We had a team meeting in the stadium today. Some of the coaches and most of the strength staff were there and they mostly talked about how the summer will go and what they expect (pretty much the same as last summer). A lot of the incoming freshmen were here today, including Brian Nelson, my good friend from my high school. The summer camps for the high school players have started, forcing us out of the north locker room. I now change at home and ride my bike. I live so close that it's faster to ride my bike than to drive.

Most guys live off campus after their first year. The rent around Lincoln is very affordable and the convenience of off-campus living far outweighs anything the dorms could offer.

My dad recently called all the coaches I'm affiliated with, such as Coach Solich and Coach Tenopir and also John Archer, and I think he even talked to our nutritionist, Dave Ellis. He basically called to thank them for the great year I had and also to find out where I am according to the coaches. The coaches all agree that I have a great attitude and am a hard worker. They also said I'm at the point now where they expect me to be. If I can keep growing like I have, I will definitely play someday. I might be on the scout team again next year. I'd rather not be on the scout team again, so I'll really have to work hard and start making some serious progress. I'm managing to keep my weight around 280, but I'm sure that will take a dive as soon as we start running.

Starting next week, we will come in at 7:30 in the morning to lift and then return at 5:30 to run. Personally, I think this is stupid. The summer may be an important time to train, but it's also an important time for working and family and vacations. We're forced to put aside about six hours a day for football with workouts, travel time, preparation, and clean up. During the summer I would much rather have fun, stay out late, party, work, and get my workouts in at times that are convenient for me. Right now, the 5:30 workouts are fine but I think it's very controlling to make us change our whole days. The argument is that it's better for us to run at one time and lift at another so we will have ample energy for both workouts. This makes sense, but not for the whole summer. It's time for a reality check.

The whole summer and winter conditioning programs are technically optional, but we require it of ourselves. We set the rules as a group and the older guys enforce these rules.

Tuesday, June 8, 1999

I got started on a workout program that is lovingly referred to as "Body By Arch." It is an accelerated chest workout that's supposed to make the upper body as strong as can be. I'm a lot stronger than I thought I was. I was working with Scott Koethe and Mike Wilford and found out that I'm as strong as Mike, who was far ahead of me earlier in the year. Scott has been having trouble lately. He has been losing muscle and strength and doesn't know how to explain it. For my last set of bench, I did 230 pounds 10 times, which is a new max for me.

Wednesday, June 9, 1999

I started my new job today. It was set up through the Huskers and I'm working at a cement plant called Nebco. It's very convenient because I live only four blocks away. Today, I learned how to change the brake pads on a train and how to arc weld. I'm not sure what my specific duties are, but I guess I'm supposed do as many things as I can and be as useful as I can be. I worked from 6:30 this morning to 4:00 and then worked my other job at the Royal Grove from 9:00 to 1:30 in the morning. It was a long day.

Thursday, June 10, 1999

We got our O-line T-shirt today and it is pretty cool. It has a pig coming through the front, a Bible verse and our four keys: courage, loyalty, passion, and discipline. The verse is "For God did not give us a spirit of timidity, but a spirit of power, of love and of self-discipline. II Timothy 1:7."

Brian Nelson and I worked out and did abdominal work and then ran some stairs. I want to get him in shape so he doesn't have to face the shock to his body that I did when I came in last summer.

Friday, June 11, 1999

Today was the first day of the summer that we came in as a group to lift at 7:30. It was kind of difficult to get up that early after getting up around 10:00 the majority of the summer. But it's nice to get that done early because then I have the rest of the day to work or do whatever. This will also be the last of those kinds of days because we will continue to work out in the morning and then run at 5:00 or 5:30 every day for the rest of the summer. I really have a lot of respect for the incoming freshmen, especially the guys who drive from Omaha every day who are here at 7:30 in the morning. That shows a lot of dedication and a good work ethics, which will pay off greatly for them later.

Monday, June 14, 1999

A couple of the guys were late today, including brothers Tim and Mike Green, Chris Loos, and Jon Dawson. (Tim, Chris and Jon are all incoming freshmen offensive linemen.) They all had to run four sets of stairs in the morning and while it nearly killed Loos, Dawson flew through them and was right back in the weight room finishing his workout. Tim Green is a huge kid who has amazing potential and a great personality. I have no doubt, even this early, that he will be a major player by the time he's a sophomore, if not earlier. Brian "Nelly" Nelson, my friend from Millard West, is also a great kid who has a lot of potential. His freshman year in high school, he couldn't even do a jumping jack and now he is a Husker. Just another overnight success story from Omaha.

> Sadly, all of these guys had their careers cut short for various reasons. Tim, Chris and Nelly had injuries that kept them out, Mike wanted to focus more attention on school, and Jon had a falling out with several players and coaches.
>
> Word got out about Nelly not being able to do a jumping jack in high school and it quickly became a great joke for everyone. He's great about laughing at this kind of stuff as well. He's a guy you just can't help but love.

Tuesday, June 15, 1999

I had my body fat tested today and was surprised by the results. It said I had gained no muscle and had gained four pounds of fat. I couldn't believe this because I feel better than I have in a long time and Dave Ellis couldn't believe it because it doesn't make sense with the workouts I've been doing. We brought Archer in and he explained some things. First, with the workout we had today, the reading is off naturally because the muscles and tissues haven't had time to return to a normal state. Also, we've been doing a base program with sets of five instead of 10 to help us gain more muscle instead of getting our bodies more toned. My food intake is not what it was during the season (with the help of the training table) so that's another factor that adds up to my new, but inaccurate, reading of 15% body fat.

We did our passing league drills yesterday afternoon, which was a pretty good workout. Today we did our option drill workout. All I did for this was hold a pad and be a human blocking dummy while the older guys ran plays. It was pointless for me.

I'm looking forward to a good night's sleep. I was totally worn out today and was hardly able to finish all of our lifts. I need tomorrow to recover, which is why I love Wednesday. If it wasn't for my two jobs tomorrow, it would be a very relaxing day.

Monday, June 21, 1999

I had an awesome day doing hang clean. It was the first day doing hang clean for a long time so I was really in the mood to get back at it and see how much I could do. I did my first two sets pretty easily and I had to challenge myself if I was going to be happy with my workout. I went to the bar where Dominic Raiola and some other guys were and decided to go for the gold. Before today, my last set was usually around 275 pounds, but today I put on 286 pounds. Eleven pounds might not seem like a lot, but anyone who has done hang clean can tell you that when you are around your max weight, even five pounds can be the difference between getting them all and failing horribly.

John Archer was watching me and probably thinking I wouldn't get it. I picked up the bar loaded with the most weight I've ever done and did five remarkably easy reps. When I set it down, Archer looked at me with surprise and sarcastically said, "Okay, what was your name again?" Matt Baldwin also saw me and I could tell he was very surprised as well. Archer later told Matt that no one was very explosive on hang clean today and Matt replied, "Dave was!"

Tuesday, June 22, 1999

Coach Tenopir had a party for all the offensive linemen at his house today. Dave Ellis was there grilling up all the meat and cooking the vegetables and also giving us his eternal advice about eating well. Coach Young was also there and there was plenty of food and refreshments, including a keg, for everyone to enjoy. I didn't stay too long; I had to finish packing and get to Omaha to get ready for a trip to the Canadian wilderness.

Mid-August 1999

I really let my journal-keeping slip over the past two months so here is a recap of the major events. I took a camping/canoeing/fishing trip with my dad, my brother, a good family friend named Dave Kay, his brother and their brother-in-law. We did a seven-day trek through Canada, covering about 60 miles by water and land. The last time I took a trip like this was five years ago when I was considerably smaller and weaker, and I discovered that this time it wasn't much of a challenge for me.

When I got back from Canada, I jumped right into the conditioning program in the horrible summer heat. We were still doing morning workouts at 7:30 and I was working from 10:00 to 4:00 at my job, which was outdoors, and then we ran at 5:30. Needless to say, this was a summer of sweat. Most days I started sweating at my morning workout and didn't stop until after the 5:30 workout. Overall, the conditioning went very well for me. I improved my jump rope skills greatly and I think my overall speed improved as well. After being on the upper-body workout program that Archer devised, I added about 40 pounds to my bench press just over the summer.

One thing that shocked me was finding out that Jim Tansey had been given a medical hardship and won't play this year. He told me that after breaking his foot during spring ball and getting pins put in it, the pins would have to come out if he wanted to play at 100% this year. And even if they performed the surgery now, he wouldn't be ready in time to have any impact on the season. He chose to get a medical scholarship and will be a student assistant coach in charge of the scout teams. Later, I heard a different story. I heard the coaches told him that he would be on scout team again this year. After some discussion, the coaches had to fight hard to get the medical scholarship from the NCAA. Either way, I've noticed a very negative attitude in him, especially when he's talking to me. To guys who are in a similar situation he's the same old Jimi, so I think he's jealous that I'm still on the team. We used to be good friends and now I've hardly talked to him in weeks.

In mid-July, I took a trip to New York City with my parents to visit my brother. We ran around Manhattan for three days trying to get it all in and ended up wearing ourselves out. For my birthday on the 16th, I saw the Yankees play the Atlanta Braves. With this trip and the trip to Canada, I missed nine days of workouts this summer and was told I would have to run one stadium stair for each day I missed, but the seniors never got around (or just plain forgot) to make me run them. Oh well!

At the end of July, I moved to a new place that I share with Aaron Patch. It costs a little more per month, but is worth it to live with fewer people and also to have an attached garage. I finished the move in about 35 straight hours and then went home to a family reunion my parents were hosting. This was on a Friday and also was the last day of organized workouts for the summer. After the morning lifting, all the offensive linemen went to Valentino's restaurant for a buffet lunch, which we absolutely demolished. The people at Valentino's were in awe at the amount of food we carried back to the party room and even more amazed when we came back for more a few minutes later. After that, I finished moving and was the most exhausted I've been in a long time.

1999 Season

Friday, August 20, 1999

The rest of this year's team arrived today for mandatory physicals. It looks like a pretty good bunch of walk-ons this year, including Brett Lindstrom, another guy from my high school, Millard West. We had a meeting in the afternoon and ate at the training table and we all received $74 for food.

I can't believe how much this city has awakened since everyone came back to college. I never really saw the city during the school year last year because I didn't have a car, but compared to how it was all summer long, the city is alive again.

Saturday, August 21, 1999

We had testing today and a few things again surprised me. Somehow I lost seven pounds in the past week. I've been 283 pounds on average for the whole summer and today I was 276. I don't know how that could be, especially since I had a buffet dinner last night. Dave Ellis has always gotten this kind of report from me. For some reason, I always seem to get tested when I'm not functioning normally.

All of the Astroturf fields have been replaced with Field-

Turf. It's kind of like green plastic shag carpet. A mix of sand and chopped up rubber is sifted down between the blades of grass and provides a very comfortable base. It looks really nice, it reduces the risk of turf-burn greatly, and it should last a long time.

The turf has caused all of the testing to be a little less productive than before so I didn't have to worry about running the 300-yard shuttle if I didn't improve my scores. Usually we have to beat a certain number of our tests to get out of doing the shuttle. Freshmen and sophomores have to beat three out of four, juniors have to beat two, and seniors have to beat one. Overall, I think I did the same or better on all the tests. I posted a 24-inch vertical, 2.02 seconds for the 10-yard dash, and 5.93 seconds for the pro agility. After testing, we had to fill out a bunch of paperwork for the NCAA about eligibility and other issues. After that we ate lunch at the training table. This was my first time back at this buffet since summer began and it felt like heaven.

The guys in two-a-days had a scrimmage today and Matt Shook, the scholarship center in my class, blew out his knee and will be out for the year. This really woke me up because a few freak injuries like these could thrust me on to the field. I always need to be ready and at my best because you never know. Also, this is the second blown knee in two weeks on the FieldTurf, which means it isn't living up to its expectations. The field is supposed to be a lot safer, especially for knees and common turf ailments like turf toe. I heard some of the morning radio D.J.s refer to it as the "Knee Shredder." I hope the injuries stop or Coach Solich could be the laughingstock of the state.

Monday, August 23, 1999

First day of school and the first day of full practice. They were both pretty much like I expected—my classes were packed and boring, and practice was fairly easy. My conditioning, as well as the confusion of the freshmen who didn't know what they were doing, made the whole practice much more friendly for me. My long-snapping talents have been overshadowed by a new guy, John Garrison, but I plan to get back into the spotlight soon enough. I'm again at the bottom of the depth chart with the fourth-string offense, which I think really doesn't reflect where I should be. I've made up my mind that I will either move up in the depth chart this year or join Mike Wilford in his move to another school. He was talking about this tonight at dinner and I really feel that he has a good point. As good as it is to be a part of one of the best teams in the nation, what good is it if you never play? I'm sure my dad won't be happy to hear this and I also know that the novelty of this idea will fade after a while and I will eventually regret writing it down.

Some of the freshmen really had trouble today; the winner of this year's prize definitely went to Brian Nelson. He was rushed to begin with because his classes run later than most and he was almost in a frenzy in the locker room trying to get dressed, all while repeatedly asking me what to do and where to go. After I finally got him and a few other freshmen straightened out, we headed off to meetings and filled out more papers. I finished my in-season lifting program in about 10 minutes because all we had to do was hang clean and Jammer Press for a total of five sets of five. Practice went fairly well and I feel I'm in a good position to impress the coaches with my growth over the past year. Let's hope all goes well.

Thursday, August 26, 1999

So far, we have received a few pieces of new gear—a new pair of shoes for the turf, a pair of grass shoes (which I returned and brought in my old grass shoes from high school because I like them better), a shirt with our new motto, "Relentless to Victory," and a pair of black mesh shorts.

Practice today was in sweats, but it was still long. I've finished my lifting for the week; we just lift four days and Friday is a rest day because of games on Saturday. Tomorrow is a scrimmage, but I'm unable to go because I have a chemistry lab in the afternoon. I took the class at this time because Friday is usually a half-hour walk-through, and I won't be traveling this year, which makes Friday the safest day to take the class.

Most of the university's classes are offered in the mornings and early afternoon. But quite a few are also offered past 2:00 p.m. and even on Saturdays. If a football player chooses a major that has one of these oddly timed classes, they're going to miss practice or even miss games if they go to class. In the end, many athletes choose the path of least resistance and settle for a major that fits their schedule, not necessarily one that fits their goals. I know I did.

I only have one class on Tuesdays and Thursdays, "Coaching Football," taught by the most qualified man in the country, Dr. Tom Osborne. He had to leave early today and instead of calling off class, he brought in Al Papik, head of football operations, and made it a full class. I think that shows the dedication and professionalism of Dr. Osborne because he doesn't let his students cut corners even when he's not there. Well, I couldn't have him as a coach, but at least I can have him as a teacher.

Saturday, August 28, 1999

Last night I worked at the Royal Grove and then went out with Patch (my roommate) until about 4:00 this morning. I got up at 7:15 and rushed to Saturday meetings. Practice was in helmets and went about an hour and a half and was just long enough to totally drain my batteries.

After practice we received another pair of black shorts, and there were sandwiches and drinks in the locker room. At noon we went out for photos and then watched the Penn State-Arizona game on the HuskerVision screens. Soon after, the floodgates opened and thousands of people came into the stadium for Fan Day. I didn't have a seat at a table like the other (better) guys, so Andy Gwennap and I found a bench close to the kickers and signed for people who were actually waiting for Josh Brown's autograph. What was really funny was that I didn't know what number to use when I signed. In the press guide my number is 71 while the number on the autograph sheet was listed as 64, but for some reason I was given a jersey with 74 on it. I signed 64 or 71, depending on what I was signing. People would notice that I wasn't signing the number on my jersey and had looks on their faces like I was messing around with them. Some people questioned me about it and I gave them some story, but overall I felt like an idiot. When I asked the equipment guys about this, their story was that with so many guys and numbers, it's really hard to keep track of all of them and mistakes sometimes happen. I find this really hard to believe. A number being changed happens every now and then. A typo where one guy has two different numbers is understandable. But I don't see how they can mess up bad enough to give me three numbers at one time. I just want to know what my number will be.

We got $34 for the weekend.

Saturday, September 4, 1999

Nebraska 42 – Iowa 7

After a highly publicized battle for starting quarterback, Bobby Newcombe came out to prove his starting spot was no fluke. Even after a few mistakes, he more than made up for it with his solid performance. Eric Crouch then came in to put the icing on the cake with some showmanship of his own.

Wednesday, September 8, 1999

It looks like the only perk I will have this year is being able to run out on the field for the games. Those few seconds are probably the only time I will be on the actual playing field on game days. I asked Coach Young yesterday what my depth is for long-snapping. As I figured, it's fourth behind Garrison, Raiola, and Hochstein. My next question was if I will see any playing time this year at all. His delayed answer was that I might be put in for a PAT (extra point) snap, but that was about it. I guess running out of the tunnel is better than waiting all season just go on the bowl trip like I did last year. If I'm making such a big payment now, I should get a pretty good return later.

In practice, former offensive tackle Jim Tansey is the new scout team assistant coach while he's on his medical hardship scholarship. One of the contingencies of keeping this kind of scholarship is that he still has to be a part of the program somehow. He's in charge of keeping the offensive scout teams running smoothly and motivating us to work hard, of which he is doing a great job. The other day, he ended up giving me my new nickname when said, "Kolowski, that's a lot like Kowalski. "Killer" Kowalski, remember him? I'm gonna call you "Killer" from now on."

"Killer" Kowalski was a professional wrestler who thrilled a growing demographic of drunken hicks between 1947 and 1977, eventually helping professional wrestling become what it is today. The nickname doesn't fit me exactly, but it sounds good.

Friday, September 10, 1999

I was able to go to practice today because my chemistry lab lasted only a fraction of the scheduled time. This was a good thing because I forgot to hand in my helmet yesterday to get the decals on it.

We got some more free stuff after practice—a new warm-up suit and travel shoes. The warm-up suit is all red and says Nebraska on the back of the jacket. The shoes are mostly white with black and red designs.

Saturday, September 11, 1999

Nebraska 45 – California 0

This was the first time I suited up for a collegiate game and the first time I ran out of the tunnel in front of 77,000 screaming fans.

The main guys on the depth chart all get locked up in a hotel the night before the game. This ensures they aren't running around all night and that they get some decent food. As for the rest of us, we're supposed to make it to the stadium by ourselves a few hours before the game. Parking close to the stadium is not an option as I soon found out. I ended up parking illegally behind one of the dorms and running to the stadium. Surprisingly, this little piece of useful information was not relayed to those of us who arrive on their own. I guess most of the other guys get dropped off by somebody instead of trying to park. I got to the stadium about 12:15, dressed in a hurry and got my ankles taped (I almost skipped getting taped, knowing that I won't play today, but I did it just to get the whole game feeling).

We had an offensive meeting at 12:45 in the main South Stadium locker room led by Coach Tenopir. He reaffirmed our belief that we are a dominating team and that we need the best game mentally and physically that we can produce. Team psychologist Jack Stark came in and we watched a psych-up tape that consisted of exciting plays from recent games with inspirational rock music blaring.

We did a lot of sitting and waiting in the locker room. Eventually the kickers, snappers, and receivers went to the field to warm up, and the crowd cheered for us when we came out just because we were the first Huskers they had seen all day. Garrison took most of the snaps and I felt pretty stupid just standing by him and watching. I tried to make myself useful so I handed him a ball when he needed one. After a while I was able to do some snaps and did pretty well with them. I did some punt snaps that were good for the most part and then I followed Russ Hochstein around for a little bit because I had no idea what to do. When the rest of the team came out, we did our warm-up running and stretching in four long lines at the south end of the field.

When stretching was done, we formed a large huddle in the middle of the field where the captains and other guys screamed about how we're not going to let someone come into our house and beat us, and how we're going to demolish California. We then broke off into our different groups and the offensive line did some practice blocks against each other on the east sideline; one pass block and one run block. Those two blocks were the only blocks I made the entire day.

After groupwork, the offense melded in the middle of the field and ran plays against us young guys who were still trying to figure out how not to mess up. There was definitely confusion. The coaches expect us to know all of the defensive terminology and positions of the guys in different formations and how they act in certain plays, but most of us are scout team players and get our information off of diagrammed cards that just tell us where we should go, nothing about the philosophy of why we're doing it.

We then ran back inside and had a big team meeting with Coach Solich who gave a really calm and collected pregame speech that focused on getting things done in the game and doing them right. When he was done, the whole team squeezed into the middle of the locker room and the captains and others gave more inspirational speeches, our team prayer, and we ended up jumping around as a group and almost got as wild as a mosh pit. After that was over, we still had some time to wait and the coaches told us to sit down and rest our legs. One thing I noticed was that when no one was giving a speech and there was no activity, the room was very quiet and everyone was focusing on the game.

At five minutes before kickoff, the music started and the crowd outside began to clap in unison and anticipation. We all got ready and the important players got up front to lead the team out. I found a place in the back third of the line and walked down the tunnel holding someone's hand next to me, I didn't see who. Once out the doors, a mass of people were waiting for us outside the tunnel, lining the path from the doors to the field, cheering us and holding their hands out for us to slap.

I could tell by the change in the crowd noise exactly when the first guys burst onto the field even though I couldn't see it from my position in line. My heart was racing and my eyes were wide open with excitement. All of the fans and players around me were yelling with excitement and this was all magnified within my helmet. I felt like I was going to explode with all the energy that was building inside me. I couldn't help but bounce around, shouting wildly.

When I finally stepped onto the field and started running, I didn't even notice the crowd. I was so focused on not tripping and embarrassing myself that the crowd was actually blocked out for a while. When I got to the sideline, I took time to look around and see that I was in the middle of a sea of red. I was part of the reason that 77,000 people gathered together on a Saturday afternoon. I was part of a group that could make the third-largest "city" in Nebraska scream at the top of their lungs. There is no feeling quite like this. None of these fans know me besides a select few, but I'm part of a group that they love. They see my helmet with the red *N* on the side and the bright red jersey, and suddenly I'm elevated to a status that I could never get in a normal public situation.

On the sidelines during the games, you can usually divide the sideline pretty easily into groups by position, as well as playing potential. The defense is usually occupying the North side with the offense on the South side. Those of the same position usually stand in a tight group, either because they will be easier to find by the position coach when it is time to be put in, or just because they will have a comrade to talk to for the duration. The first string guys are usually very active on the sideline, very talkative, and constantly moving to stay warm and loose. The second string guys are usually more stationary, but they follow the first string squad when they come off the field to learn about anything new the other team is doing. Those in the third and fourth string know that they won't get into the game barring an extreme blowout or serious injuries. For these guys, the sideline is a block-party. A few are still drunk or hungover from the night before, others are clandestinely eating food and gum that they had tucked away in their gear, others carefully check out the dance team girls and other hotties in the stands, and a lot of the guys on the third team and above gave equal concern to the events on the big screens as they do the game on the field.

At halftime, the offense went into the main locker room while the defense went into the player's lounge. As we walked in, there was a table set up with water and Gatorade as well as cut up energy bars and sliced bananas and oranges. Everyone just grabs what they want and heads in to their area. Inside the locker room, the middle area of the room, which is usually just an open carpet area, is set up with our stools just like a classroom in front of the chalk board. On the board, someone has drawn up all of our offensive formations as well as the most likely defensive formation we will see against that set. The starters and main players gather around on the stools and pay attention while the coaches quietly go through each formation and chose which plays they think would be best for that set. If they have any questions about what the defense is doing, they would ask us directly, but they lead themselves for the most part. The backs and receivers pay close attention so that they can help read the defense when they are on the field and report back to the coaches, but the linemen only have to worry about the guys in the box. As for the rest of the guys in the locker room, they are off by their lockers quietly having personal conversations about anything they want. Halftime was very quiet in general. This went on for nearly the entire halftime and was ended by a short and redundant speech by Coach Solich before we headed back out the tunnel.

The game was just like last week, a slow start but a glorious finish with a final score of 45-0. The California Bears left Nebraska thoroughly beaten, but the game statistics really didn't fit the score. We only had 301 yards of total offense and our leading rusher was our third-string I-back with only 30 yards. Really a very odd game, but a great game for Eric Crouch who scored three ways—throwing, running and receiving. He's the first Husker to do that since Heisman Trophy winner Johnny Rodgers.

After the game, I changed and met my parents and our good family friends, Dave and Judy Kay, and we all went to dinner. It was a long but great day. We were given $17 for food.

Tuesday, September 15, 1999

I-Back DeAngelo Evans quit the team last weekend. The coaches found out Sunday and the media found out tonight. Apparently, he was disappointed with his playing time and the statistics he put up, which really amounted to nothing. I never held DeAngelo in the highest regard because of his tendency to get hurt very easily and suspiciously, but this gives me a new reason to discredit him. He reportedly will come back if he is guaranteed 25 plays in this weekend's game. This just goes to show how inflated his ego is and how little skill he has in dealing with adversity. If he's going to let one unproductive game at the beginning of a season affect him, then I say let him go and forget about him. If he can be that selfish, we don't need him. We have plenty of other talented backs who are waiting to get a chance to play.

Saturday, September 18, 1999

Nebraska 20 – Southern Mississippi 13

We should have lost this game, but we were saved by two turnovers returned for touchdowns by linebacker Julius Jackson. The offense started slowly as usual and it never seemed to find the gas pedal. The majority of the plays were right up the middle and we didn't get anything accomplished out of that at all. We had some pass plays that had potential, but they were never fully used. Basically, it was a pathetic win. The offense put up 183 total yards. When we usually average twice as many yards as this, it makes you wonder how strong the offense really is right now. In all reality, the defense saved us today.

Once again, I didn't play at all and spent the day patrolling the sideline. We were given $17 for food.

Monday, September 21, 1999

The media is having fun with the news about DeAngelo Evans. The starters met as a group last week and voted that he shouldn't be let back on the team even if he wants to come back. Today, Evans met with Coach Solich and their meeting got so heated that Evans was almost forced to leave his office. Apparently, Evans really wants to come back and I think Coach wants him back, but the team voted that he is banned and that's the way it goes. Evans didn't take the news well and started badmouthing current players such as Aaron Wills, saying that he came in messed up and now that he has a Blackshirt he can pass judgment on others. Evans should have thought about what he was doing before he acted. I've been given that advice all my life and it's sad to see someone ruin his career by one hasty decision. Who knows, he could have had a great pro career ahead of him and now he will be another unknown walking around with the thought of "what if…?" for the rest of his life.

Thursday, September 23, 1999

Today's practice was just in helmets like all Thursday practices and when you don't wear protection, something might get hurt. That was proven today when we ran a play in which the linemen fired off the ball with a quick first step and then made soft contact with the defense. The guard next to me pushed nose guard Jason Lohr over to me when I wasn't ready and Jason was going nearly full speed. He ran his whole torso straight into my shoulder. I felt the mass of my shoulder get shoved into my chest and heard many ugly sounds resonate from my socket. I'm not sure what I did—I didn't get it checked out—but now five hours later it's sore and I don't have full range of motion.

Saturday, September 25, 1999

Nebraska 40 – Missouri 10

The offense finally showed its stuff today. Many were skeptical about our offense and thought this would be another close game like the last time we went to Missouri. Instead, the defense shut down the opponent like usual and the offense steamrolled over the weak Mizzou defense. This game will be a good stepping-stone to keep the offense strong all year long.

Scott Koethe, a redshirt freshman offensive tackle, traveled with the team and actually got in for a series in the closing minutes of the game. He is the first redshirt freshman from my class to actually get some playing time. I guess there is some hope after all!

I got an interesting letter from the university yesterday. It said that it's legal for me to work during the school year and it stated how much money I'm able to earn by NCAA rules. This part really surprised me—I can make a little over $10,000. That's an amazing amount of money for me and I don't think that in all my jobs combined I've even made half of that.

Something else that is job-related—the majority of the security force at the Royal Grove quit tonight after the owners failed to handle a situation properly. Jim Tansey saw the incident and told the owner that's not the way to run a business. Jim ended up throwing his vest at the owner and walking away, and soon after most of the security staff tossed in their vests and quit. I'll also quit unless they throw a lot of money my way—I don't really need the job, and it takes away from study time and makes me stay out late on weeknights.

Wednesday, September 29, 1999

If it isn't one thing, it's another. Today in practice I pulled my left hamstring running downfield on punt coverage. Not having any subs, I was forced to play the rest of practice without a break. By the end, it was pretty warm and I was able to get fairly good motion out of it and even did gassers. Afterward, however, I was hurting.

Thursday, September 30, 1999

That hamstring injury yesterday has severely limited my movement. I have to walk with a limp and have to stand up very slowly because it hurts so much when I stretch it out like that. I didn't think I was going to practice, but I ended going and I think it actually helped. I was kind of skipping—that was the best running motion I could do—but it stretched out my leg and got some blood flowing. Afterward, it felt decent, but it was still very noticeable.

Saturday, October 2, 1999

Nebraska 38 – Oklahoma State 14

This game had one of the best starts in the past two years. The whole first half was complete domination by both the offense and the defense. It was, without a doubt, one of the best offensive first halves of this season and the last. The second half was more laid back and while we still controlled the game, we let them score 14 points making us miss the defensive goal of holding the opponent at or below 13 points. Again, I roamed the sidelines during the game.

Redshirt freshman quarterback Joe Chrisman got his first taste of playing time today. He's usually with the scout team so he doesn't know the offense really well, but they put him in because the second-string QB, Jeff Perino, hurt his leg and they didn't want to wear Eric Crouch down too much. Chrisman took three snaps and finished the game for us and was even mentioned in the post-game show by Coach Solich. I guess there is life after the scout team. We were given $17 for food.

Tuesday, October 5, 1999

Today was a great day for me. I had tons of energy and gave a great effort in practice. I made all of my blocks the best I could and then went to block somebody else if my guy got away. I really was hustling all over the field and doing pretty much everything I could to do my best. I hope it shows on the tape and they at least consider me for Scout Team Player of the Week. If not, I still gave the defense a good picture. The rest of the scout team offense also did very well. During one drill, we scored on five out of 13 plays. On a later drill, the defensive man who allowed the touchdown had to run stairs.

Saturday, October 9, 1999

Nebraska 49 – Iowa State 14

This was probably one of the best total games of the past two years. The offense made over 500 yards of total offense and the defensive starters held the Cyclones to nearly nothing. About a third or more of the game was played by the second- and third-string players. That was when their offense made some yardage and put some points on the board. I still haven't played and I'm starting to think this is just another redshirt year in disguise. Got another $17 for weekend food.

Wednesday, October 13, 1999

Somehow, for some reason, somebody stole my shoulder pads off of the top of my locker. It could be that someone is playing a joke on me, but no one has said anything about it. I think somebody who wasn't supposed to be in there got into our locker room and easily swiped my shoulder pads as they sat on top of the locker. My locker is the first one you see as you enter from the back door so it's very possible somebody slipped in and out quick. This puzzled the equipment guys, but in the end they had to issue me a new set. The new pair is a size too big, but will have to do for now.

Saturday, October 16, 1999

The Hewit Center was open for breakfast today at 7:00 and we had meetings at 8:30. I showed up at 8:00, got some food, picked up my weekend money ($72), and made it to meetings right on time. Practice was at 10:00 and just in helmets so it wasn't that bad, but it was still something I would rather not do on a weekend.

This is the start of our fall break with no classes next Monday and Tuesday. Long weekends like this are never really fun because it seems like everyone goes home and the city dies. There is never anything to do and no good parties. Now I must use the whole rest of the weekend and the days off to study like a madman to catch up in my classes. I hope to pull off some really good grades this semester.

Monday, October 18, 1999

Back to the regular practice week. I have a test Thursday in Coach Osborne's class. I've seen a previous test he gave and know that I will have to study like crazy if I'm going to do well on it. Many people think his class would be an easy 'A' for a football player or he would just let us slide by, but that is not the case. He's a very good and demanding teacher and judging by his test, he expects you to know all of the important stuff very well. I've actually learned more about football from that class than I have in a year and a half of being on the team.

Thursday, October 21, 1999

The entire week of practice was rather good. The team seems well rested and ready to go for the game against Texas. The defense practiced very well against us and they seem ready to go against the dangerous passing attack of Major Applewhite. The offense seems fired up and the linemen are sure to dominate. I think it should be a good game any way you cut it.

Saturday, October 23, 1999

Texas 24 – Nebraska 20

A game filled with fumbles and turnovers ended our hopes of a perfect season. Major Applewhite dissected our secondary with methodical precision and the offense played great except they coughed up the ball too many times. We shot ourselves in the foot and handed the game to Texas. This was truly a disheartening loss and continues our streak with Texas, and will only fuel our hatred and desire to beat them in the future. Even though we lost, there is still a remote chance we could make it to the Sugar Bowl and possibly meet Texas again in the Big 12 championship game before the bowl game. That would be sweet revenge.

Monday, October 25, 1999

It wasn't as bad as I thought it would be. The team as a whole is not as downhearted as they were after the first loss last year, but the atmosphere is a little more somber than normal. Coach talked in meetings about how we are probably out of the running for the national championship and we need to focus on playing one game at a time and hopefully get to the Big 12 championship at the end of the season. Practice was in half pads on the grass and it seemed pretty normal. The defense was energetic and making jokes, and nothing seemed wrong with anyone at the end of the day. Everyone agrees that what happened in the game was a total shock and we should have won. We are hoping that the pollsters see the game not just as a loss but as a very close and lucky win for Texas. I think we are currently ranked eighth, a large drop from third last week.

My hang clean is still going up; I did 313.5 pounds for four-and-a-half times. I had a little more difficulty and

I know why—I had a weekend where I didn't eat enough and was too inactive. I need to realize that my body needs a constant flow of calories to maintain proper strength and weight. If I went on a diet right now with my current workout schedule and exercise, I could easily drop to 250 in a month. I would probably lose a lot of muscle in that descent as well. I need to gain weight, preferably muscle, and get to 300 before spring ball.

Wednesday, October 27, 1999

A very unproductive day for the team—no one had any energy or desire to practice. The coaches noticed this and were very displeased with the effort. I don't really know how to explain this horrible practice. It just happened and now we have to put it behind us and focus on putting in a good effort for the rest of the week to prepare mentally and physically for Kansas.

Saturday, October 30, 1999

Nebraska 24 – Kansas 17

This was sort of a miracle win for us. We were down 9-0 at halftime, battled for the lead three separate times and ended up winning. The most amazing thing about this win is that it was accomplished with our passing game, not the running game. The passing game has really been a key part of our offense, although it's not used to a great extent. Maybe this game will be a wake-up call and we can finish the season stronger than most people expect.

This was an away game and I was unable to watch or even listen to much of it because of a choir concert (I joined a men's ensemble with my friend and roommate Aaron Patch). I listened to most of the first quarter before the concert and was pretty disheartened with what I heard. At the end of the concert, I heard from someone who snuck a pocket radio in that the score was 24-17 with about a minute left. That really cheered me up. I stayed dressed in my tuxedo after the concert and went to some Halloween parties around town.

Friday, November 5, 1999

This week was probably one of the best weeks of the year for football practice. Monday we went in sweats when we usually go half pads. Tuesday and Wednesday, which are usually in full pads, were in half pads and then Thursday was just in sweats as usual. The coaches wanted us to take it a little easier this week since there are a lot of people with injuries who need time to recover. Coach Solich really stressed the need to continue to progress through the end of the season. We needed to keep up the intensity during this week even though we weren't in full pads. I hope this strategy will pay off.

Saturday, November 6, 1999

Nebraska 37 – Texas A&M 0

I guess the strategy paid off. We played some of the best football I've seen in recent times and seemed unstoppable in every aspect of the game. This game was one of the most exciting games, despite the score, that I've seen in the past two years. Everything seemed to come into place for us. After a slow first half, only six points off of two field goals, we got our act together and racked up the score almost rhythmically with Texas A&M having no way to stop it. The offense put up some impressive drives in the first half, but we still had problems with fumbles, and Josh Brown had a field goal attempt hit a goal post. The final score should have been something around 50-0.

The defense put on an impressive show that will be hard to beat. They recorded eight sacks, four interceptions, and many tackles for losses. They also held the Texas A&M offense to just two yards of rushing offense. I feel sorry for whoever had to pick a defensive player of the game because it would have been nearly impossible since so many players were exceptional.

If we can play like that after having no full-pads practices, I say we never have another full-pads practice again.

Monday, November 8, 1999

I did it. Finally, I was voted Offensive Scout Team Player of the Week for last week's practices preparing for Texas A&M. This really made my year. Actually, it makes my whole two years that I've been here. I know my effort is not in vain and that the coaches think I'm doing a good enough job to be picked (along with another guy who shares the honor this week) above all others on the scout team. It's hard for linemen to get this award since we don't stand out as much as the backs and receivers, and it's really hard to gauge our effectiveness against such a good defensive line. This lifted my spirits enough to make me try harder and get it two weeks in a row.

Friday, November 12, 1999

This whole week was in sweats and half pads again. I don't miss full pads too much considering those practices are the ones where everyone gets banged up and ends up crawling back to the locker room drained of energy. I think these practices really are very beneficial. We're not supposed to take people down by tackling them or knocking them down with blocks. This forces us to work harder to stay up and also use our heads to get the proper technique and pay more attention to what's happening all around. After a week of these type of practices, we have so much energy stored up and we're craving the chance to hit someone. By game day, we are ready to go like never before.

K-State should be a good game. Everyone has been talking about it and it's all over the papers. They are 9-0 right now and we are 8-1. If we beat them, we should get a better place in the BCS and have a better chance at getting back into the running for a Sugar Bowl bid.

Saturday, November 13, 1999

Nebraska 41 – Kansas State 15

This was the best game I've seen in many, many years. The crowd was utterly amazing and the energy was flowing from the stands. We even got a roar out of the crowd when the specialists went out to practice kicking before the rest of the team came out.

Every time the defense was on the field, the crowd cheered them on like wild animals and made so much noise it seemed like it was impossible for K-State to make an audible. The offense was dominant even though we fumbled the ball 10 times, losing three. Eric Crouch lit up the scoreboard with two rushing touchdowns and Mike Brown had an excellent game seeming to be in on almost every play. Today was Senior Day, making this a nice way to leave Memorial Stadium for the seniors.

I got another $17, just like every home game.

Thursday, November 18, 1999

Today was the first day in full pads in a long time. It has been about two weeks, and it felt good to get back to a full-pads practice. I could tell the guys on the team needed this because all of them were really hungry to go out and hit someone. The practice went fairly well with no major problems. Defensive tackle Jeremy Slechta is out for the rest of the season with a knee injury. This hurts the fragile depth of the defensive line, but it shouldn't cause too much damage.

We got another T-shirt today, only we got another one just like it earlier this year. I'm going to give it to my dad.

We had a Thanksgiving feast tonight at the Hewit Center.

They had everything—salads, pastas, fruits and vegetables, turkey, duck, Chicken Cordon Bleu and all the fixings. It was about as good as the food they serve during the recruiting visits, not that the regular food is worse, but you could tell they put a lot more time and preparation into this.

Friday, November 19, 1999

I was able to make it to practice today because my chemistry lab was shorter than expected. This was a good thing and a bad thing. It was good because I practiced and was able to help the team out more than if someone else was playing center on the scout team. It was bad because I wasn't able to eat lunch and was very low on energy, and it really hurt when we had to do gassers at the end.

Saturday, November 20, 1999

Florida State remains undefeated after beating Florida today, which will help us in the end. We're ranked third in the BCS with Virginia Tech and Florida State ahead of us. This is undoubtedly higher than many people thought we would be at the end of the season; we still have a chance to end up second and go to the Sugar Bowl. According to rumors and predictions, if we beat Colorado and then Texas in the Big 12 championship, it would be almost impossible for Virginia Tech to remain ranked second. Let's hope they are right, I would like to finish this season with a national championship ring on my finger.

Friday, November 26, 1999

Nebraska 33 – Colorado 30

The great escape. We began the game with a bang, scoring twice in five offensive plays. The game seemed as if it was in the bag right up until the fourth quarter with the score 27-3. With that kind of lead, the other team usually just rolls over. Colorado, on the other hand, put together an amazing offensive push with the help of a couple of fumbles on our part and a recovered onside kick. It was tied 27-27 with one second left and Colorado missed the perfect opportunity to beat us by kicking a short field goal wide right. In overtime, Colorado kicked a field goal and we got a touchdown to seal the victory and our appearance in the Big 12 championship game.

Thursday, December 2, 1999

This week of practice was similar to the weeks before with no full pads. I was getting over a stomach flu Monday and Tuesday so I didn't practice too well. The team seems very well prepared to face Texas again and this time they won't give up without a fight. The team has a score to settle, and the determination and concentration they've shown this week has really proven their desire.

Saturday, December 4, 1999

Nebraska 22 – Texas 6

We are now the 1999 Big 12 champions, just as we should be. We finally got rid of the shadow that Texas had over our heads. The whole week was preparation for domination and we showed it. The defense threw another shutout; the only Texas points were from a defensive fumble recovery. The statistics for the game show a great defensive battle with less than 300 total yards for us and less than 200 for Texas. They had nine yards rushing, thanks mostly to our defense, which sacked a flustered Major Applewhite seven times. Applewhite also threw three interceptions, which turned out to be huge turning points in the game. It was a very emotional win for our guys and now the seniors can leave saying they have finally beaten Texas. Now I just have to sit and wait for that big shiny ring.

We found out we're going to play Tennessee in the Fiesta Bowl on January 2, 2000. Under the current BCS structure our narrow win over Colorado late in the season and our loss to Texas earlier in the season really hurt our chances of making it to the national championship. Even though we avenged our loss to Texas in the Big 12 championship game, it wasn't enough to bump us up into 2nd place in the BCS. Florida State and Virginia Tech are still undefeated and that's all it takes to look better than us.

Nevertheless, we're very happy to go to the Fiesta Bowl. It's one of the biggest bowls in the nation, so we should get very good treatment and should get a lot of stuff for our bowl gifts. If last year was any indication and this year is supposed to be even better, I can't wait to see what we get.

Tuesday, December 7, 1999

Practice today was one of the easiest all year, even if you include Friday walk-throughs. We practiced for about 70 minutes, and half of that time was spent just standing around and listening to Coach Tenopir. We only had three coaches here today—Solich, Tenopir, and McBride—so there was less to do in practice. The rest of the coaches were out on recruiting trips. But instead of the team wasting a practice, everyone knew what needed to be done and the leadership on the team really shone today to make sure we got everything done.

Because the Fiesta Bowl is a major BCS bowl, we all get six free tickets for family and friends. It's a $12.5 million bowl for the university and the Big 12 Conference. This also means that we will get some pretty nice gifts from the Fiesta Bowl and Adidas. The guys on the travel squad received their Big 12 watches today. I haven't seen one yet, but I hear they are really big and really nice.

Friday, December 10, 1999

At meetings today we got sized for our Big 12 rings. We also saw one of the Fiesta Bowl gifts—a brown and black Fiesta Bowl letter jacket. It looks very nice and I can't wait to see what else we get.

Practice was very similar to Tuesday's, going a little over an hour with not much work. We were in sweats today, but tomorrow will be in half pads. There are some recruits in this weekend getting the whole tour and all of them were watching practice.

A while back I joked with Brian Nelson that everyone gets a red belly on their birthday. This isn't true but I guess he believed me and asked me yesterday, on his birthday, if he would get a red belly. I said yes. He then went to senior tackle Adam Julch and asked him. Adam said he wouldn't and that I would get one for saying that, but in the end I guess he thought the whole idea of a birthday red belly was a good one. As we were all walking over to Cook Pavilion, most of the O-line sang a very sarcastic "Happy Birthday" to Brian. Then after practice, concealed from the view of the recruits, he received his red belly. Sorry, Nelly.

We had new baseball hats waiting for us in our lockers. They are black with a Husker logo on the front. They're very nice, but I don't wear hats that often and I don't know who to give it to. At dinner tonight we got $27 for food for the weekend. That won't last long.

Monday, December 13, 1999

I really didn't want to practice today. I need to do so much work for my finals and I'm fairly confident that I won't get it all done. I really procrastinated way too much. I just have to find some way to fix it now.

Practice won't be too bad this week. Now that the regular season is done and the bowl game is so far away (not to mention finals in everyone's classes), we will practice Monday, Wednesday, and Friday, then we practice the whole weekend and straight up to next Tuesday. I wasn't too pleased to hear about the weekend schedule. We should get money for the weekend and other days when there are no classes. After Tuesday's practice, everyone who lives close enough away can go home for a little while before Christmas. I feel fortunate that my parents live only an hour away. It must be very tough for the out-of-state guys who are so far away from their families during the holidays. We have to be back here Friday (Christmas Eve day) and leave for Tempe at 7:00 in the morning. Then the fun begins. Our practices for the past week have been very short—only about 80 minutes—so it will be a real shock when we finally get back into a regular two-hour practice, especially in the Arizona heat. I just hope we don't have any of those practices that go on for almost three hours, but we should count on them.

Wednesday, December 15, 1999

Again, I really didn't want to practice today. I had finals at 7:30 and 10:00 this morning and stayed up past 3:00 in the morning studying for them. I took two naps during the day but was still tired for practice. We went half pads again and I was happy when it was all over. I have one more final tomorrow and then will be done with this semester. I think I will have a pretty good GPA for the semester. I found out that I got an A in Coach Osborne's class. This should have been expected since I'm a Husker player, but only 40% of the people who take the class actually pass it.

Friday, December 17, 1999

Another fun practice today, and by 'fun' I mean 'grueling.' I think the only reason we're going so hard right now is to show off to all the recruits who are in for their official visits. The game is two weeks away and we'll have plenty of time to prepare once we're in Tempe. Right now we should be taking it easy in practice and lifting harder. Oh well, I guess it's what the coaches think is best.

Coach Solich was named Big 12 Coach of the Year. He has really been doing a great job this year. He seems very comfortable in his role as head coach now and also seems very comfortable in front of the team.

I finally started my Christmas shopping yesterday and today I finished it up by getting two footballs to be signed by the team. Footballs make great gifts for $35 plus the effort it takes to get them signed. I hope to get a ball for my family every year that I'm on the team. I also hope one of those years will be a national championship year.

At the end of practice, Coach Tenopir pulled the scout team offensive line to the side and walked through some of our plays. He has done this for the past three practices. I think there actually may be a chance of me getting in the game, but that will take nothing short of a miracle accompanied by a total blowout. I'm doing well with remembering all of the plays so I think I should have a pretty good chance to at least get a play.

We got $69 dollars for the weekend. This is just the start of all the money and gifts that we get for the entire trip.

Saturday, December 18, 1999

Today was the first full-pads, two-hour practice we've had in a very long time. After practice, I finished getting my footballs signed by the coaches and finished up my lifting. After that, I picked up my big bag of goodies from Adidas. Along with the duffel bag itself, we received two hats, three T-shirts and matching colored mesh shorts, two golf shirts, a black wind suit, a nice black coat, and two sweatshirts. Separate from the bag, we also got a new pair of shoes. They are really nice running shoes—the kind I would actually go out and buy. I probably should have gotten a size 12 and given them to my dad or brother since I really don't need any more shoes. They're all very nice things; I estimate the overall value at about $550 retail. This made for a very nice Christmas. These make nice Christmas gifts to pass on to friends and family since my closet will probably be overflowing with clothes and merchandise after a while.

Sunday, December 19, 1999

It's never fun to practice for two hours in full pads on a Sunday, but this one was pretty good for me. Instead of going out, partying too hard and sleeping only four hours like a lot of the guys did, I got plenty of rest and was ready to go 100% for the whole practice. I used this advantage to do better than most of the guys and I know that will look good to the coaches.

Somehow, the sleeve on my practice jersey got torn yesterday. By the end of today, after all the banging around that comes with a full-pads practice, the jersey was almost torn in half.

We got $65 dollars for food after practice. Not too bad for some weekend meals.

We learned today that not everyone will suit up for the bowl game. There are only a certain number of lockers, somewhere in the 80s, and I doubt I will be able to suit up now because of this. It's rare to take any deeper than third string on the O-line if there's a restriction like this. Also, the second- and third-team centers are both seniors so they're guaranteed to suit up and possibly play. John Garrison is unofficially the fourth-string center, but he also does long snaps so he will knock out any chance of me suiting up.

Thursday, December 23, 1999

The weight room was open today from 5:00 to 7:30 this evening and since they required everyone to be there, we were able to get paid for the day. We got $84 and all we really had to do for the workout was just a set of curls or five minutes on the exercise bike. It's almost outrageous how much they can give us on days like today. Really, how is anyone supposed to spend $84 on food in one day? There are certain times that different guys get different amounts of money. Most often, guys who are on scholarship get less money for these types of days because it's already figured in to some degree in their housing allowance.

Friday, December 24, 1999

We all met at the airport at 7:00 this morning. I took a taxi so I could leave my car in my garage. They had juice and muffins in the terminal for us and we also picked up $276 to start the trip. We were really spread out in the plane and I was able to have two seats to myself all the way to Phoenix. After the two-and-a-half-hour flight, we were greeted in Phoenix by a welcoming party who were semi-enthusiastically clapping and slapped Fiesta Bowl sun stickers on us as we walked by.

We had a police escort from the airport to the hotel. The ride to the hotel told me a lot about the city and this region of the country. A lot of Native American designs decorate the highways and the side of the roads. Most of the overpasses and cement pillars are painted red or orange. It's a lot different from the stale (but efficient) way that our state looks.

When we got to the hotel, the Scottsdale Plaza Resort, we found our room (Brian Nelson is my roommate) and had more than two hours free before we had to leave for practice. I spent the majority of this time in the game room, which had two pool tables, two PlayStations, two Nintendos, two basketball games, a dart board, four arcade games, and two TVs. There also were four coolers full of drinks of all kinds and snack food like cereal bars, peanuts, raisins, applesauce, Jell-O, etc.

The practice was pretty rough, but it didn't seem very long. We're practicing at Scottsdale Community College, which is a pretty nice site. We had meetings at the hotel after practice. Coach Solich went over his expectations for the trip and a police officer explained some of the demographics of the city, such as which places to stay away from and which places are good places to hang out at.

We have shuttle vans again this year to take us anywhere we want to go for free, operating from 5:30 to midnight. I stayed in the hotel tonight and relaxed in the game room and got plenty of rest. My back is pretty sore and everyone on the trip shares my feeling of tiredness.

Saturday, December 25, 1999

Again, a Christmas day without presents. Instead, we go to practice. Our morning meeting was at 8:00, but I don't have to stay for the offensive line meetings so I can go back to the room and rest before practice. The practice was at 11:15 and it wasn't as bad as I expected. I knew it was going to be a scrimmage and I thought it would be like last year's bowl practice scrimmage that lasted three hours. Instead, it was like a regular practice for the scout team and it was actually a little easier since the top squads spent a lot of their energy scrimmaging against each other.

We had lunch and dinner at the hotel. The Fiesta Bowl sponsored the dinner and we received our watches. They're Swiss Army watches and they also came with a little knife. At dinner, starting defensive lineman Steve Warren sang grace and also led us in the singing of "The 12 Days of

Christmas" where all the positions had different days to sing. It was all pretty amusing. Then starting offensive tackle Adam Julch came out in a Santa Claus outfit and made all the little kids happy (the coaches and staff brought their families along, including many little kids).

I stayed in the lounge again tonight and played games until it closed at 1:00.

Sunday, December 26, 1999

The only thing that was required of us today was a 10:00 meeting. I napped and relaxed most of the day and later went to a mall and some clubs with some of the guys. Why we couldn't have made Christmas day an off-day I'll never know.

Monday, December 27, 1999

At an 8:00 meeting, Coach Solich informed us that there had been an "incident." He wouldn't say who did what, but he made sure to point out that there are cameras all over the hotel property. Later on, I heard that a couple guys were caught on tape sneaking around the hotel grounds. I'm not sure what they did or if they were just busted for being out too late, but the warning is out now.

The buses left at 9:30 for practice. Not much time for extra rest. The practice was full pads and very rough. My back and legs are very sore, bad enough to get out of doing gassers. I iced my back after practice and later spent some time in the hot tub.

Three busses of guys later went out to ASU's campus golf course, the Karsten Golf Course, this afternoon. It's a very beautiful and challenging course. We paired up in carts and played as foursomes. I shared the cart with Andy Gwennap. Dan Waldrop and Brian Hale rounded out our foursome. We played best ball and it was a very sloppy round.

By the end of nine holes, we weren't even playing. We were just off-roading in our golf cart all over the course, nearly tipping it over many times. We got so caught up in goofing off that we lost track of time and were the last people to get on the bus. Quite a few guys were pissed at us for making them wait, but we had fun.

We had a steak fry tonight for dinner. I can't eat very much because every time I pass through the players' lounge I grab a little something and that means I'm not hungry at mealtime. I will gain a lot of weight if I continue to eat like this for the rest of the trip.

Tuesday, December 28, 1999

Very early wake-up. We all had to leave for a Fellowship of Christian Athletes breakfast at 6:45. It was a nice breakfast, but the presentation was too long and boring. Tennessee was there also and some of the presentation included players from both sides.

We went back to the hotel and had meetings and lunch, and finally left for practice at 1:00. The practice was another long one in full pads. My back felt a lot better today after getting treatment on it. Everyone I've talked to thinks we're going too hard in practice. It's understandable because the past couple weeks of the season and the last weeks of school were a lot lighter than usual. Everyone also thinks this trip is way too long. We could have come down later and still had plenty of time to prepare. We should have at least been able to spend Christmas with our families.

Coach Solich seems very confident now in his role as head coach. The strength and confidence he's showing is, in my opinion, helping keep the team together in this stressful and conflicting time.

Tonight we went to a hockey game between the Phoenix Coyotes and the New York Rangers. This was my first

NHL game and it was a lot of fun. We had box seats with a great view, all for free. There were no fights and it ended in a 2-2 tie, but it was still a fun time. We got back to the hotel at 11:30 and made it just in time for the hot snack, which was fajitas.

Wednesday, December 29, 1999

We had another obligation today with the Kickoff Luncheon. It was very long and drawn out. I sat with a local news team, most of whom were Husker fans. One couple, however, was dressed in Volunteer colors and they weren't very pleased to have to sit with a Nebraska player.

We went straight to practice after the luncheon. Today is the last day in any kind of pads. The practice wasn't too bad, but I was still very happy to see it end.

We have police escorts to practice, which I don't think is necessary. We're fairly close to our practice site so even if we were to hit all the red lights, we would only be about five minutes later than if we didn't have the escorts. Also, while the police block off an intersection for us, we disrupt the flow of traffic in a big, fast-paced city. I see it as a huge inconvenience to the people of Phoenix and I would like to apologize for that even though I have no say in the whole deal.

Tonight is the first night with a bed check; it's at 11:30.

Thursday, December 30, 1999

We practiced at 10:15 today in sweats. It was a good practice overall, but my back problems have created another problem. The tightness has thrown off my long snaps. Because of this, Coach Bohl no longer trusts me to do the snaps and is now having me snap to a dummy punter while the real punter already has a ball.

We had the whole afternoon to relax and enjoy. We picked up another $125 at dinner. Later on, we had a small after-bed-check party in our room. I passed out at around 3:00 in the morning.

Friday, December 31, 1999

We had an early wake-up and 9:30 practice. I did not feel 100% due to the night before, but it didn't matter. I hardly broke a sweat.

I spent the majority of the day in the pool relaxing and playing with some other guys. My parents finally got here with other friends and family. This cured some of my homesickness, but not all of it.

A sizable group of players met in the players' lounge for a Millennium Party. We counted down, shouted "Happy New Year!" and threw confetti. Five minutes later, Coach Solich did a countdown of his own and said, "Three...Two... One...Bedtime!!!" (At least he has a sense of humor.)

This night really got to me. I made it through Christmas all right because I was able to go home before I left and celebrate an early Christmas with my parents. New Year's is always a fun time for me because I'm with a lot of my friends and there always are good parties. I miss my friends and the parties. Overall, this night was very depressing.

Saturday, January 1, 2000

Well, there were no Y2K disasters. All is well and the world continues to spin.

We had 9:30 meetings and then I went back to bed until 1:00. I spent the afternoon with my family. The players who will dress for the game went to the stadium to have a walk-through practice. I officially discovered that I will not suit up due to the lack of locker space.

Sunday, January 2, 2000

Nebraska 31 – Tennessee 21

Slept late again. We had 11:30 meetings and then were free for the rest of the day. We got $75 at lunch.

I went to the game with my family. They were supposed to go to a pre-game party, but it was a flop so I went and got my ticket. I ended up sitting with the other players who didn't suit up. The game was very long with a lot of interruptions, such as TV timeouts. Our offense got a quick start and Bobby Newcombe's punt return for a touchdown really set the tone for the game. It was a great game overall for us and ended the season nicely with a 31-21 win. Coach Solich finishes his second year with a 21-5 record.

One interesting fact about this game is that it was our coldest game of the year. Even after playing in Nebraska in the late fall, our coldest game was in the Arizona desert.

I finally get to go home tomorrow.

Monday, January 3, 2000

Charlie McBride, the defensive coordinator and defensive line coach for many years, announced that he is retiring, effective immediately. I guess this had been in the works for a while and a few of his close players knew about it, but it was a shock for the rest of the team and the media. With such an aged coaching staff, it seems only natural that we're going to have a couple more retirees in the next couple years.

I never thought I would look forward to being in Nebraska during the winter, but I'm glad to be home. I hitched a ride from Russ Hochstein back to my place from the airport and finally made it back to Omaha. All in all, it was a long but pleasant trip that ended very well.

End of the Year Summary

Looking back after all five of my years, this was our best year at 12-1 and the best team I was a part of. In the end, we beat every team that we played. I have no doubt that if we had been in the national championship game I would be the proud owner of another very nice ring. But as it is, the Big 12 Championship ring is the only ring that I ever earned while on the team. I had hopes for so much more, but I think, like many of my teammates, our hopes were placed on the shoulders of our better athletes and we wanted them to pull us through. I knew I wasn't going to play much, but I knew I wanted a ring. So, I did everything I could in practice to get them ready, but in the end they were the ones that had to do it in the game, not me. The benefit of this situation was that I could take pride in their success because I helped them get there. When they failed, I could either choose to feel responsible for their lack of preparation, or I could wash my hands entirely of their actions and place it all on them. Because of these mixed emotions, you won't see me wearing that ring too often.

2000 Winter Conditioning

It was around this time that I started to become much more cynical and negative about my life as a Husker. The rest of the year would be a rollercoaster of emotions. My body was aching, my strength reached it's peak before quickly fading, and my weight was a constant struggle to keep up. I always joke that I didn't just eat until I was full, I would eat until I was tired. To further compound it, it seemed as if the coaches still saw me as a freshman and nowhere near being ready to contribute. I seemed stuck. I don't like being stuck. I began to feel like I either needed to move up or move on.

Friday, January 14, 2000

We had our first team meeting today after having the rest of winter break off and the first week of school with no obligations. Coach Solich said Coach Bohl will become the defensive coordinator. Coach Solich will hire a new D-line coach, but he said it will be someone everyone knows and respects so it won't be a shock. I think it would be more shocking to get someone who wasn't a competent coach, but I guess familiarity must be the first thing they look for.

The meeting broke up and the offensive line then met in Coach Tenopir's office and discussed how winter conditioning will happen. It will be exactly like last year; lifting at 7:00 in the morning with running in the afternoon.

Wednesday, January 19, 2000

We had our winter testing/tryouts today. I think I was a little worse on my vertical, but my 40-yard dash and my pro agility were really good. My 40 speed is now 5.67 seconds, a nice improvement from last time, which I think was in the 5.8 range. My pro agility time was 4.69 seconds, which is not bad but I don't know if it is an improvement.

I've been teaching Brian Nelson how to play racquetball. He's picking it up pretty quickly, but he still has a long way to go if he's ever going to beat me.

Friday, January 21, 2000

We had another meeting today. Coach Solich made the first order of business the naming of the new defensive line coach. Jeff Jamrog, a former Nebraska player who just recently coached at New Mexico State, will take over for Charlie McBride. I don't know much about the man, but he must be pretty good.

After this, Boyd Epley went over the testing results from Wednesday. The most spectacular thing in the report was that Dan Alexander tied Ahman Green's score in the 40-yard dash. This is even more amazing because the new FieldTurf is slightly slower than the old Astroturf.

My right shoulder has been giving me trouble for a while. I haven't had any pain, but it pops when I make certain arm movements. I've been receiving treatment (ice and those electrode things) on it for a while now and haven't seen much improvement. The team doctor yesterday recommended that I get x-rays taken so today I went to the University Health Center.

They x-rayed both shoulders to get a comparison. The team doctor will look at the x-rays Monday night when he returns and we will see what happens.

Monday, January 24, 2000

Today was the first day of winter conditioning. It started at 7:00 this morning and everyone was there on time. I got up at 6:00, which enabled me to take my time and wake up before hitting the weights hard. Unlike last year, we're not the only group that decided morning workouts were a good idea. The weight room was obnoxiously packed and it took a long time just to get everybody going on their lifts. Because of this overcrowding, Archer decreed that from now on, Monday and Thursday lifting will start at 6:30. Oh well, I guess an extra half hour of sleep really doesn't matter.

I later played Kyle Kollmorgen in racquetball. This is the first round of the O-line tournament and I thought it was kind of ironic that the two of us—two of the best players—would have to play in the first round. I was worried at first because he is the returning champion from last year. He had a wicked serve that killed me last year so I was kind of nervous. This year, however, he lost a lot of his mobility and flexibility so he really wasn't as good. Or maybe I'm just a lot better than last year. Either way, I beat him two out of three games. I made a lot of great hits and really felt energized. Everyone was very surprised to find out that I beat Kyle. He even told me after the match that no one else will come close to me and that I have this tournament wrapped up. This is just another way that I am earning respect.

I saw the doctor today after dinner and he said there isn't a bone chip in my shoulder so it was probably just a stretched ligament or tendon that was a little inflamed. I was given a cortisone injection in my shoulder that is supposedly pretty successful with this kind of stuff, but it will leave me inactive for two or three days.

Tuesday, January 25, 2000

Another day of lifting at 7:00 although I couldn't do much due to the injection. I was able to do all the lower-body activities and abdominal work, but that was about it. My shoulder is kind of sore, but it is not much different. I used the rest of the day to do a lot of homework.

Thursday, January 27, 2000

It didn't take long for someone to show up late to lifting. Phil Lueking, a redshirt sophomore who threw for the track team his first year and took a redshirt football year this year, showed up at about 6:45. Shortly after 7:00 we all ran out into the cold, dark morning air and ran to the top of the South Stadium bleachers. Doing one of those isn't bad, at least it shouldn't be for any of us, and it really helps to get us warmed up in the morning. However, doing three stadiums, like Phil had to do, would be a little harder to say the least. He barely made them, but he finished with pride. I can guarantee he won't be late again this winter.

Monday, January 31, 2000

After a flawless season with no one on the offensive line quitting or getting injured badly enough to stop playing, we just lost two freshmen. Matt Witulski and John Mengles-dorf both decided to quit very recently. Matt was injured for the entire season and never did anything with the team. John, on the other hand, was a good player with an enormous frame who was still learning a lot of the fundamentals and making good progress. They're roommates in the dorm and I can only make guesses as to why they quit.

I did about half of my workout this morning. I have an 8:30 class and since I had to come back later to play racquetball, I finished early, relaxed, and enjoyed a big breakfast. My weight is really a concern for me right now. I have dropped about 10 pounds from what I was last year. I weighed 273 this morning, but I lied to Archer and told him 275. I need to put on about three pounds a week during this winter conditioning period.

I played Russ Hochstein this afternoon in racquetball and beat him two games in a row to advance to the next round. I then finished my workout and when I was completely exhausted, Jon Rutherford asked me to play just for fun. It wasn't very fun because he beat me two games in a row. I'm sure Jon and I will meet sometime during this playoffs.

Thursday, February 3, 2000

Lifting this morning started off with a little meeting about the need to get injuries examined by the trainers, no matter how minor they may appear to us. I thought this might be a good time to tell someone about my back. It's still sore from the bowl trip and flares up every now and then. Just when I think it's getting better, I move a certain way and hurt it so I can hardly move without pain. I'm afraid of being seen as a hypochondriac or someone who is just trying to get out of doing work so I have a hard time telling people about my problems, but I know I have to if I ever want them to get better.

I started a class today where I go to an area high school to observe and sometimes even teach. The principal is Jerry Wilks, an old friend of my dad whose son Joel was an offensive lineman during the mid 90's with Coach Osborne and part of the legendary "Pipeline," one of the most highly respected offensive lines ever. I talked to him about where his son was in his first couple of years and the struggles he went through. Joel and I have a lot of similarities so far—he struggled to gain and maintain his weight, he didn't play much at all his first years, and it took him a while to make a name for himself. I think he could be an inspiration to me and that I could learn a lot from his experiences.

Monday, February 7, 2000

My hang clean is finally returning to what it used to be. I did 286 pounds on the rack clean today which is near the top of what anybody else is doing. Today was also our first day of running. We met in the Cook at 3:30 and did our usual jump rope/low ropes/bags/cones workout. It didn't take too long, but by the end I was feeling pretty tired. I had some unusual trouble with the jump rope, and my foot speed is not what I want it to be on the low ropes. Other guys had some difficulty as well and it really wasn't that hard of a workout compared to some in the past. Then, just to add insult to injury, we had to run a stadium because John Garrison was late to lifting last Friday and we didn't want to run after heavy squat. I should fall asleep pretty easily tonight.

Friday, February 11, 2000

This morning I did the most on squat that I've ever done. I did 350 pounds 10 times for my last set and got all of them cleanly. I really impressed myself on that and I could tell that Archer and Coach Tenopir also were impressed. I was thoroughly wiped out after that, but it felt good. I hope I can do more next week.

Monday, February 14, 2000

My freshman year roommate Leif Sidwell has been forced into retirement because of his shoulder. Even after two surgeries, the problems were still severe enough that he had to quit. I don't know exactly what he must be going through with all of this but I bet it isn't easy. He was a hard worker and a good guy. For a brief period while he was healthy, he was playing like the best lineman in our class. So it goes.

Friday, February 18, 2000

It finally snowed today. After months of waiting and days of unanswered forecasts, we finally got some snow. The streets were still full of the five-inch snowfall at 6:30 this morning, but everyone got to the workout regardless. That just shows how much character and determination we have as a group. I'm not sure if it was related, but the seniors talked it over and called off the afternoon passing league work. I went in and finished my lifting in the afternoon and even did extra work on my form on certain lifts. Then I went into the Pit and worked on some footwork drills by myself. Also, my weight is finally getting up there again. I broke 280 pounds this week and plan to get close to 290 before this winter is over.

Tuesday, February 22, 2000

I was kind of surprised today to weigh in at 291. I had all my clothes on so that made about a five-pound difference, but it's still pretty close to my goal and it's very weird to see that weight on the scale knowing that I was hovering above 270 just four weeks ago. I don't know too many doctors who would say weight gain like this is healthy, but with all the work we do and the quality of the food I eat, I'm not worried at all. My strength continues to increase and I'm keeping an eye on my body fat. I just know that my overall size will play a key role in the amount of playing time I will get next year.

Thursday, February 24, 2000

Today's running was supposed to be easier than Monday's, but for some reason, everyone was really pumped up and we all flew through it in amazing time. It was probably the most intense running workout we have ever done and it wiped me out.

We had a special dinner tonight for Black History Month. This meant a free-for-all on some of the best food of the year. There was fried catfish, barbequed pork ribs, fried chicken, carved turkey and inside round. There were also plenty of sides with all of the food groups getting good representation. I left feeling incredibly full and satisfied. I hope this food will get me charged up for squat tomorrow.

Friday, February 25, 2000

I finally reached one of my goals for the winter. I broke 400 pounds on squat by doing 405 five times on my last set. I really had to psych myself up for this and get the adrenaline flowing, but then I attacked it and got them all really well. Archer and Coach Tenopir were both very pleased

The O-line got together for our passing drills, but we decided to play kickball instead. When we play games like this, the teams are usually the older guys against the younger guys. Believe it or not, the older guys like to make up their own rules from time to time to ensure victory, but that didn't happen today. We had some great kickers on our team and ended up beating them. They were pretty sore about it, but it really didn't matter, it's all in fun.

Monday, February 28, 2000

This afternoon's running was fairly intense, but everyone was so happy about this being the last running workout of the winter that it hardly affected us. Mike Wilford was out with a back problem and Brian Hale was out again as he has been for most of the workouts. Starting center Dominic Raiola yelled at Brian, but to no use. I don't think he's ever shown the desire or the effort to do anything.

Guard Dan Swantek learned that this will be his last semester at Nebraska. He has yet to get above a 2.0 GPA and has been given every chance to pass and slide through the system. You can only slide through life so far, at some point you have to push yourself.

Tuesday, February 29, 2000

I continued to improve on my bench today by finishing with my last set of five at 275 pounds. That's an all-time best and it felt really good. I did a lot of extra stuff in the afternoon and was sure to get a great upper-body workout, especially on my shoulders and back.

We get our body fat tested next Monday and then we do our performance testing on Wednesday. My plan for this is to put on as much weight as I can until Monday, I hope breaking 290, and then drop a lot of the weight over the next two days before testing. This shouldn't be hard because most of the weight will be water and I know that if I don't eat a lot on weekends, I can lose up to 10 pounds. This will help me out a lot with testing because I really don't want to run a 300-yard shuttle. This might not be the greatest thing in the world to do, but I think it will work.

Our testing scores are based on our weight. It's impressive when a receiver runs a 4.6 second 40 yard dash, but it's even more impressive when a lineman can do the same. Every five or ten pounds of body weight adds a degree of difficulty that can work for you or against you. Since we weigh in two days early, it gives us a chance to skew the numbers in our favor.

Friday, March 3, 2000

I knew I should have gone higher on my last set of squat, but I stayed with what my card said. I did my last set at 415 pounds and when I finished five, I knew my legs could take at least one more. I did a sixth rep fairly well. I knew I had another one in me. Scott Koethe was spotting me and went to grab the bar so he could help me rack it after finishing my sixth one. Instead I said, "one more!" and he backed off and I did a seventh rep. This one took all of my remaining strength and I barely got it up, but I did it. This topped off the entire winter.

For our afternoon workout, we all met at Hooters for happy hour. They had 35-cent wings and $1 draws, and I emptied my wallet. Nelson, Koethe and I got a plate of 40 wings and we finished them off without a problem. The waitress didn't card anybody (I wonder why), so most of us were drinking. The number of pitchers of beer they brought to our table was staggering. I think the beer tab alone was over $70. It was a nice way to wrap up the winter. (John Garrison ended up marrying our waitress).

Brian Nelson has become quite a figure on the offensive line. He's like a walking comic book character with his pleasant demeanor, easygoing attitude, and a giant belly. He also has a slight speech impediment which, when combined with the belly and overall size, make him the perfect look-alike for Lenny, the character in *Of Mice and Men.* Many of the guys have taken to calling him Lenny. At first I thought it was an amazingly erudite connection to come from this group, but then I remembered that the book was also turned into a movie.

Monday, March 6, 2000

I weighed in for my body fat test today at 292 pounds. I chugged about two pounds of sports drinks to get my weight to this, which is less than I expected to do. My percentage didn't really change, it's now 14.3%. According to this, I put on about 12 pounds of lean mass during the winter, which is outstanding. I finally broke into the 250-pound-lean-mass club, but just barely.

We had a meeting this afternoon and went over testing information for Wednesday and other general stuff. It was really a waste of time, but I had nothing better to do.

Wednesday, March 8, 2000

I was kind of worried about the testing today. If I didn't improve in three of the four events, I'd have had to run the 300-yard shuttle. We can improve in either our time, or height for the vertical jump, or the index score. Since the index score is based on body weight, getting myself to 292 helped me out in this respect. I didn't drop as much weight as I hoped I was going to by now. I'm at about 285, which added to my worries about my performance. I went to the Cook around 1:45 and had plenty of time to warm up before testing. The seniors were already testing for the pro scouts and we started after they finished.

I started off at the vertical jump. I bettered my all-time jump by half an inch to get to a 25-inch vertical. One down, two to go.

Next was the pro agility. I have always had trouble with this one because I get my steps wrong and slow down too much to compensate. This time I shaved off .05 seconds. Good enough, now I just needed one more to get out of the shuttle run.

I went over to the 40-yard dash station, did a light warm-up, tried to get some adrenaline flowing and just went right into it. Last time I ran a 40 that amazed me and I didn't really know if I could do it again. I ran the best I could and it turned out that it was also the best I've ever done. I shaved my 40 time by almost a tenth of a second to 5.60. I also improved on my 10-yard dash so in the end, I bettered all four of the tests. I was very pleased.

The test scores boosted my performance index by 200 points. I think it was 1,534 points, which isn't outstanding, but shows that I'm continually improving. All of my times and scores are respectable but there is still a lot of room for improvement and I know I'll keep getting better if I continue to work hard and stay dedicated.

2000 Spring Ball

Monday, March 20, 2000

The first day of spring ball practice. It was just what I was expecting. We went in helmets and spent the entire time learning just four of the most basic plays in our offense. It was all fairly easy and I hardly ever messed up. One time that I did mess up was funny to me but not to Coach Tenopir. Brett Lindstrom is the quarterback for the third team and he also was my quarterback in high school. When we wanted to change a play at the line of scrimmage in high school, we would put the number seven in the cadence. Brett used this for one of his cadences today, saying, "Set, 7-11, 7-11, Hut." Hearing him say this sparked my memory and I suddenly thought the play had been changed to 11 Base Option. I ran 11 Base, which was the wrong play, and Coach Tenopir was quick to point out my error.

I quickly tried to defend myself, saying "But he used a seven call to change the play."

Coach Tenopir just stared at me. "What are you talking about? We don't have a seven call." I then realized my mistake, kept my mouth shut and walked away quickly to save some dignity. Besides that, it was a good first day.

I don't know if it means anything, but after practice,

my knees were really warm. They haven't felt 100% the past few weeks and I think it may be due in part to the really heavy weight I was doing on squat. I don't know if I somehow messed up my knees or if this is just a growing pain. Whatever it is, it kind of freaked me out.

Saturday, March 25, 2000

We were greeted with our *Survivor* gift today when we got to the locker room. This was for being at every workout over winter conditioning. It's just a red Adidas T-shirt with the *Survivor* logo on it, but it has some sentimental value, I guess. We also received a pair of gray sweat shorts and a matching T-shirt, the same gray T-shirt they have given us twice before. Oh well, it's free (somewhat).

Norma handed out $27 to us non-scholarship players at breakfast, which was gratefully added to my skinny wallet. Meetings started at 10:00. A big meal, early on a Saturday, and sitting in a darkened room after getting five hours sleep doesn't add up too well. I nodded off a few times, but I didn't really miss much. We just watch the number ones run plays all the time so we never get a chance to see what we're doing well, what we're doing wrong, what we could do better, and so on. I know we're not doing everything perfectly, so why do we waste all the time looking at the group that does everything perfectly instead of getting the whole group involved in pointing out what the younger guys are doing wrong and how to fix it? The older guys know everything already and we can only learn so much on our own; I think we need to involve the younger groups in the meetings more if the coaches plan for them to be ready to play someday.

Practice started today at 12:30. The last drill we did was the scrimmage part of the day. I did okay. I don't plan to make a high grade, but I don't think I messed up too badly. My biggest problem is getting my blocks to be powerful and making them last. Too often the defensive man and I stalemate at the line of scrimmage, or worse yet, I get driven back. Sometimes, I don't hit the guy right and he slips off of me and makes the play. Leg power and my punch are my biggest weaknesses right now. It doesn't help that I'm going up against Ryon Bingham, who is much stronger than pretty much everybody, but I do a good job sometimes. I know all of the plays, I know all the calls and I know a lot more now than I did last year, but my strength and my technique need the most work.

After practice I ran home to see my high school put on its spring musical. This was a must because it's the last year of teaching for the director, Mike Janis. Mr. Janis has been a good family friend for a long time. During my time in high school, I was involved in everything with vocal music that was open to me, and this culminated in being the lead of my senior musical, *Fiddler on the Roof.* I can't begin to describe how big of an influence Mr. Janis and his classes had on me and my life, but I can say for certain that he influenced some of the most positive changes in my life.

Monday, March 27, 2000

I skipped my 8:30 and 11:30 classes just so I could sleep in and get plenty of rest. I knew today would be a big day and I would need a lot of energy. The practice was supposed to be shorter than usual, but I think that was just something Coach Solich said so we would enjoy our shortened weekend a little more. Today was very intense and I had one of the best practices I've had in a while. I made some great blocks and showed a lot of intensity and effort. I messed up only a handful of times, and I knew exactly what I did when it happened.

After dinner, I met with Jack Stark, the sports psychologist. I went over some things that recently happened to me, especially regarding relationships, and some more stuff that goes back further in my life. It was really refreshing to get some of those things said and he was very good about offering advice and direction to help me overcome my problems. I think this period in my life could be a major turning point.

> I had just been dumped, I felt like football was a curse and a burden, and I felt like I was trapped in the program with no way to get out that wouldn't alienate me from family and friends who cared so much about my spot on the team. A lot of pent up emotions were trying to get out and I didn't know how to do this productively. In short, I was pretty mixed up at this point, but it wouldn't be the last time.
>
> Looking back, it's almost comical how a couple other guys and myself would talk about how much easier our lives would be if we were in prison instead of football. We all felt we would have more freedom with our lives behind bars than on the football team. Luckily for us, no one ever acted on this philosophy.

Tuesday, March 28, 2000

I met with Coach Ron Brown after I lifted today. He is a great man and very vocal about his faith and his beliefs. We had a great talk about faith and religion. He gave me a lot of inspirational advice and showed me what to do if I really am serious about what I feel. I talked about my personal history with religion and where I am at this time in my life with all of my questions and doubts. He gave me lots of stories and personal examples and really helped me clear my mind up. Afterward we prayed together and I accepted Jesus

Christ into my life. I am taking a leap of faith and putting my life in the hands of God. I have gotten by so far in my life without ever asking for divine help and have done fairly well. I feel that with God's help I can achieve more, but it will take time and dedication. This day marks the rebirth of my religious side.

Wednesday, March 29, 2000

After dinner this evening, I met up with Chase Long, Josh Brown, Aaron Golliday, Justin Smith, and Kyle Kollmorgen. We all rode in two Lincoln Fire Department vehicles to two area hospitals where we went around and did our best to cheer up some patients. It didn't last long, but it was a good time and I got to make some new connections. They got an emergency call on the way back and we were put in the middle of the action as they raced with lights and sirens to one of the fraternity houses on campus. Unfortunately, the frat house wasn't on fire and we just drove by after making sure the situation was under control.

As far as power and authority go on campus, the football team and the greek system are about equal, but by completely different methods. The football players know that we bring a ton of money and publicity to the university, not to mention a reason to celebrate, and we are able to walk around campus with everyone admiring us. The greek system is like a parasitic leech, sucking the fun out of being a regular student and making you feel like a nobody if you aren't affiliated with a house. They keep all the school business and functions to themselves, never offering a piece of the pie to anyone else. But what really gets me about the frat boys and sorority girls is that they think they're so special simply because they can pay all this extra money so they can buy their friends, live in a cramped loft, and get trashed every weekend while trying to get some.

One of the first questions I asked my wife when we were on our first date was if she was in a sorority. She wasn't. She passed my test.

Saturday, April 1, 2000

The first real scrimmage. I was scheduled for 22 plays throughout the day. Each team is running 42 plays, giving 126 plays total for the day. Garrison took all the snaps for the first set of the threes. I then took over the next set of 10 after the other two teams cycled through. For the last set, Garrison and I traded off series for the final 22 plays. We got $27 at breakfast this morning.

It was a very good practice overall. The offense seemed very strong and pretty much shut the defense out for the day. One interception was returned for a touchdown, but that was about the only highlight for the defense. Eric Crouch didn't do anything because he is still recovering from shoulder surgery, so Jammal Lord took all the snaps for the number ones. Jammal looked amazing out there. He has great speed, agility, vision, timing, acceleration, and throwing accuracy. He looked like Michael Vick did in the national championship game with the way that he shook off tacklers and dodged defensive men like magic. He was definitely the highlight of the day.

Every high point needs a low point to bring balance to the universe. This low point for me happened no less than 10 minutes before the end of practice. We were within the five-yard line, ready to score and everyone was looking forward to getting it in the end zone and eventually going home. We ran a play off to the left, I blocked the man shaded to my right and kept him out of the play entirely. To my left, the guard must have had some trouble with his man. One of them came crashing down on the side of my calf, buckling my knee in on me. I felt a distinct pop on the right side of my left kneecap. I've been studying such injuries in my athletic training class so I knew at once what had happened. I didn't feel much pain at all and was able to hobble off the field under my own power. I passed by Coach Tenopir, who understandably asked what happened and I told him precisely: "It's my knee. I hurt my MCL."

I made my way to the training table on the sideline and the trainers confirmed what I already knew. I had a second-degree sprain of my Medial Collateral Ligament, also known as the MCL. This was the same thing that happened to Scott Koethe, and he is out for the rest of spring ball. I didn't want that to happen to me. I was just beginning to find my groove out there on the field. My mom and dad both said they hardly recognized me on the field because I looked and played so much better. I have noticed this as well and was hoping to have a breakthrough spring and get myself in position to be a contender for some major playing time.

After practice and a shower, I made my way to the training room and iced my knee in the whirlpool (not a whirlpool like one would have at home; it's just a pill-shaped metal bin with an agitator big enough for one person to squeeze into). I was wrapped up, given a brace, and told to be back at 10:00 tomorrow morning.

> In later years, this story became a favorite of my friend and walk-on fullback Andrew Wingender. He tells the story of me hobbling over to the sideline and telling Coach Tenopir that I hurt my MCL. Then he adds a little Coach Tenopir dialogue and says, "Well Dave, don't you think we should let the trainers make that diagnosis?" to which I quickly answer, "Nope, nope, it's my MCL, I'm sure!"

Monday, April 3, 2000

Everyone was very surprised to hear about my knee. Since it happened near the end of practice, those not playing were already looking forward to going home and paid no attention to what was happening on the field. Those most surprised were Dominic Raiola, Matt Shook, and John Garrison. This is because my injury evened out the distribution of us, the centers, to just one per group. Shook and Garrison are now all on their own, something foreign to both of them, but something I'm used to. They were all mad at me for being injured since they won't be on a rotation, but what could I do? I couldn't walk without a limp and I can't bend my leg more than 60 degrees.

My treatment is two times daily, for about an hour and a half to two hours total each day. It involves the cold whirlpool, electrode stimulation, and light bicycling. The main emphasis is to keep the swelling down and regain full range of motion without pain, and also to be able to run and change directions without trouble. Doak, the head trainer, thinks I could be back to practice by Friday. I guess he knows more about this than I do.

Tuesday, April 4, 2000

I stayed up really late last night and got a little over an hour of sleep because of a test I have today. I went through class and my treatment sessions and little else. I'm really glad that spring practices are every other day.

Wednesday, April 5, 2000

Everyone on the O-line, especially the centers, wants to know when I'll be back. I tell them I could be back Friday at the earliest, but that doesn't seem to please them. During practice today I did some light jogging, forward and backward, and walked five sets of stairs.

The practice was modified to accommodate all the hurt players by reducing the number of teams from three to two. This should make Shook and Garrison happy. There was a scrimmage station today and the defense finally found their groove and basically destroyed the offense. It was a really good show for them and should be a good confidence booster after last Saturday's scrimmage.

I was talking to Scott Koethe, who is also out with an MCL sprain, and he mentioned that Andy Gwennap, he, and I are the only walk-on players left from our class. I was shocked by this, but it's true. The system weeds out people pretty fast, but I think the three of us will stick around all five years.

For some bad news, our lone functioning scholarship quarterback for the spring, Jammal Lord, joined the disabled list with a torn posterior cruciate ligament (one of the four main ligaments in the knee). It's a near complete rupture; there are still a few strands holding it together. He will not undergo surgery, but will be out for a while.

Friday, April 7, 2000

Yesterday I had a treatment session in which I was put through a lot of running. I started by jogging around the field for a couple of laps, then I did six 100-yard strides, two 100-yard back pedals, two 40-yard-and-back shuffles, and then a figure *8* drill. Everything was fine up until the figure *8*. Going around the corner on those made my leg swing out and I could really feel how loose that ligament still is.

My knee was pretty sore this morning. I went in for treatment and they put me through a strength program this time. I did the Stairmaster for 20 minutes, leg press, leg curl, and a step drill. I had moderate pain with the leg press, but besides that, it was fine. For the rest of the day, however, my knee was swollen and sore. I could hardly bear standing on it during practice. I was forced to hide behind the crowd of coaches that was amassed for a clinic and find refuge on a water cooler. I iced it again after practice and finally got some anti-inflammatory drugs. This should help a lot. I will be held out of tomorrow's scrimmage as well, in the hopes that a weekend rest will have me ready by Monday.

Saturday, April 8, 2000

Scrimmage day. The offense really dominated the defense and set the tone early. Joe Chrisman took the snaps for the first string, Brett Lindstrom did most for the second string, and the surprise of the week was Kelly Cook taking snaps at QB for the third team. Kelly used to be a receiver, but he played QB at Omaha's Burke High School. There were a lot of fumbles late in the scrimmage. It was either the exchange between the center and the QB or nerves or something. Whatever it was, it wasn't good.

It was incredibly boring just standing on the sideline for the whole practice doing nothing. I did have a nice talk with the lone female on the team for spring practices, punter Beanie Barnes, who is trying out for the team while being here on a track scholarship. I hope there are some good parties tonight.

Monday, April 10, 2000

I was cleared to practice today. I was given a brace to protect my knee and also to stabilize it. I had to be cautious about what I was doing, so I was not as productive as I would have liked. I still can't run full speed or pull to the right very well; both of these things are painful. When we were going through our teamwork stations, Garrison started with me and gave me the rare chance to have a rotation so I could get some regular rest. Halfway through teamwork, Shook switched with Garrison. This made my practice incredibly easy, but I'm not complaining.

Wednesday, April 12, 2000

Typically, this practice would be in sweats. The NCAA has a rule that three of the 15 days of spring ball must be in sweats. We went in sweats last Friday because the coaches were getting tired of all the injuries, so technically today could be in full pads. Everyone was wondering what we would do, and we finally found out the strange plan in meetings. We would start the practice in full pads and go through groupwork. After groupwork, the shoulder pads come off and the rest of the practice would be like we were in sweats. It was kind of weird, but I didn't mind the break.

My knee is feeling better. I hope these next two days with no practice will give it enough rest to heal fully or just get good enough so I can play and be productive in the game on Saturday.

Saturday, April 15, 2000

This is it—the Spring Game. This is what we have been practicing four weeks for. This is why we lifted before 7:00 in the morning four days a week for six weeks. This is what will make or break many guys. This is what basically ensures that you will be invited to go through the fall camp and give you a good chance to get major playing time next year. No pressure, none at all.

We were given $27 at breakfast. I also got braces to protect my knees. Having those on provides psychological reassurance. It takes my mind off worrying about guys being thrown into my knees because I know they will be protected, and that frees me up to be more aggressive on the field.

The game started at 12:30 and the crowd was rather large, especially for the chilly weather. The first team started the game, and we (the second team) were told we would go in for the second quarter. The first-team offense struggled pretty much the entire game to get something done, but the first half was almost a total stalemate. I was the punt snapper for all of these stalemates and got on the field quite a bit for that. I wasn't able to come up with a tackle, but I did have quite a few good hits on potential blockers, including one where I blew a guy off his feet and sent him rolling. My snaps were not the best the entire day. I think part of the problem was the knee braces. There is a metal bar on the inside thigh and when I snap, my elbows hit those. After a couple of snaps my elbows were really hurting. They all got to the punters and holders, but they were not the kind of snaps I wanted.

An interesting highlight was the groundbreaking introduction of Beanie Barnes, the first female punter to play in a Spring Game, and I snapped to her for her first official kick. She was even noted in Sports Illustrated for how far her kick went. Beanie is a great athlete and wanted to see if she had the leg for football. She hasn't been the most consistent, but I'm glad the coaches gave her a chance.

When we finally got in for the second quarter, it was scoreless. We put on a pretty good drive, but were stopped about halfway. Miraculously, the return person fumbled on the punt and we recovered with great field position. We finished the drive straight up the middle with a quarterback sneak from one foot away and scored. This play made the first half highlights, which were shown before the second half and I thought it was cool because the camera was right on me and Kelly Cook.

I felt that I had a really good game. I don't think I messed up very much at all on any of the plays. I didn't put up perfect blocks, but I accomplished what I was asked. One highlight of my day happened when one of our passes was picked off by a linebacker and I made a solo open-field tackle. That felt pretty good, but it still doesn't make the interception a good thing.

The game ended in a 21-21 tie. Quarterback Bobby Newcombe hurt his elbow pretty badly and could be out for about seven weeks. Linebacker Randy Stella got a bad stinger, but it shouldn't hamper him for long. It was a good day as a whole for the team. A lot of young guys got a taste of playing and most of them did very well. That's the true purpose of spring ball.

Sunday, April 16, 2000

After a long night of celebration, I enjoyed finally being able to sleep in. I probably should have gotten a treatment on my knee, but it feels pretty good and I was not about to get up before noon.

Tonight was the annual Student-Athlete Academic Recognition Banquet. This is the first year I've been invited to it and I plan to go to all of them during my time here. The criteria for being part of this ceremony is to have a GPA above 3.0, either cumulative or for the past year. I was awarded a bronze honors medal for having a GPA between 3.0 and 3.49. There was also high honors (3.5-3.749) and highest honors (3.75-4.0). High honors and highest were given silver and gold medals, respectively. The medal is a duplicate of the athletics and academic seal for the University. This will look good on my desk along with all the other awards I've racked up over the years.

Saturday, April 22, 2000

Coach Tenopir invited all of the offensive line over to his house for a cookout like he did last summer. This time, instead of a keg, he had a big cooler full of Busch Light. I didn't really want to drink, but I ended up having one anyway. Other guys just sat at the picnic table drinking away and in the end, Coach Tenopir was kind of mad because we drank all of his beer. Another thing that was different was that he let us in his house to play pool and we didn't have to use his fence as a restroom. I played basketball most of the time in game after game of "pig." It was a pretty good time overall.

Coach Tenopir is pretty jovial when he's in his own habitat. Maybe he's just more comfortable there or maybe the beer helped break the ice. I'm not sure.

Tuesday, April 25, 2000

We had a team meeting today. Coach Solich led it and mostly talked about what will happen and what is expected this summer. After that I met with Coach Solich personally for our end-of-the-year meeting. He mostly reiterated everything Coach Tenopir told me a week ago. One new thing he said was that I may not travel. They usually take three centers on road trips. Even if I'm the third-string center, Garrison will go as the third center if he's the first-string long snapper. That means, if I want to travel (which would be awesome because we're going to Notre Dame), I need to get faster and beat out Garrison for the snapping job. I can do it; I just have four months to do it.

Friday, April 28, 2000

After a good week of lifting and also the last week of classes, it was time to party. I started out the night at quarterback Joe Chrisman's apartment where he had a surprise birthday party for his roommates, tight end Will Dabbert and cornerback Tyler Rauenzahn. This was a very good party and I was proud to see it was not a sausage fest since some of the guys have close ties to sororities.

After I got bored there, I drove to Scott Koethe's house

with Matt Shook carefully following me. I showed up for one of the biggest parties of the year about 30 minutes after the cops busted it up. Scott lives with Steve Alstadt, Dan Swantek and Mike Green, all offensive linemen and in a house that is quickly building a great reputation as a party house. Steve was talking about how he's getting screwed over by the coaches because of his grades. His scholarship was taken away because of his grades and he thought he was getting it back after a good semester, but it appears he won't.

We all got into a discussion about how much work and effort you have to put in at Nebraska when you might not even get a single play your whole time here. Just being a "lineman from UNL" could get any of us a scholarship to nearly any school in the nation but we can't even get that type of respect from our own coaches.

Mike Green is the perfect example. He hasn't played a down in three years. A Division 1 school in California has recently offered him a full-ride scholarship just because he's from Nebraska.

Also, we spend so much time with football-related activities that our social life is very limited. If we tried to have a social life like a regular college student, we'd have no time to study and would flunk out of school. If we want to do well in school, we either have to be very smart (which some guys are not) or highly restrict our free time. Any one of us would be superstars and the big man on campus at any Division 1 or Division 2 school. Here, you're lost in the crowd unless you're a starter and that typically doesn't happen until the third or fourth year.

I guess I have two choices: stay here in the hopes that one day I'll be a starter and get some recognition, but face the possibility that my turn will never come, or transfer to another school and become a local celebrity, but not have the national attention or the program I have here. If I don't see professional football in my future, why shouldn't I go somewhere where I can have an impact? Everybody loves to hear first-hand stories of how the team is doing and virtually anybody can make conversation with me based solely on football. Yet, I feel like I will always be a messenger, never a newsmaker. Will my time come? Will I keep developing? Is there a spot for me here that I can fill and make the most of? Or, should I try my luck at being a star somewhere else?

Sunday, April 30, 2000

Coach Young had a party for the kickers and snappers at his house today. Everyone was there except Dominic and Russ, both of whom longsnap. There was John Garrison and me, Chase Long, Josh Brown, Dan Hadenfeldt, and Kyle Larson. Coach cooked up some enormous steaks and had all the side dishes, including salad, baked potatoes, beans, and bread. Coach Young is hard to carry on a conversation with, especially if you don't know what his interests are. I stopped trying long ago to get on his good side. I'd much rather just stay away from him.

One thing that really surprised me was that there was no alcohol, especially since it was at Coach Young's house. I guess that's a good idea; I didn't want to drink anyway because I have to study for finals tonight. After getting stuffed and topping it off with ice cream, I made my way home and began a long night of studying.

Wednesday, May 3, 2000

I got word this week that I will move to the south locker room to be with the upperclassmen. This means the coaches think I'm ready to become a real contributor and join the rest of the team in the main locker room. This is a very good sign. The depth chart was announced today. It said I am third string.

My weight is really taking off. I'm very near 300 pounds and I don't know what I'm doing differently to suddenly gain all this weight. I think my metabolism must be slowing down or something. I'm working hard to make sure all of this extra weight is muscle and not fat.

Saturday, May 20, 2000

I started the first session of summer school last Monday and all three sessions combined go straight through the summer right up to fall camp. I'm going to summer school to stay caught up, not to get ahead. If I'm going to get done in five years, I really need to get a lot done each semester and not waste any time. I'm in no big rush to finish school. I got my report card from this semester and was very delighted to see I got a 4.0. This brings my cumulative GPA to 3.4 and I hope to keep raising it. I was one of five guys on the entire team to get a 4.0 and the only lineman.

Brian Nelson moved in with me and so far is a pretty good roommate. Later on, tight end recruit Chris Septak, another guy from our high school, will move in along with his roommate for next year, making this place very crowded. I still don't know how all that is going to work out.

I moved over to the south locker room this week. I now have a big locker about twice the size of the ones in the north locker room. They're more like an open closet with a built-in footlocker and a cabinet on top. Most guys just throw their stuff in the big open area in the middle and I guess that must be safe because so many guys do it. I can padlock the footlocker and the cabinet, but there is no way to guard the open middle. My deodorant was taken from my locker the second day, so I put a lock on the cabinet. The south locker room is definitely a lot cleaner than the north and is much more modern. There are a lot more urinals and toilets and, unlike the other locker room, these bathrooms have the extravagant feature not only of individual stalls around the toilets but actual doors on them as well (unlike the north locker room). There aren't as many showerheads and most of them don't work right, which is one of the drawbacks. The other thing I'll miss: the couches in front of the TV where everyone would relax after practice and watch *The Simpsons* or *Friends*. There's a players' lounge with couches and a bigger TV just down the hall from the south locker room, so I guess that's good enough.

The lifting schedule for these first three weeks is pretty laid back. The emphasis is getting our form back after a long break and building our base up before we go for any major strength. Most of the guys are back for lifting now, but a few who live far away will return in the next two weeks.

I have a lot of plans for this summer—lots of concerts and trips all around the country including KC, Chicago, and NY. It should be a good time.

Saturday, May 27, 2000

Ryan Ommert, a freshman wide receiver, and I went to a fund-raiser in Omaha as Husker "celebrities," even though nobody knew who we were. It was a fund-raiser for leukemia research and was an all-day bike ride across a good section of Iowa and Nebraska. We got some free food and a T-shirt, did a pie-eating contest, and signed a few autographs for some kids and that was about it. We didn't stay very long, but it was good enough for a little volunteer work.

2000 Summer Conditioning

Tuesday, May 30, 2000

After a quick three-day weekend, I had to jump right back into the swing of things.

I had a history test today and failed to get any good studying done the whole weekend, so I ended up staying up all but an hour of last night studying. I told Archer I needed to study some more, so I didn't have to lift this morning. I think I did pretty well on the test in the end, but I brought it on myself for not studying earlier. I grabbed some food over at the Union and lifted at about 1:00. I was very tired and feeling incredibly weak, so I modified my program to fit my energy level. Besides, yesterday I helped carry about 150 cubic feet of dirt in five-gallon buckets as my dad and I put in a new planting bed in our backyard. I think that was all the workout I needed for this week.

I began thinking about what I'm doing. My life will be ruled by football and school for the next three years. I've already spent two years in these shackles, and I'm just beginning to question what I'm doing. Do I really want to do this? Do I want to have the best years of my life pinned down by all of these time restrictions and commitments? I don't know. I know that I could never do this for my whole life. A pro football career would be nice, but how long do I want to keep doing this and most importantly, how long will my body last? I want to be free for a while and have the opportunity to literally get away from my life and do some self-discovery. It may sound like a romantic dream or just some nonsensical rambling, but that's what I'm feeling right now. Maybe I just need some sleep to help clear my mind.

Monday, June 5, 2000

This last weekend was a lot of fun. It was also very long. Sunday was spent at a concert in Iowa. I got back to Omaha at about 2:00 in the morning and planned to drive to Lincoln. My dad made me stay, which was probably the best choice, but then I had to be careful to not be late to morning lifting. With all the construction on I-80, it was hard to judge the time. I made it to Lincoln and ran into the weight room with 10 seconds to spare. If I'd been a few steps slower or hit one more red light, I would have been running stairs. During the past week I've been averaging about five hours of sleep a night. After this morning's lifting, I was very tired. I couldn't help dozing off in my new class today no matter how hard I fought it.

This afternoon we had a team meeting in which I learned nothing new except I think the motto for this year will be "Championship Commitment." That's a pretty crappy motto. Perhaps we're running out of catch phrases after so many years of having one. I think we should have some abstract phrase or quote that could tie in with a lot of different things at once, but I think too many people wouldn't understand it. "Championship Commitment" just doesn't strike that spark of inspiration that the past ones held, for me at least.

After the meeting I was invited to Spaghetti Works with some of the guys. It ended up being Jason Schwab, Dominic Raiola (who was recently named the number one center in the country), Russ Hochstein (number three guard in the country), and Jon Rutherford. Schwab really is a great guy. He has worked his way up from walking-on and is in his sixth year after being hurt last year. I guess he sympathizes with me or sees something in me because he's one of the older guys who goes out of his way to make me feel comfortable. At this dinner, he helped me get into the conversation after I arrived late, and really made me feel like one of the guys. As rough as it is to be a football player here with all the dedication, sacrifices, and responsibilities that we have, it's always good to know that you're accepted among people you spend the majority of your time with.

Friday, June 16, 2000

We start running next week with all the jump rope and bag drills. I'm not in the greatest aerobic shape, so I ran two stairs in South Stadium Monday and Thursday this week. In retrospect, I'm very glad I did. Today, after my alarm didn't go off, I got to the weight room about a minute late and the usual punishment is three stairs. This was after I got done with a set of 10 for heavy squat when my legs were already tired. The whole O-line went out on the field to watch me run my punishment and jeer at me for being late and wasting their time. I got through the first two stairs fine, but I really had to push myself to make the third one. After it was over, my body was entirely spent and I wasn't able to finish my workout very well. I'm pretty sure that I won't be late to anything anymore.

I can't find a job anywhere in Lincoln. Unemployment is at a record low, but the hours that I can work don't match up with very many places around town. With morning lifting, midday school, 5:30 running and a few meals thrown in, it makes it very hard to be desirable to many businesses. If possible, I want to work someplace from 8:00 to midnight. With gas prices creeping closer to $2 and a pretty busy social life, I need some money. The Huskers are usually good about finding places around town that are willing to accommodate athletes and their weird schedules, but so far nothing has come through.

I'm beginning to see just how prevalent marijuana use is around the city, as well as campus. For instance, I went over to a buddy's house recently to pick him up and all of his roommates were in the living room smoking pot. Being their teammate, they graciously offered me to join them, but I turned it down. I'm not sure how they get away with this, both legally as well as with the drug tests that we have, but they must have a system. Apparently, the team only does urine tests three times a year and they're always around the same time. If you're clean by that time, you're golden. The only real gamble is hoping you don't get called up for a random test done by the NCAA, but they only pick a handful of guys and they're usually higher profile players to begin with.

Monday, June 19, 2000

Our schedule the rest of the summer will be running on Monday and Thursday nights, passing league and option drill on Tuesday and Friday nights, and continued lifting at 7:30 in the morning each of those days. We started running today and it was hot, humid, bright, and I was tired. I should have started running stairs earlier. I didn't figure that the 20 extra pounds I've gained would work against me so much. I'm staying just under 300 pounds right now, and am not having difficulty holding this weight. I got my body fat tested and the report was pretty much what I expected. I'm now at 17% body fat, a gain of almost 3%. Dave Ellis said this isn't good, but he's not worried since it's still a relatively healthy percentage.

Thursday, July 6, 2000

Today was the first day back after a nice five-day weekend. I was able to go to Kansas City and see one of my favorite bands, Blink 182. This was fun because I was able to just walk right through the crowd without any problem all the way to the front row. All I had to do was keep moving forward until the kid ahead of me turned around to see a 6'5", 300 pound guy in a Nebraska football t-shirt behind them. One of them was even kind enough to spread the crowd by yelling, "Holy shit! Big guy comin' through!!"

I got a letter today saying I'm not going to be part of fall camp. This is really disappointing because I thought I had a good chance of going to the camp, which would have meant I'd have a chance at traveling. I know my parents really wanted me to travel so they could go to Notre Dame, but that looks doubtful now. I guess I can look at the bright side of having two weeks free with nothing to do instead of getting up at 5:30 for practice. I actually think I would have rather gone to the camp.

Friday, July 14, 2000

Courage and stupidity are a dangerous mix. I proved this today by trying to test my limits and see what I could get away with by being two days away from 21 years of age. So, off I went to a liquor store to stock up on some birthday party supplies, thinking that I was so close to the actual age that they would either say "You're close enough" or "Try again in a few hours."

I thought wrong.

The clerk asked for my ID, which I gave her. She did a quick double take and said, "You're not 21. I'm calling the cops. And I'm going to keep your license."

My heart was in my throat at this point, but I knew I could do nothing else but stand there and take it. She told me I could leave, but the cops would just hunt me down eventually to serve me the ticket. Having nothing better to do, I waited patiently and actually ended up having an enjoyable small-talk conversation with the clerk.

A female cop showed up a few minutes later, wrote me a ticket and then I was free to go until my court date. So, with fall camp only a few weeks away, I have to make sure that the coaches don't find out about this or else I could be in big trouble.

> In the end, I was able to sneak off to the court in between meetings. I didn't have a lawyer and plead guilty, knowing full well that I was guilty and that I deserved any punishment I received. I paid the fine and had a misdemeanor on my record after that.
>
> Near the end of college, as I was applying to different jobs, as well as working on my teaching license, I ran into many instances where having a misdemeanor turned out to be a big inconvenience. I went to the student legal office and talked to one of the lawyers, who suggested we go back and try to get it expunged from my record. We quickly proved that I have had a clean record since that incident and that I have done several positive things as well. The judge granted our request and now my record is back to being perfect.
>
> The coaches never found out about this, nor did the media. I guess it pays to be one of the guys who is below the radar.

Thursday, July 27, 2000

Once again, I fell a little behind in the upkeep of the journal. July 14 was John Archer's last day as our strength coach. He took a job at a different school to do what Boyd

Epley does here, which is basically being in charge of everything.

The next week was possibly the strangest, most disorganized week I have ever seen here at Nebraska. Bryan Bailey took over Archer's spot as the O-line's workout leader. Bailey is quite possibly the most educated and innovative workout technician in the world. Every player who works with him loves him. And he practices what he preaches. He runs one mile for every year on his birthday and 10 miles every other day of the year.

Some of the weight room staff were saying that if Archer came back right now, he wouldn't believe what has happened. For our morning lifting, Bailey put us into categories, such as injured, healthy, freshmen, etc. Our workouts were modified based on those categories. We're doing a lot of extra things as well. Most of these are little exercises that focus on stability, balance, flexibility, and range of motion. This is not a new idea, but it's the first time we've really focused on these things. Bailey said his intention is for all of us to develop explosive power. It's not enough to just lift the weight, we now have to lift it fast. This means that the weight of our sets will decrease, but all the little extra stuff will make sure we leave just as tired. Bailey really cares about how we're feeling as well. He constantly asks if our backs are all right or if we have any other injury. If we're hurt in any way, he modifies our workout so we can get the best workout possible while staying away from the injured area. This is a nice change from Archer.

> Bailey's story is a great one and I'll try to retell it the best I can. He was working as a personal trainer, barely making ends meet, when a friend told him about an opportunity to train a guy in another country. Bailey jumped at the chance and was soon employed by a very wealthy middle-eastern sheik as

his personal trainer. I'm not sure how long he was there, but he commented that it was always very tense because you could get in trouble for even looking at a woman and this guy had several wives.

I forgot the rest of the story about how he eventually came to Nebraska.

As respected as he was by the athletes, he was not respected by the head of the weight room, Boyd Epley. Bailey developed several different stretches and workouts, getting credit for a few, but Boyd apparently caused tension on at least one occasion when he demanded credit for Bailey's work. It even got so heated on the team that at one point, the players actually had to petition coach Solich to be able to get Bailey to travel with us to an away game so he could be there to get us warmed up properly. We were initially told that there was no room for him in the travel list but we knew that was crap. Bailey was more important than saving a seat on the plane for the University Chancellor or his wife and none of us would even notice if they weren't there. We would have definitely been affected negatively if Bailey were the one left behind.

Presently, he is one of the strength coaches at the University of Southern California. I have no doubt that he is a big part of the success they have had recently.

Saturday, July 29, 2000

Coach Tenopir had another steak fry at his house. I showed up late after taking my future sister-in-law, Stacy Markus, out to a late lunch. I was already stuffed, but managed to eat a steak anyway.

After 11 weeks straight, the summer workouts are finally done and this is the celebration. Coach Tenopir told everyone to go home and relax for the next week and I plan to do just that. My back is really sore from one of the last running days and I can use the rest.

Friday, August 4, 2000

I took this whole week off and rested at home in Omaha. My back didn't get better very quickly, so I saw a doctor, a chiropractor and a physical therapist. They concluded that I've had a spasm in my left mid-back for a long time, mostly caused by a slight misalignment of my hip bone. This should clear up pretty quickly.

My dad called Coach Tenopir to check up on some stuff and found out that senior guard Chris Saalfeld just had a major back treatment with an epidural. Coach said if Chris doesn't get better in time for two-a-days on Tuesday, I will go in his spot. This put me in a weird position because I really want to go to fall camp, but I also want Chris to have a good year. He's been severely hampered by injuries throughout his career and has not seen much playing time. If he doesn't go to camp, that will definitely handicap his chances. Coach Tenopir said I'm next on the list and he stressed that he needs more centers to step up and be ready to give Dominic Raiola a breather because he goes 100% all the time and Coach doesn't want to wear him out.

Sunday, August 6, 2000

The sports page today reported that incoming freshman tackle M. J. Flaum is out for the year with a shoulder problem. This could open up a spot for me since I was already next in line after Chris Saalfeld.

There are pros and cons for attending fall camp. The good parts are that we get some of the best meals of the year at the training table, we get to break in the new equipment, they pay us for everything, the chances of seeing some playing time are greatly increased, and I would have a much better understanding of the offense. The bad parts are getting up really early in the morning for practice, two practices a day, sitting through meetings where it's almost impossible to stay awake, and having no energy to do anything else for two weeks.

Monday, August 7, 2000

I left a message for Coach Tenopir to call me about the fall camp and he later called back and said I am going. It was actually a relief to hear this and I've started thinking about everything that will go on for the next two weeks. I called my dad right afterward and told him the news, which made his day. I go in tomorrow at 2:00 for a physical and drug tests.

2000 Fall Camp

Tuesday, August 8, 2000

I got my body fat checked today and I stayed right at 17%. I've gained close to 30 pounds since last fall, 20 of those being muscle (I weighed in at 305). Ellis gave me a big thumbs-up for this report. He told me that just to maintain my weight at my level of physical activity, I would need to eat about 7,000 calories a day. If I want to gain any more weight, I would have to eat more than that.

Since my first day here, every meal I have at the training table fills my tray with two full plates of food (always with lots of vegetables and fruits) and desert is usually yogurt, all washed down by three or four glasses of milk. During the summer I have to fend for myself, but I usually get by eating a whole large pizza or an entire thing of hamburger helper by myself, not to mention a whole can of corn or beans. And that's just for dinner, only one of the four meals I try to eat each day.

I also found out that I grew a little bit in the past year. I added a quarter-inch to my height and my feet got even bigger, forcing me to change my shoes to size 17. That is pretty amazing to still be growing at age 21. I hope I'm not done yet.

We got some new gear today. Along with two media guide books, we got a new pair of black shorts, a T-shirt, new shoes, and $57. The grass shoes this year are much better than in previous years. They have a molded plastic bottom, as opposed to the kind with replaceable cleats, and are very cool looking.

I had my physical and everything was fine. After a long summer of feeding myself, I was able to eat at the training table today. Just as I'd heard, they pull out all the stops during two-a-days and give us all of the favorites—prime rib, steaks, kabobs, and many other dishes that we only see once a week if we're lucky during the season. Later in the day we filled out a bunch of NCAA paperwork, and the coaches and support staff told us what's going to happen, what to do and, of course, what not to do. We also learned of a recent ruling affecting the Big 12 states—physical activity, such as physical testing, now counts as a full practice so we're not going to test tomorrow since the NCAA also limits the number of practices a team can have before the first game. Instead we will meet with someone from the Big 12 officiating committee to go over some new rules.

Wednesday, August 9, 2000

Today was pretty much all meetings. We met in the morning for an hour and then in the evening for three hours. Many different people from the community spoke to us about issues like agents, betting, girls, alcohol, staying out of trouble, and other such moral-guidance issues. Johnny Rodgers, 1972 Heisman winner and former Husker All-Star, was there and spoke about all the trouble he got into and told us, from his own experience, how easy it is to get into trouble and how hard it is to get out. It felt like it was midnight by the time it ended, but it was only 7:30. I hope this means I will be able to fall asleep fast tonight considering tomorrow's practice is at 6:30 in the morning.

Thursday, August 10, 2000

We started bright and early (actually, it wasn't bright, the sun had barely risen) and I actually felt pretty good, refreshed and awake, thinking I was ready for everything. The practice went about two hours with groupwork and three stations with number ones vs. number twos, twos vs. ones, and threes vs. threes.

The afternoon practice was on the grass. The temperature cooled off to make it pretty nice. We had to run two gassers at the end. I guess we're going to run two gassers after every afternoon practice, which doesn't sound very nice to me. My legs are already sore and I'm looking forward to a good night's sleep.

Friday, August 11, 2000

Practices were similar to yesterday. There are big blue plastic horse tanks filled with water (and chlorine) for us to cool off in after practice. This feels amazingly good after sweating for two hours. The rookie freshmen are a good bunch of kids. We don't have many offensive linemen, only three right now since one of them is out with a shoulder injury.

Coach Solich made it clear that there will be no hazing, but he can't be around all the time and that is when it happens. Some of the guys were playing a quiz game with Sandro DeAngelis, the new place-kicker, and if he got a question wrong, he got dunked in the tank. Of course, the questions were rigged and he got dunked on every question. We told the rookie linemen to hustle back to the stadium after the afternoon practice and grab a bag full of sandwiches and drinks for all the linemen. When they tried to collect all the food, they were told this was a form of hazing and they didn't have to do it. The scholarship linemen from last year said they had to do all that stuff and more when they came in.

Saturday, August 12, 2000

Today was typical, although we started wearing pads today. We just went in shoulder pads in the morning and then sweats in the afternoon, but it was a major change to the tempo of the practice. We were finally able to do some good hitting after four long months.

I'm on the third offense with the three scholarship freshmen, along with sophomore Scott Koethe and redshirt freshman Tim Green. We're kind of the black sheep of the offense right now because we're all still struggling to get the plays memorized and do the right thing. Coach Tenopir yells at us continually and it will probably take a few more days before we make any good progress.

After the evening practice, we got a nice surprise by not having to run gassers. This really made my weekend. I can sleep late in the morning since the first thing tomorrow is a noon lunch and meetings at 1:30.

Sunday, August 13, 2000

Before the second meeting in the auditorium and before the coaches got there, Dominic Raiola got on the computer and changed the schedule for tomorrow. For the first practice, instead of saying "Practice-Full Pads," he changed it to "Practice-Sweats and Sandals" and he changed the second practice to "Practice-maybe (tba)." Everybody was laughing while he did this and he had plenty of time before the coaches came in. When Coach Solich arrived, he started off by going over the schedule and said, "We're going to have practice at 8:00 tomorrow just as it says on the schedule..." He did a double-take at the schedule projected on the screen and began to laugh as the whole room burst out laughing. When he regained control of the room and continued on the schedule, he came to the second practice and caught the changes there, too, causing the room to break out in laughter again. He then made sure to tell us what was really going to happen and sent us off to group meetings.

Monday, August 14, 2000

I went to bed a little later than I should have last night. This morning was in full pads again and I just felt sluggish, struggling through two and a half hours of practice. I had to run a couple of errands, so I wasn't able to relax between practices. I had to be back at 1:15 for special teams meetings and was finally able to come home at 8:00. It was a long day.

When we're doing groupwork, I work with the first-string offense, including Dominic Raiola. He really is one of the best centers to ever come through Nebraska and what better way for me to learn the position than through hands on, one-on-one contact with Dom. During groupwork, he mainly goes through his proper steps, but doesn't go off hitting very hard. I don't mind this since I know he can manhandle me, but I think he does it to focus on his footwork and hand placement. Emulating that has helped a lot with my basic technique. I wish Dominic would be more vocal with the younger guys, including me, however.

He's usually very quiet during groupwork and if I mess up he hardly ever steps up to help me out. He usually just says a couple words like, "Stay low, pull flatter, pull for this backer," or some other kind of simple directions. I wish he would take a bigger leadership role and pull all the centers together and go over stuff as a group. After him, we only have three sophomore centers and one of us is going to be his backup. He probably could go a full game, every game, but he will need a break sometime and one of us has to step up. None of us has much, if any, experience so if I were him I would make sure the back-ups knew what they were doing.

We got $68 at dinner tonight. This is in addition to the $57 and $47 we got a couple of days ago. I think we get about $250 for the whole two-a-day experience.

Tuesday, August 15, 2000

This morning was in full pads again. I have a feeling we might not go back to helmets and sweats for a while. The practice was pretty intense with some live action, but it didn't wear me out too much because we were running with two stations instead of three. This put two centers on both teams and meant that I could finally get a rotation and a break. I hardly ever get a break in any practice, so this was a welcomed change. Everybody was tired this morning and the general feeling was that it was a pretty crappy practice.

I ate brunch and went home for a short nap, and then went right back to the stadium to get taped before the 1:30 meetings. The 3:00 practice was decent. We worked in a rotation again, which helped save my legs for the gassers we had to do at the end.

I have these faint memories of something called a "social life." I wonder if it will come back to me sometime soon. I kind of miss it.

Wednesday, August 16, 2000

The morning practice was typical—full pads, lots of hitting, and lots of sweating. At one point, Jon Dawson got into a fight with one of the defensive guys that almost turned into a giant rumble. Everyone who was in the fight had to do two sets of stairs. Coach Solich called us together right away in the middle of the field and talked about being a team and watching out for each other and respecting everybody. To make sure this message was clear, the entire team had to run gassers at the end of the morning practice, something that hasn't been done before. None of us expected this and we were all very tired afterward.

The afternoon practice was a pleasant break. We went half pads and just did special teams the entire time. I did my time on the punt team and then went down in the Pit with the O-line. We walked through plays for the entire time with our pads and helmets off. We had plenty of time to waste, and then went up top and did some field goal work and that was it.

Before the 6:00 meeting Willie Amos, a freshman rover from Texas, put on a jump rope show in the auditorium. He's a member of the national and world champion jump rope team and did things with a jump rope that I never knew were possible. He went under his legs, doing push-ups, quadruple rotations jumping three feet in the air and a bunch of other hard-to-imagine tricks. It was really a feat of athletic ability that a big guy like a lineman would have no chance of doing. He got a rousing ovation from everyone and Coach Solich even joked around saying that his routine is going to be worked into our conditioning program.

Thursday, August 17, 2000

With the end of two-a-days so near, we're all wearing out and the overall effort is visibly trailing off. Everyone is tired and sore and in need of a good night's rest. The only thing to say about today's two practices is that everybody was saying how horrible they did in them.

Friday, August 18, 2000

This is the last day of practice for fall camp and everybody is really looking forward to the end. This morning was in full pads and it seemed like everybody was going half speed. I met up with Kyle Larson after the morning practice and helped him work on his punting for another 45 minutes. When I got back to the locker room, on the dry-erase board was a list of everyone who has to "pay rent" for this year. They had everybody listed except me! It said rent will be due tomorrow, but I don't know if they will get away with it with the coaches' current stance on hazing. I hope they hear about it and get it stopped. I've only heard bits of stories about what happens when paying rent.

The guys who tell the stories never have that "happy memories" look when they tell them. "Paying rent" is basically the initiation process everyone new to the south locker room has to go through. They call each new person out one by one and beat them up a little or a lot, depending on the guy.

Everyone seemed certain that the afternoon practice would be in sweats. After the morning practice, however, Coach Solich said the afternoon practice would be in half pads. Everybody groaned and some guys were visibly pissed off. Coach Solich later came to the group meetings and said we would be going in sweats for the afternoon practice. Everybody was immediately happy and the whole atmosphere changed. The practice seemed short and sweet, but it was ruined in the end by having to run gassers. The first one was a full gasser, but Coach Solich had the warmth and compassion to make the second one only a half gasser.

Saturday, August 19, 2000

I knew it couldn't last long. I walked into the locker room this morning and one of the guys immediately said, "Hey, we don't have Kolowski up there." My name was officially added to the list of those who have to "pay rent."

After the scrimmage, it was time to "pay rent." They

herded all of us into the bathroom and blocked off the main entrance with the chalkboard. All of the established guys were in the middle of the locker room with plastic bats, trash cans, big water jugs, and soccer balls wrapped in athletic tape with five-foot handles to whip them around. Scott Koethe was the first to go out and get it. They called his name and he walked out into wide open middle of the locker room and into the lion's den. We couldn't see from the bathroom, but we heard a lot of yelling, laughing and painful whacks for a short time. John Garrison was next and he got it a little worse. By the time they called the next person, Coach Solich had made his way past the barricade and popped around the corner. He said, sternly, "I don't know what you guys are doing, but if it has anything to do with hazing, you are in big trouble."

All of us retreated to our lockers quickly and quietly. After a few minutes had passed, some of the veterans tried to get it organized again, but the fear of reprisal luckily got the best of them and they called it off. I guess this might be the end of another tradition.

This kind of thing could only happen during two-a-days. The media isn't as omnipresent as they are during the regular practices and classes aren't in session, giving anybody with visible bruises that couldn't be accounted for on the field a chance to heal up before school starts.

Jim Tansey got it real bad when he paid rent. They were merciless on him, dousing him with chew spit, kicking him in the chest and back, and hitting him so hard with baseball bats that he has bruises on his arms and legs for weeks. To top it all off, someone threw an apple as hard as they could at his head. It blew up into chunks of apple but not before giving him a welt and a hell of a headache.

The only funny story about paying rent was with Toniu Fonoti, a huge Samoan and one of the biggest guys I've ever known. When he was called out to receive his beating, he just said, "No, you won't be doing that." Nobody was brave enough to argue with him.

> Toniu eventually became an outstanding guard for us, earning several top honors and was a runner-up for the Outland Trophy as a true junior. He became the first true freshman offensive linemen to start a game since Will Shields in 1989.

2000 Season

Monday, August 21, 2000

First day of school, first day of regular practices. For the third year in a row it looks like I will be on the scout team. I rotated with one of the new guys and had to tell him what to do on most of the plays and he did it very well. He'll probably pass me on the depth chart pretty soon.

Wednesday, August 23, 2000

Today was probably one of the hardest and best practices I've had in a long time. Matt Shook is out sick and John Garrison is away due to a death in the family, making me the number two center. This was my time to shine and show the coaches what I think I deserve. Overall, I thought I did very well and can't think of any play that I messed up on.

I also took all the first-team punt snaps, but didn't do as well with that. I've recently been working on narrowing my stance to enable me to get back and block better on the rushes. I didn't do too well at that today. Dominic Raiola said when Coach Young yelled at me, it was the loudest he ever heard him yell. I just need more practice against a good defense like that. I hardly get any snaps against a decent defense when Garrison is here, so this was new for me.

Thursday, August 24, 2000

I heard a rumor today that fellow sophomore center Matt Shook quit last night because he was having a lot of trouble with his knees. This set off a chain reaction in my brain, thinking about what that meant for me on the depth chart, making me third string, which meant I would travel to the away games and also that I would have to miss my brother Jason's wedding in October. This issue has really been worrying my brother because he and Stacy are basically planning the wedding around my schedule. I still can't give him a definite answer about whether I can go to his wedding yet. We have an away game at Texas Tech on October 14, the day of his wedding, and he can't seem to understand my situation completely. He's desperately trying to get all of these details settled.

Shook was back at practice tonight. I didn't ask him about his knees or about the rumor. Even with Shook back, I'm still running with the number twos. This looks pretty good for me to get some playing time in the San Jose State game. I guess the real test will be what happens when Garrison comes back.

Saturday, August 26, 2000

We practiced this morning at 9:30. It was a very fun practice for me because I had a lot of energy. Whenever someone on the scout team line needed a break, I called Jack Limbaugh in to play center and I switched over to the other position. I covered every spot on the line throughout the day and had a lot of fun doing it. I liked playing tackle more than playing center. I might have to try that again.

Fan Day began right after practice. When they opened the gates, people came rushing in to line up for autographs. I was really amazed by the turnout, especially for the offensive line. I couldn't really judge the size of the crowd, but one person said the line for just the offensive line was 45 minutes long. I didn't see many objects with more than 15 signatures on them the entire day, meaning that everyone had a hard time getting around and collecting autographs.

Tuesday, August 29, 2000

The depth chart came out today. Probably the biggest surprise to me was to see that Jon Rutherford, the second-string guard, is also the second-string center. Actually, this doesn't surprise me as much as it will other people who haven't kept up with us. I understand where Coach Tenopir is coming from with this decision. Shook, Garrison, and I have little to no experience and Coach wants someone with game experience to back up Dominic. Garrison is a feisty player who puts all he has into every play, but he doesn't have the size or strength to be very effective and usually gets tossed around. Shook is hampered by bad knees, but is generally pretty good besides that. As for me, I don't yet have that hard-nosed attitude that makes Dominic such an exciting player, and I could use more speed and strength as well.

For as many players as we have on the O-line, we don't have much depth. I think the coaches might be worried about this. The same holds true for many positions, such as the secondary, linebackers, defensive line, and quarterbacks, where we have good starters, but inexperienced back-ups. It probably sounds like our team is just one man deep at each position, but we should be good, hopefully the best, as long as the starters stay healthy.

Now that I know more about the offense and the line play, I can really see that being on the scout team sucks. We don't have any rules for blocking, no correct steps or anything to tell us what to do if our guy slants away. All we do is read a card and block along the line drawn on the card. Basically, the scout team is designed to fail. The defense almost always lines up a little differently than what is written on the card, so we usually end up guessing where to go. Because of this constant indecision and second-guessing, I don't see how I'm going to get myself off the scout team and up with the number twos. Also, we hardly have enough guys to fill in for me if I did move up.

Saturday, September 2, 2000

Nebraska 49 – San Jose State 13

Finally, the first game of the season. San Jose State was a little better than we thought and we didn't play as well as we could have, which added up to a fairly exciting game for the first half. Our offense played fluidly, drove the ball down the field without much resistance, and scored on four straight drives. The defense, on the other hand, had a lot of breakdowns and looked pretty bad. There were a lot of missed tackles and many of the guys seemed to just be running through the motions like they were still in practice. By the second half, the defense was playing much better, but it didn't matter by then. Luckily, we never fumbled, but we did have three interceptions. I didn't get in this game, but I'm patient. It was also very hot today with the temperature near 120 degrees on the field. I didn't really feel the heat, but my face was sunburned at the end of the day.

We got $15 today and we also got our warm-up suits earlier this week. They are mostly black with red stripes.

Monday, September 4, 2000

Toniu Fonoti earned the honor of "Offensive Lineman of the Game." He graded out perfectly for the game, meaning he didn't make one mistake the entire day while also completing his blocks successfully. This is amazing enough, but for a true sophomore to do it means only great things for the future.

Tuesday, September 5, 2000

Coach Solich told the offense today that he expects nothing less than 40 points against Notre Dame. It would be great if the press heard about this.

I don't know yet if I'm going to the game. I asked Coach Tenopir and he said I am questionable. I should find out tomorrow.

Wednesday, September 6, 2000

It's official—Notre Dame will be my first road trip. I found out today that I will go, and I'm really looking forward to it.

Thursday, September 7, 2000

After our sweats practice today, we had to pack up our game bags with all the stuff out of our lockers that we'll need for the game. I think everyone is really ready for this game, especially the defense.

Friday, September 8, 2000

After a late night of studying and figuring out what to take on the trip, I made it to lunch at 10:30. The busses were waiting out in the south stadium parking lot and we left by 11:30. We went straight to the airport, loaded from the tarmac, and soon were in the air and on the way to South Bend. I worked on a linemen test during the flight, something the guys who play do before every game. I don't know if I will play, but it's worth it to take the test to figure out how to take them for later. Basically, they have a play listed against a series of different defenses and we have to draw in the lines for which defender we block and also list what calls we make. I didn't think it was too hard, but I tried to do every position while I was only supposed to mark the center. I didn't get downgraded, but it was my first time and no one told me how to do it. Also during the flight, Pat Logsdon, the director of football operations, gave everyone $15 for food money (being given money in these circumstances is kind of funny because we have no opportunity to actually spend the money on food during the trip).

We arrived in South Bend at about 1:30 and went straight to the stadium. South Bend looks like any other small midwestern town and then, over the trees, you see this magnificent golden dome. We drove up to the stadium where hundreds of people were gathered. We were very surprised to see many people in red—it almost reminded us of Lincoln. Across from the entrance to the stadium is a grass mall where they were setting up a commentary booth, and at the end of the mall is the famous "Touchdown Jesus." This is a giant mosaic on the side of a tall building depicting a Biblical scene and in the middle is Jesus with his arms in a relaxed touchdown signal pose. I think if they made him shrug his shoulders, it would look more like an "I don't know" Jesus.

We got into the locker room, which was entirely too small for us. A lot of guys had to double up on the lockers, including me. We got dressed quickly for our walk-through and headed out. To get to the field we had to pass through the famous "tunnel," which actually was pretty cool to do after seeing the movie *Rudy*. As I got onto the field, I happened to see someone I know. Vince Lenz, and his wife Paula, who are great family friends, were standing right there on the field. Vince didn't recognize me at first, due to the much longer hair than usual, but he finally realized who I was and we had a nice little reunion right there with some picture taking. Vince went to Notre Dame many years ago and has been an adamant fan as long as I have known him. I wasn't really surprised to run into him on the trip, but to see him on the field before our practice blew me away.

We had some time to kill before practice, so I wandered around on the grass field taking in the whole stadium where so much history has taken place. It's a very simple coliseum-style stadium with an even slope of seats from bottom to top. They recently added a couple of thousand seats by giving the top an extra ring which blends into the whole stadium nicely. There are two scoreboards, one at each end of the stadium, but there are no yardage statistics boards like we have. Their press box is a large, flat, dark-glassed structure with a couple of stories and many different compartments on one side of the stadium. Around the field are raised flowerbeds at the height of the first row of seats. This only gives about seven feet between the first row and the players, compared to the huge walkway we have on each side of our stadium.

Something unusual about this practice was that there were about 200 people in the stands watching us and more people on the sidelines. I asked Russ Hochstein if this was typical of an away game and he said we never have a crowd at other away-game practices. After the short practice where we walked through about 10 plays, we changed and headed for the hotel.

We stayed at a Holiday Inn in Michigan City, about an hour west of South Bend. At meetings, I was never so bored in my life. We were watching film from Thursday's practice and I couldn't believe we ran so many plays in one Thursday session. When that was finally over, we made our way to dinner and had one of the best spreads of food I have seen in a while. I wasn't too hungry after all the snacking we'd done all day, but I still managed to put away a good amount. After dinner we went to a local movie theater where we saw *The Watcher*. If that wasn't excitement enough, we then went back to the hotel and had a special teams meeting and a snack.

Saturday, September 9, 2000

Nebraska 27 – Notre Dame 24

We got our wake-up call around 7:30 this morning and made our way to meetings by 8:00. This was a really quick meeting in which the coaches basically told us that we already know everything and today is the day to prove it. We then had a hearty breakfast, got taped, packed and ready to go by 10:30. Before we left, we watched our psych-up tape with Carlos Polk as the main man giving the pep talk. There was a guest star—former player Grant Wistrom—who told us how lucky we are and how much he would like to be playing today because he hates Notre Dame. Right after this, we boarded the busses and were on our way with a police escort.

When we pulled up to the stadium, all we could see was a giant crowd of people dressed in red. The streets were packed with our fans and everything around the stadium was swarming with Husker fans and their vehicles. It seriously made us feel right at home.

The atmosphere in the locker room before the game was very intense. Everyone was full of energy. Everyone was acting like an anxious tiger pacing in its cage, waiting for that chance to bust through the bars and wreak havoc. After the traditional sound-off where a handful of important players make emotional speeches and incite a mosh pit, we gathered in a circle holding hands and said the team prayer, which I finally learned. It's said in a call-and-response fashion and goes, "Dear Lord, In the battles we go through life/ we ask for a chance that's fair/ a chance to equal our stride/ a chance to do or dare/ if we should win/ let it be by the code/ with our faith and our honor held high/ if we should lose/

let us stand by the road/ and cheer as the winners go by/ DAY BY DAY/ WE GET BETTER AND BETTER/ THE TEAM THAT CAN'T BE BEAT/ *WON'T BE BEAT!!*" The underlined portion is shouted, and the last three words are said in unison as loud as possible.

As we ran out onto the field, I noticed something strange—while there was a lot of blue and gold in the stands, there also was an incredible amount of red. About 25,000 people out of the crowd of 80,000 were dressed in red, which truly made it feel like a home game. The only thing that changed that feeling was when Notre Dame got a little momentum and their student section exploded with cheers and noise.

The atmosphere at Notre Dame is a lot more relaxed and fun. This can be credited to the student section, which covers seven sections of the stadium and takes up a full corner. They were packed in there and that only added to their energy. When they scored, hundreds of students were held above the others and did push-ups for the number of points they had. It looked like a dark blue ocean with waves rippling over it. They also did these cheers that had arm motions for the whole crowd. One funny thing about this is that all I could see were white arms (funny in a weird way).

About the game, all I have to say is "WOW!!" That was easily the most exciting game I've ever seen in my life. Technically, it shouldn't have been so close, but we had two major breakdowns on special teams that gave up two touchdowns on a kickoff return and a punt return. Those two touchdowns helped put us into overtime for the third time in history. We chose to be on defense first and held them with an amazing effort, and they came away with a field goal, putting them up 24-21. Then it was our turn to start from the 25. On third down, Crouch connected to tight end Tracey Wistrom for a first down. Then I-back Dan

Alexander pounded his way inside the 10. Crouch finished it off with a sprint to the left and through the corner of the end zone for the win. Everybody on the team immediately rushed the field and swarmed the end zone where photographers then swarmed us.

All in all, Notre Dame was a pretty good team. They had a lot of really fast guys on defense that shut down our option game. Their special teams were much better than ours and their offense had a big, strong line, a very quick quarterback, and a pretty good backfield. I think they are totally underrated, but they also just might have appeared to be good since it was their home game.

Since I didn't get in for any plays and wasn't very sweaty, I just dressed quickly after the game and eventually found my parents, their friends, and my cousins who found tickets for themselves in the student section. We stood around talking for a little bit and finally said good-bye and boarded the bus. We were quickly escorted to the airport and returned to Lincoln at about 9:00.

September 18-22, 2000

This was an off week, but the practices were fairly intense because pro scouts were watching. Most of the time, when we're in sweats or half pads, the defense thinks they're wearing full pads and rush hard off the line. Everyone gets sick of these "Sweats All-Americans" so we end up blatantly holding them, which gets them mad at us.

Thursday the scout teams went one-on-one with each other. The last time we did this, the offense totally dominated the defense and this week wasn't too different. We only run a very basic selection of our own plays. The defense tries to run our defense, but half the guys don't know what to do. Sometimes, just for fun, the coach sends in a defense that even the first-string guys would have trouble figuring out.

Coach McBride, the defensive coordinator, is notorious for this and would stand back and laugh at all the confusion.

Saturday, September 23, 2000

Nebraska 42 – Iowa 13

This whole week leading up to this game we did a lot of special teams work. Last Saturday's effort apparently wasn't good enough.

Coach Young said he would try to get me in for a PAT snap, but he didn't seem very dedicated to this appeasement.

The defense was looking very good this week in practice, almost as good as last year's defense. All in all, it was a typical week.

The atmosphere in the locker room before the game today was very complacent. We're ranked number 1 in the nation right now and it's hard to get excited for such a lopsided matchup. The feeling in the locker room was about the same intensity as during the Spring Game. Before we took the field, the seniors tried to get us psyched up, but I could tell a lot of the guys really didn't care. We definitely have a team with some of the best talent in the nation and we have the capability to be national champions, but we don't have the week-by-week desire.

A lot of critics and fans can't understand how a game between a highly ranked team and an unranked team could ever be close, but it is very easy to figure out. When the spread is more than 25 points, we feel like it's a waste of time to even show up and they should just give us the win automatically. The underdog thinks much differently. They have nothing to lose and if they can give us a good game. It will make their season. Every team that plays us will give us their best game; this is something the coaches always tell us. This was exactly how it felt today.

Iowa's first drive was very impressive and they scored without much difficulty. On our following possession, the offense had some trouble getting downfield. This was the story of the first half. Iowa put up a really good fight and we hung in there and went to the locker room with a little extra buffer thanks to a Hail Mary pass hauled in by Matt Davison.

During halftime Coach Solich gave one of the most heated and energetic speeches he has ever given. He must have sensed the complacency and tried to change it. Obviously, it worked and we came out very strong for the rest of the game, sealing it with a 42-13 score.

Interesting facts of the game: Eric Crouch tied a school record with five touchdown passes, Tracey Wistrom tied a school record with three touchdown receptions, and even though we had over 300 yards rushing, we didn't have one rushing touchdown. I wonder how many years it has been since that happened.

After the game, we got $15. Earlier in the week, we all got our sweats outfits. They are just basic gray, but they were free.

Saturday, September 30, 2000

Nebraska 42 – Missouri 24

Today's game was typical of the season so far—the defense looked porous and the offense had a very slow start. The special teams finally stepped it up, however. There were many key plays, most notably Bobby Newcombe's 94-yard punt return for a touchdown, and great kicking on punts and kickoffs. There were a lot of key changes made on special teams this week, especially on the kickoff teams. We currently rank near the bottom for a couple of the special teams statistics. One good thing about this is that we don't have many attempts, so a few good special teams plays will get us back where we need to be.

The defense gave up close to 500 yards, giving Missouri slightly more total yards. If it weren't for an impressive drive late in the fourth quarter that let Judd Davies carry it 65 yards in three plays, we would have been held under 300 yards rushing. It was one of our best all-around games with all three components playing well, but none of them played well for the whole game. There were a lot of other elements that went into our victory, such as their quarterback getting injured and their nut-case of a coach throwing a temper tantrum on the sidelines that gave us great field position.

It seems to me that we're only playing as well as we have to. When we play a good team, we're able to step it up and win, but when we play a bad team, it's like we toy with them to see how much fight they have until we finish them off. I don't know if it's deliberate—I'm sure it's not—but I think we don't have that desire to prove something like the '95 team did. We're too complacent and figure that as long as we can scrape by, we'll be okay. This might hold true since a third of the top 25 teams got beat today leaving fewer, yet more deserving, teams to battle for positions. I believe we have the mentality that, since we are Nebraska and are ranked number one, everybody we play will just roll over dead in front of us and we'll be handed the Sears Trophy on a golden platter.

We were able to come away with a 42-24 win. It wasn't decisive, it wasn't dominating, it wasn't even fun to watch. We're running on luck right now and soon our luck will run out and we will again have to rely on skill, intelligence, and physical domination. I know we can do it and it's about time it happens.

Monday, October 2, 2000

Today at lunch starting center Dominic Raiola said, "If this was my freshman year and the defense just came off a game like they had last Saturday, I would be afraid to practice today." This is because Grant Wistrom and Jason Peter led that ferocious defense, which would take out their aggression on the scout team. There is no force on defense like that this year, however. There is no key player who is totally aggressive, mean, and nasty. Instead, we have a tepid defense with skilled players, but no real aggressive leadership. I seriously think that all the new rules the coaches made about fighting during practice and hazing virtually castrated any overly aggressive tendencies by anyone, leaving the defense especially weak. Everyone is too kind in a sport that thrives on the destruction of others.

The report today regarding our game goals was very disheartening. The defense only reached one out of 15 goals. The special teams actually did remarkably well with only two goals missed. The offense didn't do too badly, but there is still a lot of room to improve.

Thursday, October 5, 2000

We received thick, black, down filled winter coats today after practice. We were told in meetings that we would get them and to make them legal, we had to wear them to practice today. I guess they weren't ready to be distributed quite yet, so they gave them to us after practice. Coach told us to wear them to tomorrow's practice instead. Practice tomorrow is only for those guys who will travel, and they'll practice here instead of at the Iowa State stadium, which will save them the hour-and-a-half trip from the hotel to the stadium and back. Since I won't be traveling, I can go home and relax right after my classes and take a three-day weekend from football.

The defense was looking uncharacteristically good this week. They were all very fast off the line and in hot pursuit of the ball on every play. This could definitely be the turnaround game for the defense. The special teams seemed to have its breakthrough game last week, so I hope they will keep that up. The offense is actually going through somewhat of a slump if that's possible with the amazing talent of the group. The line seems slow and sluggish, the backs unenthused, and the receivers unmotivated. They really need to pick it up for this game and the rest of the season to keep the national championship hopes alive.

This week was not an easy one for me. With deadlines slamming down in my classes and no positive reinforcement from the coaches, I had serious thoughts of quitting. Being on the scout team provides no motivation for progress since I'm not even part of the group that's learning the plays for the current game. Plus, seeing my peers and even some of the younger guys on the ones and twos makes me question whether I'm just wasting my time here.

Coach Young has nothing but criticism for me. I thought long snapping would provide a chance for me to get on the field early, but he has turned it into my vice. I have never heard one positive remark from that man. The closest he ever gets is when he doesn't say anything at all. Sometimes I have to pry a remark from him just to see if he noticed a play I thought was good. I'd say, "Am I right to block that guy coming around or do you want me to take the first guy?" and his reply is like: "No, you did it right. Just work on getting deeper." I can never win with that man.

I'm really doubting my involvement here. I feel like I was just the right guy at the right time. I was of the right size and athletic ability to join the Huskers. It was great at first, with many benefits (clothes, public notoriety and respect, bowl trips, money, rings, watches, etc.) but the demands are extreme. Football takes up a lot of time and energy, making me feel stretched thin between everything else in my life. I know that in the long term, the other things will be more important, but the instant gratification is better. Even so, I know the love for this game is gone. I question whether I can go through the process of breaking with the team, which would also mean the end of all the benefits, or should I just fake my affection for the game and bide my time. Would I be happier with another football team? The benefits would never be as great as they are here.

Some days, I wish I would just be cut from the team. I've never given them a reason to cut me, but it would make it easier for me. I'm not the right guy for football. I don't have the right mentality or tenacity or whatever you want to call it. All I have that put me in this position is my size and my perseverance. My body is in a uniform, but my heart is somewhere else. I wish I could break free and find out where it is. I figure I'll put in the necessary time to finish out everything here and then go on that quest, but until then, I just feel out of place.

Saturday, October 7, 2000

Nebraska 49 – Iowa State 27

Once again, our offense had an incredibly late start. We really couldn't do anything until the fourth quarter when we put up a massive scoring explosion. At halftime, we were actually behind 13-14. The defense played a much better game overall, but Iowa State had an amazing passing attack that we had trouble stopping. Luckily, we were able to capitalize on their breakdowns, which made the game end up looking a lot better than it actually was. The special teams had a near-perfect game, which was very nice to see.

I didn't travel with the team, but I ended up going to the game with my good friend Michael Callahan. We left Friday night and spent the night with an independent movie producer with whom Mike is planning to do a movie next year.

We arrived at the stadium for the tailgate party Saturday morning at about 10:30. I was told this was a sight to behold, but it truly is something you have to see for yourself. All around the stadium are huge parking lots filled with cars and people four hours before the game. People were grilling food, most people had some kind of music blaring, and pretty much everybody was enjoying their favorite alcoholic beverage. It was a great atmosphere, mostly dominated by Iowa State fans who were very vocal about their support. Honestly, I've never heard so many people talking so much smack.

It wasn't just a few drunk fans getting in my face since I was wearing Husker gear, it was everybody I passed walking around at the tailgate. I heard everything: "Nebraska sucks!!" "Go home, loser!" "How's it feel to be number two?" I had a lot of fun with all the smack talking and gave it right back saying, "We're number one *and* two, but what are you ranked? Oh, that's right, you're not!! That must suck since you are 4-0, too!" It seemed like everyone had something to say and I loved all of it. I walked through the crowd and laughed at all the stupid things those fans said. They won four games and their fans were acting like they'd already won the national championship.

I sat in the front row on the 35-yard line of the Iowa State bench. From there I was able to yell things at their team and get the Iowa State fans seated around me truly mad. That mission was accomplished when I was yelling at their long-snapper for having an incredibly slow snap. These college girls behind me tried to give me an etiquette lesson. They reasoned that I shouldn't single out their players if I wasn't a player. I shut them up fast when I told them I was a player. For the rest of the game they pointed out the jerk (me) to all of their friends and gave me rough looks whenever we celebrated. All in all, it was a really great, interesting day.

Saturday, October 14, 2000

Nebraska 56 – Texas Tech 3

I left for New York Thursday of this week for my brother Jason's wedding. Today is the day of the wedding and I'm obviously not traveling to Texas Tech. The wedding is in Manhattan and the game was supposed to be televised on Fox, but the Mets game took priority. All I saw of the entire game was ESPN highlights. From what I heard, this was the most complete and dominating game we've had all season. We amassed 440 rushing yards while they only had a handful.

Tuesday, October 17, 2000

This is my first day back from New York. Practice started off pretty intense and picked up more intensity as it went along. Fights broke out every couple of plays, mostly just shoving matches, but there were a couple of good fights that ended with the people involved running steps in the stadium. At one point, I noticed a bunch of guys walking off the field and later learned it was the entire second team along with the scout team walking to the South Stadium bleachers to run five stairs a piece. Apparently I-Back Thunder Collins slammed somebody into the ground and that got the whole group going. Most of the guys only ran one or two and got away with it. In all, this was a very intense day and everyone is really active. I think we're going to totally dominate Saturday. Baylor won't know what hit them.

Saturday, October 21, 2000

Nebraska 59 – Baylor 0

Like I said, they didn't even know what happened. It started off great with a punt block returned for a touchdown. Then we stuffed them again and again and again. I think they only had one yard total offense at the end of the half and we went to the locker room with over 300 yards rushing, a few passing yards and a 52-point head start. At halftime Coach Solich said he would try to get as many people in the game as possible and that the people who usually start will just have to understand that the younger guys need this experience. So, this seemed like today could be the day I finally get in.

To start off the second half, the first string was back in and scored right away. After the PAT team came off the field, Coach Young told me I would take the rest of the PAT snaps. I thought, "We already have eight touchdowns, so with over 25 minutes left, I will get a lot of snaps." Instead, the second-team offense went in and repeatedly shot themselves in the foot. For the whole rest of the game, from the time I was told I would get in, we never scored. Coach Young then said I was going in at center on the next play. I ran in, huddled the guys up, lined up and ran a 41 Sprint. That was fourth down and we didn't get the first down, but I finally got my first official taste of playing time. When I came off, Coach told me again that I would take the next series. We had a little more than a minute.

On the first snap, Joe Chrisman was the quarterback. Joe and I haven't taken a snap together for a long time. He mostly works with Matt Shook, whose snap is fairly cumbersome. On my snap to Joe, we fumbled the transition, but luckily recovered. We only got two or three more snaps off before the game ended. So, the first time I ever played as a Husker, I was able to play in the last two offensive series and finish out the game. When talking to people like my family about it later, I told them that it didn't really feel any different than practice. We practice like we play, so nothing that happens in the game should be anything we haven't seen before.

The fullback on that failed play, Andrew Wingender, who is a good friend and future best man at my wedding, will never let me forget that his first chance to carry the ball was ruined by me.

Friday, October 27, 2000

Tomorrow is the next great installment of the Game of the Century. A rematch of number one Nebraska and number two (BCS) Oklahoma in Norman. It's my opinion that the team right now is the most focused and most prepared that I've seen in my three years here. Confidence is high and the focus is not just to beat them, but how to beat them. Technique has been stressed all week long at every position and we know we'll have to play a complete, nearly flawless game to beat Oklahoma. Their defense will definitely be the best we have seen this season. Their linebackers and safeties are possibly the best players on their team and special attention has been paid to them.

Any way you look at tomorrow's game, it should be good. The great thing about tomorrow is that one team will have the road to the national championship laid out before it while the loser will forfeit nearly all hope of going to the Orange Bowl. Another great thing is that there is a strong possibility that no matter what the outcome, we will meet up again in the Big 12 championship game. Another chance for domination or defeat.

It's kind of interesting being ranked #1. It's nothing new for our program or for the coaches, and a lot of the players have the '94, '95 and '97 national championships still fresh in their minds. It's almost like this is something that should have happened anyways, business as usual. There's no celebrating by anyone. Besides, it's not over until the last game is over and that's a long way away.

Saturday, October 28, 2000

Oklahoma 31 – Nebraska 14

The game started off great for us. We scored on our first two drives, giving us a 14-0 lead going into the second quarter. Oklahoma then took over and dominated. Their linebackers were in on almost every play, stalling our offense series after series. We blocked who we were supposed to, but most of the time we just didn't block long enough and the guy slipped off and made the tackle. Our defense was shredded all day long by an incredible passing attack that seemed almost too lucky to be true.

It's funny—when you explain how you won, some people say you're bragging, but when you explain why you lost, everyone thinks you're making excuses.

Monday, October 30, 2000

The attitude on the team is surprisingly upbeat. I don't think this loss really had much of an effect on anyone. We all know what happened, we all know we'll probably see them again in the Big 12 championship game, and there are still a lot of Top 10 match-ups left in this season that could put us right back in the national championship spotlight.

Practice today was in sweats out on the grass. When we have no pads on people usually take it easy and mostly work on getting their body to the right place instead of hitting and battling on the line. I guess Patrick Kabongo never got the memo because he was battling right off the line and trying his hardest to get to the ball on every play. Brian Nelson was blocking him and was getting sick of the excessive effort. On one pass play, I was uncovered, dropped back and then went to double team with Brian on Pat, nearly knocking him over. I don't think he liked that too well because the next play, Brian and Pat almost got in a fight. Some of those defensive guys, especially the younger ones trying to crawl up the depth chart, really try too hard in practice on these days. Dan Swantek, offensive guard and poster boy for the white-trash lifestyle and inventor of useless slang, likes to call these guys jarheads. I don't really know where he comes up with this stuff, but it fits.

Saturday, November, 4, 2000

Nebraska 56 – Kansas 17

This was by far the most complete and dominating offensive game so far this season. We scored on all but two drives and one of those was stopped by a fumble at the end of the game. We didn't punt all game. Eric Crouch, Correll Buckhalter, and Dan Alexander had over 100 rushing yards each. I got in for the last play of the game. It was a 49 Pitch (I-back to the left) and even though I messed up on my first assignment, I was able to get downfield and make a key block that got Thunder Collins an extra 10 yards. My dad would have loved to have seen this had he been in town. It doesn't help that my mom set the VCR to tape the wrong channel. I'll just have to get a tape of the game from the video guys.

Jon Rutherford blew the ACL in his left knee today in the game. It was one of those freak accidents. One of our passes was intercepted and Jon was running to make the tackle, slowed down and set up to hit a blocker and his knee buckled. He has been extremely valuable to the O-line this year as the sixth starter. He can play every position on the line and has made many contributions to every game. He will be missed for the rest of this season, but will be back next year.

I guess I forgot to collect my money from the past couple of games because when I went to get the weekend money, Norma told me I have four games' worth to collect. In all, the total was $55, just enough to finance an exciting weekend.

Sunday, November 5, 2000

My picture was in the paper today. The picture is of Thunder Collins popping through the defense for a 17-yard run and shows me making a block to let him sneak by.

Back in my senior year in high school, I went to a basketball game between Millard West and Millard South. An old teammate from my freshman year, who was one of the star athletes and also very arrogant and cocky, told me I should go somewhere I will actually play. Shrugging it off, I asked him where he planned to go. His posse of idiots didn't appreciate me questioning their leader and quickly stepped up, ready to fight. After his unintelligible, monosyllabic answer proved he wasn't looking for a friendly conversation, my plan was clear. If there was ever a picture of me in any publication for the Huskers, especially an action shot, I would send it to him and show him what I can actually do. Now I have my chance and it is more than perfect.

Monday, November 6, 2000

We went through the goals today and saw that the offense met all 11 of our goals for the Kansas game. That hasn't happened yet this year and it's very rare for it ever to happen. That is just more proof that we played an awesome offensive football game. The defense also did very well in achieving their goals as did the special teams. If we can play like this the rest of the season, there's no reason we can't be national champions.

It was cold and rainy today, forcing us to move inside the Cook Pavilion. I think this winter could be drastically different from the past two, which were bearable throughout the entire season. We actually might get a typical Nebraska winter this year.

Tuesday, November 7, 2000

Today was probably one of my best practices ever. For some reason, I had a lot of energy and strength, and was able to really push around the first- and second-string defensive linemen. I was flying all over the field and just felt great. It can probably be chalked up to the fact that I have a new girlfriend and the psychological effect of a positive relationship can never be underestimated.

We got a new pair of black sweatpants and a new black sweatshirt today. These clothes finally have the Husker insignia on them unlike some of the stuff we got in the past that just had the generic Adidas logo.

Saturday, November 11, 2000

Kansas State 29 – Nebraska 28

This was a surprisingly close game for how horribly we played. Blame it on the icy turf, blame it on the wrong shoes, or just blame it on the fact that we couldn't do anything productive all day long. We looked absolutely terrible. It was best that I had to watch this game on TV so I didn't get too upset. It seemed to me that we weren't even opening up our playbook. We stuck to a few plays for most of the game and suffered terribly for it. The option game was halted at every attempt, Crouch had trouble getting the ball to the receivers, and we could not put a decent drive together.

My feelings about this loss are very disconnected. I truly don't care. I worked as hard as I could the entire week of practice to get the defense ready for this game. I did all I could. Since it wasn't me out there on the field, I feel no immediate connection to this game. I take no credit for anything. Actually, the defense did a very good job from what it looked like. It was just our offense, of which I only play a little part of now, which lost us the game. Now we have just a slim chance of making a BCS bowl. We'll probably make another appearance at the Holiday Bowl. I wouldn't mind going back to San Diego.

Tuesday, November 14, 2000

I guess the attitude about not giving the #1 ranking too much thought has now carried over into not giving our losses too much worry. Many of the guys seem totally unfazed by what's going on right now.

We had a team meeting yesterday, but we didn't have practice. Today, as a fairly nice surprise, former Husker and 17-year veteran in the pros Irving Fryar came in and gave us a speech. He basically talked about how he had been through a lot in his life, so that made him qualified to talk about a lot of stuff. Later in his speech, he kicked the coaches out of the room because he wanted us to be able to ask him any question without fear of the coaches hearing. He said some pretty interesting things about girls, money, agents, racism, and drugs, and some guys even had questions about his teammates in the pros. One thing that really shocked me, and some others I'm sure, was his belief that it's men's responsibility to lead women because they have been bringing us down since the beginning of time, and we need to let them know where they stand in the social order. He said women are incapable of leading and since they came from a part of us, we have the right to control them. Basically, he sounded like a sexist, egotistical jackass and I wasn't alone in thinking this. Oh well, at least this guest speaker said something we will actually remember.

My strength is continuing to improve on certain lifts. Today on hang clean, I did 292 pounds really easily with the help of a lot of adrenaline and a great night's sleep. Today I weighed in at 285, which means I've lost 20 pounds since the start of the season. I'm going to get my body fat tested later this week and will find out if that loss is fat or muscle.

The practices so far have been pretty intense for me. I am in for basically every play and don't even get a break during special teams thanks to my long snapping skills. I'm constantly running all practice long so it's no wonder why I'm always so tired and losing so much weight. I'm getting tired of this real quick.

Wednesday, November 15, 2000

Matt Shook was sick today, so that moved me up to the twos and I had them all to myself during practice. I did fairly well for not having practiced with those guys for the vast majority of the season, but there are still many things I need to work on. I think I'm leaning forward too much when I block and that leaves me unable to make quick direction changes. I also don't know which linebacker to chip off for on some of the plays, so that didn't help. Coach Tenopir had to help me out with some of the plays during the run station, but I think I didn't make any major mistakes.

Friday, November 17, 2000

Shook came back today, but to my surprise, I stayed with the twos instead of moving back down with the scout team. This is a very positive sign. Shook and I do a rotation where he takes the majority of the snaps and I pretty much fill in when he needs a break. This doesn't get me much work with the plays, or much of a workout in general, but it's helping me learn the plays.

Sunday, November 19, 2000

We had practice today, in half pads in the Cook, and it felt really weird to practice on a Sunday. We usually don't do anything on Sundays, but with the Colorado game on

Friday, we needed to push the week up to get it all done like a regular week. I'm still with the twos, rotating with Shook, and making fewer errors every day. Today, as a bonus for practicing on a Sunday, we got $60.

Tuesday, November 21, 2000

We practiced in sweats today. I think the coaches realize how tired, sick, and sore a lot of the guys are by this time of the year. With the temperature falling hard and finals slowly creeping up on all of us, it's always a welcome break when we can do something different. I think the general feeling on the team right now is that the dream of the national championship season is shot, but we can still finish out the season in style. A dominating win over Colorado and a win against a good team at a good bowl should help us end up in the top five when it's all over.

We got money for the weekend at dinner tonight since we will practice twice and have the game on Friday, all with no school. In all, I got $90.

Thursday, November 23, 2000

Practice was at our regular 3:30 time. My family was eating Thanksgiving dinner in Omaha at about 2:00. My brother Jason was in town from New York with his wife Stacy, so I wasn't too happy about missing all that. After practice, Brian Nelson invited me to go up to Omaha with him to his family's Thanksgiving meal. Since I would probably have a frozen pizza if I stayed in Lincoln, I happily accepted. After the meal, I called my parents and surprised them by telling them I was only four miles away when they thought I was in Lincoln. So, I spent some time with them and then came back to Lincoln later on.

Friday, November 24, 2000

Nebraska 34 – Colorado 32

Today was Senior Day. All the seniors got a chance to say something to the guys while we got dressed in the locker room and it was a mostly positive affair with a few tears shed by a few guys. The psych-up video was just a few seniors talking about how meaningful their careers have been and how much they want to go out winners. After that, it was a locker room as usual with all the yelling and screaming, and then we charged out on the field not realizing at all what was about to happen.

The Colorado team that came to play us today has had a very rough season. They are 3-6 and were 25-point underdogs, but I thought this spread was not appropriate after they lost a few close ones against some very good teams.

There were big plays happening everywhere throughout the entire game and both sides capitalized on the other team's errors effectively. There were blocked kicks on both sides and amazing plays all day long. Perhaps the most amazing was the last minute of the game. Colorado scored and had the chance to tie it up with an extra point. In a very gutsy move, they went for a two-point conversion and got it with an amazing catch in the end zone, putting them up 32-31. On their kickoff, they kicked a low-line drive that was returned to our 35-yard line. We then put on one of the most impressive drives since the final drive in the 1997 Missouri game. In 45 seconds, we passed effectively down the field and were able to set up Josh Brown for a 29-yard field goal. He missed one earlier and has been very inconsistent with field goals this season, so the whole state was holding its breath. With five seconds on the clock, they set up. Then the snap, the hold, and the kick. Barely missing the outstretched hands of a Colorado player, it sailed up and through the goal posts. Brown was immediately smothered in a giant pile on the field. Some guys picked him up and began to carry him around the field and he looked as happy as any man could be. The final score of 34-32 created a five-year string of games with Colorado where the total difference in points scored is just 15. This shouldn't be such a rivalry, but somehow it is and it definitely made for one of the most exciting games of the year.

Sunday, December 3, 2000

It's official—we're going to the Alamo Bowl in San Antonio, Texas. The game is played on the 30th and the way it looks, we might actually leave on the 26th, giving the possibility for the first Christmas with my family in three years.

Saturday, December 9, 2000

We had practice on Tuesday, Friday and today. We even got $25 for practicing today. Some recruits were in this weekend, so we had to put on a show for them and go in full pads. Most of the guys today were hurting after a long night of parties. A few guys reeked of alcohol and one of the starters only got two hours of sleep and was very hung over. I didn't get much sleep, but I didn't feel too bad considering how late I was out at the bars. I would bet the majority of the guys would rather not have practiced today.

I think a good sign that you are climbing up in the program is the number of favors people do for you. Wednesday when I was lifting, I wanted to get two days of lifting done in one day and asked Bailey how to do it. He said to do hang clean and some other stuff, but I told him my back was hurting and I probably shouldn't do hang clean. He thought about it and told me just to forget about doing anything for Thursday's lifting and that he would take care of filling out my lifting card. I'm sure there are more exciting stories of guys getting favors from their coaches, the staff, or people around the community, but I really haven't heard much stuff around here. As far as I can truthfully tell, we are a very clean program and follow the rules carefully.

Saturday, December 16, 2000

This was finals week and it was a struggle for everyone, as usual. We had practice on Tuesday, Friday and today. Friday I told the coaches I had a paper to work on until 5:00 in the afternoon and would have trouble making it to practice. Coach Tenopir said to work as fast as I could and make it to practice because they needed me. After I left Coach's office, I handed my paper in, which was already done, and went home to sleep for the first time in two days. I felt bad for lying to Coach Tenopir, but I would not have been any good in practice running on no sleep.

This morning we had breakfast, got paid $127, and had meetings at 9:00. Practice started at 10:00. The most interesting thing that happened was a fight between Kyle Kollmorgen, a junior offensive lineman, and Sandro DeAngelis, a scholarship freshman kicker. I don't know the whole story, but verbal taunting by both turned into a fistfight and the much larger Kollmorgen held Sandro down and repeatedly punched him in the face. When I was walking out of the Cook, I saw Coach Tenopir and Coach Young talking to Sandro and his whole face was cut up and swollen. I guess Sandro said he wants Kyle kicked off the team. When Coach Solich said he wouldn't do that, Sandro told him he is going to press charges against Kyle.

This brings up interesting questions. Is everything equal for everyone, or do some people get away with things others wouldn't? Are the punishments appropriate for the offenses? Is there a line between the team and our rules and the outside world and its laws? Are we an extralegal entity capable of handling something like this in an appropriate manner? It will be interesting to see what happens with this, especially when the media gets its hands on it.

I think that many athletes, regardless of the sport, think that they are above the law when it comes to certain things. They know that they are so valuable to the team that anything they do wrong will be quickly taken care of. Incidents happen all the time. It's common to see a player get suspended for "breaking team rules." In the real world, this would have given Kyle an assault charge, a court date, and a criminal record that would hang over him forever. As it is, he'll probably get a slap on the wrist and be told to go think about what he's done. No wonder so many star athletes are so maladjusted when they always get what they want and have no consequences.

Monday, December 18, 2000

Coach Solich informed the team today that he suspended Kyle for the fight, and Kyle won't practice for the rest of the year or travel to the bowl game. I'm guessing that was the agreement Sandro and the coaches came up with to avoid messy legal hearings that could put a black mark on the team.

The practices for this week look okay. We will be going every weekday. It seems we will practice in the Cook the entire time since there is blowing snow and a negative-20-degree wind chill. Except for the walk over to the Cook from the locker room, I don't mind.

I started to get a football signed for my parents today for their Christmas present. It's a lot easier to do this now that I'm in the south locker room. All the main guys are there and I can probably get it done in record time.

Wednesday, December 20, 2000

We got $84 at lunch today. This is more money, meant for food, which will be used for Christmas presents.

Today's practice was just horrible for me. Even though it was in sweats, it went too long, there was too much running, and there was too much activity on the line. I guess I was just tired, but whatever it was, I was totally dead after practice. When we got back to the locker room, we picked up our end-of-the-year gift bags from Adidas. Along with a really nice black duffle bag with wheels, we got two hats with an Adidas logo, one black, one red; two T-shirts with a big Adidas logo, one black, one white; one long-sleeved black shirt; a pair of black wind pants with white stripes on the sides; a faded black fleece vest; a faded black fleece pullover; an Adidas watch; and a pair of Adidas sunglasses with extra lenses. All in all, it was a nice bag of gifts.

Thursday, December 21, 2000

Today's practice was in full pads and was almost a repeat of yesterday. I really am getting tired of practicing. I think everybody is getting tired of practicing. No one was moving with 100% speed or effort, and I think the coaches noticed this because they said tomorrow's practice will be in half pads instead of sweats like they said earlier in the week.

After lifting, I made my way back to the locker room, half delirious, and got one more gift out of our locker—a black Adidas backpack with a Huskers logo on it.

Sunday, December 24, 2000

We were able to lift today and get paid for it. Brian "Nelly" Nelson, Chris Septak and I (all Millard West high school grads) went to the weight room at 6:30 tonight, went right up to Norma and got our money. We didn't lift, we didn't even raise our heart rate by any substantial amount;

we just told her we were there for the required 15 minutes and picked up our $76. I don't think anybody really did any kind of workout. There were guys walking out of the weight room in jeans and sweaters, looking like they had just come from a church service. Tonight I will pack and tomorrow we will leave bright and early for San Antonio.

Monday, December 25, 2000

We got to the airport at 7:00 this morning, but were slowed down from our planned departure at 8:00 by the security forces making everyone go through one metal detector. Usually, we never bother with metal detectors on team flights, but there was another group of people there as well leaving from a different terminal. Norma was there to give us all $214 to start off the trip. We got to San Antonio about 10:30 and were greeted with a small reception. We checked into the hotel soon after and got settled before the afternoon practice. The hotel is the Marriott Rivercenter, a very nice hotel located on a branch of the Riverwalk. My roommate for this trip is Cody Volk, a pairing that I'm very happy with (instead of being put with Kolterman or another one of those idiots).

Our practice site for the week will be Alamo Stadium, a site used by the San Antonio Independent School District located near Trinity University, north of the city. It was cold and rainy the whole practice, and nobody was very happy. After practice, most of the guys lifted. I was told to lift and since the guys who dress are usually the ones who lift during bowl games, I guess that means I will dress. When we got back to the hotel, we had meetings that were nice and short.

Tonight there was a Christmas dinner for us, which was pretty nice with a good spread of food. There was a small program after the food, but I skipped out early because I didn't feel like sitting through all that boring stuff.

There is a players' lounge set up for us once again. This one is actually divided into two rooms. One room has two pool tables, two pinball machines, two war arcade games, and two video game systems hooked up to two televisions. The other room has two more arcade games (including *Hydro Thunder*, a favorite of Dan Alexander, who mastered it during the Fiesta Bowl), and a table with snack foods and two big coolers with drinks. It wasn't as nice of a spread as the past bowls, but it will work.

Tuesday, December 26, 2000

Another early day. Meetings at 8:30 and practice at 10:30. In meetings, Coach Tenopir said he is going to dress 12 linemen, the 11 guys who practice with the ones and twos and me, because I long snap (he used these exact words). I'm not sure if I like dressing only because I can long snap, but it's allowing me to suit up. It was kind of like telling me that without my long snapping skills I wouldn't have a place on this team.

Practice was cold and wet again. Already, everyone hates this bowl. The only good thing about today was that it was the last practice in pads for the entire year. There is talk of the theme for next year being "Remember the Alamo."

During some free time, I was able to explore the city and saw the Alamo and an IMAX movie about the Alamo. From what I saw on my little journey, the best part of the city is around the Riverwalk and the Alamo. If you stray too far from the Riverwalk, the city gets pretty gritty.

Tonight, I went with a bunch of guys to the Alamodome to watch the San Antonio Spurs take on the Houston Rockets. At one point in the game, the Spurs mascot (a coyote) was running around on the floor throwing a football into the crowd. This one guy he threw it to wouldn't throw it back. The coyote went up to the guy and wrenched it out of his grip. As he walked away, the guy got up and tackled the mascot mid-court and stole the ball again. While walking off triumphantly, he backed up straight into Russ Hochstein and one of Northwestern's players, who picked up the guy and dumped him in a trash can to the delight of the crowd. It was all planned, of course, but it was pretty funny to watch. I stayed until the start of the fourth quarter, but it was getting really boring, so I left and walked back to the hotel.

Wednesday, December 27, 2000

Another rainy, cold practice, but the sun started to break through later in the day. Everyone is getting pretty tired of this trip.

At 6:00 tonight, we all loaded onto barges on the river and took a short trip (after waiting forever for the band to show up and lead the barges). We passed through an outdoor amphitheatre that was split by the river where there was a little pep rally. We were the last barge to pass through, so we didn't get to see any of the program or hear any of the speeches. We finally reached the Villita Assembly Hall where our function was being held.

The entire Northwestern team showed up soon after we did. After a small and unsatisfying meal, there was an even more unsatisfying program. The emcee called up some of our guys and Northwestern's guys and played this game that was supposed to test how well we know our teammates. Some of the guys filled out surveys earlier and the person had to guess what they put down. The questions were really stupid and Northwestern ended up winning that round.

Next was a dance contest. Willie Amos danced with his jump rope and blew everyone away. Thunder Collins, Wilson Thomas, Randy Stella, and Josh Brown, who posed as the equipment manager, all got up and did stuff on stage and pretty much made fools of themselves. They called for coaches to go up and dance, too, but none of our coaches would do it. They then called for trainers or managers, which is when Brown went up. Unofficially, Northwestern won that little competition, but none of us cared at all.

Thursday, December 28, 2000

We picked up our gifts from the Alamo Bowl. We received a really nice letter jacket, which is amazingly small for a 3XL. We also received a hat and a yacht sweater, and a really nice Fossil watch with the Alamo Bowl logo on it. Luckily, we didn't get another bag. I already have about 10 bags and don't need another one.

Some guys went to a hockey game tonight, but I went out with Aaron Patch, who came down with his family. We went to this bar and grill called Dick's Last Resort. They had a nice deal on 32-oz. Bud Light bottles and we both put away four of them in under two hours. The bar was full of girls, some of them at a bachelorette party, and I was drug out on the dance floor only to notice our strength coach Bryan Bailey and some other football-related guys in the crowd. They all looked shocked to see me dancing with girls at a bar, especially since it was so close to curfew. We had curfew at 11:00 and left the bar with about 10 minutes to go. I ran all the way back to the hotel, deftly flying dangerously close to the unguarded edge of the riverwalk, and made it with about three minutes to spare. Aaron was right behind me and ran into the room just in time to hide behind the side of a bed. Coach Young was soon at our door to check on us for bedcheck. From his unusual lighthearted grin and his eyes that couldn't focus, I'd guess he was in the same shape we were.

Later on, I heard from Bailey that Coach Young was

at Dick's after he made his rounds. A wet paper towel fight broke out and Coach Young was hit with a wad of paper square in the forehead. His head bobbled, stunned at the impact of the cold, wet projectile, but instead of wiping it away he sat there for a few seconds straining to look up at what was now attached to his face. I wish I could have seen that, but it's even funnier to see everyone give their own impersonation of what happened.

Friday, December 29, 2000

Luckily, we were able to sleep in until noon, when we had the Kickoff Luncheon in the grand ballroom. The food was pretty good and for the program each team showed a highlight film. Ours was more like a psych-up tape with great scenes of the year set to the song "Kryptonite" by Three Doors Down. The Northwestern tape was basically duplicated TV footage with no excitement. They had a pretty loud crowd there to support them at the luncheon. Once again, we were all glad when this was over.

We haven't seen too many videos produced by the other teams we've played, but every one that we see makes us very thankful for the video crew that we have at Nebraska. They really know what they're doing and go to great lengths to make even the most insignificant video look outstanding.

Later on, we were able to pick up the rest of our money for the trip, another $95. At 5:00 we made our way to the Alamodome for our final practice. There, we took team pictures and had our short little practice that barely gets your heart pumping, and we were out.

Apparently, last night when Aaron Patch and I got crazy, he went back out and finished the night at the bars while I waited up for him. He came back to find me asleep in my clothes and he tried to go to sleep on the floor, but was too cold. He got up and left to go back to his hotel at about

4:00 in the morning. But, in his stumbling, he left behind his hat, one of his shirts, and his wallet. When I woke up, I thought he was probably picked up by hotel security, shirtless and without I.D. and sent to detox. Luckily, he wasn't. He somehow walked back to his hotel about a mile away. Tonight I was about to run his stuff back over to his hotel when I was walking through the lobby and heard him yell out behind me. He was waiting for me in the lobby with another one of our friends and they were ready to go out again. What a trooper.

Saturday, December 30, 2000

Nebraska 66 – Northwestern 17

Late games are always nice because the first half of the day has nothing to do but a few minor meetings. The coaches want to make sure you're as fresh as can be, physically and mentally. We've got the physical side taken care of with all the hours of practice we've put in. The coaches take care of the mental side by not having hours of meetings before the game. I had a lot of time to myself today and spent most of it in my room relaxing or in the game room.

At 5:00, we got on busses to travel 500 yards to the stadium. We should have walked just as easily. There's even a pedestrian bridge spanning most of the way towards the stadium. It seemed like the height of laziness, but I guess we had to make an entrance.

We got dressed quickly and everyone seemed really focused on the game. There wasn't any talking. Every part of our pregame ritual was eerily subdued, even the parts where the seniors and starters usually give impassioned speeches to get us fired up. It was almost like we were so focused on playing the game that we didn't even pay attention to the yelling and chest-pounding ceremony that precedes every match.

We took the field triumphantly to the cheers of thousands of Husker fans. Of the 60,000 fans in attendance, I bet over 60% were our fans. We started off slow but strong, and Northwestern hung with us for a few minutes. Then we proceeded to embarrass them on national television. The icing on the cake was a play we had been saving all year where Crouch throws a lateral to Newcombe and then Newcombe throws deep to Davison who was wide open for a 69-yard touchdown pass. It was beautiful.

Finally, when it was 66-17, Coach Young told me he would try to get me in. I finally went in for a total of five plays. Since I haven't been practicing with the ones and twos for a while, I didn't have a clue what to do on three of the five plays. We didn't get anything done, probably because of me, but it didn't matter. I finished out the game and made my family and friends so proud I could see them jumping around in the stands.

Basically, we destroyed Northwestern. We put up the most points ever in a bowl game. I-back Dan Alexander had 240 yards on 20 carries and was awarded the offensive MVP; rush end Kyle Vanden Bosch was awarded the defensive MVP. It was a great way to end the season and to get a start for next year.

I went out again tonight, but everything was too packed to have a good time. Quite a few guys spend most of their bowl trip money and their free time at the local strip clubs. This seems to me like a huge waste of money, but I guess if that's what you like to do when you're in a new city, go ahead. I saved a lot of money by not doing that.

End of the Year Summary

We finished 10-2, giving my class as well as Solich a combined record of 31-7. The atmosphere on the team is definitely different now than it was when I first came to the program. I can't quite explain it, but it seems much more relaxed. We're playing well and we have a lot of young guys who are hungry for some playing time. I guess we'll just have to see where another off-season brings us.

I spent most of the season with the scout team, working my butt off and hardly ever getting a break in practice. Hopefully that means I'm more conditioned than the other guys, but I think it also means I'm more burnt out. Three years down and two to go. I'm so glad to be over that hump.

2001 Winter Conditioning

Thursday, January 4, 2001

After weeks of speculation, center Dominic Raiola declared that he would leave and enter the NFL draft. This came after many reports saying he intended to stay at Nebraska, followed by some saying he was questioning his options, and then the final news hit today. In the press conference, he said he gave it a lot of thought and talked to the coaches about it and that it was one of the hardest decisions he's ever had to make in his life. We all wish him the best and know that whoever picks him up will definitely get a great lineman.

This is already creating questions for next year and the papers are quick to show the back-ups for the job at center. They list Jon Rutherford, Matt Shook, and John Garrison, but no mention of me. I thought this was funny; apparently three people at center is good enough depth, four would just be too much for people to handle while still made to believe there are problems. There always has to be controversy. Rutherford, when he gets healthy, will most likely be the starting center for next year. This means I will have to work to beat out Shook and Garrison, which won't be easy, but is possible. This winter is going to be the determining factor in my success for the next two years.

Thursday, January 11, 2001

Earlier this week I asked strength and conditioning coach Danny Noonan about the kickboxing program he and some other players do. I've heard a lot of good things about it from many of the guys. They have all said that it helps with flexibility, quickness and coordination, which are things that I greatly need improved. I did my first session of kickboxing tonight and could immediately tell that two things: this is one hell of a workout and this could be exactly what I need to keep doing.

Wednesday, January 17, 2001

I've begun mentoring through the TeamMates program. This program was set up by former head coach Tom Osborne several years ago, and some of the players at the time were paired up with troubled kids in the area. It quickly grew and now covers much of the state with hundreds of volunteers working with hundreds of deserving youth. The young boy I mentor is Layne Armstrong. He's in elementary school and seems to be a great kid, he just needs a little structure and support in his life.

Today was the preliminary testing for the winter program. I really didn't care how I did today and I was in a hurry since I had to get to my mentoring before 2:30. I started out with a very light warm-up and really didn't do too bad overall, but I didn't shine the way I probably should have. I'm still slower than I should be with a 40-yard-dash time of 5.8 seconds. I need to get that down somehow. The rest of my times weren't that different from what I posted in the past. If I can do it, now would be a good time to put on a show for the coaches to catch their attention.

Monday, January 22, 2001

The first day of lifting. We met in the Pit at 7:00 this morning and did a rather extensive stretching and warm-up program, which is something we never used to do. I think it's definitely a good idea, but no one can prove to me why it is a good idea to lift at 7:00 in the morning to begin with. I think it's the stupidest thing ever and totally wastes the rest of your day because you're so tired. Next year, when I'm a senior, I'm going to push for afternoon lifting.

We started out light and this whole week will be fairly easy. Bailey wants us to work into the heavy weight gradually so we don't get injured, and to keep the initial soreness down.

Tuesday, January 30, 2001

Toniu Fonoti, our junior all-star Samoan guard, made news again today. He was benching and didn't get all the reps on his set. This made him mad and he punched a door in the weight room, possibly thinking he would punch through it. Instead, the door won the battle, giving Toniu two broken fingers that will keep him out of a lot of the lifting for the rest of the winter.

Monday, February 5, 2001

We started our running today. The whole team is running together now and we met in Cook Pavilion at 3:00. We were divided into groups of about 15 and put in position at six different stations. We did harness pulls, 40-yard buildups, abdominal work, an obstacle course with high ropes and bags, footwork drills that were the same as the jump rope drills minus the jump rope, and agility runs. After this, we went over to the Pit and ran some plays as a group. I guess we'll be doing this type of circuit running for the majority of the winter conditioning. It sure felt like a good workout.

My days are very busy now. With morning lifting, class from 9:30 to 12:20 every day, and kickboxing and Akido four nights a week, I don't have time to do a lot of studying. I'm far behind in my classes and I can't get myself motivated to do any of the work. My weekends are just recovery from the week and my mind won't function right if I try to do any work. Something has got to get better soon or I will have serious problems in school this semester.

Monday, February 26, 2001

I hit an all-time max of 320 pounds on hang clean today. This should hopefully open the eyes of the coaches. Hang clean is one of the most impressive lifts because it ties in several major muscle groups, shows explosiveness as well as strength, and takes incredible coordination to do correctly.

Friday, March 2, 2001

Last day of winter conditioning. I think I must be coming down with something because I felt drained of energy and didn't do well on my last set of squat. When it was all over I had to go to class so I couldn't really celebrate.

Tonight, all the linemen met at Hooters to celebrate the end of winter conditioning. They actually carded us this time, so the underage guys weren't allowed to drink, but most of them managed to anyway. I was getting tired, so I left early and went home. I was so tired that I actually went to bed at 7:00, when I should have been enjoying free steaks thanks to starting tackle Dave Volk and his dad. I eventually woke up about midnight and went out partying for the rest of the night. All in all, it was an interesting winter.

David's Senior year in High School, weighing in at 255 pounds.

October 15, 1997

David Kolowski

Dear David:

We would like to invite you to attend our game with Texas Tech on Saturday, October 18.

The kickoff for the game is 12:30 p.m., but we would like you to arrive earlier in the day for a special tour of our football facilities. If you will come to the South Stadium office building at 8:45 a.m., we will start there (see the enclosed map). NCAA rules allow us to provide you with three complimentary admissions only (we cannot help you purchase more), and you must pay for the luncheon at our dining facility. The price of the luncheon is $4.00 per person.

The NCAA does not allow us to help you with parking, but by coming earlier it should be a little easier to park. If you arrive after 11:30 a.m., go to Gate 1 and they will take care of you.

Please call Curt Thompson at 1-800-[illegible] as soon as possible and let him know if you will be able to attend. I hope to see you on the 18th.

Sincerely,

Tom Osborne

Tom Osborne
Head Football Coach

nineteen ninety-four 13-0 ◆ 12-0 nineteen ninety-five

One of the several recruiting letters I received.

Clockwise from top left: Signing with Frank Solich as his first recruit ever as head coach, Meeting with Tom Osborne on a recruiting visit, and the magnificent Husker weight room.

The Coaches that David dealt with during the 1998-2002 era. Everyone except for Boyd Epley was replaced during the restructuring that followed the 2002 season.

Nebraska's 1998 Scholarship Class

Name	Pos.	Ht.	Wt.	High School
Demoine Adams	RE	6-3	220	Pine Bluff, Ark
Jon Bowling	TE	6-4	215	Lincoln (Southeast), NE
Josh Brown	K-P	6-1	175	Foyil, OK
Jon Clanton	DL	6-2	280	Peoria (Centennial), AZ
Wes Cody	OL	6-3	255	Fremont (Bergan), NE
Keyuo Craver	DB	6-0	180	Harleton, TX
Michael Demps	DB	5-11	180	Fort Worth (Dunbar), TX
Dahrran Diedrick	RB	6-1	208	Scarborough, Canada
Aaron Golliday	TE	6-4	235	York, NE
Deantae Grixby	RB	5-8	180	Omaha (Central), Ne
DeJuan Groce	DB	5-11	185	Cleveland(St. Alberts), Ohio
Chris Kelsay	RE	6-5	240	Auburn, NE
Nate Kolterman	OL	6-3	300	Seward, NE
Jason Lohr	DL	6-3	275	Jenks, OK
Shawn McGann	WB	5-11	190	Mishawaka (Penn), IN
Matt Shook	OL	6-3	270	Medina, OH
Jeremy Slechta	DL	6-5	255	Papillion-LaVista
Justin Smith	RE	6-5	240	Sherman, Tx
Randy Stella	LB	6-2	200	Omaha (Benson), Ne
Tony Tata	RE	6-2	240	Honolulu (St. Louis), Hi
Wilson Thomas	WR	6-5	200	Omaha (North), Ne

These were all the scholarship recipients for 1998, the year I came to UNL. Most of these guys made it through their entire college career with success, but many of them faced several injuries and setbacks along the way.

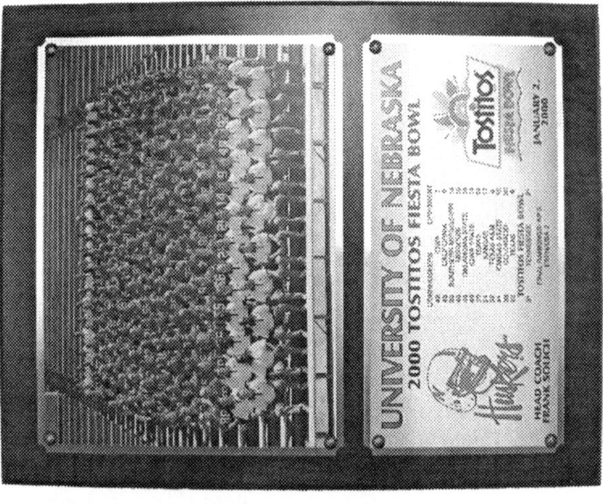

2000 Fiesta Bowl

1998 Holiday Bowl

2002 Rose Bowl

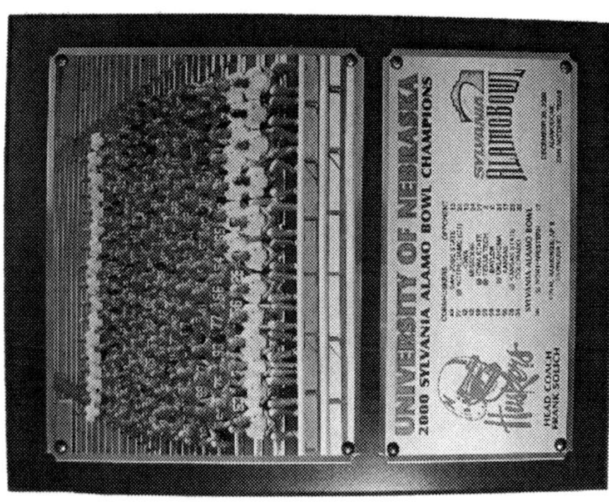

2000 Alamo Bowl

2002 Independence Bowl

Gift from Rose Bowl Committee

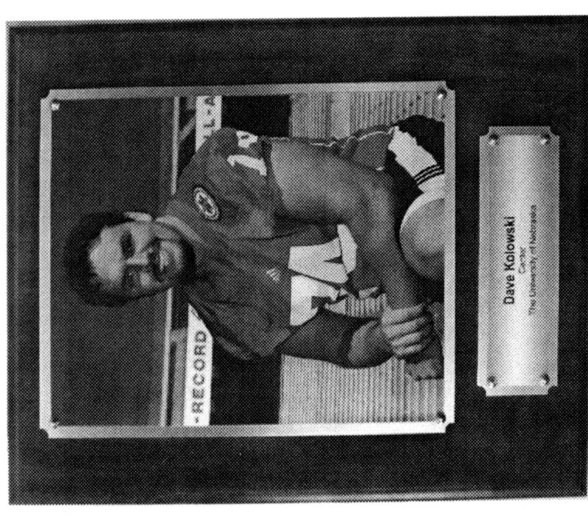

David's Senior Picture

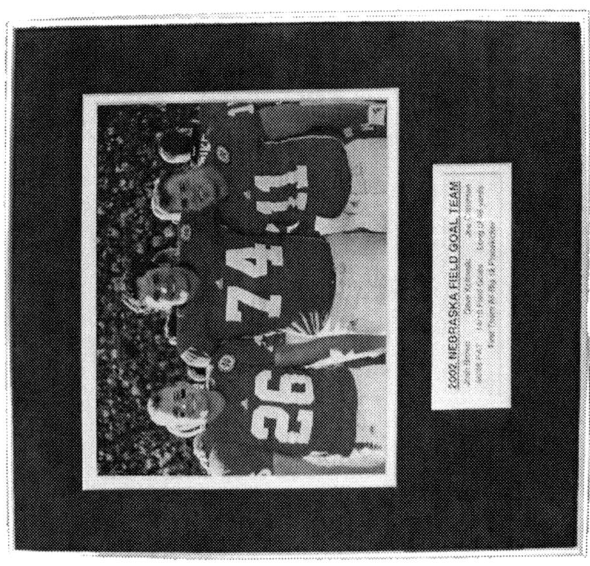

Josh Brown, David and Joe Chrisman

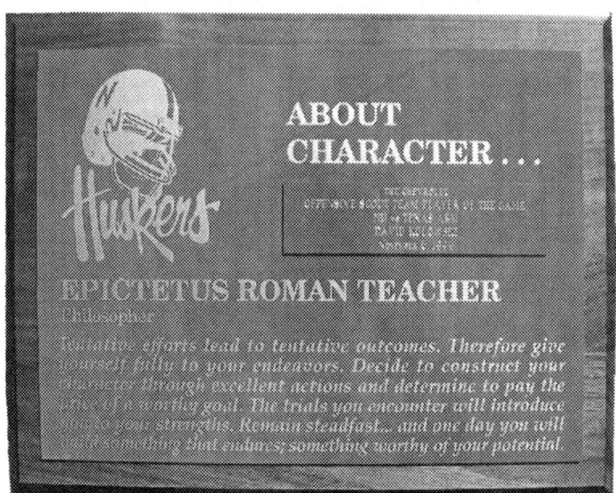

2002 Unity Council and 1999 Scout Team Player of the Game

Citizenship Team Plaque and the first jersey that was issued to David

This was the heaviest David ever was at 310 lbs. Nice gut.

Jason Kolowski, David Kolowski, and Rick Kolowski

At the end of the Independence Bowl,
the last game as a Husker.

David and his family at graduation.

■ 2002 Brook Berringer Citizenship Team

Senior David Kolowski will back up returning senior starter John Garrison and junior Josh Sewell at center and will also serve as Garrison's backup snapper on special teams.

2001: Kolowski backed up Garrison in 2001 and saw action in three games. Kolowski did not record a pancake. He did not play in the 2002 Rose Bowl.

2000: Kolowski saw time in two games in 2000 plus the Alamo Bowl as a backup snapper and center.

1999: As a reserve center, Kolowksi did not see action.

1998: A walk-on, Kolowski redshirted his first year at Nebraska.

At Millard West HS: Kolowski was the starting center and long snapper for Coach Dan McLaughlin's Millard West team. Kolowski played in the Shrine Bowl in 1998 and was a four-year academic letterman and honor roll student.

Personal: The son of Rick and Bonnie Kolowksi, David was born on July 16, 1979. He majors in secondary education and social sciences and is on track to graduate in May 2004. Kolowski was named to the 2002 Brook Berringer Citizenship Team after volunteering with the Teammates, Team Spirit and School is Cool programs. He is also a member of the 2002 Nebraska Football Unity Council.

Media & Recruiting Guide ■ 141

David's Bio from the 2002 Nebraska Football Media and Recruiting Guide

- 2002 First-Team Academic All-Big 12
- 2002 Brook Berringer Citizenship Team

Senior David Kolowski served as Nebraska's No. 3 center this fall. However, he played a key role as Nebraska's snapper for place-kicking duties. Husker kickers made 13-of-17 field goals this season and the unit had just one failed PAT attempt. Kolowski also excels in the classroom and was a first-team Academic All-Big 12 selection this fall.

2002: Kolowski saw limited action at center, but was NU's No. 1 snapper for field goals and extra points.

Career: Kolowski played in five games in 2000 and 2001 as a backup center and deep snapper. A walk-on, Kolowski redshirted his first year at Nebraska in 1998 and did not seee action in 1999.

For more information on David Kolowski, please see page 141 of the 2002 Nebraska Football Media Guide.

David's last official bio from the 2002 Independence Bowl Nebraska Football Media Guide, p. 70

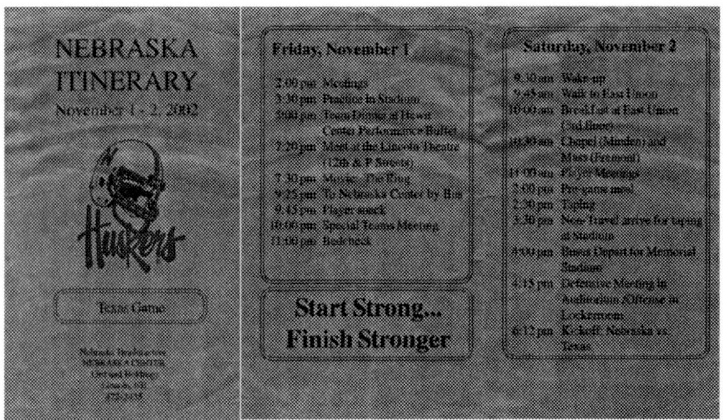

NEBRASKA ITINERARY
November 1 - 2, 2002

Huskers

Texas Game

Friday, November 1

2:00 pm Meetings
3:30 pm Practice in Stadium
5:00 pm Team Dinner at Hewit Center Performance Buffet
7:20 pm Meet at the Lincoln Theatre (12th & P Streets)
7:30 pm Movie: The Ring
9:25 pm To Nebraska Center by Bus
9:45 pm Player snack
10:00 pm Special Teams Meeting
11:00 pm Bedcheck

Start Strong... Finish Stronger

Saturday, November 2

9:30 am Wake-up
9:45 am Walk to East Union
10:00 am Breakfast at East Union (2nd floor)
10:30 am Chapel (Minden) and Mass (Fremont)
11:00 am Player Meetings
2:00 pm Pre-game meal
2:30 pm Taping
3:30 pm Non-Travel arrive for taping at Stadium
4:00 pm Buses Depart for Memorial Stadium
4:15 pm Defensive Meeting in Auditorium /Offense in Lockerroom
6:12 pm Kickoff: Nebraska vs. Texas

Itinerary Pamphlet for a Home Game against Texas

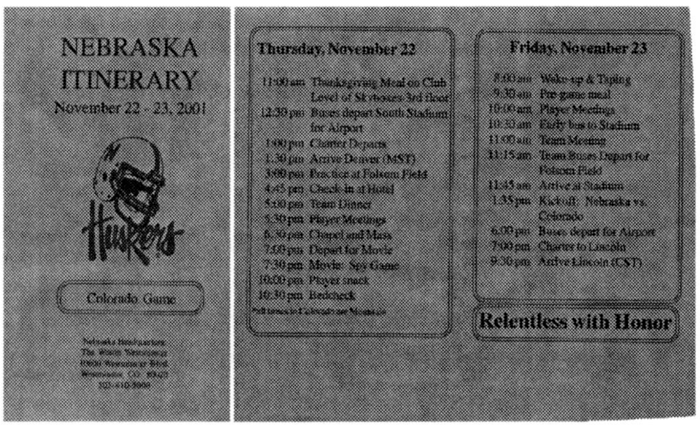

NEBRASKA ITINERARY
November 22 - 23, 2001

Huskers

Colorado Game

Thursday, November 22

11:00 am Thanksgiving Meal on Club Level of Skyboxes 3rd floor
12:30 pm Buses depart South Stadium for Airport
1:00 pm Charter Departs
1:30 pm Arrive Denver (MST)
3:00 pm Practice at Folsom Field
4:45 pm Check-in at Hotel
5:00 pm Team Dinner
5:30 pm Player Meetings
6:30 pm Chapel and Mass
7:00 pm Depart for Movie
7:30 pm Movie: Spy Game
10:00 pm Player snack
10:30 pm Bedcheck

Friday, November 23

8:00 am Wake-up & Taping
9:30 am Pre-game meal
10:00 am Player Meetings
10:30 am Early bus to Stadium
11:00 am Team Meeting
11:15 am Team Buses Depart for Folsom Field
11:45 am Arrive at Stadium
1:35 pm Kickoff: Nebraska vs. Colorado
6:00 pm Buses depart for Airport
7:00 pm Charter to Lincoln
9:30 pm Arrive Lincoln (CST)

Relentless with Honor

Itinerary Pamphlet for an Away Game at Colorado

Various tickets from different events.

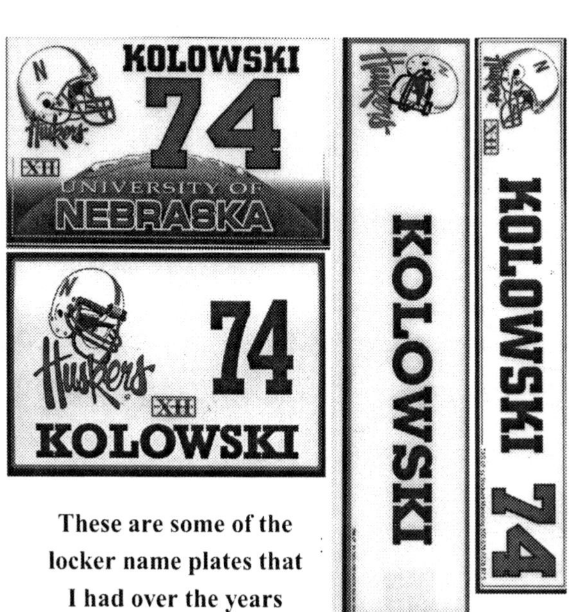

These are some of the locker name plates that I had over the years

Some random game souvenirs. Helmet decals from Rice and Baylor and the commemorative coin for the 2002 Rose Bowl.

My Collection of Autographed Footballs From Each Year

David's Letter Jacket and special Fiesta Bowl jacket, given as a Bowl Game gift.

All the watches that David accumulated over the years.

Top Row: 1998 Culligan Holiday Bowl, 1999 Big XII Championship Game, 2000 Tostitos Fiesta Bowl, Gift watch from Adidas

Bottom Row: 2000 Sylvania Alamo Bowl, 2002 Rose Bowl National Championship, 2002 Mainstay Independence Bowl

1999 Big XII Champions Ring

Two of the official Home jerseys, given to the players after the last game. These two still have the Rose Bowl and Fiesta Bowl logos attatched.

David and Lauren, back for a game.

Wednesday, March 7, 2001

Today was our testing day to see how well we did throughout the winter program. This was not good for me. I was feeling sick today with a sinus and eye infection and it really affected my performance. I didn't even feel well enough to go to class today, so I slept in and then went to the Cook to test out. I didn't have much energy but figured I should give it a try.

I only needed to beat two of my four events to avoid running the 300-yard shuttle. I came within a few hundredths of my best times in the 10 and 40, but didn't improve in the agility run or high jump. I talked to Coach Solich about possibly getting one more shot at the 40, but he said he didn't want people doing too much as a way to avoid injuries.

At this point, I was screwed. I had to run the shuttle and I knew I wasn't going to make it. I didn't have the energy and would probably pass out from it. I told Boyd I was sick, but he just questioned my manhood and told me to do it anyways. I walked over to where they were running the shuttle, gave them my card as if I was getting in line, and walked out. I didn't want to put up with their crap and I knew I wouldn't get anywhere arguing with them, so I just left. Damn the consequences. It probably wasn't the best choice, but I didn't care.

Thursday, March 8, 2001

Another low day for me. I didn't get a phone call from any of the coaches last night wondering what happened to me, nor did I see anyone who asked me about it until dinner. One of the weight room staff told me Bailey wanted to see me to set up a time to run the shuttle. I went to the weight room and Bailey was immediately upon me wondering what happened. He couldn't believe I would just walk out, and

I think he knew there must be a good reason. I told him I was sick, which he noticed as well, and he told me to have the doctor talk to Boyd to get it all cleared up. I then did that, so as far as I'm concerned, it's over.

When I got home, I opened my email which included a typical email from my dad about football, going on for a page or two about what I need to do and what I should think about doing to help myself. Something in this, along with the way I was feeling and the stress I was under, made me write this reply:

> *Dad and Mom,*
>
> *It's time for me to be very blunt and honest. I am sick of football. I am sick of hearing about it. I am sick of answering everybody's questions about it. I'm sick of everyone who thinks they know everything about the Huskers trying to correct me when I don't even care.*
>
> *There are only a few guys on the team that I would even consider my peers, the rest are wastes of life who were given exceptional physical ability. The coaches and trainers are all two-faced (maybe more). They show their public face, talking highly about everyone. They show their compassionate face saying that school, church and family come before football but then ridicule you if you actually use these reasons. If you're hurt or sick, they never take you seriously at first, unless you are a starter and then you can get away with murder (or rape).*
>
> *I would love to be cut. If they called me up tonight and told me that I got cut, it would be a blessing for me. I'm actually in trouble with the coaches right now for not finishing part of my testing, and I don't care. I don't see a future in this, it's not for me. Does this mean I will quit? No.*

This is where my internal struggle comes in. Playing football means more to everyone around me than it does to me. I enjoy seeing how something I do makes people happy. And I know, and you can't deny, that it makes you extremely proud.

It's not that it's too hard. It is fun at times, the rewards are great, and the possibilities that could be opened from being a part of the Huskers are unlimited. I know that I could spend five years playing football and then go along my merry way into the real world. But I have all these questions.

If I stay, will it have been worth it? Will I have just wasted five of the most prime years of my life doing something that didn't make me happy? Will the benefits that I receive from my participation mean anything to me? So far, none of it does. The watches, the ring, the clothes; they are all just possessions that I use because they fit my needs, not because I feel that I earned them.

If I leave or transfer, will I find a place that truly fits who I am and what I am looking for? Will I find better friends? Will my credits transfer? Will I be happy? Will I look back on this in the future and question my decision? Will everyone around me understand?

I would rather focus on school and having fun with what I do, whatever that may be. I don't think it's fun to be a fifth wheel on the O-line. I don't think it's fun to spend all my time and energy on an activity that has become more of a business instead of a game. You know what I mean, too. Ticket price hikes are just one of the signs. It's not about the game and letting the players have fun, it's about winning and making more money than ever before. This boils down into the coaches mentalities, creating the two faces, and giving them ulterior motives

> *for every action.*
>
> *My spring break is coming up. It is a full, uninterrupted week of no football-related activity whatsoever. I am going to relax, forget about football, and enjoy it. This means that I will be going to K.C. This means I will be partying.*
>
> *This means you probably won't hear from me the entire time. And I need this.*
>
> *Ray, the kickboxing instructor, always talks about widening your vision and seeing everything around you at once. Since it is only natural that I take something that I learn and apply it to my life, I have seen all of this more clearly now. Only now that I see everything, I don't know which path to take.*
>
> *For now, I see it as another year and a half of floating through my life. My inspiration is gone, my desire is gone, my love of the game is gone. Basically, I am just doing this for everyone else. So don't worry, you'll still get your tickets to next year's games.*
>
> *-Dave*

Of course, they were pretty surprised by this and it probably raised a lot of concerns in their minds. I have hit a low spot in my life. Not exactly a depression, but something very similar. The whole winter conditioning, my classes, and my increasingly disgruntled outlook on my slow improvement all added up to this. Luckily, spring break is right around the corner and I will be able to relax for a week.

Thursday, March 15, 2001

My spring break was going well until today. I was driving to Kansas City with a friend. We left at night, during which time weather reports warned about a big snowstorm moving in. We had just gotten into Missouri when I hit some ice and skidded head-on into a row of barrels and a portable flashing arrow sign. Luckily, we were able to walk away without injury, but my Chevy Blazer wasn't so lucky. The whole front end took it pretty hard and the bumper got pushed all the way to the motor. We have to wait and see what the insurance people say about the damage before we attempt to do anything with it.

I think this experience really snapped me out of my rut. Before, I viewed myself as disconnected from everything, as if I was watching my life on television. I had no emotions about anything, I was just going through the motions and was miserable. Now, I have a new set of values for what I think is important and I think this will be a big step for me. I could be dead right now, and if I was, how would people remember me? Who would remember me? Have I've been wasting my time trying to rebel against something that I knew was right? I still have plenty of time to make myself happy when I'm done with college.

2001 Spring Ball

Monday, March 19, 2001

I ran into Boyd Epley while walking to class today. He apologized for not trusting me when I told him I was sick. I guess that means it's all cleared up.

Today was the first day back from spring break and also the first day of spring practice. I remembered all the plays pretty well and helped out some of the younger guys. Practice lasted over two hours, but it went by quickly.

Some new developments have come about recently. Most notably, sophomore fullback Judd Davies is questionable for next year and even the rest of his career due to back problems. Judd was impressive last year and should be a shoe-in for the starting spot if he can get healed. Linebacker Randy Stella might be off the team for a while due to academic problems. Trevor Johnson moved from tight end to rush end; Phil Peetz moved from rush end to tight end; and Junior Tagoa'i moved from D-line to O-line. Quarterback Eric Crouch is sitting out due to shoulder surgery, along with utility o-lineman Jon Rutherford for knee surgery, and offensive tackle Tim Green looked questionable after today due to the strength of his knee. There are a lot of holes to fill and we're running out of good talent. This should be an interesting spring.

Saturday, March 24, 2001

Today was our first practice that had a scrimmage section. We can't actually call it a scrimmage because NCAA rules restrict us to only three scrimmages, but part of our teamwork session was full speed. This was kind of hard for a lot of reasons. For one, it was only our second day in full pads and our fourth practice of the spring, and it was hard to switch it over to full speed after walking through stuff for the whole week. Basically, I don't think I did very well.

Monday, March 26, 2001

I saw my grade for the scrimmage and was very surprised by how horrible I did. I graded out at a 1.3 out of 2, when 1.85 or higher is the level they expect us to play at. That officially makes me one of the worst linemen at Nebraska. With my physical testing scores, my strength comparison, and my on-field ability, I'm now one of the worst athletes on the entire team. I'm surprised I haven't been cut by now and I won't be surprised if I get cut after this spring. That was just plain horrible.

For the grading, you get a '2' for going to the right guy and blocking him effectively. You'll get a '1' for messing up slightly. You'll get a '0' for getting everything wrong.

Wednesday, March 28, 2001

Jon Dawson, a sophomore guard, went down with a knee injury at practice today. It appears he blew out his ACL and MCL, and will be out at least six months. It happened on a screen pass when he was running downfield, passed a receiver running his way and their knees collided. On film it didn't look like that could possibly hurt anything, but freak accidents like this happen more than we like to think.

Thursday, March 29, 2001

There is an article in the *Omaha World-Herald* sports section, front page, titled "NU Duo Eager to Fill Hole at Center Position: Garrison, Shook Battle to Follow All-American." The article details how the departure of Dominic Raiola is going to create some interesting competition for the center position, even going so far as to mention Jon Rutherford as a possibility if he can recover from knee surgery. There is even a huge picture of Coach Tenopir, Matt Shook, and me. However, the article doesn't mention a word about me. Now, the media gets all their information from the coaches. Given this fact, apparently the coaches think I'm not even a contender for the center position in my junior year. I guess the coaches are saying indirectly that I should just stop trying. I'm one step ahead of them.

Friday, March 30, 2001

Either I'm finally getting some more recognition or I'm just being used to help Shook and Garrison get a break in practice. Today I learned that I'm finally going to be working with the second team instead of being stuck with the threes. Shook and Garrison were both on the ones rotating with each other. I was the only center on the twos.

The second teamers go against the first-string defense while the number one offense goes against the two defense. This was sort of a trial by fire. Luckily, memorizing plays is a lot easier for me this year. I guess if I do it long enough, it should finally sink in. I think I did pretty well against the first-string defense. I know I made a few mistakes. Near the end of the day, I was getting pretty tired, but I made it through without a break. After practice we did some P.A.T.s and I found out that my feet were quickly becoming blistered right on the balls of my feet. The trainers said they are deep blisters that will probably cause me some discomfort for a couple of days until they surface. Fun.

Saturday, March 31, 2001

Today was the first official scrimmage of the spring. It went well, without injuries and good things happened on both sides of the ball with all groups. The number one offense went against the number one defense, and so on, and this caused a lot of good battles. It seems like the one offense really has a lot of work to do to get the group gelling a little better. That's typical. It usually takes the offense a little longer to come together than the defense just because there's so much to learn.

The highlight of my day was one of my last plays. It was a pitch reverse to the right where I go straight for the backers making them flow left, peel back to the right and wait for defenders to chase the reverse and then pick them off from the front. This play just developed perfectly, and when I got out and looked back for defenders, I saw big Patrick Kabongo. He didn't even see me and I just ran as fast as I could, lowered down to his belly level, and laid into him with all my force. The hit knocked me down before I even knew if it was effective. I immediately heard everyone on the sidelines start shouting. I looked back and saw the runner racing along the sideline heading for the end zone.

Behind me, I distinctly heard Coach Tenopir yell out my name in an excited manner. That was a first. I got up, brushed myself off and looked to the end zone where my dad was sitting in the stands and he was jumping up and down, looking very proud of my block. As I jogged over to huddle for the extra point, I noticed that my vision was kind of messed up. Everything that was white was now a bubbling yellow color. Bending over for the long snap gave me a head rush and didn't help my situation at all, but I got through it and the cobwebs eventually cleared out of my head.

I had a few more plays to run, got through those and then went to the sideline to recover when I learned that my block took out Pat and another guy behind him, and cleared the way for the touchdown. That play really made my day.

Afterward, I was pretty sore after only 21 plays, and was ready to get home and rest for the remainder of the weekend.

Monday, April 2, 2001

I graded out at a 1.9 in the scrimmage. This was the fifth-highest grade on the O-line and is my best score ever. I must have impressed Coach Tenopir because during meetings he told me I would be on the number ones for today. I switched off with Garrison, getting about a third of all the plays. It was definitely a lot harder than going against the number three defensive line, but I think I did fairly well.

Coach Young even went out of his way to tell me he thought I had a nice block in the scrimmage. Someone must have left the freezer door open in hell.

This school semester is probably going to finish out as one of my worst ones ever. Last semester, I hardly missed a single class and did really well in my classes. This semester, my classes are expendable. If I think I need more sleep to be productive in practice and lifting, I'll skip my classes and sleep until noon. It really doesn't make sense to even go to my classes when I know I'll fall asleep. It always happens—I go to class tired, stay awake for about the first half hour and then sleep at my desk through the rest of class. I never learn anything and most of the test info is straight from the book anyway. It would also be better to get more sleep so I'd have the energy to study after a long day of football. If I don't have the energy to even drag myself through practice, how am I supposed to study when I get home? Too many people have control of my life with too many conflicting demands. I wish I had control of my life.

Thursday, April 5, 2001

Former player Will Shields paid us a visit today and talked about the NFL. He laid out some facts and figures about the averages for number of years played, salaries, and other fun stuff, giving us a look at the reality of the NFL. He also talked about his own experience and how he built himself into one of the best with a relentless work ethic, unstoppable desire, and the brains to make the right decisions at the right time. I really enjoyed listening to him and he gave me a lot to think about as we finish spring ball and head into the summer workouts. I think if I focus myself like I never have before and set realistic goals, I can develop into something that will shock the coaches. Here's to the future.

Saturday, April 7, 2001

Our second major scrimmage. After last week's good showing with my 1.9 grade, I got quite a few more snaps today. On the sheet, I was scheduled for 33 snaps, 26 with the number threes and seven with the twos. The whole offense started off slowly and was surprisingly unproductive for quite a few series. The threes didn't fare too much better when we stepped on the field, but we did all right. The offense still has a lot of work to do if we ever hope to be productive in the fall. There were a few injuries—Patrick Kabongo apparently hurt his ankle, I don't know how seriously, and Tony Tata, a linebacker, apparently blew out his ACL, which will keep him out for about six months. It doesn't help our defense to lose two guys like that, especially when we are so thin for productive players as it is.

The defense actually scored first. The number one offense finally got a touchdown and then sophomore fullback Andy "Primetime" Wingender followed that up with his second score in as many weeks. The kicking game was crippled by the wind that blew unmercifully, preventing all field goals and even two extra-point attempts. The coaches even had to coordinate the various offenses and defenses today to keep some of the drives alive for certain groups. It's a little insider cheating, but it gets us some experience.

Matt Shook and I were going to trade off series at one point. On his third play, he got into a fight with a defensive lineman, Mitch Manstead, and ripped his helmet off. The refs threw him out of the scrimmage and that tossed me right back into the action. I took the final four plays and finished the day with 37 plays.

Saturday, April 14, 2001

We had the annual Spring Game today. I was on the white squad for the first half of the Spring Game, backing up Shook. For the second half, I was on the red team, backing Garrison up. I only had 17 plays the entire day and didn't really do too well because the guys around me didn't really know what they were doing and their missed assignments messed me up. I won't be surprised if I grade out fairly low. Finally, when it was all over and I knew I'd made it through the entire spring without any injuries, I was very happy. Now I can focus on being a regular student with only school to worry about.

Wednesday, April 18, 2001

This is truly the best time of the year for me. I love it. It's getting warmer, school is winding down, there are no football requirements to deal with, and my days are much more free. Although, with this freedom comes responsibility. Without football controlling my extra activities and energies, I've let those relaxing things take priority and going to class has become an expendable choice. Oh well.

Sunday, April 22, 2001

Tonight was the Student Athlete Academic Recognition Banquet. It was held at the Devaney again and tonight was a lot more interesting than last year, if only for 10 minutes. At the start of the meal, we were informed that a tornado might be coming toward us and that we should all leave the floor and move to the wrestling rooms where it is safer. I took my plate of food with me which got a lot of laughs from people around me. I guess a big man who likes food is funny.

When that plate ran out, I went back out for more and, soon after, everyone else started to come back out. Former Husker Trev Alberts was the key speaker tonight and gave a good, short speech. I received my gold medal for highest academic honors (3.75-4.0 GPA for the past year). The whole night lasted a long time, again, and then I had to return to my apartment and work on a sociology project, just like a good student should.

Thursday, May 17, 2001

For the past two weeks I've been doing nothing but relaxing and whatever I please. This is the best time of the year. School is over, there are no workouts or any football-related activity, and it's springtime. Nothing can be better. I went golfing, partied with friends most nights, and got a lot of little things done that I haven't had time for until now.

I found out that I got all Bs in my classes this semester. This really surprised me because I was sure I'd get one or two Cs. This makes the semester GPA a 3.0, which is the lowest I've ever had for a semester, but I'll take it considering my lack of effort. I really need to concentrate in school now and I can't slack off when I get home from workouts any more. I would like to get my cumulative GPA above a 3.5 before I'm done. Right now it's a 3.385.

I went to the weight room today for the first time in a month and worked out on my own. I did some hang clean and shoulder work, and was pleasantly surprised that I haven't lost too much strength.

Friday, May 18, 2001

I went to work out on my own today again at 8:00 this morning. Bailey was there and I joined the little group he was working out—former Husker and Detroit Lion's fullback Cory Schlesinger and fullback Steve Kriewald. He put us through an entire running workout with a lot of form running, stairs, and doing high knees in place for 45 seconds at a time. All of this was too much and my body had to make a sacrifice, expelling the cereal I had for breakfast. This is the first time I've ever puked from physical activity. After that was all over, I felt a lot better and finished the rest of the workout. We did a circuit workout with leg curls, leg extensions, bench, one-legged squats, and bicep curls. It all took about an hour and when it was done, I was exhausted.

2001 Summer Conditioning

Monday, May 21, 2001

Today was the first day of our summer workouts. Not everyone was there this morning; a lot of guys are home for the pre-session. I heard that Andy Gwennap quit. This means that Scott Koethe and I are the only walk-on offensive linemen left from our class. We started at 7:15 this morning in the field house with a warm-up and then went to work out. This was a lot easier than what we did last Friday and I left without feeling too tired. I'm trying this new stuff called Juven along with the regular creatine. Juven is supposed to help shorten the recovery time and so far, I believe it. I take a packet of creatine every morning before the workout and then come back and take a packet of Juven. This needs to be a very productive summer for me and I think these supplements should help.

Thursday, June 7, 2001

We started running tonight, although the strength coaches told us this is not yet the official running workout. What this means, I have no idea. Basically, this running workout is just to get us in shape for the real workout. However, with Bailey, everything is done to the extreme.

We started as a group in the Pit and did some exercises to work on our steps for blocking. Then we got together and ran through some plays for the young guys. Bailey then joined us and put us through his own workout. We did some long-stride running, side-running, and back-pedaling. We also did this thing that should have been really simple, but we kept messing it up. We all lined up in six rows, one for each position. Then Dave Volk yelled out what kind of step to take (iso, stretch, pull, or pass), which way to go, and the count. He gave a cadence, and then the guys just had to do the step and run out 10 yards. The next group would line up and then both of those groups would go and so on until they had marched their way across with about five reps.

This sounds simple, but we kept messing up the count, having guys jump offsides. We all had to do push-ups when someone messed up, but this wasn't enough. Eventually, Bailey had to put an end to it by threatening stadium steps for the next mistake. After that, only one person messed up, but that still meant we had to run stadiums. Before we did that, however, we ran in place doing high knees for about 20 seconds with the same kind of marching down the field organization.

I think some of the guys don't really appreciate the effort that Bailey expects from us. A lot of guys whine about all the hard work, and I'll admit I do the same at times, but I know it's for the best. I hope the rest of the guys realize that Bailey knows more about working out than all of us combined many times over. With his leadership, we can be the best prepared O-line in the country.

We have two freshmen in for the summer right now—Nate Manley and Carson Schott. Both of them have been a source of laughter for all of us, as I'm sure I was as a freshman. Carson fell backward, losing his balance on the snatch squats and losing control of the weight in the process. It wasn't a very graceful move, especially for a big guy, and everyone around had a good laugh at his expense.

We only have two scholarship guys coming in and not very many walk-ons. This isn't good news for the younger guys hoping to move up to the main squad for practice instead of being on scout team again. As for me, we will have to wait and see. I don't know if we brought in any centers and if we didn't, then I could be on scout team one more year. I really hope this is not the case; four years on the scout team will not be a fun thing to look back on.

Friday, June 22, 2001

This morning's workout was one of the hardest ever. Bailey put us through a workout of his own creation. We put on weighted vests of 40 pounds or more and then walking lunged from the sideline out to midfield. There, we did 25 squats, and then walking lunged the rest of the way across. We then did 15 more squats before lunging our way back across the entire field. At this point, my legs were aching and my butt felt like it had sand grinding away between all the muscle fibers. Then, just for fun, we side-lunged out to midfield and back.

After this was over, I was going to go inside and loosen up my back on the bike when Dave Volk, Nick Povendo, and Tim Green invited me to do some stadiums with them. How could I refuse that fun?! So, we put the vests back on and walked two South Stadiums.

Monday, June 25, 2001

I've been trying to find part-time work in Lincoln on my own for the past month without any luck. I really didn't try too hard, but every place I went said the same thing: my hours of availability aren't what they were looking for. I can only work from 1:00-4:00 most days or at night after the running workout. Mornings are taken up by lifting and class.

Finally, I threw away my pride and talked to Coach Turner Gill, who only had to make one phone call to get me a job. I say that I threw away my pride because this job, like most of the other jobs they find for athletes, is the business basically doing a favor for the athletic department. Most of the jobs are really easy and pay pretty well. I don't like people doing favors for me just because I'm a football player. But, in the end, when no other choice was available, I used the power that was in front of me. I'm now working at Harris Data Storage, which is owned and operated by Neil Harris, a former Husker football player. From the sound of it, he's really thankful for all the doors that playing for the Huskers opened for him and he's giving back to the program by hiring some of the guys. I really don't know what I'll be doing; I only did about a solid half hour of work for the three hours I was there, but I'm making $8 an hour. Tackle Kyle Kollmorgen and tight end Kyle Ringenberg both work there as well. Kollmorgen said this is the easiest job I will ever have in my life.

Up until now I've been spending my afternoons either napping, getting stuff done around the apartment, doing homework, or going swimming with my neighbor. He and I have figured out that wasting an afternoon by the pool can be done very inexpensively if you just sneak into the pool of one of the many apartment complexes in town. This way, we avoid paying to get in a public pool, the noisy kids, and the crowds. All you have to do is find a complex that doesn't have a locked gate around the pool, or else wait by the gate for someone who lives there to let you in. Either way, it's a free day in the sun by the pool. Nothing is better in the summer.

On a sour note, two of our guys have recently been in

the paper for doing bad things to their girlfriends. Thunder Collins was arrested for supposedly beating his girlfriend in the Campus Recreation Center. I don't know the full story, but from what I've been told, he bounced a basketball off her head when they were arguing. Josh Brown is the other player to be arrested this summer, this time for beating up his ex-girlfriend's new boyfriend. Apparently he was drunk one night and decided to pay his ex a visit. I was told he was trying to get back together with her, but her new man stepped in and Josh beat the crap out of him. He was arrested a short time later and the next day it was all over the news. Needless to say, the coaches weren't too happy. Coach Solich called a meeting before running one night and told us that the next person to screw up will face severe consequences. So, I guess our quota for the summer has been filled—no more than two girls can be beaten by any of our players.

Thursday, June 28, 2001

I think today was the beginning of something very bad for the O-line, maybe even the whole team. Tuesday, during our passing league work, Jack Limbaugh left to do some long snaps to Kyle Larson. He told me he was going over there, which makes sense because I was in his huddle for the passing league. The problem was that he didn't tell Volk or any of the other seniors what he was doing and they all were mad that he left passing league to go snap without telling them. Because of this lack of communication, they told him he had to run three stairs since they thought he was skipping out.

After running tonight, Toniu, Jake Andersen, Dave Volk, and a couple of others were screaming their heads off at Jack to run his stairs. Jack tried to explain the situation, but in the end, he had to run the stairs and a spike was driven deeper in the unity of the offensive line.

There seems to be a lot of division across the entire team. This has started in the past couple of months and I'm worried about the future of our program if this trend continues. There is a definite lack of leadership on the team. No one has emerged to lead the team in a positive way. There are the obvious choices like Eric Crouch and Tracey Wistrom, but everyone else seems very complacent. I think this traces back to the Peter brothers and Grant Wistrom era. They were amazing figures on the '97 team and before, but their leadership style was intimidation and domination. Everybody was scared of them and no one ever got in their way, as some of the seniors now still talk about them. When they left, it seemed like everyone was more relaxed and relieved to have guys like them gone. They didn't really train a protégé, so their influence stopped when they left.

Since then, divisions have developed. I think the divisions on the O-line started in my freshman year. We worked out that winter by ourselves in the morning, the first group to set an official workout time. That was a good idea to build camaraderie, but we soon grew separate from the rest of the team. We only thought about us, and this selfish mentality has finally boiled down to individuals. The O-line is now divided into many little overlapping groups. Where there once was one single group that pushed each other to be the best we could be, these little groups are now competing with each other. Even worse, some of the young guys have a very selfish attitude, trying to improve themselves while criticizing others who are struggling instead of helping them out. They figure they will do better on the depth chart with less competition. I hate that. I know I'm not going to be an All-American and I might not even ever start a game, but I will push everyone around me to be the best because I'm part of a team and the team needs the best people to step forward, not the people who got there through the downfall of others.

I don't think the coaches are helping either. Coaches Tenopir, Young, and Darlington are all near the end of their careers. Their departures will take away a cornerstone of this program—nearly 70 years of experience is between those three. Coach Solich really could do a lot of good if he dropped his diplomatic, limited liability, adoptive father figure role. He should give it to us straight instead of dancing around issues with vague references. He should say, "Josh and Thunder did some bad things and now we are all going to go out and watch them run stairs until they puke." He could change the mentality of the team, but I don't think he's aware of it. I have no idea what he does all day, but I would bet a lot of his time is spent in meetings talking about how football could bring in more money, better recruits, better sponsors, higher paying donors, and better equipment. I wonder what his reaction would be if he saw what was actually happening within the team.

Friday, June 29, 2001

Coach Tenopir had his annual summer cookout at his house tonight. He always has great food, but this was the best yet. He had two big trays full of slabs of ribs, each slab the kind you would pay $10 for in a restaurant. I had three slabs and was full, along with some potato salad, macaroni salad, beans, and corn. As always, there was a giant cooler full of Bud Light and Busch Light. I didn't stay very long because I had to go to Omaha, so I thanked Coach and went on my way.

When I got to my house in Omaha, I discovered one very good benefit of being 300 pounds. My neighbors, who are watching the house while my parents are in Europe, locked the door between the garage and the house.

Before going out with a group of friends, I put a note on my neighbor's house asking them to unlock the door if they returned. When we got back and my neighbors hadn't returned, I threw my shoulder into the door twice and it opened rather easily. The door frame was shattered and pieces of wood were everywhere. I've always wanted to break a door down like cops do on TV, and I must admit it was pretty cool.

Monday, July 9, 2001

Today was the start of the three weeks Bailey said would be like boot camp. The morning lifting wasn't anything new, just the same lifts with slightly different weights. The afternoon running was the thing Bailey was talking about. Not only did we do our whole base program of jump ropes, low ropes and bag drills, but we also did stairs, high knees, and 10-yard plays. He said if we messed up the plays, we would have five stairs for every mess-up. It didn't take long to get to 15 stairs. Luckily for the rest of us, Wes Cody started having back spasms near the end of our drill, forcing Bailey to focus on him and forget about the stairs.

Bailey is pushing us to be as good as we can by working us harder than we ever have. This is great, but he's relying on threats of stairs to get performance out of us. This has hurt him because his threats are unrealistic. None of us could do 15 stairs after a full workout. I doubt it's even possible. One time, after we were done with our running and tallied up about five stairs as punishment, we just ran two half gassers as hard as we could instead. We were all thankful for his change of heart, but his respect across the O-line took a hit because of it. He would do better to make us run two stairs as fast as we could, but he knows what to do much better than I do, so I shouldn't criticize.

Monday, July 16, 2001

To celebrate my 22nd birthday today, I got up at 6:45 to lift. Then I went to work for five hours, and went to afternoon running. Happy Birthday to me.

I heard Coach Solich told Bailey to back off on us because so many guys have had back problems recently. Bailey took the order and the weeks of boot camp have changed to give us time to heal. We're doing less running and backing off on its intensity. The goal for this week, according to Bailey, is to get through it without any more back problems. We're even backing off on lifting. I thought what we were doing was great and I had no problem with any of it, but some of the guys just couldn't handle it.

Also in the news this week was the retirement of Dave Ellis, our director of nutrition. Apparently he has been hinting at quitting for the past four years because he was making more money contracting out with pro teams than he was here. I guess he finally had enough and wanted to focus on the pro teams full time. Well, whatever makes him happy. Good luck, Dave.

Thursday, July 19, 2001

The tradition of hazing the freshmen is alive and well. Two scholarship guys—Richie Incognito and Gary Pike—have joined Carson Schott and Nate "Nate Dog" Manley, who are walk-ons. So far, they're all doing pretty well keeping up with us. They can't officially do the afternoon running program because of new NCAA rules, but they do it on their own, alongside us, just not directly with us. Whoever made this rule is an idiot. Sometimes the NCAA makes rules with no logical sense.

Tonight, instead of doing our typical passing league stuff in the pit, we sat around while the freshmen went one-on-one against each other in a receiver-defensive back matchup. They all must have run about 20 routes each. Dave Volk was the QB and made them run long on every one. One time, Nate Kolterman was the QB and sent them downfield. Before he even went 5 yards, he threw a bullet at Nate Dog, hitting him square in the back of the head and all of us just laughed for a couple minutes. Another time, Carson was chasing down a long pass, but it was a bit too far for him and he tripped over his feet and crashed into the hitting net for the baseball team. Pike and Incognito didn't have any embarrassing moments but we pushed them as far as they would go. They both seem like pretty good athletes and very competitive.

2001 Fall Camp

Friday, August 3, 2001

The summer wrapped up nicely with a nice trip out to New York to see Stacy, my sister-in-law. I also had a chance to see Jim Tansey down in New Jersey. He is still very supportive and remains a good influence on me. He wants me to succeed and so do I.

Today was mostly just a meeting day. We listened to the same old stuff about new rules and regulations, what not to do in certain situations, how to make yourself and the team look good when we're in public—that kind of stuff. Then we had forms to fill out and all the legal stuff to settle. We learned that Josh Brown will be held out of two-a-days and also will miss the first game until his court case for assault is settled. Randy Stella finally got in trouble one too many times and is officially cut from the team. Coach Solich wouldn't say specifically to the entire team what the reasons were, but word spreads fast amongst teammates and friends and the reason didn't surprise anyone.

Team psychologist Jack Stark presented his ideas for our theme this year. The one he proposed was "Relentless Men of Honor." I disliked it immediately. He showed some clips from the movie *Men of Honor* with Cuba Gooding,

Jr., just to try to drive the point home. It still didn't work. Linebacker Jamie Burrow said he liked the meaning of it, but didn't like using a movie title for our theme. Someone then proposed "Relentless With Honor." This is only slightly better than the original theme, and it still makes me cringe. I think someone should just sit down with a thesaurus and make one up. All the good ideas are quickly becoming old and tired.

We received our first bit of money for the camp at dinner tonight. I think by the end of camp we should have about $511. The scholarship guys get much less, but they can't really complain.

Saturday, August 4, 2001

Just as I expected, today was a long first day. We started at 7:30 this morning with meetings. We received a new gray T-shirt and a pair of black mesh shorts. We're also given new shoes, which haven't been rated very highly by most of the guys.

We introduced some of the most basic plays to the younger guys. Practice started at 9:00 and it was warm without a breeze in the stadium. The health and safety of the players in this heat is a main concern of the coaches and the staff right now. There have been a string of heat-related deaths across the country, most notably Korey Stringer of the Minnesota Vikings. It's very scary to think that practicing this sport and trying to stick it out through the pain and the heat can be so dangerous.

As a precaution, we're required to weigh in before and after every practice and write it on a big chart in the locker room. This is to record how much weight we lose during practice. Since nobody can lose even one pound of fat or muscle in two hours, all the weight lost is water and must be replaced. The Gatorade company is making out like a bandit because of this—for every pound we lose, we're told to drink one bottle of Gatorade. It's provided free all day long on carts near the meeting rooms and outside the locker room. So far, I weighed in at 304 and lost about three pounds at both practices today.

The morning was fairly easy. We're only in sweats and helmets because NCAA rules don't allow pads on the first day. This made it easier because there wasn't a lot of knocking around. I was on the third team and switched off with Richie Incognito. Richie also is a long snapper and is pretty good at it. He will probably take my spot as back-up long snapper. I just don't have the speed and quickness that this level demands. This morning went about two hours and then we had lunch. The next hour or so was free and then we were back in meetings until practice at 3:00. This practice was a little tougher, mostly because it was 100 degrees outside. I was moved up to the twos and switched off with Matt Shook. I'm feeling really good out there on the field—I have more quickness and strength than I've ever had before. We had one and a half gassers at the end and they were incredibly easy for me. Then, as if two meetings today weren't enough, we had a third meeting tonight at 6:00. In the meeting, we went over the afternoon practice film and then went to dinner.

Sunday, August 5, 2001

Today was the first day in shoulder pads. We started at 7:30 this morning, which is ridiculously early for a Sunday, but the days of the week have no meaning during fall camp. You just try to get through to the next day. This practice went really well for me. I have a lot of energy, I feel like I have a lot more strength and quickness, and I'm doing better against the defense. Because of this, and running with the twos which go against the number one defense, my confidence is really high.

I've started taking a supplement that is a thermogenic metabolizer. I checked it out with a nutrition person and she told me this stuff would show up on a drug test because it has ephedra, a metabolizing agent. It's giving me a lot of energy. The only problem is that it has been linked to heart problems in young athletes. I think I'll try to find an over-the-counter drug with ephedra and if I get caught claim that I was taking that instead. Otherwise, there's this drink that claims to clean your system out and pass drug tests. This is probably a stupid thing to do, but it will help me get ahead. Also, it gives me a little more energy, which will help me stay awake in classes and meetings, and get my homework done at night. So, now if I die from a heart attack on the field, everyone will know why.

After practice, we were free to go to church or do whatever we wanted. I grabbed the bag of food they had for us, went home and took an hour nap. We had to be back at 1:30 for another session of meetings and then we were free the rest of the day.

> I know what you're thinking. Pretty stupid, huh? Even with all the problems that ephedra and similar chemicals were proving to have, especially on young football players, I was not deterred. And I wasn't alone.
>
> Desire will get you so far, talent can take you a long way, but if you still come up short and you need to get there quick, there's always an answer. It's usually not the best answer, but when the pressure is on to perform because your position on the team and possibly your future in the sport depend on it, you'll do anything. It's sad, but that's why we have to drug test. That's why so many guys push themselves to the limit every day just to prove that

they can be something better than the sum of their parts. At this level, it's no longer a game, it's a war. Those with the biggest weapons survive.

I believe that the tests need to become more difficult to fake, need to be taken more often by more players, and the players should face public humiliation for their actions. Too many guys get passed off for "breaking team rules" and their penalties do not show the other players on the team the seriousness of their actions.

Monday, August 6, 2001

Today is the first weekday of two-a-days. The weekdays start with getting to the stadium around 6:30 in the morning, getting some fruit and supplements, then getting taped, suited up and on the field by 7:30. The morning practices are in the stadium and go for about two hours. The O-line is in the Pit with Coach Tenopir and Coach Young reviewing plays and working on technique. Then we go up to the field, do two stations for option drill and full-team skeleton, which is pretty much live blocking and pass rushes and doing mostly pass plays. Then we punt, take a break, and we're right back into stations for teamwork. We do three stations for teamwork, and then we're done. The three stations consist of pass, run and mixed.

After practice we shower and eat lunch, and relax from about 11:00 to 1:00. The second set of meetings starts at 1:30 and goes until about 3:00. The afternoon practice starts soon after and goes for about 1 hour and 45 minutes. This practice is always on the grass, I guess because it's cooler with a breeze. This practice is similar to the morning, except there's no punt, no option drill, or full-team skeleton. After practice we shower and take a little time to relax, then another set of meetings starts at 6:00. These are supposed to go until 7:30, but Coach Tenopir usually lets us out early so we can get first picks at dinner. I get home by 8:30, rest, and get ready for the next day.

They're doing a bunch of remodeling all around the stadium right now. They redid our locker room and put in new carpet and painted the walls. The carpet really needed to be cleaned or replaced, so I'm glad they did that. This new one is red and in the middle of the floor is a big red *N* outlined in black. They also replaced all the showerheads finally. However, the new ones they put in really suck. After the morning practice, everyone is covered with the little black pieces of rubber that make up the FieldTurf. The water pressure isn't even enough to blast those off of us.

Tuesday, August 7, 2001

Today I took my first try at doing long snaps in practice. Until now, freshman Richie Incognito has taken all of them for our group. I finally got in there and did pretty well. Actually, for the first time in a long time, not only did Coach Young not yell at me, but he actually gave me a compliment. Just a little thing like a compliment helps out so much sometimes.

This afternoon's practice was all special teams. The guys not on a special team, like most of the linemen, did groupwork. We mostly talked through the plays, but Coach asked questions and called on people for the answer. Some of us have a lot to learn about our system—most of the guys were lost about the plays. Coach Tenopir stresses that we should have a clue about what everyone on the line does for each play so we'll know how to react in case the defense does something unexpected.

Wednesday, August 8, 2001

This morning was the first day of full pads. It took a little adjusting for most guys to get used to their pants, especially since everyone's legs are so tired. It was a typical practice and everyone is moving around well, but obviously tired.

We had a lighthearted start to the afternoon meeting with a few jokes by Coach Solich. The people on kickoff and kickoff return were watching film and Coach had them play back one of the kicks for everyone to see. On it, Coach Young was in the middle of the field looking back at the returners. He didn't see the guys running downfield after the ball carrier, and one of them got blocked right into his back, knocking him over. They must have replayed that scene five times and everyone in the whole auditorium was laughing.

Then Coach Solich started talking about how everyone was doing a good job hustling during practice and doing what they're supposed to. Right then, on the video screen behind him, was a picture of the two kickers, Kyle Larson and Sandro DeAngelis, sitting on water coolers doing nothing. Coach continued saying that nobody is just sitting around or being lazy and that everyone is doing all they can to be the best. Once again, everyone was cracking up and we had a good laugh at the kickers' expense.

At this afternoon's practice my legs were feeling really dead. I thought the defense would be feeling the same way, but they were playing their hearts out and really moving well.

Thursday, August 9, 2001

This morning was in full pads on the field again. Everyone is really tired and mistakes are happening more frequently. It has gotten a little cooler, but it's still hot, even in the morning. I'm running on the second group with Richie, doing three out of every five plays. This gives me a little break, but it still wears on me.

We got the new press guides and highlight videos today. They finally have my picture and bio in the guide, but they messed up a little bit. It says I only played in the Alamo Bowl last year when I actually played in the Baylor and Kansas games as well. Also, they misspelled my parents' name. Oh well, at least they got the right picture and spelled my name right.

Friday, August 10, 2001

This morning's practice was in full pads on the field again. We're still doing the two groups for offense, which gives a better rotation for most of the guys, but wears me out. I'm still going three out of every five with Richie Incognito and I'm really hurting. My whole upper body is sore. Both my elbows were banged up in last night's practice and they're still swollen. My left hand got stepped on by a cleat today and skinned the inside of my pointer finger. My shoulders are tired and have no punch in them.

Tonight's practice will just be a special teams practice, which will be a nice break. Tomorrow is a scrimmage, and Sunday is off. I can't wait to do nothing for an entire day.

Saturday, August 11, 2001

The scrimmage today started at noon and went for about 120 plays. The offense put on a pretty good show, scoring on the first two possessions. The defense had a slow start, but a couple of their main guys are on the disabled list. Overall, the offense looks very strong, especially on the O-line.

The running backs put on a good show also. Most of them are young and untested, so they're hungry to show their stuff. Steve Kriewald, DeAntae Grixby, Dahrran Diedrick, and Jammal Lord were only a few of the guys who shone today.

The younger guys struggled a little bit, but the two freshmen quarterbacks, Mike McLaughlin and Mike Stuntz, really put on a good show. Both have excellent speed and great vision on the field. They made big plays today and I see big things in their futures. It's going to be hard for one of them since only one will start at QB. They've also been running receiver routes in practice, so we'll see what becomes of them in the future. Eric Crouch put on a dominating show, as expected, and also had a great day throwing the ball, putting to rest some of the doubts that have plagued his career.

I did pretty well, I thought. The offense is making a lot more sense to me now and I'm getting more comfortable at center. I had about 25 plays and by the end I was feeling pretty good. Mike Stuntz is having trouble taking some of our snaps and there were about four plays where the ball slipped out from the center-quarterback exchange.

My first play was when Coach Solich threw Matt Shook out of the scrimmage for fighting. He wasn't really fighting though, he just pushed one defensive guy who was fighting with one of the offense guys. When Coach threw him out, he sort of smiled, looked at Coach and said, "Are you serious? I'm thrown out?" That sealed it and then I was in running center. Shook only missed one play, but this has been a recurring theme. I think Coach has thrown him out of the past three scrimmages.

Monday, August 13, 2001

Yesterday was our first day off since two-a-days started and it went by way too fast. Everyone was really dragging today, especially me. I just couldn't get my body or mind ready for this morning's practice. The afternoon practice was a little better, but not by much. I also caught a cold, which doesn't help the situation.

Coach Tenopir likes to play mind games with the linemen, especially the younger guys. For example, say there's a play where the guard pulls for the playside linebacker. Coach will ask about a similar play, and if the guard says he has the playside backer, but hesitates with his response, Coach Tenopir looks at him questioningly and asks, "Do you?" The inexperienced young guy, if he doesn't know the playbook well, questions his own answer, but if he knows the play and answers "yes," Coach Tenopir moves on to the next play. He does this a lot, so we really have to know what we are doing on all of the plays.

Wednesday, August 15, 2001

It was raining this morning. Plus, I was more sick than I've been in over a year. I could still function pretty well physically, but my head felt like it was 10 pounds heavier than usual. The weather has gotten a lot cooler since the start of fall camp and I think the change affected a lot of guys. It's also allergy season, so a lot of guys are as sick and congested as I am.

This afternoon's practice was supposed to be a special teams practice and also was supposed to be the last day of two-a-days. In their infinite wisdom, the coaches changed this at the last minute. Instead, this afternoon was still in sweats. And, instead of having only one practice tomorrow like everyone was dreaming about, we're going to do this all over again and have two. Oh well, one more day.

In the team meeting tonight Coach Solich talked about how it's necessary to maintain our strength during the season. He told us to be sure to get into the weight room. He added that even the staff takes care of their physiques, prompting a picture of Coach Darlington with his shirt off displayed on the screen behind him. Everyone started cracking up, even coach Solich. He is one of the oldest coaches and his appearance would not be characterized as "trim." He isn't obese, but many years of low-intensity workouts do not leave the skin very tight.

Thursday, August 16, 2001

Today was full of surprises. It started this morning when I was in the training room waiting to get taped for our full-pads practice. The coaches sent a message that we would be going in half pads, which is late to make a change like that. Eric Crouch delivered the message and no one believed him. The trainers said: "Sure thing, Eric. You don't need to try so hard to get voted captain."

Switching from full to half pads doesn't really make much difference, everyone still goes pretty hard during practice, but I think everyone is more comfortable overall when we're in half pads.

The other surprise came during the morning practice when I heard a rumor that the afternoon practice had been cancelled. I was immediately much happier, but skeptical. At the end of practice, Coach Solich confirmed it and you could see the approval on everyone's face. We just had to return at 3:30 for meetings and that was it for the day. It was very nice.

Friday, August 17, 2001

Another day of surprises. Only this time, one was good, the other was disappointing. Our second scrimmage was today, but it was very different from last Saturday. Aside from the fact that only 89 of the 105 original guys were healthy enough to participate, we had to run scout offense and defense against the top two units. And, just like always, I was on the scout team offense. This was very disappointing. I didn't run a single one of our own plays during the entire scrimmage; I just had to look at the card and run the TCU offense. The TCU blocking schemes are ridiculous, especially against our defense. For example, I'm supposed to scoop with the backside guard around a backside shaded nose and try to get the middle linebacker on an outside play. If our defense doesn't just destroy them, I will be very surprised.

The good news came at the end of the scrimmage when we found out that the afternoon practice was cancelled again. This meant the rest of the day was wide open, and I loved it.

Saturday, August 18, 2001

Apparently I had a little too much fun last night at a local house party. I got home at about 6:00 this morning and went to bed, dreading the thought of meetings and practice in just a few hours. Meetings were scheduled for 8:30, and practice started at 10:00.

I woke up at 10:00.

I raced to the stadium, got dressed and out on the field, and luckily only missed a couple minutes of practice. Coaches Tenopir and Young and the rest of the O-line, who obviously noticed my absence at meetings this morning, were surprised to see me and asked what went wrong. I told them I forgot to set my alarm, which actually was true, but didn't give any more information. I didn't really have to. The coaches have been doing this long enough that they don't even need to ask when something like this happens. They just know. I wasn't alone in my condition. A couple of other linemen were actually still drunk from the night before and one of the guys reeked of tequila. Luckily for us, the practice was in sweats and we didn't do a whole lot.

After our half-hour teamwork station where I was once again on scout team, the linemen retired to the benches to watch the kicking practice and relax. A grasshopper was hopping around and became the center of attention as it was thrown on unsuspecting people to freak them out. One time it got away, but not far enough from the grasp of Jon Dawson. Tim Green told Dawson he would pay him to eat it. Everyone else chimed in and said they would pay him five bucks a piece if he ate it. Jon didn't have to think about it too long. He bit off the head first and chewed it loudly, which caused Shook and Koethe to gag and almost throw up. He continued eating it until the whole thing was in his mouth. He just sat there chewing it for the longest time, occasionally sticking his gut-coated tongue out at people who didn't believe him.

After practice, they had pizzas for us at the Hewit Center. There must have been 150 pizzas stacked on the tables and everybody got their own box. At 1:00 everyone was back out on the field for Fan Day and for the next hour and a half I signed my name so many times that my hand was sore.

Captains were chosen today. They are Eric Crouch, Tracey Wistrom, Dave Volk, Jeremy Slechta, and Keyuo Craver.

Sunday, August 19, 2001

I went in for treatment on my hand today. Something is wrong with my right thumb—it gets really sore during the season and it's hard to grip the ball. Sometimes when it gets hit in practice I can barely stand the pain. They x-rayed today at the stadium and the initial diagnosis is that nothing is broken, which I already knew. This has been a constant injury, occurring every season going back to high school. It's probably tendonitis or something like that, but I have to see another doctor tomorrow night.

Monday, August 20, 2001

I knew I wasn't going to get away free from missing meetings on Saturday. I had to run three stadiums after practice, and after that we just did one and a half gassers. I did two and called it even; my legs were about to fall off.

A few more guys got in trouble this weekend. Linebacker Tony Tata and I-back Dahrran Diedrick were downtown Saturday night. Around closing time they were standing outside of one of the bars where a large group of people usually gather. The police came through and asked the crowd to disperse since this has been the scene of many fights. When the cops came through again, apparently some profanity was used and Tony was arrested. Dahrran, who was not drinking, argued about the arrest and the cops arrested him as well. They were ticketed for disturbing the peace and failure to disperse. The media immediately got hold of this and it made the front page. This is a really minor ticket and the coaches don't know what the punishment will be. During meetings today we made the coaches leave and the captains talked about what will probably happen and how we should deal with it. Nothing really was dealt with officially; basically a bunch of people spoke their mind on the issue and we ended up right back where we started since no consensus could be reached.

Practice today was rough. Mondays usually are, but today was just painful for me. I had no energy and also my hand hurt so badly that I was snapping with my left hand, which caused some bad snaps and limited my blocking ability. This is supposedly the last day in full pads until the game.

Tuesday, August 21, 2001

Today's practice was a little better. I got to the training room at 7:00 to get a brace made for my hand. This took a long time because they had to try a couple of different things before they got it right. Eventually they got my whole right thumb immobilized. This caused some difficulty blocking, but provided good protection from getting it hurt like usual.

Since our first game is a kickoff classic and not just a

regular season football game, we can receive special gifts for participating in it, kind of like a bowl game. We voted that we would like video cameras, which we received after practice today. They are pretty nice, but nothing spectacular since they could only spend $300 per player. They're Panasonic Palcorders with some nice features and should come in very handy later on.

Thursday, August 23, 2001

Rank has it's privileges. Upperclassmen are privy to a lot of information and I'm enjoying it.

Richie Incognito was caught breaking team rules recently. The details are a big secret and are not being discussed, even on the team, but a few of us on the O-line know. As punishment, he had to run five stairs at the end of practice today. The coaches will be monitoring him closely over the next couple months to make sure this doesn't happen again, but for now it's certain that he won't play in the first game. This makes me the second-string long snapper once again. Garrison wants me to take over the first-string position, but that decision is up to Coach Young.

We received some more free clothes after practice. We were given our team T-shirt with the "Relentless with Honor" motto on it, and we also picked up our warm-up/travel outfits along with a new pair of shoes.

I finally was able to see the doctor about my thumb. He gave it a shot of cortisone. It was really sore and swollen for a couple of hours afterward. I hope this works.

Friday, August 24, 2001

The cortisone must have helped because I finally was able to snap today without a lot of pain. It's still tender, but the majority of the pain is gone. Today's practice was a typical Friday and only lasted about a half hour. After practice

I got more treatment and went to dinner.

The rest of the team showed up today for their physicals and paperwork. A lot of the guys are pissed off that they won't be able to suit up and play in the game like they were told a while back. Apparently the NCAA considers a game like this to be like a bowl game, so only the players who have been part of the team for this camp are able to play. They're still going to suit up about five seniors who weren't part of the two-a-days.

On the other hand, some guys not suiting up saw this as a perfect opportunity to party the night before a game. I'm not staying at the Nebraska Center tonight, so will be free to do whatever I want. I'll most likely go to bed early since I have a pretty good chance of playing tomorrow.

2001 Season

Saturday, August 25, 2001

Nebraska 21 – Texas Christian University 7

This was a slow, unexciting game from the first snap. Our offense had no power all day long, but luckily we had enough good athletes, such as Eric Crouch, that we were able to get the score up a little bit.

Since this game was played before the official start of school, we weren't able to have the full team for practice, just the 105 from the fall camp. This meant that we didn't have the numbers to have a really effective scout team for the offense to go against. Because of this, we got caught with our pants down on many plays. In fact, there were 15 plays where we were stopped behind the line of scrimmage. Coach Solich said that's the highest number of negative yardage plays he's ever seen from us. Most of the time it was just a simple missed assignment by one of the blockers, but other times we simply ran the wrong play into their defensive set up. A couple times their guys just were too quick over the line of scrimmage and we couldn't get a finger on them before they tackled the ball carrier.

On the other hand, the defense put on a great show, giving up only six first downs the entire game. Kyle Larson debuted at punter and had a great day, averaging 48.6 yards for eight punts. Sandro DeAngelis was the place-kicker since Josh Brown was held out for disciplinary reasons. He made the first extra-point kick, the second one had a bad snap and didn't get to kick it and then on our final touchdown we went for two points and got it. This should have been an indication for Coach Young to put me in for PAT snaps since Garrison is the starting center and will probably get tired while he's on the field. But, once again, I didn't get in for a single play.

Saturday, September 1, 2001

Nebraska 42 – Troy State 14

Once again, it wasn't pretty, but we got it done. And, once again, the defense did a hell of a job. There were plenty of highlights on the defensive side of the ball, but not too many from the offensive side. We were stopped many times within the 10-yard line, even going for it on fourth down and not getting it. We just couldn't finish the job. Before the game, Coach Young told me he would probably put me in for the extra-point snaps. In the second quarter, he told me I would have the rest of the extra-point snaps. We then made it into the red zone where our drive ended. One chance lost. In the second half, the same thing happened two more times. So, I guess I can say that I almost played, but almost doesn't count in this game.

Coach Tenopir was very disappointed in the week leading up to this game,. The first-string line performed poorly in the last game and this week of practice didn't show any vast improvement. The second-string guys, which I'm now officially part of, have been doing very poorly, but we've been consistent. Every day someone gets yelled at for some stupid mistake and it seems that Coach Tenopir loses more faith in us as each day. I'm not sure what the main problem is, but

I have a few ideas. I think we need to go back to square one and start with the basic terminology of the offense and also the basic techniques of our assignments. As I see it, on both the practice field and the game field, we're missing some of those key components which basic technique work would teach us. We have guys who know what they're doing, where to go, and who to block, but they're not doing it as well as they should.

We received $15 after the game.

Tuesday, September 4, 2001

I had an interview with our radio announcer, Warren Swain, after practice today. He asked me beforehand if I had any interesting hobbies or things about me that we could talk about. I mentioned that about every two years or so, my dad and brother and I go to Canada for a fishing and canoeing trip. He started the interview asking what he would experience if he were to join us on our next trip. I told him the basics of what we would do and what he would see. He asked if there have been any harrowing experiences and I mentioned the time when I was about half the size I am now and fell on one of the portages and couldn't get up because the backpack was so heavy, even though it was the lightest one we had. He said later it was a really fun interview and I think it went pretty well. I have no idea when it will air.

Friday, September 7, 2001

Lt. Shane Osborn, the pilot of the spy plane that was recently shot down over China and a native Nebraskan and alumnus of this university, came to practice today and gave us a short speech afterward. He talked about how we should do as much as we can to prepare ourselves for our future right now. It was a short speech, but it was very good. He will do the coin toss at the game tomorrow.

Saturday, September 8, 2001

Nebraska 27 – Notre Dame 10

This was a beautiful game. We came out strong and showed what we can do. We scored 17 points in the first quarter and capitalized on many of their mistakes. It didn't take long for the offense to set a rhythm. After that, it was all over. It was 27-3 at halftime.

The coaches decided to play ultraconservative football in the second half to try to keep us from giving the ball away. This worked well in the turnover department, but left the offense disheartened because they really weren't trying to score, they just wanted to gain possession and waste time. Apparently, it worked.

Again, the defense played their hearts out, holding the Irish to just 162 yards total offense. Our defense is really looking good this year and I think they will be unstoppable all year long.

Before the game Coach Ron Brown told us we have been in a situation like this before (in 1997) when we didn't play too well in our first two games and then in the third game we blew up Washington and made a name for ourselves. He said a lot of people doubt us right now and that we have our back to the wall. I thought of the image of a wild animal that's cornered. The animal will get crazy and fight with every bit of strength in its body to get out of that corner. I think we did just that tonight. I heard that 67% of our fans thought we would lose this game. A lot of people had lost faith in us, but I think we got it all back now, and then some.

ESPN's *Gameday* crew was in town today and did a live show from Memorial Stadium. Our fans set a new *Gameday* record for attendance when as many as 16,000 people flooded in for the free show. It was taped so early that I was able to be in the stands for this. Commentator Lee Corso ended up wearing a big red foam cowboy hat that was parachuted in by Army paratroopers, his trademark way of showing how he was going with Nebraska to win the game.

We received $15 after the game.

Tuesday, September 11, 2001

This was a day that will always be remembered. I woke up this morning to frantic phone calls and then my roommate tells me that the World Trade Center buildings in New York have been hit by planes and collapsed. We watched it on TV before I had to run to class and it was amazingly surreal. I stared at the television in disbelief. They showed footage of a large commercial jet slamming into those great buildings like a missile and exploding in a ball of flame with people in lower Manhattan running for their lives. My parents were quick to call and report that my brother Jason and his wife Stacy, who live in New York, were safe. There were reports of other planes hitting the Pentagon and a car bomb somewhere in D.C. I wanted to watch this unfold, but I had to go to class.

As the day went on, televisions everywhere and on every channel were tuned into the events in New York and D.C. I was not only amazed by the events themselves, but by the reaction of those around me. Some people were laughing at footage of a person running through the street in terror. The scene of the plane diving into the building brought ooo's and aaah's as if it were some Hollywood movie. I fear that we as a nation have been too complacent. There is no great unifying event, especially for people my age and younger. For us, World War II is old history and the Korean and Vietnam wars are footnotes that we've only glanced over. After the Persian Gulf War we had so much faith in our country's safety and dominance in the world (especially with the Cold War having ended) that we just went about our merry lives with no worry about our safety and security. That changed today. We are vulnerable. We have enemies. These enemies have shown that they're capable of the most despicable acts of violence and can attack without remorse.

If there is a war, I'm enlisting.

In football news, apparently I had a pretty bad week last week and have been moved back to the scout team while Richie Incognito moved up to the twos. I also heard that his parents are in town, so that might be the reason he moved up. So, basically, this is the fourth consecutive year that I've had to do some scout team duty and I'm not happy about it at all.

A national tragedy isn't even enough to make us stop practicing. As practice went on, I got more and more mad and on the last play I punched d-lineman Manaia Brown in the facemask while we were in a pushing match after a play was over. Luckily, none of the coaches saw it or his hit in retaliation, so we didn't have to run for it.

While we were sitting on the benches watching the kick-off practice, I heard that Matt Shook hurt his knee. I don't know exactly what he did, but they said it sounded bad. Then, right in front of us on a kickoff return, Clifford Brye was running and all a sudden fell down in pain, clutching his knee. In the locker room he said he tore his ACL, so he will be out for the rest of the season. If Shook is out, I don't know if I'll be second string or not because I'm not sure the coaches have that much faith in me. Rutherford will most likely be first-string guard and second-string center, and then if Richie is still ahead of me, who knows? I'll just wait and see.

So, this has been a weird day.

> As I'm writing this in February of 2006, the military occupation of Iraq is still going on, forever looking like a quagmire. I said I would enlist and I

meant it, however I do not agree with what the war has become. I would have fought in Afghanistan where we had adequate reason to invade, not Iraq where we had to invent reasons to be there. Our misguided failure of a president got us into this mess and he's consistently shown that he doesn't have the leadership ability to find any way out. Even after "borrowing and spending" trillions of dollars, there seems to be no end to governmental oversights while the administration keeps digging this country into a social and economic black hole.

Wednesday, September 12, 2001

It's the day after the terrorist attacks and everyone in the nation is glued to the news coverage. We learned that the Big 12 cancelled all games for this weekend. Eventually all games around the nation, including professional sports, were cancelled. The Rice game will now be played next Thursday night. This will be really weird because we've never had a Thursday game during school before. This brings up a lot of issues such as Wednesday night class attendance, Thursday class attendance, and what to do for Thursday night classes.

Friday, September 14, 2001

We got today off from practice, but I had to go in and lift after classes. It seems that my strength is really improving. Today we did heavy squat for sets of two. The last set I did was at 365 pounds and I got it really easily. I told Bailey I wanted to do more. He didn't want me to, but I reassured him how easy it was and he let me try 405. This is the most weight I've ever squatted for sets. I did this for two reps and got it very easily as well. My bench has been the same way—I raised the weight 20 pounds and still was able to do more than was required on my last set. Next week should be a good test to see how high I can max out.

Sunday, September 16, 2001

Today was supposed to be our team picture day, but it was overcast and rainy so it was postponed. We did get our individual pictures taken in the Cook before practice.

The following is from an email my brother Jason sent out to a bunch of friends and relatives. He did it mostly to get what was in his head out into words and to keep up his sanity through these incredibly difficult times. He has been working at the Office of the Chief Medical Examiner in New York City. This office handles all of the forensic work for all of the crimes that occur in New York and my brother thought he had seen some strange things before 9/11. That all changed in a blink.

I woke up on Tuesday morning to a ringing phone. My mother-in-law from Michigan was calling to see if Stacy and I were OK, and if we were near the World Trade Center. For the rest of the day, I watched in horror as the replays of the second plane flashed across the screen, followed by the reports from the Pentagon and Pennsylvania. As the first building collapsed, I held my breath, knowing my co-workers were down there as first responders. My normal world ended when the second tower came down as well. As the day slipped into night, relief came from the news that my friends, broken and battered, had all survived and would be OK. In the early morning hours of Wednesday, I got dressed in the dark, kissed my wife goodbye, and made the 64-block trek through a ghost town called Manhattan to the Office of Chief Medical Examiner where I work as a criminalist in the Department of Forensic Biology, which is the DNA lab for the city of New York.

Arriving at the office at dawn, I found a makeshift autopsy suite set up outside, several hundred cops and firemen milling around, and my co-workers, exhausted from the night shift, looking relieved to see me. As I got dressed in scrubs and protective gear, the next refrigerated truck pulled up and I began my day helping process the remains of the victims who had died in this terrible tragedy. For the next four days, I witnessed more grim and unspeakable things than anyone should in a lifetime. What countered this dark task was the most unbelievable outpouring of support and encouragement that I have ever witnessed in New York.

The rumors of the typical New Yorker are not true, not now, for I have seen people no different than you or I drop off boxes of food, clothes, flags, cots, blankets, raincoats, scented candles, gallons of water, and toiletries, just to name a few items. A local lumberyard donated a truckload of lumber and a crew of carpenters volunteered to come down and built us ramps for the gurneys, stairs up to the trailer doors, and benches and tables for us to sit down and rest. People from all over the country have shown up to volunteer for the Salvation Army, to help in the morgue, to drive trucks, to help take out trash even, just to try to help.

It's odd, in the middle of all of this death and destruction, my background and training allow me to be stoic and professional while examining the remains of the victims of this disaster, but nothing could have ever prepared me to see grown men crying, having found the body of their fallen fellow officer or fireman. No class or internship could have prepared me to read the personal messages, attached to individual granola bars saying "hold in there, you are brave, and will be home again soon." There is no scientific way to dissect a letter from a little girl, included in a batch of homemade snack bars, asking if we come across her uncle or daddy to please give her mommy a phone call. There is no way to not feel torn, broken, bruised, but in a way no one can visibly see.

In the end, we are all victims. No one close to this, either by family ties or by simply being American will ever be the same again. I understand, now, what it means to be shell-shocked. I understand, as best as I can, what my grandfather must have seen on the beaches and in the jungles of the South Pacific in WWII, and what eventually led him to take his own life several years after the war had ended. I understand now, only too well, that there is a human side to my job, to my responsibility as a forensic scientist who, on a daily basis, normally deals with rape and homicide, but always at a comfortable distance. I understand that families need closure, and I fear that if we fail in our duties, we fail these families as well.

This letter comes after my fourth 12-hour shift in as many days since that Tuesday morning. I'm tired, but ready to go back again in the morning, and will keep going back until there are no more remains, no more DNA tests, no more questions. So, I will return, and help in any way I can.

Monday, September 17, 2001

The major news of the day was that I'm not going to spend Wednesday night at the Nebraska Center, which would have been a pain since I have Wednesday and Thursday night classes.

It looks like Richie Incognito has moved up past both Shook and me. I don't know for sure what the coaches' plans are for him getting playing time and losing his redshirt year, but it looks like he could be playing if they need him.

Thursday, September 20, 2001

Nebraska 48 – Rice 3

This game was treated very differently from those in the past. It was the first Thursday night home game ever at Memorial Stadium and was our first game since the terrorist attacks. We went through our usual warm-up routine and locker room rituals before the game. Then, with eight minutes to go, we quietly walked out onto the field. We lined up along the sideline as did Rice on the other side. The band was on the field and when we were all in position, they played the national anthem and the entire stadium sang along. It was a very emotional moment for many. When the song was over, the tunnel walk music started up, and the crowd erupted at the sound of the intro. On the big screens many of the computerized graphics that travel the state had been changed to fit the evening. On the Kearney overpass, a banner was hung that read, "United We Stand," there was a flag at half-mast on the Woodmen tower, and the opponents' helmet wasn't there to get squashed by our Sears Trophy like the previous ones. Then, when it showed the tunnel doors open up, instead of the usual scene of Coach Solich followed by us, we saw a group of police officers and firefighters carrying an American flag. The crowd cheered while I fought back tears. When the procession ended, the cheerleaders held up large signs with "U.S.A." instead of the usual "Go Big Red." The emotions of the entire crowd were very high, and this was quickly followed by the kickoff.

After such a stirring opening, we didn't disappoint. We came out strong and scored quickly, and nearly everyone who suited up got in for a few plays. Eric Crouch broke the Big 12 all-time rushing yards total for quarterbacks and also moved up to eighth on the all-time rushing list here. He should be able to keep climbing that list and end up fairly high, but we need to get more of a well-rounded ground game going. For a program that prides itself on moving the ball on the ground, we haven't been able to make this happen so far. We're very accustomed to earning rushing titles much more than conference titles or national championships, but we really need to pick it up if we intend to repeat this year.

It was interesting how the fans reacted to the game. We had a really good passing program for the day and completed 12 of 15 passes for 205 yards. The first bomb that made everyone realize we actually could throw was a beautiful 42-yard pass to Wilson Thomas who dove into the pylon while making the catch. Wilson later said he thought the ref called it incomplete since the crowd was silent for a couple of seconds. Actually, they were just in disbelief. We've never been a highly effective passing team, but now I think most teams would respect the fact that we can throw the ball.

I got in for two extra-point snaps, the first long snaps of my college career. The first one was perfect with a good kick; the second one also was a good snap but Kelly Cook, the holder, bobbled the ball and eventually was tackled, leaving us stranded on 48 points. As we were walking off the field, I saw Coach Young immediately go for Cook instead of me, so I knew I had done my job right.

Kelly later told me the snap was a little to the outside, so I guess I could have done a little better and it might be my fault, but it's useless to point fingers. At the end of the game I got in for the last series and got three or four plays that I thought went pretty well. We didn't move the ball too far, which was expected since all the reserves were in, but we ran the clock out and walked away with a resounding win.

Tuesday, September 25, 2001

Today Coach Solich talked about some incidents that occurred last week. One dealt with a big cooler full of Gatorade and water that was set outside the north locker room last Wednesday. After practice that day someone broke the lock on the cooler and everyone in that locker room helped themselves to as much Gatorade as they could grab. In all, nearly $200 worth of drinks were stolen and Coach told us that when he finds the person responsible for breaking the lock, the penalties will be severe. He said he might dismiss the player or take away some of his benefits like tickets for the games, suiting up for the games, and so on. With threats like those, it's unlikely the person will come forward. If the person is a scholarship player, they would never cut him, so it was a lot of hot air, but Coach Solich had to say it to lay down the law.

The other incident involved Jake Andersen. Last week he and a few other guys, all under age 21, were caught going into a bar downtown. The guys with him were scholarship linemen as well, but only Jake was given a citation because he was using someone else's identification. As punishment, he was put on scout team this week and he's not sure what else will happen.

Saturday, September 29, 2001

Nebraska 36 – Missouri 3

In the end, this was a good game, but Missouri put up a good fight for most of the first half and made it a close game for a while. Our offense couldn't get much done, and our defense had some trouble stopping them, but that all changed with a little bit of Eric Crouch magic. On third down, from our own five-yard line, Eric dropped back to pass, saw no one open, slipped away from a potential tackle in the end zone, and took off on an amazing run. He juked his way down the field, making even their best defensive backs stop in their tracks and trip over their own feet. Ninety-five yards later, he set a new school record with the longest run ever. After that, Missouri was done. Our offense found its groove, right over Missouri's broken spirit, and marched in for touchdown after touchdown.

I didn't travel for this game, but Coach Tenopir said he would try to take some different guys to every away game.

Wednesday, October 3, 2001

Some of the linemen have too much time on their hands. Before practice today some of the O-line guys played a prank on place-kicker Sandro DeAngelis. They completely wrapped his helmet in athletic tape and then took a marker and drew on the decals, facemask, eyes, nose, and mouth. They laid it in his locker on top of a pile of clothes and then laid his jersey below it and his pants below that, so it looked like he was laying in his locker. This was probably the funniest thing I've seen in a while. Sandro didn't say much about it when he came in and just went to work undoing the tape. I guess he's gotten used to having a locker so close to the offensive linemen.

Friday, October 5, 2001

We've received some more gear in the past two weeks. We were given a long-sleeved white spandex shirt, a gray sweats outfit, and two red short-sleeved collared shirts (one Adidas, one Huskers). We were issued a new winter coat. It's black fleece with an old-school letter jacket look with a big red *N* on the front and "Nebraska" in cursive on the back.

I bought a cell phone finally and was able to pick my phone number. Luckily, I was able to pick one that includes my jersey number. This, along with my NU OLINE license plates, might be overdoing it a little bit, but it's fun while it lasts.

Saturday, October 6, 2001

Nebraska 48 – Iowa State 14

Iowa State came into this game after a very good season last year, which ended in a bowl game, and after having a very productive start this season. Their quarterback has proven himself to be a very effective passer, setting a Big 12 record with 18 consecutive pass completions last week. They got a wake-up call this week.

They received the opening kickoff and looked like they could move the ball pretty effectively. Then Keyuo Craver picked off a pass and took it all the way back for a score.

Their next drive got stopped and by that time the momentum was clearly on our side. By halftime, it was 41-0 and it looked like we were just getting warmed up.

We only scored once in the second half, but the game was already in the bag so it didn't matter. I got only one play in the entire game and that was the snap for the last extra point. Kelly Cook was holding again and we got it perfect this time.

Eric Crouch scored four rushing touchdowns tonight, which set a new NCAA career record. He simply looked amazing with his speed and quickness. His ability to stutter-step and freeze the defenders in their tracks is something he makes look way too easy. The Heisman Trophy is as good as his.

Offensive guard Toniu Fonoti hyper extended his elbow midway through the game. He was on the sideline bench getting attended to and I happened to be sitting next to him. The trainers tried to fit him with an elbow brace, but couldn't find one big enough for his massive arm. Eventually, they brought out a knee brace and after trying a couple to get the right size, he had a large knee brace fit over his hulking elbow. I couldn't help laughing at his size and he found it pretty funny, too. He's 350 pounds, and a rather trim 350 as well, so every part of his body is just an enormous pile of muscle. His arms are probably as big as my legs. I will be greatly surprised if he doesn't go pro.

We received another $15 after the game.

Monday, October 8, 2001

Even after getting only four hours of sleep last night, I felt great today. In fact, I felt great enough to destroy my old record on squat. Today was the first heavy squat day in the past three weeks and I've been waiting patiently for it. My old record was 405 pounds; I put on 455 and began to psych myself up while everyone around me was wondering who was doing all that weight. They couldn't believe it was me. When I was ready, I got under the bar and ripped out two repetitions almost too easily. It felt great. Bailey was very impressed and I challenged him to get me up to 500 by the end of the season. He said I was already there. I know he's right.

Saturday, October 13, 2001

Nebraska 48 – Baylor 7

This game was in Waco on a grass field during adverse weather conditions, which made it more interesting than it should have been. I didn't travel to this game; instead I went home and worked off a $100 parking ticket doing odd jobs around the house. I took a nap before the game and actually slept through the first half. When I woke up, I expected the score to be out of control and the game already set, but it was only 14-7. There were a lot of fumbles in the first half, seven total with five lost, which really put a damper on any chance of getting a solid drive going. Baylor's lone score came when Crouch fumbled in their end zone and they recovered.

At halftime, Coach Solich supposedly got really fired up, which is a rare thing to see, and the guys knew he was serious and we needed to get something done. In the second half, it was like we had a totally different team. We kept it on the ground for almost every play, but this was still tough. It rained the night before, and there was a 35-minute rain delay during the first quarter. All of this combined to give us the worst field conditions ever. The game was only on the radio, but the announcers were talking about how the players just couldn't get their speed up since the field was like running on sand.

We kept pounding away and eventually ended up with touchdown after touchdown. Also, for the first time in

Husker history, four of our backs—Eric Crouch, Thunder Collins, Dahrran Diedrick, and Judd Davies—each racked up 100 yards or more on the ground. The second- and third-team guys who traveled got quite a bit of playing time as well, and proved that they could move the ball just as effectively. In all, it was a good game.

Friday, October 19, 2001

I found out today that I'm going to stay at the Nebraska Center with the rest of the team tonight (actually it's just the top two or three strings, but this is the first time I've been with them). This was a surprise, but I should have guessed I would be called up when Mike Erickson hurt his shoulder earlier this week. When I saw my name on the list, I had to double-check it because I didn't believe it. I had to go to Coach Tenopir's office and take the linemen test. Coach Tenopir handles the run test and Coach Young handles the pass test, and we have to take both of them.

After practice I found a note in my locker from Jon Rutherford, Toniu Fonoti, and Wes Cody telling me to bring three two-liters of Sprite and three bags of Reese's Pieces to the movie tonight. Apparently everybody, especially the linemen, brings a lot of food to the theater and it's the job of the Nebraska Center rookies to bring the food.

After another Friday night dinner of crab legs, I ran a few errands and got dropped off at the theater to watch *Iron Monkey*, a new martial arts film. This movie was incredibly horrible and we were all laughing the entire time.

After the movie we went by bus to the Nebraska Center, which is on East Campus. I'm not sure what this place is used for throughout the year, but there's a hotel there that the team uses the night before games. My roommate for the night was Steve Safranek, a sophomore middle linebacker. There was a snack for us in the lobby consisting of hamburgers, chicken patties, granola bars, cookies, fruit, and all kinds of juices. Since the game is tomorrow evening, we had a late bed check at 11:00.

Saturday, October 20, 2001

Nebraska 41 – Texas Tech 31

We got up at 9:00 and walked to the East Union for breakfast. They had another great buffet for us with everything one could want for breakfast. We had our team meeting afterward in which watched some film on Texas Tech and did some last-minute analysis. We then split into groups; Coach Tenopir let us out pretty quickly after reminding us to play hard and leave it all on the field.

Our pre-game meal was at 2:00 and we got taped after that. There were a few games on TV and a lot of the guys watched those. I took a nap and got more sleep than I probably needed, but it was worth it.

At 4:00 we headed out to the busses which took us to the stadium, It's only about three miles away, but we still had a police escort. The busses pulled into the Vine Street loop and dropped us off at the east side of the stadium. We then filed through the sizable crowd that was awaiting us. Everyone there watched with a certain awe and confusion, like they didn't really recognize us outside of our pads and uniforms. They could run into any one of us during an ordinary day in Lincoln and would never know who we are. That's a good thing about football; you can be worshipped on the field, but when you're off the field and out of your gear, you can blend in with the rest of the crowd if you want to, unless of course you are a walking land-mass of a lineman.

Coach Tenopir tells us he likes close games, but he also likes those 70-to-nothing blowouts just as much, if not more. This definitely was a close one.

The Red Raiders hung in with us through the whole game and made us work hard on both sides of the ball. Their backs and receivers were incredibly fast and really gave us a scare on too many occasions. They had deadly returners for kickoffs and punts, taking it from deep in the end zone and getting to the 30-yard line or farther while the punt returners took two punts back for touchdowns, but one of them was called back.

As if they needed any more help, the officiating crew for this game was by far the worst ever. They called us for every penalty they could think of while only calling two or three on Tech the entire game. It's truly amazing that a team can pass for the majority of the game and never once get an offensive-holding call. The fans, players, and coaches quickly hated the refs and there were pockets of chants coming from the crowd criticizing and threatening them.

It was 28-28 at halftime and Tech came out just as hard as we did in the second half. Eventually, we were able to get ahead, despite the bad calls and their incredible speed. Through all this, we managed to be just a little better and pull off the win. The game truly went to the last minute and we were all very happy when it was over.

We had a lot of guys go down in this game. Tight end Tracey Wistrom didn't play because of injuries from last week, cornerback Keyuo Craver was hurting pretty badly during the game and eventually was taken out, fullback Judd Davies came out with an ankle injury as did offensive tackle Dan Waldrop, and offensive tackle Dave Volk came out after his shoulder popped out of joint. Near the end of the game, we had a good amount of our starting crew laying on the benches.

At the start of the game, senior rush end J.P. Wichman was walking out of the tunnel and putting on his regular show of wild, psyched-up moves, when all of a sudden he slipped and fell on the slick concrete. The camera followed him down for a brief second, as if expecting him to do something special, but then people in charge figured out that it wasn't on purpose. Of course, this all was on the big screens in the stadium, so everyone saw J.P. fall on his face. He was the center of attention on the sideline with people coming over to laugh with him and congratulate him on a graceful fall. This should definitely make the highlight films.

Wednesday, October 24, 2001

This is the deciding week of the season. We face Oklahoma this week and we've been waiting for this all season. The BCS report came out Monday and has us listed at #2 and Oklahoma at #1 while the other polls list us at #3 and #2, respectively. In preparation, we've added a few new plays. They're variations of plays we used a year or two ago, but have been reworked to fit what we think will happen on the Oklahoma defense. They have a very strong defensive line with big, quick guys who are taught to avoid getting cut-blocked and have proven to be very tough to knock down.

In meetings the coaches have been showing us clips from famous Oklahoma games of the past to give us a flavor of the tradition that this match-up has developed. Yesterday Coach Solich showed the 1978 game and asked us a few questions about it. Carson Schott, a walk-on O-lineman from Osceola, spoke up and answered every one of Coach Solich's questions, except who kicked the winning field goal. If he had answered that, Coach Solich said we wouldn't have had to run gassers. Today, he showed us film from the 1971 "Game of the Century" and Coach Solich made the same offer. Carson came through for us and answered his question right, baffling Coach Solich and making everyone cheer since we wouldn't have gassers.

After practice, and to no one's surprise, we still had to run one gasser. We also went in half pads today, mostly because a lot of guys are working off injuries and hoping to get back by Saturday.

Thursday, October 25, 2001

We received more gifts today to accommodate the recent cold weather: a white cotton long-sleeved shirt, black spandex pants, and a red stocking cap. After practice we picked up a new pair of shoes as well, and everyone with size 16 and above, including me, were issued a pair of old-school black shoes with three white stripes on the sides.

Coach Solich started today's meeting with a tape that he said would show us how to get pumped up. It was the film from the tunnel walk of the Texas Tech game and it slowed down right when J.P. came by doing his wild maneuver and falling down. The whole auditorium was laughing hysterically and J.P. was flushed red as we watched this over and over. Then they showed some sideline shots of him getting laughed at, and his own re-enactments.

Saturday, October 27, 2001

Nebraska 20 – Oklahoma 10

This game was hyped as the Game of the New Century. #1 vs. #2 (in the BCS polls) and a classic Nebraska/Oklahoma matchup. Everyone knew coming into this game that it would be a defensive battle and that the score would be very low. This definitely held true. After the first quarter alone, each team had only two first downs and it was 0-0. Oklahoma scored first on a dump pass over the middle into the end zone, but we answered that on our next drive with a touchdown. A field goal later on would give us a 10-7 lead, but it looked like it wouldn't hold at the half. Right at the end of the second quarter, Oklahoma was deep in the red zone and came within a few yards of scoring the go-ahead touchdown. Luckily, our defense held and they settled for a field goal, which tied the game at 10 at halftime.

The second half was much the same, but they never got close enough to give us a scoring threat. We got close at one point, but had to settle for a field goal. Later in the game, the play of the season happened when Crouch pitched the ball to Mike Stuntz on a reverse, who then stopped, set up, and unleashed a pass to Crouch who snuck downfield past the secondary. The throw was perfect and 63 yards later Eric had another touchdown, a Heisman highlight, and the crowd on their feet. We were all so excited that we were called with an excessive celebration penalty. We were then able to stuff Oklahoma's offense and ran the clock out for the victory. This was easily the biggest game of the year for us and with this win we will be in the driver's seat for a trip to the Rose Bowl.

Tuesday, October 30, 2001

Practice is so boring for me now. I'm rotating with Shook on the twos and I take one play for every four he takes. Basically, I'm just there to give him a break now and then. I'm not motivated to try hard because this situation almost guarantees that I won't see much, if any, playing time.

The coaches also never give any positive encouragement. They seem to believe that constant criticism will inspire us to do better. All this has taught me to do is to ignore anything negative they say and do anything I can to avoid being noticed. Also, I need to focus more on school, which is quickly slipping behind, and I also would like to spend more time with my new girlfriend.

Friday, November 2, 2001

There was an addition put on the South Stadium complex underneath the stadium. It's connected to the player's lounge area and so far has only been used for defensive meetings during games and also as a place for post-game interviews. We were told some entertainment things would be put in this area, such as a pool table and video games, and the pool table has finally arrived. Before one of my classes today, I went into the room and Cody Volk and Jake Andersen were playing a game. I joined in on the next one and beat Jake pretty soundly. It's a very nice red table with very nice cues and balls to match. This truly has got to be one of the best colleges for an athlete.

Saturday, November 3, 2001

Nebraska 51 – Kansas 7

It was a pretty typical game against Kansas. For the 33rd time in a row, we beat them soundly and without much effort. It was a very slow first quarter with no score and it looked like our offense had a lot of trouble getting going. That quickly changed when we scored our first touchdown on the second play of the second quarter. By halftime it was 20-0 and the Jayhawks had only six yards of total offense.

Our defense played magnificently once again and came within minutes of posting our first shutout of the season. Another first for the season was the first punt return for a touchdown by senior Ben Cornelson. This was the first touchdown of his career and it was a perfect 71-yard run.

Our offense continued to pick up steam throughout the game and by the end we were looking unstoppable.

Tuesday, November 6, 2001

About two weeks ago, two of our offensive linemen—Junior Tagoa'i and Jon Dawson—got arrested. Junior was arrested for assaulting his girlfriend who is about seven months pregnant, and Jon was arrested in his dorm room for smoking marijuana and having a bunch of drug paraphernalia. This was all reported in the school paper last week and the team and the coaches were pretty shocked by it all.

Today was Jon Dawson's first day back at practice since blowing out his knee in the spring. After groupwork we all went up to the field to wait for the option stations. While we waited, Steve Alstadt, who doesn't like Dawson very much, said, "I bet it sucks being back on the team now, doesn't it?" Dawson asked why and Steve replied, "Because now you can't smoke out every day." Some more words were spoken and then Dawson unleashed a punch right on Steve's left temple. The coaches broke it up and Dawson screamed, "I don't need to take this kind of shit, I'm leaving!" The coaches didn't stop him. As he was walking off the field he told Derek Clark, one of the head trainers, that he was quitting.

Wednesday, November 7, 2001

At the end of practice today Coach Tenopir told us that he isn't sure if Dawson will come back or not. But he told us that whatever happens, we should be supportive of him, like we were his brothers, and not to judge him for anything he has done. I'm sure if the coaches didn't have a scholarship invested in him, they wouldn't have cared at all.

Friday, November 9, 2001

I made a very late change to my class schedule this week. I was having trouble in my history class, "The History of Britain Since the Glorious Revolution," and decided it was time to take decisive action. I went to see Dennis LeBlanc, the man in charge of academics for the football team, who suggested that I drop the class, which would put me down to

10 credit hours, and pick up a football credit and a weight-training credit to have the 12 hours I need to stay eligible. This is a pretty lazy way to take care of a problem, but I really don't mind. It might be cheating to get school credit for something that I have to do anyways, but I do have to pay for the two hours and they don't really count for anything towards my major.

Here's the basics: every athlete needs to take at least 12 hours of classes. You have to declare a major by a certain time and then you have to show successful completion of a certain percentage of your major's courses by the end of each year. You don't need to pass all 12 hours, but you do need to pass a certain number and you have to have a 2.0 or higher GPA. The NCAA makes these rules and they keep getting tougher every couple years. When carried through, these academic rules are much tougher than the University's rules for the average student to stay in school and on track for graduation.

I now have no classes on Tuesday or Thursday and I love it. I use one of those mornings to see Layne, my TeamMate mentee, who is currently a sixth-grader at Mickle Middle School. As a special treat, Layne was able to watch our practice today. Afterward I gave him a tour of the weight room, Hewit Center, and the locker room. I had to let him go pretty early because I had a special teams meeting, but I think he had a good time.

The other day I was sitting across from Eric Crouch at lunch. We were talking about the possibility of both of our high schools, Millard North and Millard West, meeting in the state finals and how great that would be for Millard. It was then that it hit me how great of a person he is. Eric is undoubtedly the best athlete on our team and easily one of the best Huskers ever. This fame and constant publicity could have caused him to have a huge ego. But that is totally not true. Eric is a very quiet person most of the time, but he's very approachable and friendly, and he acts just like any other person I know. He's very humble, and I don't know how he can do it when all the talk this season has been about him, especially now that he is a finalist for the Golden Arm Award and the Heisman. I truly admire him and I think he will go very far in this world.

Saturday, November 10, 2001

Nebraska 31 – Kansas State 21

The score doesn't make this look like a convincing win, but all the papers and columnists agreed that it was good enough to lock us into a solid first place in the ESPN/Coaches poll. We fumbled and threw an interception on our first two possessions, going all the way until the second quarter before Crouch broke off on a 14-yard play and dodged his way into the end zone. Kansas State came back right before the half and we went to the locker room down 14-13.

The atmosphere in the locker room was horrible. Everyone was down and it was like we had already lost. We needed to come out in the second half and put it away.

It wasn't until halfway through the third quarter that we were able to score again. Then a few minutes later DeJuan Groce added another touchdown with a punt return. With another field goal in the fourth, the score looked better for us, but Kansas State rallied one last time and scored with five minutes left to make the score 31-21.

In all, we totally controlled the game, especially up front. Our line was playing amazingly well and Toniu Fonoti was tossing guys around like they were little kids (compared to him, everyone looked like little kids). The K-State guys actually were playing very poorly, doing everything they could to cheat for their own advantage. Their players took many cheap shots at our guys, driving them over into a pile after a play was over or even wrestling our guys to the ground violently after the play. They also held and clipped as much as they could on special teams and basically played very dirty the entire game. But that's what we expect from K-State.

Tuesday, November 13, 2001

I went in to talk to Coach Young today. After Garrison's bad snaps last weekend, I need to find out where I stand. He said I'm the second-string long snapper, right behind Garrison, and he would like to use me in the games, but isn't sure if he will because I don't have game experience and he isn't sure I can block properly. I reminded him that I haven't had a guy run by me for a long time, but he wasn't convinced. I guess I'll have to practice harder and show him what I'm talking about.

We practiced in sweats today, which was a nice surprise. Everyone is looking forward to a short week with Friday and Saturday off.

When I was being taped before practice, a newscaster from Channel 8 was in the training room doing a story where he steps in and does someone else's job for a day. For this day, he was taking over as an athletic trainer. He used me as the example and did a small part of the taping, making sure to make a big show of it. Afterward, he asked me what I thought of the student trainers and the job they are doing here. I said they are very important because they keep us healthy, help prevent injuries, and when we are injured, they help us heal up. It should be on next Monday night.

Wednesday, November 14, 2001

When we were doing special teams today, instead of going to snap for the field goal unit, Coach Young called me over to work with the punt team instead. I guess our little talk the other day made an impression. I did pretty well, blocking the guys I was supposed to, making good snaps, and then running downfield hard and making good plays. We were in full pads, which doesn't help my long-snapping because we have to wear knee braces with full pads and they affect my flexibility. Also, my elbows hit them when I snap, making them really sore.

Sunday, November 18, 2001

After having Friday and Saturday off, practicing today wouldn't have been too bad if it weren't for the incredible hangover I had. I was out late last night and drank a different kind of beer than usual. Well, this morning it seemed like I had a combination of food poisoning and a hangover. I vomited once, which helped considerably, but I was still feeling very weak and in pain. To top it off, today's practice was outside on the grass and it was one of the coldest days we've had so far this year. I was very uncomfortable, couldn't think clearly, and couldn't move effectively. I tried to hide it the best I could, but I know I didn't look too well. Let this be a lesson—don't overdo it at parties with drinking or staying out too late. I did both and I'm paying for it.

Monday, November 19, 2001

My stomach pains are still around, which makes me think this could be some type of poisoning. I have had the worst case of diarrhea all day long and nothing has been able to stop it. I couldn't even make it through practice.

After my performance in practice yesterday, I was demoted to the scout team for today. I guess I deserved it since I couldn't do anything right yesterday and couldn't tell the coaches that I had alcohol-related stomach flu.

Tuesday, November 20, 2001

Today's meeting was probably the most important meeting I've been a part of in all my years here. The seniors asked for some time alone with the team, so the coaches left and Tracey

Wistrom, Dave Volk, Eric Crouch, and Jeremy Slechta led the group. Tracey started it off by addressing the issue of theft going on in the locker rooms. Various things have turned up missing, including money, and he said it has to stop because there is nothing worse than stealing from a teammate.

The next issue was the most important. He said that so far this season we've won 11 games, which is outstanding and most schools would love to have a record like that, but we have nothing to show for it. We don't have a north division championship, a Big 12 championship, nothing. And if we lose to Colorado, we will probably play in the Cotton Bowl since the BCS only takes two Big 12 teams. He said that if he has to spend the last month of his career preparing for the Cotton Bowl, he will be miserable beyond words. We have a chance to prove that we are the best and to do that, we have to beat Colorado. We have three games left and we need to be 3-0. When we beat Colorado, we are in the Big 12 game and are pretty much guaranteed a BCS bid. We need to start practicing for the biggest game of our lives, because if we don't win this one, the season and all of our dreams are lost. We have the talent and the skill and the people to get it all done, and we need to prove it to everyone.

I think I will take some of the long snaps in the game this Friday because Coach Young actually pulled Garrison out of the field goal work and put me in there to snap all of them. He hasn't told me officially that I will handle the long-snapping duties, but I can only assume that I will take some of them.

Wednesday, November 21, 2001

Today is the first day of Thanksgiving break, but we still have practice, of course. We got a nice surprise at brunch today—apparently we missed some money from two-a-days, and with the money for this weekend, I received $147.

A couple of weekends ago, four players were at a party

together. One guy saw another walking out of the house with a full cooler and asked what he was doing. He replied, "Shut up, I just need a new cooler," and threw it in his car. The other guy apparently wanted to steal stuff now too, so he went to the unattended basement and grabbed a whole stack of video game CDs, keeping them under his coat and walking right out the door.

On his next trip, he saw some things that couldn't fit under his clothes, so he knocked out the basement window and tossed two speakers onto the lawn, walked up the stairs empty handed, and then threw them into the car. This wasn't enough, so he went back and stole a very nice, very expensive subwoofer as well.

The driver, who was the first to steal the cooler, then turned into the voice of reason. He noticed the latest addition of the stereo equipment to his car and thought the lineman had gone too far so he carefully put everything back in the basement without getting noticed. The lineman noticed his haul had been returned and then ran back again and tossed it all out of the house and back in the car again while the driver was busy trying to get the other two he came with rounded up.

The last guy to hop in the car, who was thoroughly inebriated, had swiped a jar full of loose change at one point and stashed it behind the wheel of a car parked in the driveway. When he went back to retrieve it, the car had left over the jar, spilling change and broken glass all over the ground. He recovered most of the coins, stuffing it into any pocket he had. The driver finally found him with his pockets weighed down with his plunder and all he could say was "I've got a pocket full of quarters!" By the time they finally left, they had about a thousand dollars' worth of stuff.

The next day they heard that the cops were looking for the stolen stuff. They got scared and tossed all of out on the side of a road in a secluded part of Lincoln. Somehow, someone got their names and in the past couple of days, the cops have been calling everyone constantly, trying to find out the whole story. The cops know all the guys play football, but this was a felony so they're putting pressure on them to rectify the situation before the press catches wind of it. They told the driver that if they replace all the stuff or give them money for it, the charges will be significantly less if not dropped entirely. Two of the guys are pretty much clear in all of this, but since the fullback was driving and the offensive linemen stole all of it, they were the main two guys.

After a few days, the lineman rectified the situation by paying for most of the stuff and the fullback got a small theft charge, which was later dropped. No harm, no foul.

Thursday, November 22, 2001

We had a Thanksgiving lunch on the third level of the skyboxes today. It was a very good lunch with the full spread of all the good food they usually have for special meals. After this, we loaded up the buses and headed to the airport. After arriving in Denver, we took about a half hour bus ride to the University of Colorado campus in Boulder. It looks like a very nice campus, but I was very surprised by the stadium. From where we drove up, it's hard to notice it's even there. Once inside the stadium, it seems very small from the field. The sidelines are very tight and the bleachers come right up to our sideline, so I can just imagine how the crowd must react being so close to the enemy.

We had our short walk-though practice, then hopped back on the busses and headed to our hotel, the Westin Westminster. This hotel was as good as any of the ones we've had for bowl trips—extremely elegant with very opulent features. We were all impressed.

After a very good dinner, we had a team meeting that almost put me to sleep. Then we had a little break before we went to the movie. We watched *Spy Games* which was kind of long and boring with a very thin, predictable plot. Some of the guys liked it, but most of them were indifferent.

There has been some inter-team hostility today. The first incident was on the bus after the plane ride in which Jammal Lord and Josh Davis got into an argument over something, and it appeared that Josh was ready to go crazy on Jammal. Luckily, there were plenty of guys around to hold him back. The other incident was between Wilson Thomas and Jon Clanton. Wilson didn't like the movie and said he would kick our ass if he found out that we had voted to see that movie. Jon made fun of him saying that Wilson would only like the movie if it had Ice-T or L L Cool J in it and then shoved Wilson as he got off the elevator. Coach Gill was on the elevator with us and held Wilson back as Jon got off, which stopped any chance of a fight.

After the movie, we had a snack waiting for us which was very good as well. Then we had bed check at 10:30.

Friday, November 23, 2001

Colorado 62 – Nebraska 36

This was an embarrassing day for Nebraska, but I'm not so much embarrassed as I am infuriated by Colorado. I truly hate them and their fans. We knew they would give us their best shot after we squeaked out a win in each of the past five years. But this day was stacked against us.

There were many reasons, as I saw it, that we lost as badly as we did. For starters, we came into this game expecting to win, thinking of the Big 12 championship game and dreaming of the Rose Bowl. Our minds weren't in this game from the start. For our psych-up tape, starting defensive tackle Jeremy Slechta put forth a very weak effort. I have nothing against Jeremy, I think he's a great guy and one of the best human beings on the team, but when it comes to psyching us up, he's no Grant Wistrom. So, we left the hotel for the game with no real energy.

The locker room at the Colorado stadium was another factor. It was very small and was sectioned into many parts. There was no open area for us to gather as a team like we normally do before a game, so that added to the disconnected feeling. Then we had to go single file outside, which took a long time, and run down a short hill and straight to the sideline. This was a very different feeling from running out of the tunnel in Memorial Stadium because it took all the fun out of taking the field.

When we were on the sideline, the stands were so close that we could hear everything people in the first five rows said. Many people took the opportunity to verbally abuse and taunt our players, yelling "wide right!" to our placekicker, Josh Brown, and even trying to fluster Eric Crouch. Some of them were halfway entertaining, but many were simply vicious, showing how shallow the gene pool is in Colorado. They had shirts that said, "Huck the Fuskers," and at one point I saw a bed sheet pulled out and displayed above the heads of some fans across the way that was spray-painted with "Fuck Nebraska." Even after the game, some young Colorado fans made it their goal to taunt our entire fan section. They slid around on the grass and danced in front of our stands, which was also the area we had to use to walk back to our locker room, so I made sure to bump one of these kids as I trudged by.

Another reason I think we lost was that our emotions were flat. We came out of the locker room with no enthusiasm; everyone was looking forward to the next game. This lack of emotion was evident throughout the game.

The announcer for Colorado also really bothered me.

He had a very slow, boring, and monotonous voice. When he referred to us, he used a very sarcastic and demeaning tone. I don't know how much effect this had on the guys who actually played, but I couldn't stand it. Anyone who's ever been to one of our home games will note that the announcer is completely unbiased and very gracious to the visiting team throughout the game. He has received much praise for his job as well as many lucrative offers, but remains loyal to the Huskers.

The final things that helped us to lose were the referees. They used every chance they had to call us for the minutest detail. Near the end of the game, they seemed to be a little too flag-happy, and some of their calls surely put the nail in the coffin for us.

Then there was the game itself. Our offense couldn't get anything done in the first quarter and our defense couldn't stop anything. Everything Colorado ran worked extremely well. Our defense could have stayed on the sideline and had the same effect. Before we knew it, they were up 35-3. Our offense finally got something going in the second quarter and near the end of the half it appeared that we were getting ready to pull off a comeback.

At halftime, Coach Solich told us to keep our heads up. He said that we were not out of this and could still pull it off. We came out in the second half feeling like we could do it, with the most energy and emotion we'd had the entire afternoon. But it wasn't enough. We fumbled, faltered, and were flustered on offense. On defense, they continued to run straight through our backfield like there wasn't even a defensive team out there. Early in the fourth quarter we knew it was all over. The only thing to do was to play for pride. Our dream of playing in the Big 12 championship game was gone, our dream of the Rose Bowl was gone, and it looks like we will end up in the Cotton Bowl. We won 11 games, but we have nothing to show for it.

Monday, November 26, 2001

After a wild weekend in college football in which Oklahoma lost to Oklahoma State and Miami demolished Washington, we didn't fall as much as we expected and we are actually sitting fairly well to get into a BCS bowl. There is also the outside chance that we could get back into contention for the Rose Bowl and the national championship. We're fourth in the BCS today; if Colorado beats Texas, and Florida loses in the SEC championship, we will be second in the BCS and able to go to the Rose Bowl. Those are unlikely, but it's nice to know there is still a chance. Miami could also lose to Virginia Tech, but that is another long shot.

We just had short meetings today in which we watched the game film. They want us to lift and run twice this week, but other than that, this week is free of football.

Tuesday, November 27, 2001

We did some light running work today, similar to what we do for winter and summer conditioning with the low ropes and the bags. It wasn't much, but it was enough to show me that I'm out of shape. I didn't do anything last weekend except watch movies and sleep, so that may have some correlation.

Thursday, November 29, 2001

Our workout today was similar to Tuesday, with just some running and lifting. Bailey said that the running would be more difficult than Tuesday, so I wasn't looking forward to it. His actual words were, "We're going to have some fun today," and his idea of fun is very different from most of the offensive linemen. He loves to push us to our limit and a few of the guys really dread his workouts, myself included, but I know I will feel great afterward and that his workouts really get something done.

There was a new gray hooded sweatshirt waiting for us in our lockers today. I also received a new pair of shorts.

Sunday, December 9, 2001

These past two weeks have been the most amazing two weeks in college football. It all started right after our game against Colorado when Oklahoma lost to Oklahoma State. Then Texas, the next number two team, fell to Colorado in the Big 12 championship. Tennessee was the next number two team in the BCS, and LSU beat them this weekend in the SEC championship. Oregon struggled against Oregon State and Miami nearly got tied by Virginia Tech. Also, TCU won its game, which increased our strength of schedule. In all, from the end of our game against Colorado, everything that had to happen to keep our hopes of being in the Rose Bowl alive actually happened. Dr. Tim Gay, who does a little show called *Football Physics* on the big screens during the home games, figured out that we had a 3% to 5% chance of having everything fall into place to put us in the Rose Bowl.

At 2:30 today, the announcement was made that we will play in the Rose Bowl against Miami for the National Championship. I was ecstatic. Right after the announcement, Coach Solich and Colorado's Coach Gary Barnett were on TV talking about what just happened. Coach Solich looked like he was trying his best not to smile too much and Coach Barnett looked like a two-year-old who just had his favorite toy taken away. I heard that the Oregon coach had a few choice words about the whole BCS system, saying that it was like cancer. Some might say we're lucky to have all of this happen this way, but I say we're unbelievably lucky. In the BCS score we were only .05 points ahead of Colorado.

In both polls, we were number four with both Colorado and Oregon ahead of us. With just one vote going another way, the results could have been much different. Either way, the BCS is the system that's in place to choose the teams for the championship game, and we happen to be the one chosen. I'm going to Pasadena to play in the national championship game and I don't really care how we got there.

Also, on no small note, Eric Crouch was awarded the Heisman Trophy this weekend after receiving the Davey O'Brien National Quarterback Award and the Walter Camp Player of the Year Award as well. Toniu Fonoti was a finalist for the Outland Trophy, but lost to Bryant McKinnie from Miami.

Friday, December 14, 2001

Eric brought the Heisman into the locker room today. It came with an impressive-looking metal case that has a telescoping handle and wheels on the bottom. The inside of the case is lined with foam and the trophy is placed face down with the stiff-arm to the ground. There were only a few guys still in the locker room at the time, so we got a good view of it. He let some of the guys hold it and pass it around, but I didn't want to because I'd feel horrible if I dropped it. There already were some dents and chips in the base of the statue.

Saturday, December 15, 2001

We practiced four times this week—Monday, Wednesday, Friday, and today. Most of these were in some form of pads, which doesn't make these practices very fun, but we need to keep working hard to get ready for this bowl game. We had to run gassers after every practice. This next week will be similar and we have to lift four times.

Another story of how great our fans are—before practice today there was a man outside the field house eagerly waiting for players to sign his photo album. Most of us were busy trying to get to practice on time, so I don't know if too many people signed it. Two hours later after practice was over, this man was still there. He asked my number and flipped to a page where he had two pictures of me that he took last year. He had doubles of the pictures and asked me to sign one of each. He then gave me the copy, which was very nice of him. This man, Jerry Schulte, is truly one of the great fans of Nebraska football.

As soon as everyone got back to the locker room, we had a signing party. Everyone brought everything they had to get signed, which was mostly footballs and posters. Eric Crouch was a little late for all of this, so in his place, defensive safety Mic Boettner did a very good job of signing Eric's name on several items.

Earlier this week, I heard an interesting story about Athletic Director Bill Byrne from one of the student managers. He said that when Bill took the job, he wanted to make some drastic changes to the football team. For starters, he wanted to cut the entire coaching staff and fill it with "his people." Coach Osborne stood up to Bill and told him that as long as he was coaching, he had control of the team and the state would back him. Another thing Byrne wanted to do was change the decal on the helmet to a big showy *N* like the *W* on the Wisconsin helmets. Again, Osborne turned him down.

Wednesday, December 19, 2001

This is finals week, but we're still going pretty hard with our practices. We're only practicing on Monday, Wednesday, and Friday, but the practices will be in full pads. Today after meetings I picked up my reimbursement check for the charter flight back since I plan to stay in California after the game. The Huskers can provide us travel money up to the cost of the return flight. This check was $203 and the return ticket I purchased was only $111, which means I'm getting paid to stay in California.

During meetings we also went over all the money we will receive for the trip. We're getting only about $50 a day, which isn't bad since we have some meals taken care of and really nice hotel rooms, but $50 a day won't last too long in Los Angeles. We'll be staying at the Beverly Hilton, which is supposedly a very nice hotel with rooms that run $450 a night.

After practice we were given our gift bag from Adidas. Along with a very nice red travel bag with an *N* on the side, there was a black sweats outfit, a black warm-up suit, two long-sleeved spandex workout shirts, and a red hooded Nebraska sweatshirt. All in all, this was probably the most disappointing gift bag in my four years here. Before, we always received cool stuff like watches and sunglasses and nice collared shirts, but these gifts were pretty generic. I know I shouldn't complain about getting free stuff, but compared to previous years this was a letdown. According to one of the equipment managers, the Adidas representative plans out our gifts before the year even starts, so where we sit at the end of the season has no bearing as to the kind of gifts we receive. But he also said this year we were going to get some really nice stuff. While this stuff might be worth some money, there's nothing that you can wear out and make an impression in, only sweat suits and warm-ups.

Friday, December 21, 2001

At lunch today we received $100, our first installment of money for the holidays. It's a pretty good start.

After another full-pads practice, the last practice before taking off for Califonia, and the seniors stated the precedent of no gassers for themselves on the last in-state practice. So while everyone else ran gassers, the seniors did their best to rub it in our faces. After this, we finished up our lifting for the week and packed up our football equipment. We have a relaxing weekend to look forward to until we have to be back here at 8:00 Monday morning to fly to California. I can't wait.

Monday, December 24, 2001

Everyone arrived at the airport at around 8:00. The security of the airport had been heightened with the presence of the National Guard and one of the guardsmen was Brent Reno, a high school friend. It was cool to see him but it was also sad that it was necessary for him to be there fully armed and on alert.

Along with some fruit and breakfast snacks, we were issued $200 to start the trip. We took off on a gigantic 747 nonstop to Los Angeles and arrived about 10:30 local time. There was no one there to greet us as we got off the plane so we just hopped on our busses and drove to Beverly Hills under a police escort. We're staying at the Beverly Hilton, which actually doesn't look too extravagant from the outside. It sort of looks like any other halfway run-down hotel from the '50s that you can find in most cities. The inside is very clean and nice looking, but once again, nothing really amazed us. The welcoming committee doesn't seem to be doing its job because throughout the entire hotel, the only thing that says Nebraska or Huskers is a small banner hung high in the lobby.

We had a little time to relax before we had to get taped and on the busses again, so I took a quick nap. We had another police escort as we left for practice at the University of Southern California. Those guys are nuts to mess with LA rush-hour traffic to get four huge tour busses on and off the freeway, so I tip my hat to these escorts. I guess they didn't expect so much traffic because when we finally got to USC, we were a half hour behind schedule.

We had a two-hour practice in full pads that ended as the sun was setting. We all went pretty hard and everyone was looking very tired at the end, especially after the two gassers.

The USC facilities are very nice. The locker room is even better than ours, except we have more open space and TVs all over. Their showers are a thing of beauty and are as nice as the most expensive hotel room showers, only these are used by many people to shower at once.

We lifted after practice in the USC weight room which looks impressively similar to ours. They have a few machines we don't have, but I'm sure that's because our strength coaches feel they are unnecessary.

We had a team meeting back at the hotel and went over the ground rules of the trip with the help of two LAPD officers who gave us some information about this immense city. They basically told us to be careful about where we go and at what time of day because the scenery can change very drastically by going only a block or two. They also mentioned that prostitutes are illegal and that many of them are undercover cops, but I doubt any of our guys would be desperate enough or stupid enough to do something like that.

After this we were free, but it was dark and we were tired so Andy Wingender and I just went to our room with o-lineman Mike Erickson and cornerback Kellen Huston, and played Simpsons Monopoly. We had a hot snack of chicken wings and sandwiches at 10:00 and had bed check at midnight. I guess they wanted to make sure our first night in this city wouldn't be too wild.

Tuesday, December 25, 2001

For the fourth year in a row, I'm away from my family for Christmas. I actually think I'm getting used to it, which is kind of scary.

We had meetings at 8:30 this morning after getting taped and eating a small breakfast of supplements and fruit. Luckily, Coach Tenopir stopped meetings right as I was falling asleep and then I had about a half hour to waste before leaving for practice. I wouldn't be surprised if we encounter some road-raged drivers who get fed up with our police escort.

Practice again was in full pads and even more grueling than yesterday, probably because we were tired. One thing I've noticed—we work just as hard whether we're practicing for a pud team or the national championship. There's a strong desire on this team to win this game, and I believe, along with everyone else, that we will win.

After lifting, there was a very good lunch prepared for us by the people at USC. Then we had nothing to do until 6:00, so I took a nap back at the hotel. At 6:00 we had our annual Christmas dinner in the Grand Ballroom of the Beverly Hilton. We had to dress nice for this occasion. There was a pretty nice buffet followed by a short program. There was a video of a bunch of different groups of football players spliced together singing Christmas carols, which was pretty bad, but the best part was when tight end Phil Peetz came on at the start. Phil is a great kid and one of the hardest workers on the team, but it has been noticed that he has a very prominent and very hairy brow, making him look just like Phil Hartman's Unfrozen Caveman Lawyer character from *Saturday Night Live.* He started off saying: "I don't understand all this Christmas stuff. I am just an unfrozen caveman and these decorations and flashing lights frighten and confuse me." I didn't actually hear all that he said because I was laughing so hard at the whole thing. It was easily the funniest thing I've seen all year.

After the video, Dave Volk came in dressed as Santa and put on one of the funniest Santa routines I've seen. As he made his way slowly to the front of the ballroom, he didn't have much prepared, so he just kept saying, "Ho Ho Ho! Merry Christmas!" Just when you thought he would say something new, he would say it again, and Dave has the comedic ability to make it funny. He stopped by two little kids and asked if they had been good this year. When they answered, "yes," he just said, "That's good," and moved on. He made his way to Coach Nelson Barnes and asked the same question, and then followed it up with, "Have your rush ends been getting broken off by the tackles?" After a good laugh, he took his spot on the stage to await all the young kids who came to him while the rest of us quickly grabbed our bowl gifts and left.

The bowl gifts this year were pretty nice. Along with a very nice Tissot watch with a special Rose Bowl emblem on the face, we received a travel bag with the emblem on it and a Rose Bowl edition football inside along with a permanent marker to get it signed, a Kodak Advantix camera with film, a black Rose Bowl hat, a silver commemorative coin similar to the one that will be used in the game, a nice Rose Bowl blanket, and a card congratulating us on making it here. And, since the bowl game itself is sponsored by AT&T, it wouldn't have been complete without a pre-paid phonecard.

There was no bed check tonight, but we just stayed in and played Monopoly again.

Wednesday, December 26, 2001

Today's practice was in sweats, which was a very nice break. Again, we had lunch at USC and then took the bus back to the hotel and had the rest of the day off.

Andy and I walked to a mall a few minutes away, but

left soon after we found out that every store was well beyond our price range. I don't mind not going out too much right now. I don't need to be running around late and getting too little sleep before practice and having a hangover. Also, I'm saving the money the team gave me to use during my extended stay in California after the game.

Thursday, December 27, 2001

Today's practice was similar to yesterday's, only a little shorter and we had to run gassers. We had lunch at USC after lifting and then hurried onto the busses. Some Disney people were there at USC to escort us and even had another set of box lunches and Cokes for us. Even though we just ate, it didn't stop us from having seconds.

After the 45-minute trip to Disneyland, we were led through the back gates and divided up into groups of 10, each with two park guides. We were given badges that allowed us to get right on all the rides. We also were given a $15 food coupon and spent most of that on two corndogs, a bag of chips, and a pop. Midway through our visit we went to one of the park's studios where they do their own version of *Who Wants to be a Millionaire?* Ten of our guys, the most popular names on the team, were chosen to be on the show. Regis Philbin finally came out after we were initially disappointed to see the regular host for this park studio. Regis made many cracks about us beating Notre Dame, his favorite team, and always asked the guys if they thought Notre Dame was tough. Chris Kelsay, Keyuo Craver, and Jamie Burrow all made it into the "hot seat" and they won hats and pins and shirts for the different levels of points they hit since they can't win any money because they're amateur football players.

We then went to the ESPNZone building and were given cards for unlimited games in their arcade. This place was really cool and had all the top games. While we were there, Eric Estrada from the old TV show "CHiPs" showed up and mingled with our guys for a while. They eventually closed down at about 8:00 and then we headed back to the hotel for another night of Monopoly.

Friday, December 28, 2001

During meetings Coach Solich warned us to stay away from unknown girls. He said that if they are in our hotel rooms, all they have to do is run out screaming "rape" and we would instantly be in jail. Also, someone was supposedly hanging out in the lobby telling some of the guys that he could get them into the Playboy Mansion. Coach Solich warned us that if this guy wants to do this "favor" for us, he might want something from us in return or even try to give us gifts or other things that could possibly hurt our eligibility, especially for the national championship.

We don't have practice today, so this is a very nice day. After lunch, Andy Wingender, my girlfriend and I drove out to Marina Del Ray and went to the Cheesecake Factory for a second lunch. This place was really good and I didn't mind eating a second meal of this quality.

The team was invited to the Lakers game tonight, but I didn't go. I'm not really a big basketball fan and Shaq wasn't playing, so I had no interest in going. The guys who did go came back with some pretty good stories. They said they had a couple of skyboxes all to themselves with free food. A few of the higher profile guys were asked to come out on the floor before the game and during halftime to do some little games for prizes. Apparently LA people don't like us much because they booed our guys both times we were on the court, and they even booed when we were shown on the big screens. I wouldn't doubt that the media has had a role in this. One of the *LA Times* sportswriters constantly says we have no right to be here and that our team is a bunch of hicks. However, everyone we've interacted with has told us that we're the best behaved and nicest bunch of guys they've ever seen at the Rose Bowl. Especially when the Miami players are involved in the event with us or when people have had the chance to compare both teams, they always say we're their favorite group of guys. For example, the Rose Bowl princesses, who are all just high school girls, told my parents that they're not supposed to choose sides, but if they could they would root for Nebraska because we have been the nicest group of guys. The princesses said the Miami guys all act like rude thugs with no manners or decency. I already knew that, but it's nice to hear it from another source.

Another good story of the night involved Brad Pitt. He was there enjoying the game and after it was over, he was walking out near our team. There were dozens of girls screaming his name and he just shrugged it off. One of our players wives, who is normally very calm and collected, was very eager to get Brad's autograph, but was too shy to yell at him. Lineman Kyle Kollmorgen stepped up to the challenge and started yelling, "Brad!! Hey, Brad, get over here!!!" When Brad turned around and saw a 6'5", 315-pound man yelling at him, he quickly hurried to his limo and was gone, leaving all the players laughing.

Saturday, December 29, 2001

After our last full pads practice of the year, we had a light lunch at USC and then headed back to the hotel to get into our warm-ups before leaving for Lawry's restaurant. Lawry's is a family-owned prime rib restaurant in Beverly Hills and this has been a Rose Bowl tradition for 45 years. The teams are invited on different nights and get to dig in and eat as much prime rib as they can handle. There was a short presentation by the owners of Lawry's in which they showed a very-well-made video about the Rose Bowl and our season. Coach Solich then presented them with a Nebraska jersey with the number 88 on it for the 88th Rose Bowl. I put down three pieces of very good prime rib and then had the rest of the night to rest and let it digest.

Sunday, December 30, 2001

We started a little later today because Coach Solich and a few of the players went to the City of Hope cancer hospital. At 10:00 we left for Pasadena and the Rose Bowl media day. We picked up our jerseys in the locker room and went out to the stadium to get a view of the whole bowl. It's a massive stadium—very round and all on one level. The slope of the seats, especially in the end zone areas, is very shallow so I feel sorry for the people who sit in that area and have to contend with the people ahead of them for a view of the game.

After we had some time to soak in the stadium, we went to side tents for the media interviews. There were some Danishes and juice set out for us and we devoured these while the high-profile guys all got interviewed.

Then it was off to practice in half pads for two hours back at USC and the rest of the night was free.

A good friend of mine from high school, Michael Callahan, is now living in LA and trying to break into an acting career. We met up and went out tonight. This is the first night I've gone out to actually see the city and it was a really great time. We started out at Mel's Diner on Sunset Strip, which was the scene for *American Graffiti*. We then cruised up and down Hollywood Blvd.

Monday, December 31, 2001

Today was a pretty standard day. Meetings, practice, and the afternoon free to do what we wanted. I lounged around reading most of the day, and later went out with Andy and Brian Nelson to Santa Monica and walked out onto the pier before heading back to the hotel. There was some posh party going on in the hotel ballroom when we returned, but we were unable to get in because Coach Solich told the people selling tickets not to allow players into the party. Instead, I counted down to midnight standing in the lobby. It was pretty depressing not being with good friends or family, so I went out to stock up on beer but was unsuccessful in finding a store close enough before bed check. It's just another lonely day.

Tuesday, January 1, 2002

We had to get up early today to go to team meetings at 7:30. This is way too early for anything after a night of partying. We had our last real practice of the season today. I've been working with the second team offense for all the bowl practices, which surprised me because I thought I'd be working with the scout team a little. Our practices haven't changed much. We've done the same things in the same way as we have all season long.

This feels just like any other game. I haven't listened to the media or read a lot of the hype in the papers, mostly because those people make themselves sound like they know everything when they actually know nothing. The other night on ESPN they were trying to diagram one of our options, but they had a mix of about three of our plays in their pathetic diagram. We have no play in our playbook like the one they showed, but they still made it sound like they were the ones who designed the plays for us.

At 3:30 we loaded up the busses and left for Burbank to see *The Tonight Show.* About 100 guys went and we took up a third of the seats. We were all dressed up semi-casual with slacks and nice shirts. Miami came in behind us and they were all dressed down and looked like a big gang of thugs. The whole show was pretty cool with Kelly Ripa, Johnny

Morton from the Detroit Lions, John Ritter, and the rock group Adema.

During the commercial breaks, the band plays music and a woman sings. In one of the breaks, she came into the audience and had one of the Miami guys try his best at rapping. He started off trying to freestyle, but didn't do too well. He then had a prepared rap which was actually pretty good. The lady then needed a Nebraska guy to try rapping and we volunteered Titus Adams, a freshman defensive lineman. He grabbed the microphone and just blew the Miami guy away with a very quick rap. I couldn't understand much of it, but it sounded great and we walked away from the commercial break a winner.

After the show I met my parents for dinner on the Santa Monica pier.

Wednesday, January 2, 2002

We had later meetings today at 10:30. Then we had a special teams meeting at 1:00 and another team meeting at 4:00 where we watched the pre-psych-up tape which was very good. After the team dinner we went to see *Ocean's Eleven* at a nearby movie theater. Bed check was at 11:00.

Thursday, January 3, 2002

Miami 37 – Nebraska 14

We had meetings at 9:30 and watched a ton of tape on the Miami defense. I would have thought we'd see this earlier in the week rather than the day of the game, but I'm not a coach. I started to fall asleep while watching all the tape. I did my best to stay awake, especially since Coach Solich was sitting right next to me controlling the VCR, but sleep got the best of me. I fell asleep and then Coach Solich slapped me on the thigh like my dad does at church when I fall asleep. Luckily, that was all he did and meetings were over shortly afterward, but I felt pretty bad about it.

We picked up $86 at lunch. At 2:00, we had another short meeting where we saw the game day psych-up tape and then drove to the stadium.

Former all-American rush end Jason Peter showed up for the Rose Bowl and gave us a pep talk in the locker room. Jason is one of the most intimidating guys I have ever seen. We gathered around him and I was unlucky enough to be on the inner part of the circle. If I hadn't been wearing pads, I would have been scared. After a lot of yelling and cursing at us and talking about how ashamed he was of the defense and how the media has been calling them the "Blackskirts," he put a $1,000 price tag on Ken Dorsey's head for anybody who took him out of the game. This piqued the interest of every one of our defensive guys.

We left the locker room the most prepared and the most pumped up we could ever be mentally, physically, and emotionally. However, this could not stop the incredible talent and force of Miami. It was 34-0 at the half and we walked to the locker room feeling like we did at Colorado.

Coach Solich was abnormally unmotivating in his half-time speech, even for him. He said, "We have two choices now, we can either give up and take the loss or we can go out there and give it our best." Pausing quickly, he thought over what he had just said and added, "No, we have just one choice. We have to go out there and do our best. I don't care whether we win or lose, I just want us to do the best we can." I looked around the locker room and saw only disbelief in everyone's eyes. Did our coach just tell us it was hopeless and that we should just play for pride? What kind of motivation is that?! We left that locker room feeling like we had just taken a cold shower. We knew we still had half of a game to play, but we weren't sure why we were playing it.

We battled back a little bit, but we never really got it going. They hit very hard, threw very well, and ran faster than we did. We were definitely beaten by the best. Everyone realized this and it was sort of reassuring knowing we lost to a superior team, and everyone seemed very glad it was over.

After getting beaten this badly by Colorado and Miami in back-to-back games, I wonder if we have what it takes to recover. It seemed like once we get behind in a game, our spirits are completely broken and we are lost. We are so used to getting a strong start and coasting to the finish that we don't know what to do when we start out behind. I think we've lost our killer instinct and our will to win has been replaced by the idea that if we do as we're told, we will win. This is definitely something to work on in the future.

There were some sandwiches and drinks for us after the game, and I grabbed a few and went outside the stadium. I tried to find my parents, but we never discussed where or how we were going to meet. I called them on my cell phone, but apparently everyone else at the game had the same idea and all the circuits were busy. Instead, I just sat outside the gates, waiting for everyone else to finish changing so we could get on the busses. There were tons of Nebraska fans still hanging around the bowl trying to get a glimpse of some of the players, and we were actually received pretty well by the fans.

When we finally got back to the hotel after a very long bus ride, there were a lot of fans in the lobby and they were nice enough to give us a standing ovation when we came in. This choked me up, but I managed to smile and walk on by to my room. I had hoped to go out tonight in celebration of a victory. Instead, I just crashed early and got plenty of sleep.

End of the Year Summary

Close, but not quite. We had an interesting year with some close games, some great games, and two absolutely lousy games leaving us with a record of 11-2. We have a lot of talent on the team, but we seem to have lost the spark. We're a power-football team who's used to being strong, slow and steady throughout the game. This was changed when we got stuffed repeatedly and were put in a position to start fighting back.

Our fans were wonderful, as usual. We truly have some of the best fans in the world and I think Nebraska as a state is unique in its dedication to its team. We don't have any other major colleges or professional teams, so nearly everyone in the state is unified in their love for the home team, the Nebraska Cornhuskers. Our fans travel to our away games in huge crowds and many other states even have their own fan clubs like "Californians for Nebraska" and so on. There's no other college program in the nation where a football player could be so revered by so many people in the state.

As good as our fans are, we knew there had to be a few fair-weather fans. We saw them come out at the end of the season. Apparently making it to a National Championship isn't good enough for some people. I wish I had a finger to point at someone, to explain this season for the fans, but I don't. We seem to be missing something from our team mentality. I still think there are too many guys on the team who don't care at all about their situation. They're just here for the gifts, the trips, and the notoriety. We need to thin the herd a little bit, but none of the coaches have ever shown much fondness towards cutting anyone. I guess we need as many healthy bodies as we can for practice. I also guess that the coaches believe everyone deserves a chance to mature and develop. For example, I should have been cut after my freshman year for how terrible I was in practice, but now I'm in position with my size and strength to be a contributor.

2002 Winter Conditioning

Saturday, January 12, 2002

Soon after the game was over, it was time to speculate whether any juniors would go pro and skip their senior year. Our star junior guard, Toniu Fonoti, said he would go pro. He definitely has the size and speed to go pro right now and make a dent in someone's program, but he's only 20 years old and still has much to learn. He and Dominic were pretty good friends, so I wonder if Toniu saw what all the money could do and couldn't say no. We all knew it could happen, but we just assumed that since he's so young and since he didn't win any awards, he would be back to get either the Outland or Lombardi and help us to another national championship game. Well, good luck in the pros, Toniu.

Monday, January 14, 2002

Second semester classes start today. We don't start anything for football for another two weeks. The only thing we have to do is go to meetings on Friday to go through the winter conditioning plan.

My girlfriend's dad was recently at a sports collectibles show where some kid was selling a Husker football helmet. The kid said he just finished his career at Nebraska as a defensive back. The helmet was pretty beat up and he told a story about how there are two helmets, a practice helmet and a game helmet, and we get to keep the game helmet after the season's over. This isn't true; there is only one helmet per guy and when they are given to the seniors as going-away presents, they are cleaned up better than this one was. There was a special forces sticker on the back of the helmet, which was only given out this past season. And to top it off, the kid said he didn't know me and blamed it on being a large team. Her dad also could tell that a number *2* had been removed from the back of the helmet. The only number *2* on the team who is also on special forces is Aaron Terpening, so this made me very suspicious.

I asked Aaron about it and said his helmet was stolen the week of the Oklahoma game. Somehow this guy had Aaron's helmet and was trying to sell it for $200. I gave all the information to Pat Logsdon, the director of football operations, and she said she would look into it.

Thursday, January 17, 2002

I recently heard some good news—it appears that I'm now second string. Matt Shook, who has battled chronic knee pain the past four years, has decided to take a medical hardship and not play his final year. Richie Incognito, who looked to be a ringer for second string and even battle John Garrison for first string, is moving to tackle. That leaves me in the second spot, which means I can get a scholarship if I can hold on to this. I finally have something tangible to work for.

Friday, January 23, 2002

We did our preliminary testing on Wednesday. Once again, I didn't eat or rest properly and performed very poorly. I met with Coach Tenopir today and went over these scores. He said I will have to improve my speed greatly if I ever want to get a lot of playing time. He mentioned that Matt and Richie are no longer centers and he isn't sure if he will move anyone else to center. So, the position is mine for the taking. I just have to work my ass off and secure the second-string spot.

Monday, January 28, 2002

Today is the first day of winter conditioning and once again we're lifting at 7:00 in the morning. We won't start running for two weeks, so we have time to get adapted to the lifting.

Tuesday, January 29, 2002

Several years ago, Jack Stark, our team psychologist, had the idea to form a council of players that would act as a liaison between the coaches and the players. The "Unity Council" is represented by every position on the team and it is the job of the representatives to bring forth any issues that their group is facing. Then, the players concerns are given to the coaches directly and handled very efficiently with Dr. Stark as the intermediary. This council has worked very well to build a great deal of unity and ownership among the players.

I volunteered when Coach Tenopir asked who from the O-line wanted to be on the council. The O-line only needs five guys on the board, but I made it six. Because of this, my official title is an alternate, according to Jack Stark. I'm not sure what that means exactly, but I'm going to consider myself a full member.

We had our first meeting tonight. Jack Stark had a few issues to talk about. We finalized our jersey styles for next year. For away games, we will wear all white with a red stripe down the side. It will be interesting to see how the public reacts to this since there were a few Husker teams in the past who chose all white and didn't fare so well in those seasons. The home games will be the same, with white pants and red jerseys, but I think there will be a white stripe down the side of the jersey and a red stripe down the side of the pants. Jack then asked if there was anything we would like to change about the locker room. No idea is too ridiculous apparently, because Jack even talked about doing what Baylor has done and put personal TVs in our individual lockers. I would be happy with different showerheads and better soap, and think the TV idea is a little much. Jack said there are a couple of local businessmen who are ready to sign a check for whatever we want in our locker room. That just seems amazing to me, but I'm sure this is not the first time.

Thursday, January 30, 2002

Today was light squat day, but this was followed by one-legged dumbbell squats and leg curls. I'm not sure if I was a little sick to start off, but halfway through all of this, I threw up. I guess doing that much leg strength work in one morning was too much.

I got a list of all the guys on the O-line and made up a telephone roster for everyone. I'm looking for some kind of leadership role this season. I know I probably won't play much, so I want to be someone behind the scenes who the younger guys can look up to for guidance and support.

It still amazes me that I'm finally a senior. When I came in four years ago, I looked up to all the seniors, even the ones who didn't play. Now I'm one of those guys and it feels weird for many reasons. I'm so close to the end of my college career, so close to freedom, and am in a position of power. I'm now in the group that makes all the decisions for the O-line. I can make suggestions and changes, and can easily take time off for school or other activities that in the past required me to tell the older guys and then hope for their approval.

Monday, February 4, 2002

Bailey is now in charge of a wider range of players, not just the O-line. His pet project is a new treadmill workout he borrowed from his own rehab work when he had surgery on his leg this past year. Basically, there's a pneumatic pulley system above the treadmill which holds a special harness that allows us to run with reduced weight. This does a few things—it helps our posture, takes a lot of pressure off of our backs, especially for the bigger guys, and reduces the amount of impact per step, making it very useful for people recovering from an injury.

Before we got on the treadmill, we had to do a couple of things for documentation. We took off our shirts and shoes, and were photographed to look for symmetry, flexibility, and muscle tone. Then we had to walk to and from a video camera to document our walking style in the hope something might be found when it's analyzed, and also to compare it to the end product when this is all over.

When we're on the treadmill, they take about 30 pounds off of us with the harness and then we walk forward, backward, and sideways, and run in these same positions for about 12 minutes. I have to do this two days a week; some guys have to do it four days a week because the coaches want them to lose weight and they see this as the best way to do it.

We no longer have a nutrition staff. Since Dave Ellis quit, the whole nutrition department (about three people) has scrambled to fill his shoes, but now everyone is gone due to graduation, family commitments, and other factors. The nutrition people made sure there were drinks and plenty of cups. The weight room staff now has to do this and they are doing a horrible job. It's not easy to mess up a Gatorade-type drink, but somehow they do it. The recovery drink mix, which is more like thick, calorie-rich meal supplement, has separated into a watery mix and looks disgusting. Art McWilliams, the head guy for the training table, is now the interim nutrition guru.

> After my senior year, everyone continually asked me what went wrong to make us fall so far. My best guess was that it wasn't any one thing in particular, it was several small things that added up together. The nutrition staff dissolving was just one of these things. Later on, several of the people on the strength and conditioning staff would take positions at other places too, leaving a void for many of the players that the other strength coaches struggled to fill, overloading themselves in the process. During this year as well, we saw many changes around the stadium, including a lot of construction work in the weight room. Much of the high traffic areas of the stadium were under construction, which was never the most wonderful thing to see, smell, or detour around.

Monday, February 11, 2002

Today was our first day of afternoon running. I wasn't looking forward to it, but knew I'd have to suffer through it. I went home after class, planning to nap until it was time to run. I slept right up to 3:30, when running starts. I drove quickly to the Cook Pavilion, ran inside and mixed in with the O-line during one of the drills. I knew I'd have to run stairs for being late, and if anyone pointed out my tardiness I was just going to say I would run my stairs when I was finished. Fortunately, no one pointed this out. I'm not sure if it's because I'm a senior and the younger guys don't want to point out the flaws of the older guys, or if no one noticed. Jack Limbaugh later asked me if I had a class before running and I decided to save myself a lot of trouble and said "yes." So, I got away with it.

Tuesday, February 12, 2002

Somehow it happened again. I think I turned my alarm off this morning and went back to sleep. I awoke at 7:45 and couldn't believe it. I knew I wouldn't get away with it twice and would have to run three stairs. I saw Wes Cody at breakfast and told him I overslept and would do my stairs later today. He said: "No one noticed. Don't worry about it. If anyone asks, just tell them I saw you in the drink room and you told me you had to study for a test today."

Wes was right; no one even noticed. With Wes' go-ahead, I dodged the bullet again. But this bugs me for two reasons, and I don't know if it bugs me more that I let myself down by being late or that no one noticed. I'm a senior now, and should be one of the most visible guys. Maybe it helps that I'm the one who takes roll in the morning.

Wednesday, February 13, 2002

Coach Tenopir met with the O-line at 3:30 today. He had pens and notebooks ready for us and went through a handful of plays, hoping we would take notes and learn something. It was helpful, but it lasted too long for as few plays as we looked at. This is supposed to be our day off so I would have liked to do nothing related to football, but I guess I have less control over my life than I thought.

Thursday, February 14, 2002

Richie Incognito was late again this morning. He was late earlier in the week, so this time he had to run four stairs since it was his second offense. We went out as a group to watch him run and we were huddled around each other on the field because it was so cold. Richie is just a freshman, but he has a mouth that doesn't know when to shut up. He's a pretty funny kid and already is fairly popular, but everyone keeps talking about how tired they are of him running his mouth all the time. The other seniors have all said we should just beat the crap out of him sometime, but he wouldn't shut up even if he was beaten within an inch of his life.

I guess Richie knew I was late on Tuesday because he joked that I would have to run with him, but he knew his place as a freshman and didn't push it too far. After his third stair we knew he would have trouble with the fourth, so someone asked who wanted to push him up the stairs. Scott Koethe volunteered, but Richie said, "I think Kolowski should run with me." I got up there and Scott and I tailed behind Richie as we all sprinted up the stairs. Richie was pretty worn out after this, nearly vomiting a couple of times on his way down, so I think he learned his lesson.

We ran again this afternoon; Bailey is in charge of our running workout, which makes me feel better about what we're doing.

Friday, February 15, 2002

My back was really sore this morning. I think it's from our strength coach, Zach Duval, trying to get us to have "better" form on hang clean. Hang clean has always been my favorite lift, but now that he's trying to change it, I'm losing interest in it. Bailey and I worked on a lot of warming up and stretching today to get my back working. After that I asked Zach what I should do for lifting today and he just said, "nothing." A decent lifting coach would have figured out something for me to do. Nothing doesn't help. I told him I felt like I could do something, but he didn't want to waste his time figuring out something for me to do. Instead, I just did some lat pull-down and arm curls and went home.

Thursday, February 21, 2002

I am getting very tired of all of this. After four years of doing the same things, I am very ready to get out and be in control of my life. It seriously feels like football has more control over my life than I do. Football is a major motivating force, but right now it's only motivating me enough to get by. One of the main thoughts that gets me through the day is that football will be over in less than a year and then I can live like I want to. I'm just afraid that once I'm done, I'll be so pleased to have nothing to do that I'll turn into a couch potato.

I don't care about school anymore. I just want to do enough in classes to get a passing grade and get out of college. I don't want to go to graduate school. My parents aren't the same motivating force they used to be. I'm in a rut right now. During the week is the worst. The weekends are a great relief because I can actually have some fun. There's nothing in Lincoln for me anymore. I don't have a strong group of friends here and I feel like an outsider everywhere I go. I'm tired of this city and I'm tired of this state. Maybe I'm just depressed right now, but something has got to change, either within me or in my life.

Lifting in the morning has turned into a joke. I go in and do what I need to do and get out. I'm cutting corners and even skipping some lifts entirely, like many other guys who can get away with it. Some of the lifts I skip are ones that I feel don't do me any good, like clean shrugs which I think are responsible for my tight back. I used to feel good about lifting and actually look forward to it. Now I just want to get the hell out.

Friday, February 22, 2002

Tonight was a pretty fun night. Fullback Judd Davies, cornerback Pat Ricketts, split end Ben Zajicek, and I went to Andersen Middle School, my old school in Omaha. We signed a bunch of footballs and shirts with our numbers on them, and then got free pizzas and sandwiches. Afterward we went into the gym and crowds of people streamed in for autographs. I must have signed over 200 autographs for the 500+ in attendance. I signed everything from shirts and jackets to footballs, shoes, pants, and even arms. One pair of guys wanted to take a picture with me and they wanted me to act like I had them in a headlock.

When the autograph session was over, we were worked into the program for the evening. Johnny Rodgers was there with his Heisman Trophy (his granddaughter attends Andersen) and he was the main attraction for many people. Li'l Red (our inflatable mascot) and four cheerleaders were there along with three twirlers and they put on an energy-filled show. There was a raffle of prizes donated from the community and also some mock jerseys with our numbers on them that we signed. One of the prizes was the chance to catch a pass from a Husker. There were four chances given away which should have worked well since four of us players were there, but one of the kids picked Johnny Rodgers to throw him a pass, leaving me out of the whole thing. Then, there was a short question-and-answer session. I was told I should answer one of the questions for the football guys, but they only asked two questions: "What's it like on game day running out of the tunnel?" and "What are you most proud of?" I passed these off to the other guys hoping there would be a question more suited to me, but that was it. I came to this event at my own junior high school and I didn't even get to play much of a part in it. I had a lot of fun though, and saw a lot of former teachers who were really happy to see me. That, and I got free food.

Monday, March 4, 2002

I was stranded in Omaha over the weekend when I took my car in to get serviced and the mechanics discovered some serious problems. It was done at noon today, which means I missed morning lifting. I didn't mind.

I called most of the seniors and said I'd be down for running in the afternoon and would make up the lifting later.

We switched the running up a little bit today, and put away the jump ropes. Instead we did 10-yard dashes from our form start like we would for testing. We did about six of these and then finished the day by doing five-yard sprints from our position starts. If someone jumped the count, we had to do it over again. We were only supposed to do eight of these, but we ended up doing 12 because of so many mistakes.

After the running we had passing league where we just played football—upperclassmen versus lower classmen. The upperclassmen always cheat, so we never lose and usually the younger guys just give up and the game is called off when no one cares about it anymore, which only takes about 15 minutes. Jack Limbaugh, who has become somewhat of a black sheep on the O-line, doesn't get along well with Richie Incognito. Richie plowed right into Jack's back on one of the plays, taking Jack out and leaving him on the ground. Jack finally got up, grabbed his stuff and walked out. I talked to him later and he said that he was tired of that shit and got pissed off, so he just left. I don't blame him. In fact, I was in entire agreement with Jack for our whole conversation.

When this was all over, I still had to do my lifting for the day. Luckily, all we had to do was heavy squat and bench press. I finished squat today with 350 pounds for my last set of 10. On bench, I followed the chart for the sets of 10 that would give me a one-rep max of 330 pounds, the last set being 245 pounds for 10. In all, I think that went pretty well, especially after running.

Thursday, March 7, 2002

We finished out this week in the weight room by maxing out on all the major lifts. The amount of time spent in the weight room has greatly decreased this week. They just want us to come in and do a couple of lifts and get out.

They decided to make running a little more fun today. Instead of running, all we did was play tug-of-war. We divided up into 12 groups that were a mix of different positions. We did a single elimination bracket and the last group standing got the chance to face off against the coaches. The coaches looked like they might have a chance, for about the first half of a second. After that, it was all over. Nate Kolterman pulled Coach Jamrog, who had the rope looped around him, down the field 30 yards while Nate just ran off in victory with the rope in tow.

Friday, March 8, 2002

This morning was the last workout ever for me in winter conditioning. The strength coaches yesterday said this workout would be optional, but the O-line as a group decided we would lift today anyway. Everyone was there on time, but most of the guys obviously had no intention of working out. Some didn't even take off their coats. They just stood around and for 20 minutes and then went to breakfast. I did a quick arm workout with Scott Koethe and soon joined the guys at breakfast. Since I have no classes on Friday, this makes the day even sweeter knowing that this is the last time I will have to get up this early to work out during a semester. We'll probably work out in the morning during the summer, but that's not as bad since I won't have to save energy to stay awake during classes.

Monday, March 11, 2002

We had a meeting to talk about testing and to debrief after the whole winter conditioning. I will test out at 1:00 on Wednesday along with the rest of the seniors. We're going first because there will be pro scouts there who want to get a look at us. I don't plan on going pro, so that takes a lot of pressure off me.

I went to see Dr. Albers after the meeting. I had a really strong irregular heartbeat this morning. I told him about it and how it happens about once a week or more. I've had this since high school and have never gotten a straight answer about it. He came to the conclusion that it's a common thing caused by an excess of blood in the heart, which causes it to pause a bit while it flushes out and then it gets going again. He said it's nothing to worry about, so that put my mind at rest.

We talked about other things on my mind and he said I might be depressed. He went through a list of depression symptoms and I have a majority of them. I actually don't doubt that I'm depressed. I've known this for a while, but I just figured it was caused by football and would go away once football is over. He talked about trying some antidepressant medication, but I would rather not do that. He said if we did start medication, the records would be kept confidential. He said he types up those reports himself and stores them in a separate safe, and they would not follow my other records if they are sent to a professional team. He said he does this because there is a stigma against people on antidepressants, even though over 10% of the population is depressed. The only way another person would ever see the record is if I say it's okay. I think it's very nice that he does this, but I wonder how ethical that is.

Tuesday, March 12, 2002

I called Jack Stark tonight and asked if he can set me up with a therapist in town. He said there are a few in private practice he could recommend, but he and I agree that it might be best, and cheapest, to use the psychology staff at the University Health Center which is free for three visits.

All day today I tried to put together what exactly has depressed me so badly and so recently. I think the majority of it has to do with football. I'm pretty much forced by pride and personal honor to continue, while being told what to do by coaches I don't respect and who don't respect me. I'm forced to maintain a weight and a physique that I'm not comfortable with. I don't have much respect for some of the guys on the team. I don't get the same encouragement or results that I used to in the weight room, and my general motivation for the sport has decreased. I hope something good will happen now that I know where to start.

Wednesday, March 13, 2002

At noon I headed over to Cook Pavilion. Some of the pro scouts were there to get our times and they had us fill out some paperwork. They took our weight and height, and measured our hand-span and arm length. As I was filling out the forms, I was listening to the scouts talk about some of the players they've recently picked up and the conversation turned to some of the weird things players do. One of the stories was about a guy from Nebraska who drank eight ounces of his own urine every week. He was a tight end who played for the 49ers but they couldn't remember his name. They ended the conversation by agreeing that there are a lot of freaks in the NFL. I'm not a freak and I don't want to work with a lot of freaks. Right now, I'm much more interested in doing a job that I enjoy even if I don't make much money, than going pro and making a lot of money but not being happy. It's just not for me.

After I finished all the paperwork and was sufficiently warmed up, I put the last nail in the coffin of my potential pro career by turning in an average testing day. After this, the pros will write me off, much like the coaches have probably done already.

Oh well, just a few more months.

After the testing Coach Solich called a quick meeting to tell us he has picked up a pre-season game. We will play Arizona State the night of August 24. This means if we play in the Big 12 championship and a bowl game, we will have a 15-game season. That has to be a record.

Coach Solich said the sole reason for adding the game is to get us ready to play in the Big 12. He stressed that money was never an issue and that neither he nor the coaching staff was pressured to take the game because of the revenue it will bring in. I believe him, but why would anyone try so hard to convince someone so strongly it wasn't for money unless it was indeed a motivating factor?

2002 Spring Ball

Monday, March 25, 2002

After a nice spring break that included a trip to Chicago and a visit with my family, today was our first day back and the first day of spring practice. A snowstorm dumped five inches, however, so classes and afternoon practice were cancelled. The main field wasn't cleared off and Cook Pavilion was being used by the soccer or baseball team. So, instead of practice, all we did was have meetings. Coach Tenopir and Coach Young are changing up a few things to make some of the blocking assignments a little easier. I think they make a lot more sense, but we'll see when we start practicing. I'm not sure if we'll make up this practice later, but we only have 15 practices total, so I wouldn't be surprised if they try to throw in another practice somewhere.

Tuesday, March 26, 2002

I talked to Coach Solich today while we were in the elevator together and he said practice was called off for the same reason that school was called off. He wasn't sure if everyone had gotten into town on time with the snowstorm and he didn't want anybody to miss a practice. The papers say we will make up the practice on the Friday before the

Spring Game with a sweats walk-through.

I got some disturbing news today as well. I heard yesterday in meetings that the lifting would be intensified over the spring period, but I thought that meant we would do more lifts on the days we work out. Instead, we will lift four days a week now, Monday through Thursday. We really don't do much, just enough to keep our strength up, but this puts a cramp in my schedule, especially with classes all day on Thursday.

Coach Tenopir wants us to meet on Tuesdays and Thursdays, as well as on our practice days. The NCAA allows 20 hours a week for football-related activities, and we are squeezing in every second. Today we just watched a bunch of old film on some of the plays we will add tomorrow.

Wednesday, March 27, 2002

The first day of spring practice. We were in sweats in the stadium and it was a typical practice. We only have a handful of plays at this point, so we ran the same plays over and over. Both sides of the ball worked well and the day was pretty good overall.

We had a Unity Council meeting tonight. On the agenda was the issue of blazers and the Black Coaches Association (BCA) money. The game against Arizona State is the BCA Classic and because it's a special game, we get a gift. Jack Stark is trying hard to sell us on blazers, which would make us look like a very clean cut and respectable team, but there were many objections. The guys who aren't part of the 105 group for two-a-days would have to buy their own blazers and suit pants, and this is not an option. We have $300 to play with for the gifts and we can get a discount buying in bulk. Other gifts Jack has looked into are portable DVD players, but he can't find them cheap enough unless a sponsor helps out. Some of the guys started talking about how a big TV would be a great gift, and this branched off into a discussion about what kind of electronic gift to get. I broke up the discussion by suggesting we get $300 gift certificates to Best Buy and this immediately satisfied everyone. Jack said the only problem with gift certificates is that we need to make sure guys don't trade them in for cash. We should know by next week what we'll get.

Friday, March 29, 2002

Today's practice was in sweats again, but today I worked with the first team. I think Coach Tenopir thought Josh Sewell knew the plays well enough and didn't need me to help him, and he wanted me to get up with the number ones and give Garrison a break. I did a 6-2 rotation with Garrison, so I really didn't get many reps. By the end of the practice I didn't feel like I had done anything.

I guess it could be a good thing or a bad thing being on the first team like I am. It could be that Coach thinks I'm ready to work with the top unit and wants to break me in to it, or it could be that he wants to give Sewell more snaps with the second team and develop him as a good back-up center. So either I'm good enough to be there or I'm just being used to give Garrison a break and I'll be pushed aside later on. I wish I knew.

Saturday, March 30, 2002

Today was the first day in pads. I switched off with Garrison for most of the practice, but at the end I had to give Sewell a break since he had been taking all the snaps for the twos and was getting worn out.

I feel like I'm doing a lot better on the field. We did some one-on-ones in the Pit and I did pretty well against the defensive guy. I even got a compliment out of Coach Young. I'm moving around better and I think it has to do with my recent plan to lose a little weight. My body really doesn't work well at 300 pounds or higher, so I'm going to slim down over the next couple of weeks and see if I can get to 285 and see if this has any effect on my playing. I hope I'll get quicker on the field and not lose any strength. I'll have to be careful to still lift hard in the weight room to keep my strength up. I weighed myself as I got out of the shower after practice and I was 290.

Wednesday, April 3, 2002

Today's practice sucked. Everyone was tired and beat up from Monday's scrimmaging and my legs didn't want to do anything, especially after being kicked hard on the side of the shin. I started off okay, but by the end of practice I couldn't block anyone at all. I'm sure it looked really bad on film. I would be down on myself if I cared about all of this, but I don't.

We had another Unity Council meeting tonight and we just go over the same issues again and again, even though Jack keeps telling us we need to make a decision. We still don't know what to get with our BCA money, and we continue to deal with some of the common complaints, like the lack of soap in the locker room. There is finally some sort of traction surface leading down the ramps into the Pit to prevent guys from slipping in their metal spikes on the bare cement. The idea of the blazers has officially been shot down and we still need a motto for next year.

Friday, April 5, 2002

Demoine Adams was named Lifter of the Year today. He's very deserving of this award and should probably get something else for how hard he has worked on the field, in the classroom, and in the community as well as in the weight room. He is a great guy and he beat out some tough competition.

Saturday, April 6, 2002

Before meetings today, former Husker and 49ers full-back Tom Rathman gave us a talk. He is currently the running backs coach for the Niners. He talked mostly about how we are Nebraska and have a tradition and an expectation to live up to. He told us we need to play with a lot of heart and be relentless on the field in our attempt to get better. It was a very good, quick speech and he really made his point about how everyone needs to work hard.

Monday, April 8, 2002

I got my grade back from the scrimmage this last weekend. It was a 1.76, which isn't bad, but still needs lots of work. I think the thing that hurt me the most was not finishing blocks against some of the guys, and other times I just couldn't get the right position on the guy to make the block in the first place. The tape of the scrimmage didn't lie.

The seniors had a private meeting today with coach Solich. The main thing on the agenda was the development of leadership among the seniors and how we need to find our own way to lead the younger guys and the team as a whole. Coach Solich has said that he's disappointed by the lack of leadership and how the team is deteriorating during practice with too many side conversations instead of paying attention to what's going on. The papers must have gotten wind of this and now one of the hottest topics is how the team has to "rebuild" and that we will be fortunate if we get our typical nine wins this season.

Another hot topic is the status of Randy Stella. He has been in the paper for weeks now and the issue of his suspension has been batted around. Today it was finalized when Coach Solich said the suspension has been replaced with an expulsion. As we learned in the Unity Council meeting, Randy had to clear certain guidelines with three groups; the

NCAA, the university, and the football team before being eligible for inclusion on the team. He has pointed a finger at Coach Solich, saying he had the power to let him back on the team, but Solich was doing nothing. The truth is that Coach would love to have Randy back, but it wasn't his call. I guess finalizing the expulsion was something that was within Coach Solich's power and the issue is finally settled. Randy has been given every chance in the world to extinguish his bad behavior, but he just hasn't gotten the hint.

The O-line had to take a drug test after practice today. This is usually a small thing, but it was pretty heated today when a freshman lineman was caught trying to get another guy to fill his sample cup for him. We have to stand around two garbage cans and fill a cup under the watchful eye of one of the trainers. Somehow, everyone made a mad dash for the cans and blocked off the trainer's view and when he got it straightened out, he caught him. I'm not sure what he was trying to hide, but we'll find out soon enough.

I talked with Boyd Epley candidly a little while ago about the status of the weight room and the nutrition staff. He said he's as surprised as anyone about how many of the weight staff have moved on to better jobs. We now have only a minimum staff with no more than six people for the entire weight room all day long. We still don't have a nutrition staff, so these people have the duties of filling up drink containers and giving athletes their supplements. Boyd said the nutrition staff placement has been held up because there's a difference of opinion between Coach Solich and Athletic Director Bill Byrne. Byrne wants a nutritionist for the entire athletic department and Solich wants one just for the football team. Three very qualified candidates applied for the job, but they all pulled their application after it took too long to make a decision.

Wednesday, April 10, 2002

We had another Unity Council meeting tonight. It appears that our choices have changed once again and an Xbox video game system is now at the top of the list for potential gifts for the first game. I don't like this idea because I waste enough time without a video game, and the games for those things are so expensive I wouldn't even want to buy them. Besides, every couple years a better system will be out making this one obsolete. My idea for the gift certificates was turned down because they couldn't find a sponsor.

Art McWilliams, who runs the training table, talked to us about the food. Some of the guys have said they want some changes in the food. Art told us there are certain rules this cafeteria needs to follow, such as serving the same food that's found in the dorms, but Art does his best with the help of Bill Byrne and some boosters to give us the best-quality food. He assured us that nothing on our plates is ever canned (except for some beans), and that most of our food is better than what we find at the grocery store. He also said he has requested $230,000 for new tables and chairs, new trays, a bigger and better organized serving area, and many other great things. He doesn't know yet if he has the money, but I'm sure it will find its way to him.

Friday, April 12, 2002

We had another full-pads practice today. That's seven practices in a row in full pads. I don't think we've ever done that before, even during two-a-days. Everyone is tired and beat up, but there's a reason why we had to go so hard today. There is a coaching clinic going on this weekend and over 1,000 coaches from across the nation, and even from Mexico, are here to learn from our staff. So, in order for them to watch and learn something, we had to go in full pads and give them something to analyze. After practice Coach Solich introduced Monte Kiffin, the defensive coordinator for the Tampa Bay Buccaneers. Kiffin got his start at Nebraska, first as a player and then as a coach. He gave us a very good speech about what it means to play here and how the tradition has carried on even after so many years. He was very fiery and threw in a few jokes here and there, but he really made a good point about putting forth a good effort because we are all playing for the tradition of Nebraska football.

Monte Kiffin is the type of coach our team needs. We don't have anyone who can give inspiring speeches and make us feel that we can get the job done even after he chews us out. Monte is the type of coach you would really fight for and I think that is a huge thing missing from this team.

Saturday, April 13, 2002

Today was a long day. We showed up for meetings at 10:30. All we watched in group meetings was film from the number ones. Luckily, we didn't watch the twos, because I had a horrible day. Ryon Bingham keeps destroying me and anyone else who tries to block him. The guy is so strong and has such a firm base that he's impossible to move and can just toss you aside like a trash bag. He will be a great player for us, but he still has a tendency to jump offsides on a long count. That's his only drawback, unless you count that he doesn't try to read the offense much. He just plows through and makes the tackle. Well, it works for him.

At 12:30, the offensive line had to do demonstrations for the coaching clinic and luckily I wasn't chosen to be in that group. By that time, I was already back home eating lunch. I then had to run over to see Layne, the boy I mentor, and wish him a happy birthday. Then it was back to the stadium by 1:30 and on the field by 2:30 for kicking demonstrations. I took all the snaps for the field goals and Garrison took all the snaps for the punts. After the demonstration a bunch of the coaches came up and asked me for tips on how to long snap. I did the best I could to answer their questions and to give them advice they could pass on to their athletes.

I took two of the live punts in the scrimmage while Garrison took the first two and did pretty well.

The scrimmage started off slowly. The defense has proven they are very strong, but the offense wore them down today by picking up better drives as the day wore on.

There were a few key injuries today, some of the worst ones yet. I-back DeAntae Grixby went down with an injury to either his knee or ankle, cornerback Willie Amos went down with a knee injury, and center Josh Sewell came out during his last series with an ankle injury. I filled in for Sewell on the last few plays. Guard Brian Nelson is out again with a re-aggravated shoulder and is having surgery today, guard Carson Schott tore his ACL, offensive tackle M.J. Flaum hurt his good shoulder with the same type of injury as on his other one, and guard Wes Cody spent a couple days out of practice with a back problem.

Monday, April 15, 2002

After a weekend with a very long scrimmage and a massive increase in the temperature, the coaches gave us a little break today. We started off going full pads, but were allowed to take our shoulder pads off midway through practice. This was supposed to keep the hitting and injuries down, but it didn't decrease the intensity of the practice. John Garrison had a class today and Sewell is out due to his ankle, so I was up on the number ones, trading the center job with Junior Tagoa'i. Without a doubt, this was one of the most intense and mentally tough practices of the entire spring session. We were going very quickly through the plays and each one of us was watching out for the other, making sure we did what we were supposed to. By the end of practice, I was as tired as if we had been in full pads. It was about 90 degrees for the first time this year and was such a change from the cold conditions we had at the start of spring practice.

After practice, the strength coaches wanted us to do some extra work on our shoulder muscles and other stabilizing muscles. I don't really see the point of this, but apparently there is a reason for it.

Wednesday, April 17, 2002

The members of this year's Brook Berringer Citizenship Team were named at meetings today and I was among the 16 guys selected (Brook was a quarterback for us back in 1995 and traded the starting spot with Tommie Frazier. He did a great job and also was very active in the community. He died shortly after his senior season when the small plane he was piloting crashed, leading to a huge outpouring of support including the formation of this group). I received a very nice plaque with two pictures of Brook, one of him speaking to students and the other of him playing quarterback in a game. This is a real honor although I don't really know what goes with it. I'm not sure if this is just something to put on a resume or if we actually do something as a group. From what I can gather, we are the guys who will be considered first when people from the community request a Husker to come and speak to them. That should be easy enough.

Today was the last full-pads practice of the spring. I am so glad it's over. I was on the number two offense and will be the first to admit that our defense is very, very good. The linemen are very strong and quick; the rush ends are fast and in on almost every play; and the linebackers avoid blocks well and pursue the ball. The poor secondary hasn't had much of a chance to prove itself because the quarterback is usually under so much pressure he can't throw the ball. Ryon Bingham leads the defensive line in brute strength and can simply toss anybody to the side and pursue the ball carrier. If he plays all of our 15 possible games this next season, he should break some records. Of all of the defensive linemen I've gone up against in the past four years, he is undoubtedly the strongest and one of the quickest. If he doesn't jump offsides, he should be golden.

Saturday, April 20, 2002

Today was the culmination of spring practice with the annual Spring Game. A cold front moved in yesterday and it was only about 45 degrees the entire day. We had breakfast and meetings, then sat around until we had to snap to the kickers at 11:30. I could tell my snaps were going to be off today by how I was warming up because I didn't have the control that I usually do. I think it was due to the unexpected cold.

The game started at 12:30. I was on the white team, backing up Junior Tagoa'i at center. Junior switched from D-line to O-line and can play guard and center. I'm guessing he is the choice for second-string center, which is a smart decision on the coaches' part. By moving a scholarship guy to the second-string spot they don't have to waste a scholarship on Sewell or me. Typically, when a walk-on earns at least a second string position, they will be given a scholarship. It's not a rule that's written in stone, but more of a common courtesy.

The red team started the game with the ball and did fairly well on their first drive although they didn't score. I overheard one of the head trainers say the early series were scripted to make sure the offense looked good in front of the public and the media. The defense destroyed the offense in earlier scrimmages, but this time the defense was put in a position to fail. That's pretty sneaky, but will anyone be able to tell?

Junior took most of the snaps. I only got 16 snaps total and actually graded out with a 1.813. That's high for me, but middle-of-the-pack for the rest of the guys. I had all the snapping duty for the white team and ended up with the extra-point snap and four punts. One of my punt snaps was perfect, but the punter really had to reach for the rest of them because they were high and to the right. All of them got off, except for one that got blocked by Ira Cooper whom I was supposed to block on the line. The funny thing about his block is that there were no blocks called on the punts at all. He just had a golden opportunity and took it. I ended up redeeming myself and not even knowing it when I recovered a fumble. It was another high snap, but he finally got it off with a high, short kick. It landed near me and I thought I was just downing it when I dove in the pile. I came up with the ball while other guys were clawing for it, and the ref stood over me pointing "white ball." It didn't even register until I started to walk off the field and remembered that I'm on the white team and the ball was ours again. Then I was happy.

The red team won 17-7, which was expected since they had the first-team offense. After these past four weeks, and a cold and rainy second half, I'm very glad this is over. My last spring practice ever is done.

Sunday, April 21, 2002

Tonight was the Student-Athlete Academic Recognition Banquet. The guest speaker was Rulon Gardner, former Husker All-American wrestler and the 2000 Olympic gold medal winner in Greco-Roman Wrestling. He made history when he defeated the world champion Russian wrestler in the finals, ending his nine-year undefeated reign. Rulon claimed he had a fear of speaking to crowds in college and got a C+ in speech class, but he really did well tonight. He talked mostly about being positive, being very proactive, and setting high goals for yourself. He related all of this to his life and how he has worked hard for everything he has, from his college degree to his gold medal. For some reason, this speech really struck a chord with me and I thanked Rulon personally when I received my medallion by telling him he is a great role model. I'm going to get a copy of his speech and watch it again. Who knows, this might be the start of a turn-around from the state of mind I've been in.

Tuesday, April 30, 2002

I worked out today for the first time since spring ball. I did a pretty good all-around workout and then ran two sets of stairs at the north end. After those stairs, my body was done. I guess a week and a half off really takes a toll.

I recently found out that my locker has been moved. I'm out in the middle of the locker room now by the rest of the offensive line. I guess this isn't too bad, but I liked my area back in the corner because it was quiet and private. When I cleaned out my locker I found three pairs of shorts, eight T-shirts, two long-sleeved shirts, a couple of spandex shirts and a pair of spandex leggings, as well as my shoes and leg pads and a still-in-the-wrapper warm-up suit. I didn't even know I had that much stuff in there.

We had a meeting yesterday at the last minute. Coach Solich explained how the professional football draft works. Apparently there have been a lot of questions posed to him about it and he ran through some numbers for us. He told us to have a good summer, stay out of trouble, and work hard with our conditioning program.

Friday, May 10, 2002

Today was the last day of school for me with my last final getting out at 11:00. I spent the rest of the morning tying up loose ends around campus, selling my books back for a whopping $20, and then going out with Brian Nelson to play keno at Brewsky's. I also stopped in the locker room and picked up a gift waiting for us. It's a commemorative plaque from the Rose Bowl with the team picture that we took in front of the stadium and a list of all the guys below the picture. It's a very nice gift and I didn't expect it.

While at Brewsky's, we met Steve who manages the restaurant and is also the editor of a Husker football web page. He guessed correctly that we were both Huskers and sat and talked with us for over an hour. It was the usual, "How's the team look?" kind of talk, but I threw in a few good stories about the players and coaches that will probably make their way to a Web page somewhere. Nelson ended up paying for the meal after winning $250 in keno. I didn't win anything, but I got a free meal and would have done the same if I'd won.

Monday, May 13, 2002

I started working today at Meginnis Ford, a car dealership here in Lincoln. I'm working with freshman wingback Mike McLaughlin (another former Millard North quarterback just like Eric Crouch), who is a great kid and a really good worker. When I got to work and met the man I talked to on the phone, I learned I'll be helping out in the wash bay cleaning and detailing cars. He jokingly told me not to kill myself by working too hard. There isn't really that much work to be done, so I should take my time and pace myself. So far, even after just the first day, it's the best job I've ever had. I get to drive cars around most of the day and I've always got something to do so I'm not just bored out of my mind.

> Any job arranged by the coaches for their players at these places around town has to be by the rules. For instance, an athlete can't get paid more than a non-athlete doing the same work. Beyond that, it's

up to the employer to keep the athlete accountable. Now, this is where I could get the program into hot water, but I'm sure every program has similar situations. I know of a few guys that have been paid a little more than others for the same work. I know of guys who maybe had a total of a half hour of actual work during their whole day. I know of others who wouldn't even show up but still get paid. Several guys on the team have been driving around in nice Cadillacs recently and I can only wonder how they got the money for this. The NCAA has not placed a limit on how much a student-athlete can earn during the summer, so all earnings go unquestioned.

One of the more highly decorated players from a few decades ago had a summer job where all he would do was drive by the grounds of a building once or twice a day, if he felt like it, to make sure the sprinkler system was still working. Only in America.

On a side note, several players, and I would probably sound racist if I tried to categorize them, seem to be spending their NFL paycheck before they're even out of college. I have never seen firsthand or heard anyone on the team talk about it, but it wouldn't surprise me if money was being dispersed illegally.

I'm sure everyone's heard stories from a friend of a friend who knew a guy who saw money illegally handed out in unmarked envelopes or performance enhancing drugs being used, but I can honestly say I never saw anything like that. But I did see many athletes drinking and smoking pot on a regular basis. After all, it was college and there was nothing else to do in the small town of Lincoln.

2002 Summer Conditioning

Friday, May 24, 2002

This was our first week of summer lifting and we were all back in the groove by the second day like we had never had a break at all.

On Wednesday night, Andrew Wingender (now simply known as Primetime) learned that my girlfriend broke up with me last weekend. He insisted that we go out to the bars to forget/celebrate the breakup. We stayed out for a long time and I think I finally passed out around 4:00 in the morning. Thursday, I woke up at around 10:00 on the floor of my living room and realized I'd missed lifting. I lifted later in the day and thought for sure I'd have a valid excuse for missing lifting since I just broke up with a girlfriend. Friday morning, I was proven wrong. Wes Cody and John Garrison called a meeting for the entire O-line and discussed how we all need to change our attitude and push each other to work really hard this summer. They don't want any more talk in the press about how the O-line is questionable for next year. They want to bring the dominance back to the O-line and keep it there. They finished by going over the rules one last time—if you're late, you run three stairs no matter if you're a freshman or a senior. At that point, I knew I was going to have to run stairs because I'm a senior and need to be a role model and leader for the younger guys.

When I was halfway through my lifting, Wes Cody asked me when I was going to do my stairs. I said I would probably do them next week, but he insisted I do them right then. All the O-line guys went out to the stadium and watched as I ran all three sets of stairs. I didn't think I was going to make it since it was the first time in over a month that I've done anything really athletic, but I paced myself and got through it really well. Afterward, I slowly made my way back to the weight room, and laid down in the floor for about 15 minutes to catch my breath and get my heart rate down. When I got up and started to move around, I knew it wasn't over. I made my way to the nearest trash can and emptied the contents of my stomach. Then I finished up my workout the best I could and left. It was definitely not the way I wanted to end the first week of lifting. God, I can't wait until this shit is over.

Thursday, June 6, 2002

We have two of the new freshmen linemen in for the morning workouts now. Jermaine Leslie and Cory Timm joined us this week and have been doing well adapting to our system and getting comfortable with the other guys.

As a not-so-shocking surprise, Richie Incognito came late to lifting today. Everyone remembered all the fun we had with Richie when he was late during the winter, and we couldn't wait to do it all over again. Midway through the workout Wes Cody called all the linemen outside to watch Richie run his stairs. This is his first week back, so I'm sure he wasn't in the best shape. He got through the first one fine, occasionally running his mouth like he always does, making jokes about Tim Green's weight and Josh Sewell's awkwardness. On the second one, he began to show the strain and had trouble with the last couple of stairs. While he took his time coming down, someone asked how many he had to do. Wes, John Garrison, and Jake Andersen began thinking about the rule and suddenly realized they had it wrong. Before, as I thought it still was, the rule was if you're late to a workout or miss one, you have three stairs and each subsequent absence or tardy adds another stair. Apparently that rule has been revised to say if you miss a workout entirely you have to run five stairs. "Dave, were you late or did you miss the workout that one day?" Wes asked.

"Well, I missed you guys in the morning, but I made up the workout later in the day, so I guess I was just late," I said.

"But you missed the time that the rest of us were there," he said. "You ran three that day, right? You've got two more. Do them now with Richie."

Now, I respect Wes, don't get me wrong. I think he's a hard worker and a very good lineman and hopefully will be a captain. But I thought this last minute change was really underhanded. But rather than challenge his position, I decided to make him look good and just do it. I was going to run one set of stairs today anyway, so I didn't mind too much.

There is a lot of remodeling going on in the weight room now. New carpet is being put down on the east side and the rest of the weight room will soon be covered with black rubber mats. There are three huge automatic racks that can adjust to the perfect height for hang clean with the touch of a foot pedal. I think we're getting three more of those. The rest of the weight room has been re-arranged. Still, losing so many quality staff members really leaves a hollow place in the weight room leadership. Even though we lift as a group, everyone is very individualistic. Being on time is the only thing we do as a group. We have our lifting partners—mine are Cody Volk and Dan Waldrop—and that's who we spend all our time with in the weight room. We simply do our stuff and get out of there.

The supervision by the strength coaches is a joke. There aren't enough of them to watch us all and the apathetic attitudes have caused a few of us to shorten up our programs any way possible. Instead of doing a full set of 10, we round it up from six or seven. Instead of doing three sets, we do two. Instead of doing sit-ups, we just lay down in an out-of-view area and talk until enough time was wasted that they might think we actually accomplished something. Maybe this isn't a prevalent attitude among the O-line, but it's mine and I'm not alone. I just want to get out of here.

Monday, June 10, 2002

We started a new lifting program this week. It's a longer workout with a couple more lifts. On Monday and Thursday, we will do strictly an upper-body workout to save our legs for the running program we will be doing in the afternoon. On Tuesday and Friday, we'll do all the leg stuff like hang clean, squat, and lunges.

At 5:30 today the whole team was on the stadium field for the start of the running program. Coach Solich talked to us before we ran and reminded us to work hard and be sure to use the summer wisely since the season will be upon us very soon. He said he was recently showing a recruit around the stadium and actually avoided the locker room because he was embarrassed by the mess. He's fed up with the mess in there and has enacted a new policy that sets standards for how our lockers can look. We can no longer have any kind of decoration on the outside of our lockers, not even team decals or family pictures, and we have to store all of our gear out of view. The only things we can keep out in the open are our helmets, shoulder pads, knee braces, and one pair of shoes.

Coach Solich kept the seniors around after the team meeting to talk about a couple of things. He first wanted to place the responsibility of the locker room cleanup on our shoulders and get everyone else to fall in line. The other thing was about next year's warm-ups. He asked whether we want our names or our numbers on them. We decided to put "Football" underneath the Nebraska symbol on the breast and put our number on the sleeve.

Tuesday, June 11, 2002

We had our first session of passing league today. We went through a lot of footwork, blocking techniques, and talked through various defensive situations that we might see in a game. After that, the linemen ran plays. We got the younger guys involved more since we had a chance to give them more in-depth coaching. Kurt Mann, a freshman from Grand Island, joined us today. He's very tall, has a huge frame, is fairly quick, and is very strong. He should be a powerful weapon for us in the future.

After passing league we circled up around the freshmen and started the traditional "fight club." We told the freshmen they had to fight each other and then the winner would wrestle Cody "Five-Time High School State Champion" Volk. In the past the freshmen would start tentatively, but we would egg them on and then step in and stop it right before the actual fighting started. But today we just let them go at it. Corey and Kurt went first and actually went at it pretty well. Jermaine wrestled the winner. Then Cody wrestled Kurt, who won both previous matches, and pinned him in less than 10 seconds.

Wednesday, June 12, 2002

I went to a local Chinese buffet for lunch today. I sat next to a table with an elderly couple and I could tell they noticed me, much like when I saw the manager cringe as I came in the door. As I was sitting there eating my first of four plates of food, the lady came up to me, put her hand on my arm, and said, "You remind us of our grandson and how much he loves to eat." I had no idea how to respond to that.

Saturday, June 15, 2002

Coach Tenopir had us over for a cookout tonight. He grilled up some huge 20-oz. ribeye steaks and served roasted corn, potatoes, carrots, and rolls. There was a large cooler full of beer and a smaller cooler of pop. John Garrison showed up at about 5:30 to fill up with some food before returning to his daylong drinking binge called a bachelor party. He's getting married in a week to a girl he met during one of our other O-Line functions (lunch at Hooters after lifting) and it's probably a good idea that the stag night happens a week in advance.

Monday, June 17, 2002

I got a call today from one of the football secretaries on behalf of Coach Gill, saying that my locker still needed to be cleaned according to the new policy and if it wasn't clean by tomorrow morning, I would have to run stairs Wednesday morning at 6:00. I didn't think my locker had anything on it, but when I checked, it still had a Baylor helmet decal on the top door. I took that down along with anything else that might be scrutinized.

During the running program today, Bailey led us through an abdominal workout that no one could do correctly. The station only lasts three minutes, but he had us do this thing where we lay on our backs, lift one leg up to the sky and the other leg just a couple of inches off the ground and then do crunches trying to touch the toe of the foot up in the air. We did about 10 crunches, switched the legs, and then did 10 more, and then repeated this cycle for two and a half minutes. Bailey is probably the only person in this entire program who could actually do this workout successfully.

Monday, July 8, 2002

After a long two-week vacation of camping in Canada, it was back to the grind today. The trip was terrible with lots of headwind, large waves, heat, humidity, and millions of flies. It was great to get away.

Today was over 100 degrees, which made for a very tiring day at work where all I did was walk around the car lot inspecting the used cars. By the end of the day I was drained and sunburned, and I still had the afternoon running to look forward to.

I showed up at the stadium at around 5:00 and saw Dr. Albers so he could check up on me after two weeks of being on the antidepressant Celexa. I don't really know if it's working yet; I guess being on vacation helped.

We started running at 5:30 with Bailey leading the group of linemen and tight ends. Bailey has finally found his niche and really took control today when he told us the new rules. He said no one would just go through the motions. We would all do everything with a full effort or we would do it again and again until we either got it right or couldn't move.

We did a couple of 40-yard buildups, some 10-yard sprint starts, and 10-yard position starts with proper footwork. Then Bailey had us do these new things where we got on all fours, alternated one knee to the chest and the other leg straight out as fast as we could and then on the whistle we sprinted out. Then we went to the stairs and did one set of every step, one every-other, and one sideways shuffling each way. After all of this, we went back down to the turf and did our position starts with a five-yard dash on Bailey's whistle. Sometimes he would go on the second or third whistle and just as before, if someone jumped we would all have to go back and start over again. We got to midfield and then had to go back when Bailey saw people slacking. The punishment wasn't too bad, but it is very hard to concentrate fully and move well after such an intense workout.

When that was finally over, we circled up and Bailey led our abdominal workout. He's a small guy who is very fit and very athletic and always seems to put us through abdominal workouts that no one can possibly do, even when it appears that he has no trouble doing them. And then, as if that wasn't enough, we ran plays as an offense when this was all over. We didn't run too many, mostly because everyone was tired and it was still very hot. I finally returned home at 7:00.

Tuesday, July 9, 2002

Today was our agility day. We did a lot of different things including jump ropes, low ropes, and lots of ladders. It was another very hot day and we were all very happy when the workout finally ended.

Friday, July 12, 2002

While we were doing the last of our lifts this morning, one of the funniest things of the summer happened. Starting tackle Dan Waldrop, in an amazing display of athleticism, was practicing his footwork against a padded sled in the weight room. He took a stretch step to the right and set up for a powerful punch, but his left foot slipped out from beneath him causing him to miss the pad and hit it with his head first and then his whole 330-pound body came crashing down with a mighty smack on the floor. It was very quick, but a few of us saw it and many more came to investigate after hearing the laughter and seeing Dan lying on the ground laughing.

I was quoted in an *Omaha World-Herald* article today about how the summer workouts are "voluntary," with no coaches involved (in accordance with NCAA rules), but in reality there are many unspoken rules and a commitment to work hard.

Monday, July 15, 2002

Instead of going to work today I went to an apartment complex with my roommate Joel and swam in the pool all day while drinking beer and eating pizza. By the time I left for the stadium for running, my stomach was full of pizza, I was tired from swimming, sunburned, and drained by the sun. Luckily, the running program wasn't that hard tonight. We did a lot of short sprints and some stairs, and that was about it. It could have been much worse and I was very happy when it was over.

So far this summer I've been very impressed by the freshmen linemen who are with us. Corey Timm, Kurt Mann, and Jermaine Leslie have all worked very hard and, in my opinion, they all have a legitimate chance to see some playing time this year if we need them. It's good to have these guys around during the summer because they remind us how much work we need to do on the fundamentals. They've needed help learning the basic footwork of our blocking, which forces us to become the teachers, and through teaching we analyze our own actions. This helps open our eyes and watch everyone—even the top guys and ourselves—to make sure we're providing the correct example.

Tuesday, July 16, 2002

I turned 23 today, but I kept it a secret to avoid getting a red belly. I don't think it would have mattered because our running program was so tough tonight that everyone would have been too tired to expend the energy for the red belly. Bailey really worked us hard. He has set a lot of standards and we're proud to say we've met them. He wants us to do everything perfectly as a group and with a positive attitude. He doesn't allow cursing during workouts anymore for fear that an outside person might hear something and be offended. False starts also are a penalty and we pay these penalties at the end when we run extra for them. In all the time I've been here, I think this group right now is one of the hardest-working, best-unified groups. We push and support each other. There are no individuals, and I think this will be a big factor this season.

A lot of publications say we will have a 9-4 season or worse, end up third in the Big 12, and that we're on the decline as a program. These sportswriters don't have a clue what they're talking about. The only legitimate sportswriters are those who post the facts—the scores, statistics, and so on. All of this speculation is nonsense. They try to convince you that they know what they're talking about, but they don't know any more than anyone else outside the team. If I've learned one thing in my time here, it's that a lot of things happen that are never meant to go public. This is the stuff that makes the team and makes the season. These things, just like with an inside joke among friends, unify a team.

There are two sides to every story and a columnist can influence how you feel about a certain issue by the way it's written. The fact is, we are a good team. We have been working very hard for the past six months, and we have the desire and the ability to be the best in the nation. I can't see the future, but I'm fairly confident that we will be a lot better than most people think.

After the running, Jack Stark had a senior meeting at Aaron Terpening's house, catered by Famous Dave's. He wanted to get us together, hear about any issues, and let us know what's going on. He said the gift for the first game still hasn't been chosen, but the coaches really like the idea of the portable DVD players because we'll soon have the ability to produce DVDs right after the games and then we'll be able to watch them and critique the game on the way home. They're still trying to find units that fit the $300 limit, but we'll probably be able to swing a deal with Nebraska Furniture Mart. Also, the motto for next year was narrowed down. Someone suggested "Start Strong, Finish Stronger," which I think is a very good motto, but Troy Hassebroek tonight said we should make it "Start Strong, Finish Strongest," referring to how we want to be the strongest and best team in the nation. Jack also made a list of 10 standards we should strive to live by over the next six months. They were things like "demanding the best from each other all the time," "telling the new guys how to act while acting the part ourselves," "watching out for each other," "being positive leaders," and so on. This was a very good meeting and we plan to have another one shortly.

The rumor is that Coach Solich has been talking to a lot of pro teams to find out how they run their fall camps as well as their whole season of practices to learn how their players last for their long professional season. We have a very long season coming up and Coach Solich obviously wants the best out of us. According to these rumors, we'll only have six practices in full pads during the entire two-a-day session. This makes me very happy. I'm sure a lot of the other practices will be in half pads which is almost as rough, but when you don't have to wear the pants it just makes you feel better. Some say the whole season will be like this, too, with scaled-back practices. I guess the coaches have decided that after the Colorado loss, we felt like we needed to redeem ourselves in the national championship game and practiced very hard leading up to the Rose Bowl. A lot of us feel that the Rose Bowl practices were some of the hardest practices all year and that we might have gone into the game too worn out to play well.

Wednesday, July 17, 2002

After a little birthday celebration in Omaha last night, I met up with the seniors and starters on the O-line at The Champions Club golf course this morning. The Bugeaters, a group of guys who love the linemen, sponsored a golf outing as a fund-raiser and really laid out the red carpet for us. We had free food and drinks all day long and played 18 holes on a professional-level course. I was grouped with Dan Waldrop and two of the Bugeaters, Mr. Morgan and Mr. Munson. The course was very challenging and I had a rough day hitting well, but it was a very enjoyable time all around. This was the first time Dan had ever played 18 holes and when we started he really struggled to make good shots. By the time we finished, after much coaching by the experienced Bugeaters, he was hitting fairly decent shots consistently. This just proves how good of an athlete he is.

The Bugeaters later had a dinner for us—huge T-bone steaks, potatoes, and salad. There were flag prizes on certain holes and some of our guys got gift certificates for the pro shop.

Coach Tenopir has been growing his beard out for a while now, which is completely white, and he wore a straw hat today. He had an uncanny resemblance to Ernest Hemingway, but I doubt many other people made that connection. At the dinner Coach Tenopir introduced all the offensive linemen. He started with me and said very nice things. He said I'm a great student, a great person, and will be a factor this year. He stressed that I have stuck it out for five years and he's very proud of me for that and is very proud to have me on the team. I was honored by these words and I'm thankful for moments like that which remind me why I'm doing this.

On a lighter note, Junior Tagoa'i and Wes Cody were paired up and drank a large cooler full of beers between them. On the 18th hole, Junior hopped in the cart, spun it around fast on a hill and tipped it over. I guess the whole top of the cart was bent and they were lucky not to be injured. No one knew who was going to pay for the damages, but we were all laughing about it so much that I don't think anyone cared.

Thursday, July 25, 2002

After taking the last four workout days off to visit my brother Jason in New York City, I returned for the last two days of the summer conditioning program. I had to max out on hang clean and barely beat my record from two years ago. Hang clean has reached a plateau and hasn't gone much higher in two years. On Tuesday everyone did 225 pounds on bench for as many reps as possible like we will be doing when we test out. Josh Sewell led this effort with 31 reps and also led the hang clean max with a 380-pound one-rep max. Wes Cody, still one of the strongest benchers on the team, put up 225 pounds 29 times.

Friday, July 26, 2002

This morning's workout started off with running on the field at 7:00. Today's lifting was just squat and whatever else we felt like doing. I started warming up with 135 and 225 pounds, but my left hip started getting sore during the reps so I called it a day. I think it's slightly out of socket but I can't tell. It has been sore since I went rock climbing in New York; I plan to see my chiropractor on Monday to get it fixed. I just took a guess at what I could do based on what I have squatted recently and came out with a one-rep max of

420, which sounds right for how my legs felt this summer. Technically, we're supposed to do our max lifts in view of a strength coach, but Scott Koethe, Cody Volk, and I all vouched for each other and the coaches had to accept it. I then had to make up the bench max by doing 225 pounds as many times as I could; the same test that the pros use. I put it up 17 times, which wasn't great, but respectable. That gave me a one-rep max of 340, which sounds about right. After that, I was done and I strolled out of the weight room thinking this was the last time I would ever have to get up for a morning lifting session ever. I was happy.

2002 Fall Camp

Friday, August 2, 2002

The last couple of nights leading up to today have been nothing but partying and celebration, and also dreading the start of two-a-days. This included last night, which might explain why I missed the short morning meeting at 9:30, arriving 15 minutes later just in time for all the body tests. I had my height and weight checked—6'5" and 288 pounds— passed the blood pressure and eye test, and then had to drink a lot of water for the urine test. One new thing we did this year was to finally use the Bod Pod for the body fat test. This is a big white bubble that looks like an escape pod from a space movie. I'm not sure how it measures body fat, but it said I have 25% body fat, which is ridiculous. I never believe what those tests tell me, so I don't care.

We then had lunch and relaxed before our next session of meetings. At 2:00, the chief of the university police talked to us about common sense stuff like what to do if we get pulled over, what to watch out for at parties, and how to act in public.

We finally have a new nutritionist, James Harris, after nearly two years without one. James has been around here for a while so he should be a good fit. We also have a new head equipment guy, Jay Terry, who told us about the new system they are instituting. There's a bar code for each of us and all the gear is bar coded as well. That way they know exactly what we have and what we still need.

Our guest speaker for the evening was Don McPherson, former college football star from Syracuse, Heisman runner-up, and pro player. He spoke to us last year as well and once again did a great job of getting his point across. He talked about how we need to treat women with respect and how we need to treat each other with respect as well and not try to live up to some lofty cultural standard, but instead just be a good person. He talked for a long time, but it was very good.

I picked up $70 at dinner as the first installment of the money we'll get. In accordance with a new NCAA regulation, we had to count all the money when we received it and sign off that we were given the right amount.

After dinner, we had yet another meeting where we filled out all the NCAA paperwork. Coach Solich reiterated that there is to be no hazing this year. This may be the end of "paying rent" for now, but I'm sure it will be back one day. Shawn Marcelino from an investment firm here in town talked to us about how to handle our money better and what we should think about doing when we leave college and start working or go pro. Once again, common sense, but it was still needed for some guys.

I received a lot of new gear today. For starters, I was issued a new pair of red-and-white basketball shoes, which are very ugly and will probably never be worn. I also received a new pair of molded cleats and turf shoes. On top of that, we received a gray T-shirt, black shorts, a black Adidas spandex sleeveless top, Under Armour boxers, three pairs of socks, and a new pair of padded gloves.

Saturday, August 3, 2002

Today was the first official day of two-a-day practices, although we really only had one practice. We met in Cook Pavilion at 8:30 to do our athletic testing. I breezed through mine quickly, and my goal was to better one of my times to avoid doing the 300-yard shuttle run. I beat my old pro agility score by a mere 0.05 seconds, but that was all I needed.

At the 10:00 meetings we just watched some old film of plays that will be introduced today. Then we had lunch and I went home to take a nap and was back for more meetings and practice. We had another meeting after practice and then went to dinner at 8:00. Basically it was a full day of football, which will be our lives for the next two weeks.

The practice today was pretty good, considering it was the first day. It took a while to adjust to little things, like the snap counts, which were recently changed slightly to throw the defense off. This is a small thing, but we're all so used to doing it a certain way that it was a problem for the first few minutes. We really hit the ground running today and it seemed as though none of us had been gone from the game very long. Practice was very fast paced with three 10-minute stations at the end. We didn't have that many plays to choose from, but I hope this quickness keeps up for the remainder of the practices.

I was long snapping with John Garrison and Richie Incognito before practice and thought I was doing really well. If I do anything this year at all, I would like to be the starting long snapper for punts and extra points. I know John and Richie don't want to do them since both of them will be starting, and this would guarantee me an athletic letter if I can actually do it. I hope so.

Sunday, August 4, 2002

This morning's practice started off really well. It felt good to be in shoulder pads for the first time since the Spring Game and felt like I was moving well. We did some punt work today and I did really well with that. I'm still not sure if I will beat out Garrison for the job on punt team. Our place kicker, Josh Brown, thinks Garrison will keep the job for this year because it will be his ticket to the NFL. That may be true, but he already has a good enough track record for scouts to look at that he doesn't really need to do it this year. After practice we did some PAT work and this went very well, too. Quarterback Joe Chrisman, who will be the holder for the field goal team, said all of my snaps were right on target and he didn't even have to spin them.

The afternoon practice was on the grass in sweats but it was still really hot. The new freshmen are doing well overall. Jemayel Phillips from Winnfield, Louisiana, has joined us on the offensive line and really stands out, mostly because of his size. He's 6'7" and 335 pounds with size 18 feet and has so far been very quiet but very attentive. Coach Tenopir has reminded him to be physical and not just walk through plays. On film he moved fairly well and made some good blocks. After practice Jemayel was one of a few guys, including Richie Incognito, who cramped up so badly that they needed IVs of sodium chloride. Jemayel sat through most of the meeting in Coach Tenopir's office with the IV in his arm and Dr. Albers holding the IV bag for him.

Monday, August 5, 2002

Today's set of practices went pretty well. This morning was in half pads and it was overcast with clouds that looked ready to give us more rain, but the skies cleared midway through practice. It was a cool morning which made practice much more bearable. I was running with the number ones, mainly giving John Garrison a one-play break for every three plays he took. This puts me in a position to get very little attention from the coaches since I have fewer plays to show them what I can do, but for two-a-days it's fine because I'm not getting as worn out as the other guys.

I knew when I came here four years ago that I would have to mature and develop a lot to see much playing time. Now in my senior year, I think I'm a pretty good athlete, which must be true if I'm at a program such as Nebraska, but I'm not the caliber of athlete who can make a difference on the offensive line. That doesn't bother me because I never planned to make my living being an athlete, and I also believe there are other sports I can excel in or at least just have fun in.

Overall, I think the defense will surprise a lot of skeptics this year. They're playing very good all around at every position and they have great depth all over. The defensive line is stacked with big, fast talented guys who are hungry for the ball. The linebackers are unbelievably fast and hard-hitting. The rush ends are playing out of their minds and always in on the plays while the defensive backs continually pick off passes or at least make spectacular breakups. I can't wait to see them in action in a game, mostly because I'm sick of them making us look bad. I would be surprised if we play a team that has as good of a defense as we do.

After dinner a bunch of the older offensive linemen went to Bryan LGH to see Tim Green, who just had back surgery. He looked good and said he has no pain in his back at all, but he's still on a lot of medication. He was already walking around after early-morning surgery. Coach Solich stopped by to see how he was doing and to wish him good luck.

Today will be repeated for the next four days with 7:30 and 3:00 practices, and 1:30 and 6:00 meetings. At night, I usually get home from dinner, relax a little, type this journal, and then go to bed before 10:00 if I can.

Tuesday, August 6, 2002

This morning was in half pads again. I think a lot of the guys are getting worn out physically and mentally. There have been a few little fights here and there, mostly by guys getting beaten on a play and then fighting out of frustration. Nate Kolterman has been one of the guys to run stairs for fighting both yesterday and today, which is no surprise to anyone.

For the afternoon practice we just had a special teams session. We worked on kickoff and kickoff return, punt and punt return, and PAT and field goal block. While most of that was going on, the O-line just walked through plays on the side with the younger guys getting all the reps so they can learn a little more. The young guys still need a lot of work on the plays, but they are coming along as well as any of the groups of the past couple of years. Jemayel could be a starter by next year if he just would get his plays down and show a little tenacity on the field. I think Coach Tenopir could have another All-American on his hands with Kurt Mann as well.

At the 6:00 meetings, Coach Tenopir and Coach Young drew up formations on the board and called on us individually to draw up what everyone has to do on certain plays. I got called up for a 43 Tackle Trap and I knew what the guards and centers do, but didn't have a clue what the tackles do. The other guys had to help me out, but even some of them didn't know what to do, so I didn't feel so bad. As I left the board Coach Tenopir told me as a joke not to become a coach. This hurt since I'm working on getting a coaching endorsement on top of my teaching degree.

I picked up another $60 at dinner tonight.

Wednesday, August 7, 2002

Jammal Lord is really throwing well. He has been throwing darts right to the chests of the receivers while he's on the run and he's even thrown some perfect lob passes that slip right over the hands of the defensive back and straight into the arms of the receiver. If he keeps it up, we will see something that hasn't been seen at Nebraska in a long time—a quarterback who can actually throw the ball well. I hope he can; it would really help our all-around game if we could back up the run with the threat of a pass.

Thursday, August 8, 2002

When everyone came in last weekend, it seemed like we were mentally ready for this season. We worked out together all summer, we've been through the rougher past seasons, and we all know how close we came to winning it all last year and not finishing it off at the end. Because of this bond I think this team has the best chemistry I've seen in my five years. Everyone is looking forward to this season and I think all of us have the right mindset to do well. We will just have to prove it to everyone else. It's actually kind of nice not to be picked very high in the preseason polls. It takes a lot of pressure off us and makes us less of a target for other teams. But it also tells us that we have work to do and can't be complacent if we want to regain our status at the top of the polls. I think everyone is very positive about where this team could go this year.

Fatigue is starting to take a toll on everyone. We're all still trying to work hard, but it's evident on the film that people aren't moving as fast as before and more mental mistakes are occurring. Coach Solich told us no progress was made in tonight's practice due to all the mistakes. That's kind of insulting, but it's the truth and needed to be said.

Coach Solich really has taken full control of the team and every aspect of the practices. He's involved with virtually every group and freely gives constructive criticism. I see him as a much more confident authority figure this year compared to previous years. His speeches have gotten much better by focusing on the positives while putting a positive twist on negative points. He now has a team that's entirely his. Besides the sixth-year seniors, everyone on the team has had only him as a coach and he no longer has to try to be better than Dr. Tom Osborne; he can just be himself.

We found out tonight that we will each get an Xbox for the BCA game. That's a nice gift, but I'm not sure if I'm going to keep it. Today we also picked up our new T-shirt with this year's motto on it, "Start Strong, Finish Stronger."

Friday, August 9, 2002

This morning's practice went a lot better for me. I had a hard time making a good block yesterday because my legs were just dead, but today I was moving around well and making some really good plays. This afternoon's practice was another special teams practice. I took a lot of the punts, but so far it appears that John Garrison will be the main punt snapper this year. The coaches haven't said anything to the contrary and they know he can do the job. I was the only snapper for field goals, however, so this seems to be something I will do this year, finally. All of my snaps were great and Joe Chrisman told me that he hardly even has to spin the ball at all and they are always right where he wants them. Josh Brown is really positive about my snapping as well and I think he has put in a few good words for me to Coach Young. All I want is to earn my letter this year, and this will be the best way to do it.

Monday, August 12, 2002

After our first full day off, this morning's practice was a lot less active than usual. I think everyone is still remembering all the fun they had doing nothing for an entire day. We didn't get a lot accomplished, but it was still a fairly good practice overall.

During the afternoon session we finally implemented some of the Arizona State stuff. They run a defense similar to ours so we don't have to change too much, but they do some things a little differently with the linebackers that we had to adjust to. Also, to make it a full five years in a row, I ran a few of the scout team plays against the defense at the end of the teamwork session. I mentioned to Matt Shook, now a student-assistant coach, that my motto should be "Relentless to Mediocrity," a spin-off of a previous motto, "Relentless to Victory." Another spin-off, suitable for the many guys who have been on the disabled list for so long like Brian Nelson, Tim Green, and Chris Loos, would be "Relentless to Injury." A couple of us plan to make up shirts that say this for these guys, but so far no one has taken any initiative.

We received another $70 at dinner.

Tuesday, August 13, 2002

This morning's practice left a lot to be desired. There were a lot of mental mistakes all over the field. Tempers were very short today as well, and it's probably because two-a-days are close to being over. At one point during one-on-ones, center John Garrison and nose guard Jon Clanton had what amounted to a facemask-grabbing contest. Rush end Chris Kelsay jumped in on Clanton's side and yelled at Garrison, trying to provoke a fight. Garrison stood there on the defensive, holding a guy with each arm and Coach Solich ran in, as did others, to break it up. Coach Solich is so much shorter than Kelsay that it took Solich three tries to grab him by the shoulder pads and pull him away from the potential fight. Once Coach got Kelsay off, he grabbed him by the facemask and calmed him down. No one got in trouble for this, but it started the downward slide for the day.

At afternoon meetings Coach Solich told us how terrible

today was and how much of a waste of time he thought it was. The afternoon practice was supposed to be just a special teams practice, but Coach decided to make up for lost work by putting in a 13-play session. He also threatened to extend the number of two-a-days if tomorrow morning doesn't go better. He said he doesn't want to go into the game feeling like we haven't done enough work, so we will work until he's confident in our abilities. I think part of the problem might be that we are all tired.

The mental mistakes wouldn't happen if we only had one practice a day. That's just my opinion.

Wednesday, August 14, 2002

This morning's practice was the one to decide whether we would have two-a-days tomorrow or not. We started off slow and it didn't really pick up. After the full-team skeleton session, Coach Solich told us: "I don't know what you guys thought of that station, but from the sidelines that was the worst display I have seen. You didn't even have one good pass play there. That was a poor-ass display. If you play like that, you won't even beat an average team. You'd better pick it up right now and start making plays. You need to finish everything off and get places on the field." We started to practice better right after this. All of us know he means business when he gets that close to cursing. We immediately started to work harder and quickly turned the practice around.

By the end we thought we did pretty well, but weren't sure if it was good enough to keep tomorrow at just one practice. Coach Solich started the afternoon meeting saying: "We'll practice tomorrow morning at the same time and then we'll have you come back (at this point everyone held their breath) for meetings at 2:30 to go over the practice film. We won't have any type of official practice tomorrow, but if your position coach wants to run something on the field you might do that." We know Coach Tenopir respects our desire not to run, so we're pretty much guaranteed to just have meetings and go home. That sounds very good to me.

The afternoon practice was used to implement more of the Arizona State offense and defense. I ran with the number twos; I really wonder if I will see much action at center this year. I'm locked in at the third spot on the depth chart so I probably won't see the field unless we're blowing someone out. I know all the plays and what I'm supposed to do, but a lot of times I just can't physically do it. I'll admit that I've been outmatched in strength and speed by a lot of guys, but I've also had times where I did pretty well against them. But, overall, it hasn't been enough to put me in a spot to get a lot of attention.

After practice we had to run two gassers just to rub in the fact that our legs are tired, and then it was done. Two-a-days are officially over.

Thursday, August 15, 2002

We practiced in half pads this morning at 7:30. Even though it's the only practice of the day, we're practicing this early because some guys are still in classes. The practice went well and we implemented a lot more of the Arizona State stuff. I worked with the scout team all day, alternating with Kurt Mann.

After meetings I picked up the boy I mentor and took him to (what else!) football practice. So instead of going through a practice myself, I watched a bunch of 12-year-olds running around trying to learn some of the fundamentals of the game. It's really a change to go from a level like the Huskers to that level, but I was able to pick out the kids who had a lot of heart and the kids who knew what they were doing out there. Layne is the age I was when I started playing football, and I'm sure I looked just as helpless as a lot of his teammates. Layne was actually a standout in the practice. He gave all he had in every drill and chased every loose ball he saw. If there was a Mr. Hustle award, he should get it.

Friday, August 16, 2002

We had our last scrimmage of fall camp today, which is also the last scrimmage I will ever participate in. We had an interesting start when it began to rain very hard during warm-up and lightning hit no less than a mile away from the stadium. We were quickly led inside to avoid being hit with lightning, which is a good thing considering we were wearing nothing but metal and plastic. We waited about a half hour for the storm to pass, then did another quick warm-up and got the scrimmage under way.

This scrimmage was set up differently from those of the past. The coaches wanted to get the first and second strings a lot of the action today, so everyone below these guys didn't really do too much. There was one session each of ones-on-ones and twos-on-twos for 21 plays each. Then the offense ran against the scout team running Arizona State defense and then vice versa. I alternated with Kurt Mann again at center when we ran the scout team against our defense. We did all right, but it's hard to judge how we did on scout team since we run off of what a play diagram says to do. We don't have rules to follow or certain blocking assignments so when something happens that isn't on the card, it's difficult to figure out what exactly you're supposed to do to solve the problem.

The only major setback today was when Jason Lohr went down with what appeared to be another knee injury. He had just come off of a previous knee injury and was looking very promising on the defensive line, and we were all very eager to see what he could do out there. He was wearing a knee brace as we all do now, but he planted his leg a certain way and Nick Povendo said he heard a loud pop as Jason went down. This is a terrible loss because Jason is such a great guy, but we have so many other good defensive linemen that this shouldn't be a big setback for us as a team.

At lunch today we received another $90.

Saturday, August 17, 2002

After our morning practice, it appeared that the old tradition of "paying rent" has not completely died. In the locker room, the guys new to the south locker room were called out and made either to lay on the *N* in the middle of the carpet or else be pinned down on the *N* while everyone else beat on them. Someone had a plastic wiffle bat wrapped in athletic tape, others used the big trash cans, others dumped water and Gatorade on the guys, and others just added a few kicks and slaps. If the guy fought back or resisted, everyone was more ferocious in their attack so the best thing to do was to just go out in the middle, curl up in a fetal position, and take it. Luckily, Coach Solich didn't come in during all the fun. Nobody advertised this session of "rent" so we not only completely surprised the players but the coaches as well.

The gates opened at 1:00 and a couple of thousand fans poured into the stadium for Fan Day. The weather was on our side and gave us a fairly cool day instead of the horrible heat in the years past. Many interesting people came by today and it's always nice to meet the fans. It really reminds us of who we are playing for and what we mean to this city and the state as a whole.

Afterward they had a large pizza for each of us as we left. I munched on that as I made my way to Omaha for the rest of the weekend and a much deserved rest.

Monday, August 19, 2002

The weight room is really coming together. Nearly half a million dollars in improvements have been made including new flooring and 15 new machines called "Husker Power Transformers," which are mechanized racks that raise and lower with the push of a button. These are an outstanding addition to the weight room and we can guarantee that no other school will have this type of equipment since it was all made in Lincoln. There's a huge new platform in the middle of the weight room now, enveloping the huge transformers. All this work was done by the strength staff and will really look impressive for recruits. The drink room also has a new addition, possibly the greatest addition of all: Gatorade dispensers. Just like a soda fountain, ice-cold Gatorade is ready for us whenever we want it. It took them three years to find a good drink for us, and they finally did it.

The locker room also has a new addition—they took out three of the sinks and added a very big whirlpool. This might be a little excessive, but I think we'll be able to find some use for it.

Wednesday, August 21, 2002

We picked up our Xbox's after practice. I took mine straight to a local game store and sold it for $166. I used that, along with other money we'd gotten earlier, to buy a PlayStation 2 and a couple of games.

Thursday, August 22, 2002

We had our typical Thursday practice today. As a nice break from routine, Coach Tenopir gave us a chance to test our skills and catch some passes. He gave us one quick button hook and one long pass each. Today, I served as the relay person and at the end went straight out for an over-the-head catch, but missed it. I'll be sure to get it next time.

Joe Chrisman and I have an inside joke going as we practice. We're counting down the days until January 3 since that's the last possible day we will officially be done with football, and he uses that number in his cadence. For example, today we had 134 days until we're done and he calls out, "Set, 1-34, Hut."

Neither of us can wait to get this over with. We know we're only here to practice and to be emergency backup to the guys ahead of us. Statistically, I should be safe. It would be amazing if both of the centers ahead of me had career-ending injuries, but it would be even more amazing if Coach Tenopir didn't move somebody ahead of me in that scenario just to ensure one of his favorites gets playing time.

A lot of people don't understand my frustration with football. To the rest of the state, what I'm doing everyday is a dream come true. But this dream gets really old really fast when it becomes all that you do, leaving you very little time and energy to do anything else. This dream quickly turns into a nightmare when you realize all your effort will get you nowhere. I'm sure I could give myself lots more free time if I just skipped more classes and didn't worry about school, but I can't do that. And this frustration isn't just my own. I know of two players who vented their frustration by urinating on the "N" at midfield one night.

I dread every day, fearing that I might go out there and get severely injured so close to being done. I just want to finish my career with my body intact. After seeing so many major injuries right in front of my face over the past five years, I feel very fortunate to not have needed any surgeries, and I hope to continue the streak. It's probably a good thing that my job now is essentially to give the main centers a break now and then. I only run one out of every three or four plays. This ensures that I don't get worn out and it also decreases the risk of injury.

In a full-contact sport, you're always going to have guys who take it a little too far and start a fight. Most of the time it's just a result of frustration at being beaten one-on-one during a play, but there are times when somebody is just a true jackass and deserves to get the crap kicked out of him. Nate Kolterman is one of those guys, although there aren't many people who are willing to get into an all-out fight with him. He knows this and uses it to his advantage. I guess he earned a little street credit when he was in a fight early in his career here and he broke his cheekbone when his own helmet was used as a club on his unprotected face. Coach Solich always has to remind him to keep his energy focused on the play and not to do anything foolish that could get him in trouble. That doesn't seem to work.

The coaches praise the people who are tenacious, but there's a thin line between tenacity and dangerous behavior, especially in a game where penalties for such behavior can severely hurt the team.

Friday, August 23, 2002

We picked up a new T-shirt today. The group of guys who have to get locked down in the hotel tonight before the game are supposed to wear it to the team movie in an attempt to display our unity. It's a red shirt with a stitched *N* on it. Nothing special, but it's another shirt to add to the collection. We had a late practice and just went through our regular half hour walk-through before the game. After a special teams meeting, we went to see *Serving Sara* at a downtown theater. When the movie was over, there were coach busses waiting to take us to the hotel on East Campus. We all went straight to our rooms after briefly pausing at the snack table.

2002 Season

Saturday, August 24, 2002

Nebraska 48 – Arizona State 10

There are a lot of issues when you have a game late in the day. For one, it cuts down on the time we have to go out after the game. We also have to sit around the hotel with nothing to do for a long time before the game. Some guys pass the time reading the paper, doing homework, watching TV or playing video games. Most of us take a nap at some point, but there is a lot of down time to fill. We got up at 9:30 for breakfast, had meetings, then went back to the rooms for a couple of hours. We had a little walk-through in the grass outside the hotel before the pre-game meal. After that we waited around until 4:45 when it was time to leave.

This game was a great way to start the season. We came out with a strong first possession that ended in a field goal, but it seemed that ASU had the momentum for the rest of the first half. They put together some good drives and stopped our offense from doing anything productive. We went to the locker room up 10-3. It was still anyone's game.

That all changed in the third quarter when we finally got some steam going. The defense, offense, and special teams all played magnificently, putting up touchdown after touchdown.

Jammal Lord put to rest any questions about his ability to be the starting quarterback. He resembled a very limber Michael Vick in the way he shed would-be tacklers and scrambled forward for the first down. He put some moves on guys to make them miss, he made some great decisions on when to pitch the ball, and he threw some great passes. In all, I don't think anyone could say he doesn't deserve this job.

Offensive tackle Richie Incognito finally got his trial by fire, starting as a redshirt freshman and going up against ASU's Terrel Suggs, the number four rush end in the nation. Suggs played a great game and showed that he has the quickness and ability to be a big-time player. He came away with four tackles, but he probably could have had more if Jammal hadn't been so elusive.

I also got my trial today—I was the snapper for all the extra points and field goals. In the end, we made them all and all the snaps were fine, except one after a returned blocked punt where I was still pretty excited and went a little high. Luckily, Joe Chrisman is a good holder and was able to get it down and ready for Josh.

I had one little incident during one of the drives though. I was standing on the sideline waiting to see if we would get the first or if we would kick it, and I must have spaced off for about five seconds. Next thing I know, I look out on the field and the field goal team is out there yelling for me. I rush out, give Joe a perfect snap and Josh makes the kick. As I'm jogging off the field, Coach Solich and Coach Young are both waiting for me.

Coach Young began tearing into me, saying, "Where were you? Why weren't you paying attention? You've got to keep your head in the game. You've got a great opportunity here, don't blow it. Do you want us to get someone else to do this because we're running out of centers." And then, without a break in his berating, Coach Young said "Good snap." He actually looked very pleased after that. I'm not sure if it was because he was able to chew me out in front of 77,779 people and a live ESPN audience or if he was truly happy about the snap. I was reaffirmed later in the locker room when he came up to me and shook my hand with a big smile and said that I did a good job. This is the nicest he's ever been to me and it has only taken five years.

The joke after this was that I finally hit for the cycle. I've been late for lifting, running, meetings, practice, and now I've been late in a game. It's not really something to be proud of, but it holds certain bragging rights.

Monday, August 26, 2002

We had our first practice today as a whole team. We have four new walk-on linemen. They reminded me of my first day—they all look like they don't know what's going on. In actuality, they really don't know what's going on because they're just thrown out there and expected to pick it upon their own. I remember this well. There is no time spent on getting the new guys up to speed on anything. I ran on the scout team with the newest guys, probably so I could show them the ropes a little bit. Given that we had a lot of new faces who didn't know what they were doing, nor were they properly conditioned, I'd say practice went pretty smoothly. 130 days and counting.

Thursday, August 30, 2002

The news of the day, which isn't yet public, is that I-Back Thunder Collins apparently quit the team. From what I heard he was caught trying to sell his tickets and when confronted about it he said that he quit. I don't know if this is true or when the media will notice his absence, but it's an interesting story. I never considered him the most mentally gifted athlete on the team, but I thought he was a little smarter than that.

My dad recently wrote Coach Solich a letter thanking him for all the assistance he has shown over the years, but also trying to coerce him to play me more by stating that this journal could be used as a recruitment tool, noting how a positive senior season with lots of playing time and earning a letter would be a good end to the story. I received a copy of the letter from my dad after it had already been sent to Coach Solich and I was very embarrassed how this appeared.

I talked to Coach Solich in his office today and explained my feelings about the letter. I told him I thought it was tactless and that my father acted without my approval. I also told him that whatever happens here and whatever playing time or honors I receive, I want to earn it. I don't want it given to me because my dad requested it or because it would make a good story.

Football is business and sometimes guys like me get passed over. That's life. I know I'm not going to get All-American honors or even Big 12 honors and I'm fine with that. Even if I don't get recognized by the team, it won't be a big deal. I'm part of a group of exceptional athletes and I'm proud to say that I am one of them. There are thousands of guys like me in the annals of Husker history and many more in all college sports. I'm just one of a few of those people who managed to stick it out the whole time. That either proves I'm oblivious to the fact that I've been outmatched for five years or that I'm dedicated to a goal. I know the first statement is true, but I choose to believe the latter.

> In retrospect, I should clarify a few things. My father and Frank Solich go back a long ways to when he blocked for Frank when they both played on the Omaha Mustangs (Continental Football League)

semi-pro team. They've kept in contact over the years and for me to be on a team coached by Solich was quite a thrill for my dad.

My dad had his football glory days as a standout lineman at Lake Forest College and was drafted by the Kansas City Chiefs in 1967, playing a preseason before being cut and heading to Omaha. He would have loved for his sons to pick up where he left off, but when my brother injured his back in high school, all the athletic hopes and dreams were transferred to me.

He always worked hard to give us the best opportunities in every circumstance. By sending this note to Solich, he was once again using the tools at his disposal to give one of his sons the best chance for success. I know he had the best of intentions and I can't blame him, but at the same time he should have consulted me about it before he sent it.

On the other hand, I wonder if anything would have been different if he never told me of the letter's existence, but that would have been really unethical. I have no idea whether Coach Solich would have seen the potential use of this book and played me more, or if he would have just seen this as another pushy parent trying to get their kid more playing time.

Saturday, August 31, 2002

Nebraska 31 – Troy State 16

At the morning meetings today Coach Solich addressed the team about Thunder Collins for the first time. He said Thunder would be held out of today's game and the coaches will continue to look into the situation. They will let us know what's going on when they know the whole story.

Troy State didn't seem like a slouch last year and this year they played even harder. Their defense nearly shut down our offense by attacking the line and getting people around blocks to make plays. Basically, our offense looked horrible with little bursts of hope now and then, but nothing really kept it going. We only had 199 rushing yards, far from our typical 250 to 300. Troy State finished with 34 more offensive yards than us, but the score didn't reflect this.

The biggest factor in the game was the special teams. DeJuan Groce played one of his best games ever by returning two punts for touchdowns and a total of 155 yards. He also had two interceptions. The night was all his and he's the main reason there was such a difference in the final score.

Our defense played very well tonight, pressuring the quarterback to make a lot of hurried throws but only getting one sack late in the game.

Troy State is definitely on the path to becoming a great team and I hope to see more of them in the future.

Monday, September 2, 2002

I set a new personal record for laziness today as I ran with the first-team offense. I was there to give Garrison a break now and then, which wasn't crucial since we were just going in sweats. We did a rotation where he would go in for four and I would take one. By the end of practice, I had only taken 12 offensive plays. I consider that a great day.

Wednesday, September 4, 2002

For some reason, the coaches decided to make today the hardest practice of the year. For starters, it has gotten warmer each day and is probably in the '90s right now. In full pads, this doesn't make for a nice practice. On top of that, we ran every station possible; one-on-ones pass pro, skeleton and option drills, two teamwork stations, and ended the day with one-on-one and two-on-two for 10 minutes. We were all so dead by that last part that it wasn't even worth it. And then, just to rub salt in our wounds, we had to run gassers. Although as we were walking over to the line Coach Tenopir named the guys who didn't need to run gassers, something he has never done before, and I wasn't amazed when he named all starters. I got through my gassers, lifted quickly, and then returned to my apartment where I did nothing because I was so tired.

Thursday, September 5, 2002

In the news today we learned that I-back Thunder Collins is under suspension because he failed to complete the pre-trial diversion program for his assault charges. This is his own fault, so I don't blame the coaches for their decision. After practice, coach Solich said they have to follow NCAA rules and suspend him for four games. Since he sat out the last game, he only has three more to sit out, but I'm still curious if the coaches suspended him for that first game for reasons other than his assault charges.

Saturday, September 7, 2002

Nebraska 44 – Utah State 13

This game was another solid performance by us, especially in the first half. We came out strong and put up 37 points before halftime. The Aggies really played well in the second half, but by then we already knew we had the game won. For the third game in a row, I took all the PAT and field goal snaps, but today wasn't perfect. After the last touchdown of the half, I was pretty hyped up and didn't get settled down before making the snap. I forgot to focus on my keys (Joe Chrisman's hand and my grip of the ball) and my snap was a little low and to the left. Joe had to reach for it and couldn't get it controlled so Josh Brown took it and tried to run it in for two, but got stopped short. It's reassuring to know that my mistake didn't make or break the game. However, the spread on the game was 32 points and because of my bad snap we stayed under the spread.

The defense combined for six sacks on the day, with rush end Chris Kelsay getting two of them by himself. DeJuan Groce also had another outstanding game with two interceptions. DeJuan is really making a name for himself nationally and also is making our defense look very good against the pass.

I thought I was going to get in late in the game for some offensive snaps, but Josh Sewell finished out the game instead. Coach Solich was trying to run the score up a little and tried to convert on fourth and long late in the game but failed. After that, I knew I wasn't getting in. I'm content with just taking the field goal snaps, but I go to practice every week to also be an offensive linemen. It would be nice if I could do it in a game once in a while.

We received $90 at the pre-game meal.

Friday, September 13, 2002

This week leading up to the Penn State game was pretty standard. However, today we were supposed to leave for Pennsylvania around 1:30, but found out before practice that our plane wouldn't even take off from it's current location in Florida by that time. This caused a lot of changes in our schedule such as not being able to go to Beaver Stadium tonight, not having an evening meeting, and also not being able to go to the movie. A minor setback.

After we finally landed (we all got $10 during the flight), we boarded busses and drove to Altoona. We got a good view of the stadium on the way; it looks pretty big from the outside and is lot more modern than Memorial Stadium with metal pillars instead of cement.

Earlier this week we were issued our new warm-ups for this year. They are mostly black with a broad white stripe down the side, and both the jacket and the pants have our number embroidered on them.

Saturday, September 14, 2002

Penn State 40 – Nebraska 7

After sleeping in later than usual, we had a late breakfast, meetings, and all the usual pre-game stuff. The local newspaper is very negative about their home team, casting a lot of doubt on their ability to play hard against anyone on their schedule. It's a little odd to see the local paper to be so down on its own team.

We gathered for the psych-up tape at around 4:30 and then headed to the busses. We had a police escort the entire way, but they didn't really help much. Most of the roads leading to Beaver Stadium are two lanes and the congestion was horrible even three hours before the game. There were hundreds of RVs in the nearby fields and nearly everyone appeared to be having fun at this massive tailgate. It's always funny to see an opposing team's fan recognize that the bus they're looking at contains the invaders. At first, they're kind of taken aback, but then they proudly display their shirt or hat or anything else with the home team logo. Most of them also give the "we're-number-one" finger sign, but a few also give a different version of the same number.

We pulled into the stadium and were able to walk onto the field and take it all in before it started to fill with fans. The place is huge. Both end zones have upper decks and the south end zone has an upper, upper deck. It looks amazing and really makes you feel small when you stand in the middle of all that massive height. We headed back to the locker room and got ready for the game, passing by a few Penn State fans who took the opportunity to say a few choice words to us.

As for the game…wow.

No other word better describes the night. Penn State took all the wind out of our offense's sails and pounded on our defense all game long, racking up impressive stats and an equally impressive score. They controlled the ball for nearly six minutes more than we did, ran 13 more plays, and had 148 more total yards. Jammal threw three interceptions, Richie Incognito got ejected from the game for fighting and will miss the first half of the next game, and the Blackshirts looked just as embarrassing as our offense that routinely went three and out.

With the stadium packed with a record 110,753 people, the sound they generated was deafening. Their chant of "We Are…Penn State" raised hairs on my neck. Their fans did a good job of holding on to their tickets and not selling out to Nebraska fans like Notre Dame did, and they played a big factor in this game.

We were supposed to be the better team, but Penn State really came out fired up and never gave up. No one would have guessed the outcome would be so horrible for us, but sometimes truth is stranger than fiction.

After the game, Coach Solich had nothing positive to say about us or the other coaches. He said we didn't play like the athletes he knows we are and we failed to keep our composure. There were several personal fouls he noted that should not have happened. He was very disappointed in us and kept his speech short, leaving us with a very bitter taste. We showered and changed quietly, and grabbed boxed KFC dinners before boarding the bus.

To add insult to embarrassment, our plane showed up two and a half hours late. We were supposed to take off at 1:00 in the morning, but we didn't get off the ground until 3:30. By the time we got back to Lincoln, it was nearly 6:00

in the morning. In all, it was a horrible trip.

One positive thing I will say is that the Penn State fans are probably closest to being on the level of Husker fans with their loyalty and class. Many others might say the Penn State fans didn't have much class—our cheerleaders had beer and other objects thrown at them from the student section and had to be escorted out by police in the third quarter for their own safety. Penn State fans haven't had much to cheer about lately, so a win like this gives them a reason to be happy and revel in the win. Some said mean and derogatory things to us as we walked by, but that's pretty common. There were also many people who thanked us for coming, shook our hands, wished us good luck with the rest of the season, and genuinely offered their condolences for the loss. I went to the sideline of the section where my parents were seated along with my brother and his wife, and a few Penn State fans there in the mix said only nice things. As our busses passed all the fields with the tailgaters, most of them raised their drink to us and many others waved. I left with a very positive view of Penn State, their program, and their fans. Joe Paterno is a living legend and I feel honored to have played on his field against his men, even if it was only for one extra-point snap.

Monday, September 16, 2002

We didn't practice today, but we still had meetings. We went over our goals and were very surprised to see that the defense only made one out of 15 of their goals. Coach Solich said he couldn't remember a single game where the defense ranked this low. After sharing more facts to make us realize how horrible we were, we watched the game film. I fell asleep in meetings, but I know I didn't miss anything.

After meetings we went out on the field and took group, team, and individual photographs. Then, just to make sure we got some kind of workout on our off day, Coach Solich had us line up at the goal line for 100-yard strides. We did six of them, and everyone was okay with stopping there instead of doing the 10 that Coach Solich earlier said we would do.

Right after the running, Coach Solich had a meeting in the auditorium with all the seniors who went on the Penn State trip. He started off by saying how much he depends on us to set an example for the rest of the guys. He talked about how much he hates to lose and how much it hurts him to lose, having to visibly hold back his emotions at this point in his speech. He asked us to offer any input or advice that might be beneficial to the team. Chris Kelsay suggested that the defense get in a huddle before each play as a way to build unity. This would give the defensive guys a chance to congratulate each other for a good play and also encourage a player who might have made a bad play. If they need to, they can go back to the no-huddle approach if the offense is going no-huddle. Chris also said he would be willing to come in on his own time to learn all the defensive calls so he could be the relay man on the field taking signals from the sideline and giving them to the defense.

This meeting was good—a lot of good ideas came out and Coach Solich heard directly from us what we think should happen.

Wednesday, September 18, 2002

For some reason, Josh Sewell didn't show up for practice today. He called Coach Tenopir at around 2:00 saying his keys were locked in his car. He could have called his girlfriend, a taxi, or found another way to get here, but he didn't show up all day. This meant John Garrison and I had to take all the snaps at the teamwork stations, which was not fun in full pads and surprising heat. He'll be getting a red belly tomorrow before we make him run stairs, and John and I get the first smacks.

Thursday, September 19, 2002

It turns out that Josh locked his keys in his car at a shopping mall 10 miles from the stadium and didn't have any money to take a taxi or bus. This seems like a valid excuse, but we still had fun giving him a red belly today.

Saturday, September 21, 2002

Today, I helped out at a car wash fund-raiser for a local family who has a three-year-old boy named Keithen who has terminal cancer. I was the player-liaison for the organizers of this event and got place kicker Josh Brown and cornerback DeJuan Groce to help out at the car wash. We washed and dried cars, played with the little boy and his brothers, and stood out on the corner of 25th and O street holding signs to get people to come and help out. The turnout was tremendous and we raised over $5,000 from donations, bake sale and auction. People even gave us money right off the street. However, one completely thoughtless person noticed our signs that said "Huskers Washing Cars Today" and "Carwash Fund-raiser For Three-Year-Old Boy With Cancer" and yelled, "I'd help out if you could win a game!" Josh Brown yelled, "This isn't about football!! It's about a little boy!" Josh also threw in a few colorful words and probably would have pulled the bastard out of his car if the light hadn't turned green. It's incredible how someone could be so careless and inconsiderate.

This fund-raiser really gave me a lot to think about. This boy only has about six months to live. His family and friends don't expect him to see Christmas this year. This is incredibly sad, especially when you see this little boy who is so young and beautiful and surrounded by people who love him. I can't wait for these next three months to pass while these next three months might be the last that he is alive. While I'm wishing this time will pass quickly, his parents wish they could slow it down. This really affected me and helped put things into perspective. My life could be a lot worse. I'm waiting for these three months to go by so I can start my life while another might not have a life in three months due to brain cancer. Life is too short to do something you hate for too long.

Wednesday, September 25, 2002

Apparently I'm the only one who got a positive impression from our trip to Penn State. The media has been referring to the horrible behavior of the fans for the past week and many people sent letters to the Penn State president, which prompted him to publish an apology in our newspapers. It was very well written and I think it will do a lot to heal any wounds between these two programs.

I've been asking the coaches if I will be on the travel roster this weekend and they still don't know. We can only take 70 guys to a conference away game and I needed to know by today if I would be going so I could sign up my tickets. I signed them up anyway, not knowing for sure. I told Josh Brown, our kicker, about my precarious position and he immediately went to Coach Young to press him about my traveling possibility. Josh loves my snaps and is willing to go to bat for me. At the end of practice today, Josh told me I will be going. It's about time I was told something in a timely manner.

Friday, September 27, 2002

We had meetings at noon today, followed by our walk-through practice on the field before we packed up and headed to Iowa. We took five Coach busses on this trip, with room for everyone to have a two-seater to themselves. The trip was pretty quick, mostly because we watched *We Were Soldiers* on the bus televisions and napped most of the way (one of the stars of *We Were Soldiers* is Chris Klein, a former high school teammate of mine at Millard West). We arrived at our hotel in West Des Moines, unpacked, had dinner, and left for our movie, *Barbershop*. I picked up my $10 for the weekend before the movie. The movie was really well done and I think everyone enjoyed it, even the coaches. We then went back for our night snack, had a short meeting, and went to bed.

Saturday, September 28, 2002

Iowa State 36 – Nebraska 14

The main difference between this loss and the Penn State loss is that Penn State embarrassed us and at Iowa State we embarrassed ourselves. We played absolutely horribly today; it looked like we weren't even ready for the game. Penalties and fumbles put the nail in the coffin, having nearly as many penalty yards as we did rushing yards (75 compared to 81). Usually we continue records of excellence when we play, but tonight we set records of ineptitude. This was the largest margin of loss to Iowa State since the 1800s and the first consecutive regular season losses since 1976, and the first conference opener loss in 28 years. It's also the first time we will be off of the AP poll since 1981.

There were some highlights, however. Chris Kelsay had a solid game, getting seven tackles, two hurries, and putting lots of pressure on Seneca Wallace. He also allowed Pat Kabongo to get in and finish Chris' pressure and get a team high 15 tackles. In all, the defense played much better than they have in the previous losses, but not well enough to stop a juiced-up Iowa State offense. The special teams played extremely well tonight, too. Josh Davis had two amazing returns on kickoffs, but both of them were nullified by penalties. Our punt return team blocked one of their kicks deep in Iowa State territory that set up one of our touchdowns. Kyle Larson had a 47-yard punting average and Josh Brown showed consistent leg strength by knocking all three of his kickoffs out of the end zone and making both extra points with ease. Special teams is the only thing we are doing right this year so far.

Our offense was pathetic. We had just 16 rushing yards in the first half. The only scores we had came off of a 90-yard pass from Lord to Ross Pilkington and a punt block that set up a short run by Judd Davies. The 90-yard pass looks like a fluke compared to the rest of the statistics, but it was actually the best play called all night. We finally called the right play at the right time and it worked. Without these two plays, we could have easily been shut out. Luckily enough for me, those scores meant I got to snap the extra points, the only playing time I had all night. My job was done perfectly and that's all I can be thankful for.

I don't even remember what was said during halftime or after the game. We were all in such a state of disbelief that I don't think anybody heard. I just remember that Coach Solich had the same expression, but with a little more panic in his eyes since his job and his livelihood depend on his performance.

If people didn't question us after last year or after the Penn State game, they sure are now. Our own fans are cursing us, blaming the coaches, calling for firings and cuttings, and demanding sweeping changes. They aren't too far off. If I was to point to one main thing that must be changed, it's that our offensive coordinator (Coach Solich) is on the sideline and not up in the skybox as he was for Coach Osborne. This is a huge handicap and I think the pressure will be on him to do something about this.

Coach Bohl, the defensive coordinator, should be safe for now after the defense played better this game, but he's not hanging on by much. Coach Gill or Coach Brown are rumored as the possible next head coach or offensive coordinator. This might be a good solution, but we need to look at the big picture. Our coaches have a combined number of years that make us look like we know what we're doing, but perhaps this ancient staff is now too slow to keep up with the changes in college football all over the country. We've been doing the same thing for over 30 years and teams are finally stopping us with ease. There are no surprises anymore. When we get behind, the average fan can guess what play we will run next and be right a high percentage of the time.

Another factor is that our coaching staff doesn't motivate well. They just expect things to be done. They expect the players to provide the leadership. After Wistrom and Peter left, there was a huge leadership vacuum and no one knew how to take control because no one else was allowed to have any say when the most dominating Blackshirts where in power. The coaches also don't have the charisma that coaches of more successful programs have, which turns out to be a big factor in recruiting. The top recruits go to the teams with the most charismatic coaches. Coach Solich is a great guy, but he's not exactly someone I would want to hang out with on a regular basis.

Another huge outside factor is that we are finally seeing the results of NCAA rule changes such as the 85 scholarship limit and restrictions about what can be done for players. This has leveled the playing field drastically across the country and has allowed many teams to gain some national power while other teams, like us, slowly slip as the NCAA loosens our grip on domination. The best teams in the future will be the ones with the best fans and donors, largest stadiums, and best locations. Notre Dame, Penn State and

Nebraska all have big stadiums and loyal, deep-pocketed fans, but our locations leave a lot to be desired. We are all in small towns in the middle of nowhere, the only difference being that Penn State is relatively close to many major cities. Miami will probably stay at the top for a while, until they set up a schedule where they actually play someone decent. They might be able to win a national championship, but I doubt they could run the table for a Big 12 championship.

Monday, September 30, 2002

A lot of changes have taken place. Quarterback Jammal Lord has been bumped down to third string with Mike Stuntz starting and Curt Dukes in second. Cornerback Fabian Washington will start where Pat Ricketts was and rover Lannie Hopkins will start in front of Aaron Terpening. Robin Miller and Rodney Burgess quit today and I'm sure others are pondering that move.

The coaches have placed some of the blame for the recent losses on the scout teams, which could be true, but sounds like they are looking for a scapegoat. They are saying that we aren't giving the top groups a good picture of what to expect and that we need to work harder and play better.

It's hard enough to find the motivation each day to face being on the scout team, but now we're being blamed for a loss. There's no glory in being a scout teamer. We run different offenses every week because we are simulating what our next opponent has been seen doing. We are forced to run plays that are diagramed on a piece of paper with no clue about the strategy or the specific techniques that these players are using. Most of the scout team guys are overmatched by the first team guys, so rather than risk injury with an all-out effort, many guys choose to play in survival mode. These are the guys who know that they don't have much chance being a starter, but they're hanging around to get all the benefits and maybe someday they'll get a few plays here and there. And, with so many guys on the depth chart ahead of them, they are so well insulated from the chance of another person's injury catapulting them into playing time that they can remain inconspicuous for as long as they want. Whenever we do get a guy who really shines and does well with lots of great effort, he's promoted off the scout team and the guys he left behind return to mediocrity. However, those promotions happen so rarely that they offer no inspiration.

We went in half pads today, which is something that never happens after a game. The practice was shortened, but at the end we ran the top two units against the third-team guys. I was running on the third-team offense, running scout team plays against the first- and second-team defense. In all, it was a pretty intense practice. A lot of the focus in groupwork was on basic fundamentals, apparently in an attempt to fix the foundation before trying to continue to build.

All of the media is bashing us. They are bringing out all these statistics about how horrible we are compared to past Husker teams. All the facts they're presenting are true, but what they don't show is that while we always have been at or near the top, other teams are starting to catch up and pass us over. It's not necessarily that we have gotten worse, other teams have gotten better.

Tuesday, October 1, 2002

The weathermen were right today. There was rain in the forecast and it started to rain lightly about midway through practice. It got steadily stronger up until about 15 minutes before the end of practice when the clouds ripped open and poured out everything they had. The wind and the downpour off of the South Stadium bleachers combined to look like huge waves crashing down the rows of seats. With thunder rumbling and rain so thick it was hard to see, we got inside quickly and Coach Solich conceded to Mother Nature and called practice off a few minutes early.

Wednesday, October 2, 2002

Today started off well. We were in full pads in Cook Pavilion since it was still very wet outside, and I was doing my usual thing of staying at the run station all day and giving John and Josh breaks every few plays. Near the end of the first station, someone rolled into the side of my leg and I felt my ankle twist. It didn't hurt initially, but I got up gingerly and hobbled back to the huddle. Then it started to hurt and I couldn't press off on my left foot at all. Doak Ostergard, the head trainer, showed no sympathy for me and told me to just walk around and get back to practice as soon as possible. Sorry, Doak, but I don't trust your judgment when all you do is watch me walk around. He could at least have checked out my ankle right then, but he didn't seem to want to take that initiative. This could be another sign of how when you're not an important contributor to the team they don't care about your well-being as much, but I might be looking too deeply into this. Anyway, I sat out the rest of practice and did the best I could with lifting.

When I got to the locker room, I found that a practical joker had filled my turf shoes, which were sitting in my locker, with water. The water spilled into the bottom part of the locker, getting most of my clothes wet. Then, when I was in the shower, someone took my backpack and hid it in Kyle Ringenberg's locker and also tossed my grass shoes into the same aisle. I don't know who did it, but I'm pretty sure it was Richie Incognito. He and Garrison were in the locker room before most of the guys and Richie had a large water cooler bottle. He wouldn't take credit for it—I didn't expect him to—and John failed in his role as a team leader and captain by letting this stupid shit happen. As I left the locker room, I was pretty pissed off and spread Richie's shoes over the entire locker room so he will have something to do tomorrow.

There is a potential hurricane brewing in the South and McNeese State has opted not to wait around for the weather to clear before making the trip. They flew into Lincoln today and will practice at our facilities. It's been organized so the teams won't come into contact with one another until Saturday.

We recently received our new sweat suit. It's all gray and simply says "Nebraska Football" on it. We also received a long-sleeved black Under Armour shirt and black tights, both of which are valued at $45 or more in the stores.

Thursday, October 3, 2002

Apparently Richie didn't notice that I threw his shoes around because he never got mad. He taped up the lock on Josh Sewell's locker, though, so maybe he did notice and blamed Josh for it. I passed on a note about the whole thing to Coach Solich, but left out my little retaliation. Coach Solich must have talked to Richie and John because in the huddle Richie claimed that Chris Kelsay said the coaches said the pranks need to stop. Dan Waldrop later told me Chris never said anything to Richie, so Richie was just trying to cover himself and make it sound like Chris, who has more power on the team, was enforcing the rules. I guess Richie doesn't like to be held accountable for his actions.

Friday, October 4, 2002

Today after practice Junior Tagoa'i threw a handful of liquid soap in Richie's face. Some of the soap got in his eyes and was apparently very painful and hard to wash out. After Junior left the locker room, Richie squirted liquid soap all over Junior's stuff, including in his shoes and in his helmet.

Even if this retaliation was warranted, to do it the day before a game is inexcusable. Junior is going to have very little time to clean out his stuff before the game and he will almost definitely get soap in his eyes when he puts on his helmet.

Saturday, October 5, 2002

Nebraska 38 – McNeese State 14

Either the managers noticed the soap or Junior didn't, because nothing was said about it. We all thought there was going to be a brawl in the locker room today, but neither Richie nor Junior said anything about it.

This game had a number of outstanding performances, such as Mark LeFlore's 64-yard touchdown on a reverse, and David Horne's debut as I-back with 12 carries for 81 yards. Horne has a very smooth and patient running style. He carefully watches the blocks develop in front of him and then explodes through the hole with great acceleration. I think he'll do very well, and that's probably an understatement.

It was a pretty good game all around, and we really needed it to gain some confidence as a team. McNeese State wasn't a pushover. They are ranked number two in their division for very good reason. They have some good athletes and they have a very good team as a whole. They played us hard and gave us a good game. I hope to see at the end of the season that they are the national champions for their division.

Once again, I took all the snaps for the extra points and the one field goal that we had, all of them being good, continuing a solid performance on the year.

Monday, October 7, 2002

Once again, we are going in half pads on Monday. All of us are beginning to wonder how long this will keep up. We know we need to be a little more physical in practice so it will carry over into the games, but going in half pads is just like going in full pads and doing it too much doesn't give us any time to recover.

My ankle is still very sore and is hampering my playing and running. It doesn't matter too much because I don't take too many plays each practice, but it's still hard for me to do a good job. It's discouraging not to contribute at the level that I can, especially since that level isn't very high to begin with.

Wednesday, October 9, 2002

Rush End Chris Kelsay hurt his hamstring in the last game and it looks like he won't play in this week's game. This could be bad since Missouri's quarterback, Brad Smith, has made a name for himself as a very potent weapon for the Missouri offense. He looked very impressive as he led his offense through an amazing romp of the Oklahoma defense, but was still unable to get the victory.

David Horne's performance in the last game has sparked some controversy among the I-backs. The other I-backs have been quoted in the paper sounding jealous of his playing time and the yards he has racked up. If they have a problem with it, they need to re-evaluate themselves and see where they really are. If they think they should be playing above him, they need to prove it with actions, not words. We have a very talented group of I-backs right now and they're all playing very well, which poses problems when you try to divvy out playing time. The stars won't get the stats they desire and the other guys might not get any playing time. At the same time, if they have good cohesion, they will inspire each other to work harder and keep getting better instead of working to undermine each other. I hope they get it together.

Saturday, October 12, 2002

Nebraska 24 – Missouri 13

After a slow start, our defense really got it going and put on an impressive show. They really played out of their minds and simply looked amazing. The Missouri offense was slowed down to 220 yards and 13 points.

What was even more amazing is that we were able to fight back from being down and come away with a solid win. Missouri scored first and they were up 13-7 near the end of the half. We scored with 43 seconds left in the half and added the extra point to make it 14-13. When we came out in the second half, we still played well, but the offense couldn't get the job done, so we turned to our special teams. DeJuan Groce proved for the third time this season that he's the best punt returner in the country by taking a punt 89 yards for a touchdown. Josh Brown later added three points with a field goal to give us the final score. He could have had one more, but he missed a 35-yard field goal late in the game. It was from the left hash and he said earlier in the week that he doesn't like kicking from that hash.

On the other end, Kyle Larson had a very tough day punting. He averaged only 27.2 yards on six punts and looked like he was really struggling. I later learned that there is a very personal reason for this. His mother has been battling cancer for a while and just underwent surgery to remove the tumor. I'm sure his mind wasn't focused entirely on the game and I don't think anyone can blame him.

This was another very good win for us. It improved our confidence even more and proved that we have what it takes to overcome a deficit. We're not strangers to being down now, and we know that we can come back and win. This could be the turning point of the season.

Once again, I took all the extra-point snaps and the field-goal snaps.

Friday, October 18, 2002

This was an interesting week. On Monday we learned that starting quarterback Jammal Lord was taken to detox Saturday night after being charged with disturbing the peace. We don't know the whole story but from what we were able to piece together Monday night in the Unity Council meeting it appears that Jammal didn't do anything wrong. He just went outside to see what was going on and the cops took him downtown. This became big news very quickly, especially after having a good game against Missouri earlier in the day. We discussed what should happen to Jammal in accordance to our point system and we decided that since we didn't have enough information, especially the official police report, we shouldn't do anything. Coach Solich was at our meeting and agreed with our decision. It turned out later in the week that Jammal would be allowed to start the game.

Another weekend occurrence that didn't make the papers was that offensive guard Jake Andersen drove home after drinking quite a bit and got into an accident south of downtown. The cops showed up and gave him a DUI, making his case the most serious. The media still hasn't heard about this, but he won't go to the game this weekend and will have to go through pre-trial diversion to get this erased.

Also, after the Missouri game Thunder Collins mentioned to a few guys that he was going to quit because he was discouraged about his lack of playing time. No one believed him because he's always complaining about something and not too many people care what he says anyway. Well, he turned out to be a man of his word and didn't show up all week for practice or classes. Near the end of the week, there was a statement printed in the paper saying that he's quitting the team because his scholarship check has been cut in half and he can't support himself and his brother on $200 a month. It was a well-written statement, which makes me doubt that he actually wrote it, but there were quite a few sympathetic souls who replied on the *Omaha World-Herald*'s Web site. No one on the team really cared. We have replacements. Go have fun, Thunder.

On top of all of this, offensive linemen took our drug tests and we also were given flu shots. Everyone passed the drug test, as far as I know. The NCAA recently made a new rule that a certain chemical in Red Bull, a popular energy drink, is now illegal. This shouldn't have much of an effect on us, but it's an inconvenience for some.

We were issued a new pair of shoes and our winter jackets on Wednesday. The shoes are pretty nice, for the guys who have feet under size 16. The shoes I got are still nice, however. They're a mid-top black-and-white classic Adidas design and are really shiny. The jacket is a big, puffy black coat, exactly like the one we were issued last year or two years ago. Now I have two identical coats hanging in my closet.

Classic Coach Young story: During practice Coach Young was rounding up guys for the kickoff team. I-back DeAntae Grixby is usually on this team, but was injured earlier. Oblivious, Coach Young called out "DeAntae!" while looking around on the sidelines for him. Someone nearby informed Coach that DeAntae was hurt and not practicing. Coach Young, after being told this, looked around again as if to yell for someone else and yelled out "Grixby!" His senility keeps getting funnier.

My old teammate, friend, mentor, and all-around great guy Jimi Tansey is in town for a while. He's staying with me and living life to extremes. Every night is a new adventure and my sleep and homework schedule have begun to suffer, but I don't care. Jimi was such a help for me that I will do anything for him any time. True friends are hard to come by and to have someone who will always be there for you is very special and I really appreciate Jimi for this.

Saturday, October 19, 2002

Oklahoma State 24 – Nebraska 21

Once again. This time, in an uncharacteristic losing fashion, we didn't get blown out. We could have won this game easily, but too many little things piled up to weigh us down in the end. We had the chance to kick two field goals, both over 45 yards. Josh was kicking great today and I have no doubt he could have made them.

Both teams got off to a slow start, leaving the first quarter scoreless. Oklahoma State started the scoring with a field goal, which we answered with a touchdown, but Oklahoma State proved to be too consistent and steady to be slowed by our Blackshirts. They kept putting points up, and our offense kept getting stopped midway down the field. Kyle Larson had another tough day statistically, but only because we kept punting from midfield. He hasn't really been able to show off his amazing leg yet, but people will know it when he does.

The temperature was fairly cool, especially when I was standing on the sideline waiting for the offense to score so I could get out there. I had to put on one of those big jackets after halftime just to keep my arms warm and ready. A light drizzle fell most of the day as well, making it that much more uncomfortable. The cold made it a little tougher to make good snaps, but we made all the extra points so I can at least be happy with my performance.

The stadium at Oklahoma State has very thin sideline areas between the field and the stands, similar to Colorado, however these fans were much better than Colorado's. They didn't try to degrade us constantly, just some of the time, and the things they said made me laugh because they obviously had a much smaller vocabulary than the Colorado fans. In the end, the fans got their win and they celebrated by bringing down the goalposts. We just made our way back to the locker room, past Husker fans who offered both optimistic support and disgraced looks. A true fan stands by the team, especially when they're down. Fans who chastise the team aren't really fans, they're just along for the ride.

We picked up $10 on the plane ride in, and on the way out of the stadium we had KFC meals waiting for us.

Monday, October 21, 2002

The theme of today's meetings seemed to be "Where do we go from here?" Coach Solich told us that we have to keep our heads up and remain focused on playing one game at a time. Our goal of a national championship is gone. Our goal of a conference championship is gone. Our nine-win season is in jeopardy. A winning season is in jeopardy. Even the bowl trip is in jeopardy. From what I've heard, either the Arizona State game (because it was a pre-season game) or the McNeese State game (since they are division I-AA) will not count for the number of wins we need to be eligible for a bowl. This means we have to win two more games. Kansas seems like the only guaranteed win. Texas, Kansas State, and Colorado are all ranked and Texas A&M is one of the toughest places to play in college football. If we could just win our home games, that will do wonderful things for us. This is a very shaky time. None of the players or coaches have been through anything like this, and I'm not sure we really know how to react.

Tuesday, October 22, 2002

My ankle still hurts. Even after getting a cortisone shot in it last Thursday night, it's still sore, although it's much better. Late in practice someone was thrown into the back of my calf, causing my ankle to shift forward. The pain went away quickly, but a new area, at the front of my ankle, is sore now. This sucks.

Wednesday, October 23, 2002

I found out today that I have been listed along with 13 other guys as Verizon/CoSIDA Academic All-American candidates. This is given to anyone who has enough playing time and a 3.2 GPA. Only one of us will end up with the award, but I think two or three guys have a very good chance. The other guys are Philip Bland, Chad Buller, Judd Davies, Troy Hassebroek, Trevor Johnson, Chris Kelsay, Chad Sievers, Phil Peetz, Pat Ricketts, Kyle Ringenberg, Barrett Ruud, Mike Stuntz, and Aaron Terpening.

After practice today I was told that the sports information office wants to do a feature article on me for an upcoming home game program. This should be exciting, but I have no idea what to talk about because I know I'm supposed to make it sound positive.

Saturday, October 26, 2002

Nebraska 38 – Texas A&M 31

This was easily the most exciting game I've been a part of in my time here. We started off strong, scoring on the first drive. It seemed almost too easy. The momentum quickly switched over to A&M when they blocked one of our punts and took it in for a touchdown. On our next drive Jammal pitched the ball right through Dahrran Diedrick's hands and A&M recovered the fumble and soon scored again.

We were able to tie up the game with a touchdown from David Horne, but A&M found the end zone again with a short pass just a few seconds before halftime.

We came out of the locker room hungry for a win and knowing we could get it. A&M added a field goal on their first drive of the second half, however, and then returned a fumble for 66 yards and a touchdown on our first possession of the half to make it 14-31. It looked like we were completely out of it. We needed big plays by the defense and scores on all of our remaining offensive drives to get the win. That's exactly what we did.

I-back David Horne and Dahrran Diedrick lit up the field, along with some great runs by quarterback Jammal Lord, to get us three straight touchdowns. Our last drive ended with a 42-yard field goal. Defensively, we stalled them on their first two drives and then Pat Ricketts and Phillip Bland came up with big interceptions, the last one by Bland was in the end zone and took away all chances they had for a comeback.

Our fans, which filled two sections at the tips of the horseshoe stadium, went crazy after the win. We had not only caused an upset, but we came back from a huge deficit to pull off a victory on the road and in one of the most intimidating venues in the nation, and our fans loved it. Many of them tried to storm the field after the win, but the A&M security, which was just their military guys, stopped them. A couple of them pulled out their billy clubs and even used them on a few of our fans. I think that was uncalled for and so did Nate Kolterman who was right there when one of our fans got hit. Nate scared the shit out of the security guy.

The Texas A&M fans were quite amazing. Their collection of cheers and chants, along with their choreographed motions were very impressive. One of the most awe-inspiring sights was when they all put their arms over the people next to them, overlapped their legs, and then swayed in unison. It was almost nauseating to watch this huge wall of people move, but it was still very exciting to see. Their fans were also very well behaved. I don't remember hearing one negative thing uttered from them. That could be because of the distance between us and them, or because most of the people closest to us were in their band. Their band was also very amazing. I could have stood there all day and listened to them play, and I thought about doing just that as I was stretching during warm-ups. I wish I could have seen their halftime show.

With this win, we now have new life for the rest of the season. We know we can pull off a come-from-behind win, we know we can win as underdogs, and we know we can win on the road. If we win the rest of our games we could be in the Big 12 championship game, and if we win that we would automatically be in a BCS bowl game.

Even after losing three games this season, I think this year has been the most beneficial for the team as a whole. In this game we learned how to battle for everything. We gave them 21 points and were still able to win. We've learned how to battle back, something that wasn't there a year ago because we never had to do it. The Nebraska teams of the past came out strong and dominated for four quarters. When we got down early, it was such a shock that we didn't know what to do. Now when we're down, we know we still have a chance.

We've also become a more unified team. The defense plays for the offense and vice versa. Special teams work hard for both sides. We were placated with Eric Crouch being the team. We played off of him and he led us to victories. Now the leaders are less prominent, forcing the whole team to step up a notch to fill that void.

Today marked the beginning of a new mentality for Nebraska football. A new mentality that will adapt to all the changes and still produce great teams.

On the flight in we were issued $10, and before we left the stadium we also received a new travel T-shirt because a lot of guys haven't been wearing theirs when they should.

Wednesday, October 30, 2002

Coach Solich is cracking down by implementing a zero-tolerance policy involving anything in a game or in a practice that would be penalized. After Josh Davis punched one of the Texas A&M guys after a late kickoff, and was very lucky to not get thrown out of the game, Coach Solich apparently had enough of all the penalties and the lack of discipline we are displaying to the country. From now on, for every penalty committed in the games or in practice, we have to do extra running. The more severe the penalty, the more severe the punishment. This also includes getting in fights during practice. Nate Kolterman even got extra running for pushing one of the Texas A&M guys hard as a play was winding down. He didn't get flagged for it in the game, but Coach Solich thought he deserved it anyway.

It has been a very rainy October so far, but it hasn't gotten too cold. It's still in the high 30s and 40s but we're hoping the cold will put a damper on Texas this weekend. We got black stocking caps tonight to help us combat the cold, but they're so small they don't even cover my ears.

Saturday, November 2, 2002

Texas 27 – Nebraska 24

Former head coach Tom Osborne spoke to us before the game. He talked about the traditions here at Nebraska—the coaching philosophy, the coaching staff, and the work ethic of a power football team—and how they have remained unchanged over the past couple of decades. He's an excellent speaker and makes very good points, and he left us with a renewed sense of pride in this team and the program.

The game started off with all of us in a very clear and determined frame of mind. We came out strong and put up a field goal on our first drive. Texas later answered with their own field goal. Another field goal by Texas early in the second half was the last score before halftime. We could have taken the lead with two more field goals, but mistakes were made. On the first one, we all rushed out there with 1:50 left on the clock and Coach Solich told Steve Kriewald, who told Joe Chrisman, that we should eat some time off the clock. This message wasn't relayed to the rest of us, and I figured we were going to follow our normal rhythm of getting on the ball and getting the kick off soon. I was down over the ball and ready, and I looked back and saw Joe waiting. I didn't know what we were waiting for, so instead of mentally focusing myself to get the snap done, I started wondering what was taking so long.

When Joe finally called for the snap, I wasn't prepared. The snap was high and slow and Joe fell on it for a seven-yard loss. There is no one person who gets the blame for this. In the end, we should have stayed in the huddle longer and then gotten on the ball. Also, being upside-down over the ball for that long is hard enough, especially when I'm supposed to throw the football accurately seven yards between my legs. I was getting a head rush and pretty much knew as soon as I was about to snap it that it wasn't going to be my best snap.

Then at the end of the half, we had another chance to tie it up. This time Joe called for the ball and I snapped it right away because I wasn't sure how much time was left, and Josh was looking at the time just as the ball was snapped. When he looked back, the ball was already down and it was too late. He kicked it, but it was cleanly blocked by a Texas guy coming off the left side and he actually had to slow down, otherwise he would have over-run the block. This is the first kick Josh has had blocked all year. All of this really hurt going into halftime.

Josh, Joe, and I left the locker room early during halftime and got on the field as soon as the band got off. We took some more kicks and got back into our normal rhythm and felt very good as the game got under way again.

The second half started off really well, with both teams scoring on their first drives. Texas scored again late in the third quarter, but we answered with authority early in the fourth with a 60-yard touchdown grab by Matt Herian. The game became a complete dogfight with both sides playing very well. Chris Simms of Texas was putting up impressive passing yards and getting first down after first down, and our QB Jammal Lord was running the ball like he was going against the scout team. Texas scored again late in the fourth, making the score 27-17. With three and a half minutes left, we knew we had to score quickly, stop them on their subsequent possession, and then score again quickly. In less than a minute, Dahrran Diedrick took it in for a touchdown. We were able to stop them on defense, they punted and DeJuan Groce almost broke his most crucial return of the year, but got stopped at the 16-yard line. With 34 seconds left and 16 yards to go, Jammal tried to run but got nowhere. After a quick spike, Coach Solich sent in a pass play to go for the win instead of the tie. If the pass was caught, it would be a touchdown and if it was dropped or incomplete, we would kick a field goal. The worst possible thing would be for the ball to be intercepted. Well, the worst thing happened. All the excitement in the crowd and on the sideline just shut off like someone pulled the plug. Texas ran out the last 10 seconds and then triumphantly took the field to celebrate their win.

I grabbed my gloves and headed into the locker room, avoiding eye contact with everyone since my face was now red and my eyes were tearing over. I got into the locker room and cried quietly. I took it very hard because with the points we could have had off of my bad snap, we could have tied the game. Also, I wasn't sure if Coach Solich had lost faith in the field goal team because he decided to go for the win instead of the tie.

There were a lot of things that could have turned this game around quickly. We had a pair of fourth and ones that we didn't convert; there was a missed catch that was deflected and intercepted; there was a missed interception that was tipped and caught by a Texas receiver who turned it into a 40-yard gain, and the list goes on. I guess we just made one too many errors. Occam's Razor states that when all things are equal, the simplest answer tends to be the right one. The simplest answer is to go for the field goal and try our best in overtime, which is why I took this loss so hard.

In all, it's fairly amazing that the score was what it was. Chris Simms threw for a career high 419 yards and gained 27 first downs. Usually when a team does that, they score more than 27 points. This is positive for our defense which has sputtered this year. Jammal Lord had another career night, running for a new record of 234 yards.

In all, this was the most exciting game I've ever played in. I know that even though we lost, our fans are still proud of us for coming so close to beating a team ranked in the top 10 in the nation, especially since we are still unranked. It's a loss that gives us a lot of crucial things to work on in the future, but it also gives us even more confidence as we finish out our schedule and still hunt for our bowl game bid, a winning season, and a nine-win season.

Wednesday, November 6, 2002

Coach Tenopir weighed us today for the first time in a while. Everyone seemed to be right where they were before, although Dan Waldrop is again in the 340's when the coaches want him at 320. The biggest surprise of the day was when Jemayel Phillips got on the scale and it read 379.8 pounds. He had his street clothes and shoes on but this means he gained 20 pounds in the past couple of weeks! He's a huge kid. He's got a belly but he doesn't look too fat. He's just enormous. He moves well and has great strength but I'm sure the coaches will be all over him about keeping his weight down and eating better. I'm sure this made Dan Waldrop happy, though. Now the coaches will be on Jemayel's case. Jemayel is officially the largest Husker football player ever and he's just a true freshman.

Thursday, November 7, 2002

Tight end Phil Peetz amazed everyone today. He's the one guy you can depend on to do the right thing and keep everyone else in line while also being one of the hardest workers on the team. However, today he came to practice in a black wig, looking more than ever like the Unfrozen Caveman Lawyer. He even wore it under his helmet, which looked hilarious with all the long hair spilling out the back. I heard that when the coaches saw him, they all laughed their asses off, especially Coach Solich. He wore it the entire practice.

Saturday, November 9, 2002

Nebraska 45 – Kansas 7

This wasn't a surprise to anyone, but it was nice to have a win like this after the last few games. Kansas showed up for its annual ass-kicking and didn't disappoint yet another sold-out crowd.

We opened up the running game and ran all over them all day. In the end, we totaled 352 yards on the ground, adding more yards to put us back in contention for a national rushing title. Dahrran Diedrick and David Horne both had over 100 yards rushing, although David's average of 13.6 yards per carry was much higher than Dahrran's 8.9. Horne is really proving that he will be a huge part of our offense in the future and I bet the coaches can't wait to see what he can do after an off-season in the weight room.

Today Jammal Lord became the third Husker and the 18th player in NCAA history to pass and rush for 1,000 yards each in a season. This is an incredible tribute to him and I'm sure it was a shock to most of our fans who, like me, didn't realize he has been that good this year. He's not a flashy player and the press doesn't get much from him when he's interviewed, but he has very quietly been racking up these statistics.

We kicked Kansas all over the field all game long. A season-record 111 guys got into the game. With this win, we guaranteed our bowl game bid. I should have been happy but late in the game, when it was already put away, Coach Young asked over his headset to whoever was listening (probably Coach Tenopir) if they wanted to go with me at center for the last minutes of the game. I never heard the answer, but I was never told to go in for a series, so I can guess what the answer was. I took the snaps for all the extra points and the field goal, but I really thought I would get in for some center as well. If there was any game I should have gotten in this year, this should have been it. It just pisses me off that I spend all week being a center in practice, but come game time, I'm just a short snapper. What the hell am I wasting my time for in practice when I won't even play? I told Josh Brown that he needs to talk to Coach Young and see if I can specialize and just snap all day in practice. He understood and laughed.

The best thing that happened today was that my article was in the game program. It was a very well-written article and said many nice things about me. The most surprising thing is that Coach Young said very nice things about me and my commitment to the community. Just when I think I really can't stand a guy, he goes and does something like that and totally redeems himself.

Friday, November 15, 2002

We left Lincoln at 1:30 today on busses to Manhattan, Kansas. The offensive and defensive linemen shared one of the big coach busses so there was plenty of room to spread out. We watched two movies on the TVs in the bus and also stopped in Marysville for a quick snack of Subway sandwiches.

When we got into Manhattan, we stopped at the stadium and had our quick walk-through. Their stadium could look nice, but it's in too many odd pieces. It looks like they're still trying to build the whole stadium and just waiting for the money.

We then headed to the hotel, checked in, had dinner, and then went to another movie. In all, we saw three movies today—*Mr. Deeds*, *Spiderman*, and *I Spy*. We picked up our $10 for this weekend before the movie. Bed check was early tonight at 10:15, but I was tired enough that it didn't matter.

The team seems pretty confident about tomorrow. We're looking to get nine wins this season, even though this hasn't been brought up by the coaches at any point recently. I think their desire to follow our goal of playing one game at a time makes them hold back from mentioning anything about the nine wins. We've got a bowl trip locked up; now we're just working hard to make sure it's a fairly respectable bowl.

Saturday, November 16, 2002

Kansas State 49 – Nebraska 13

Kansas State is ranked as the number 11 team in the nation on both polls, and they proved this tonight. They shut us down in all three areas of the game: offense, defense, and special teams. There was very little we could do right. At the end, we had less than 100 yards rushing for the second time this season. Kansas State walked away after putting up more points on us than they ever have before, and my class of seniors leaves this field without knowing what it's like to win at Kansas State.

There were some good points about the game, however. Matt Herian continued to prove that he can be a deep-threat tight end by catching a 28-yard pass. He only has four catches for the season so far, but he's already totaled 165 yards as a true freshman. Out of all his catches, this one today is the shortest so far.

Josh Brown had an impressive day knocking every kick-off out of the end zone and making two of his three field goal attempts. The one he missed hit one of the uprights.

Rush end Chris Kelsay came back for the first time in five weeks after hurting his hamstring and proved that he is a dominating force on the defense. He chased down the quarterback from the backside of plays, showed great agility, and overpowered the offensive linemen and tight ends all game long.

Quarterback Jammal Lord added a little more to his statistics column today by gaining a few yards, most of which came on a very impressive pass play which he scrambled out of, was almost knocked down, and then took it the other way for the touchdown after a very nice downfield block by one of the receivers. He may not have Crouch's speed, but he makes up for it by being so incredibly agile and with his ability to shed tacklers.

There were numerous bad points of the game. One was that our offense got overpowered by their defense. Their defensive line played the run very well and our offensive line looked pretty bad all around. They were also able to rush the passes fairly easily and sack Jammal five times. The defense also gave up some huge plays, including a 91-yard dash by quarterback

Ell Roberson. Finally, the special teams didn't do much by having a punt blocked and recovered for a touchdown.

It seemed like the refs had it out for us today. Their guys held all day long and weren't called for it. The Kansas State fans were also very rude, especially the students. They yelled a variety of things at us all game long, letting us know that we were about to have our fifth loss and picking on individuals for their performance. When we recovered one of their fumbles and it was still a relatively close game, I motioned to the crowd to "bring it on." Apparently someone took my challenge and chucked a water bottle at me from the stands. It missed by two feet.

Finally, their announcer was very biased and sounded very demeaning when we were on offense or when our defense was getting pushed down the field. This just reaffirms my belief that our announcer at Nebraska is one of the best in the country (along with our fans) because he sticks to the facts of the game and makes no inflections to indicate which side he's on.

On the ride home we watched yet another movie, *The Sum of All Fears*, but I didn't care to watch it. I was more interested in the two liters of Long Island Iced Tea I made for this trip, along with the whiskey and Coke that another guy brought. We weren't drunk by the time we got back to Lincoln, but we sure felt better than when we left Manhattan.

Monday, November 18, 2002

We didn't have practice today. Instead, we just had meetings at 3:30 to watch film and go over some notes about the game. There was no "Offensive Lineman of the Game" this time, which means Coach Tenopir thought no one was worthy of the honor. We graded out lower than on all of our previous games and on film it looked like we couldn't move them or slow them down at all. It looked horrible.

The coolest thing I saw on film was during the last field

goal, which we missed, Kansas State had a middle jump to try to block the kick. I heard them say this as they lined up, so I was ready when the two guys started to jump up the middle. As soon as they jumped I stuck my arms out and ran forward, catching both of them in the waist and thigh pads, flipping one of them and holding the other one from getting a good jump. It looked pretty good on film, but we only brushed by it quickly so I didn't get to savor it.

Wednesday, November 20, 2002

We went half pads yesterday and full pads today. We're supposed to go full pads tomorrow. I don't understand why we are doing this. This is an off-week. Shouldn't we be trying to fine tune things instead of getting worn down and injured? We know we have to prepare really well to play Colorado, but I don't understand the logic of going in pads three days in a row on an off week.

All of my classes are starting to kick into high gear right now and this has really put the restraints on the amount of sleep I'm getting. My effectiveness in practice has been compromised, but I'm not going to play anyway so why worry about it? I've also lost a bit of weight in the past couple of weeks. I've steadily dropped one or two pounds each week without even trying and am now on the brink of being in the 270s for the first time since my freshman year. The coaches haven't said anything so I'm not going to worry about it.

Tuesday, November 26, 2002

The media found out that Josh Brown was picked up for a DUI this past weekend in Omaha. This is very disturbing news for Josh and the rest of the team. Coach Solich announced at the end of practice that Josh will have to sit out for the Colorado game according to team rules. This is definitely not the way Josh wanted to finish his senior year at home so I'm sure he's very disappointed in himself. This now means that Dale Endorf, who joined the team midway through the season, will be the starting place-kicker for the game. He joined the team late because Sandro DeAngelis went out with a broken toe. I'm sure he's feeling a lot of pressure. I'm confident he can get the job done, but it will be a good test for his nerves.

Near the end of practice today, I once again witnessed a horrific injury. Freshman guard Jermaine Leslie was pulling to the right when he got caught in a group of guys and his left ankle buckled. But not only did it buckle, it dislocated and was nearly on the side of his leg. It was bent at a 90-degree angle out to the side. It looked very similar to Tim Green's knee a few years ago. They carted him off for x-rays to see if anything is broken. We later learned that he broke one of his leg bones in five or six places and had plates and screws attached throughout his leg. One of my biggest fears right now is something like that happening to me in these last few weeks. I just want to get out of here with no serious injuries and no surgeries.

We should know which bowl game we will go to by this weekend. Coach Solich has been talking with the other Big 12 coaches and the bowl committees to help figure it out. It's complicated since nine of the 12 teams in the Big 12 are bowl-eligible this year. To have three-fourths of your conference going to a bowl game certainly says something about the strength of the conference. The Big 12 is definitely the strongest group in the nation.

Wednesday, November 27, 2002

There is no school today because of Thanksgiving break. Because of this, I picked up $164 at brunch this morning. It makes the whole weekend worthwhile when I can walk away with a full wallet.

Friday, November 29, 2002

Colorado 28 – Nebraska 13

We looked very good at the start of this game. We had a good drive going on our first possession which is not very typical for this season, but that ended shortly after it started and we had to punt. Our next possession was intercepted, followed by another punt. In the meantime, Colorado scored on a 40-yard pass giving them the lead. We answered this with our first drive of the second quarter by throwing an 80-yard bomb to Matt Herian who broke away from the defender and jetted all the way to the end zone. Once again, he proved that he is a deep threat.

Dale Endorf, who was named the starting place-kicker due to Josh Brown's suspension, made the extra point easily and then raced back to the sideline. I turned around after seeing the ball go through, expecting to see Joe and Dale there, but Dale was already near the sideline and Joe was just standing there looking like he was wondering where Dale went. I congratulated Joe as usual and then waited for Dale to get done with the ensuing kickoff to congratulate him. He got a big break on the kickoff because Colorado drew a flag on the extra point that allowed him to kick from the 50-yard line. He easily kicked it out of the end zone and then raced back to the sidelines. I've never seen anyone so proud and beaming with excitement as Dale was at that moment. I congratulated him and he did the same to me, and I told him next time we want to congratulate him on the field so he should stay out there for a little while. He understood but he was still on such a high that I wasn't sure if I got through.

At the end of the half Dale proved himself with a 33-yard field goal, his first-ever field goal at Nebraska. He made it through easily and was about to run back to the sideline when he remembered that we want to congratulate him on the field. Nate Kolterman picked him up with a big bear hug.

We entered the locker room with a 10-7 lead. When we came out we stopped Colorado on their first drive and recovered a fumble deep in their territory. It looked like we had a guaranteed score, but Richie Incognito spoiled this when he retaliated against a Colorado player right in front of a ref. While the flag was deserved, the Colorado player should have received one too for trying to push Richie backward over a pile of guys, but the ref didn't see it. We were then forced to try a 49-yard field goal. None of us was sure Dale would be able to do it, but we went out and got ready to do our best. Josh Brown usually marks off the yardage and Joe sets up to get ready to take the snap. Dale didn't do this so Joe set up where he thought was seven yards deep. He accidentally set up a yard too deep, which made my snap a little low when it got to him, but Joe made a good hold and Dale made a great kick, putting us at a more comfortable lead of 13-7. This didn't last long.

Colorado's next two possessions resulted in touchdowns, and they added another one later in the game as well. After our last field goal, we weren't able to do anything at all on offense and our defense looked just as bad.

We now fall to 7-6 and there is no chance of a nine-win season. That's just one more record to fall by the wayside this turbulent year. I didn't really care to listen to what the coaches said after the game, I just wanted to change and get out of there.

On somewhat of a bright side, today was Senior Day. There was a video played while we were warming up, with all the seniors talking about our memories and our feelings. It was put together pretty well, but my part was hard to hear because my voice is lower than a lot of the guys. I even had a hard time understanding what I said, but it was something about the pride that I take in being here in this program because we have always operated with a high level of class and respect.

The best part of the day was when we were introduced and ran out onto the field one at a time. I jumped the gun a little bit and started to run out before they announced my name, but it didn't look too bad. I guess that was an unconscious gesture that meant I can't wait to get this over with. Before running out I shared an awkward hug with Coach Solich. It was awkward because I didn't know if I should hug him or shake his hand. I guess he was thinking the same thing and we kind of split the difference on the two. I said, "Thanks for everything, Coach," and he thanked me as well. I then took off waving to the fans as I went. It was a good feeling to run out by myself and have 78,000 people watching me, although I'm sure quite a few were just clapping to be nice and had no clue who I was.

Monday, December 2, 2002

After a whole weekend of media speculation, Coach Solich brought us in for a meeting and informed us that he has made some coaching changes. He had a very stern demeanor as he told us all of this and it was apparently a very emotionally taxing weekend for him. It seemed just as tough for him to face the team and tell us. He informed us that Coaches Craig Bohl, George Darlington, and Nelson Barnes would not be with us anymore, and that he would relinquish the offensive coordinator job. He said he has been in contact with a few people to fill the spots, but wants to leave all names out of the discussion right now so that this process can go smoothly without those people getting a lot of pressure from the press. Coach Solich wanted us to know that if we have any questions, he will be available at any time for anyone who wishes to speak with him. He also said he was going to have a press release about this later today, but he was not going to hold a press conference.

This information was not really a surprise except for defensive ends coach Nelson Barnes getting fired. I overheard rush end Chris Kelsay say later that he saw it coming. I guess he would know. Coach Barnes hasn't produced anything over the past five years and has failed to bring in outstanding recruits. Coach Darlington (Defensive Backs) was another slight surprise, but he has been here for 30 years and it's probably time for some new blood. Also, our pass defense is ranked in the middle of the whole NCAA this year and was never really too good in the past anyway. As the last remaining member of Tom Osborne's def ensive staff, I know he took great pride in his job and it meant a lot to him. I later heard that Coach Solich first asked him to retire. When Darlington refused, Solich fired him and Darlington took this very hard. He allegedly threw a bit of a tantrum in the office, but that's just a rumor.

The media had a field day with all of this and it was the top story on all the news channels. I didn't care to watch any of it. I knew what happened and the news programs would tell me nothing more than what I knew.

Tuesday, December 3, 2002

Just as the news about all the coaching changes was sinking in to the public psyche, more shocking news hit. Bill Byrne, our athletic director for the past 10 years, is leaving for Texas A&M. Apparently this news broke in Texas earlier today. Byrne had wanted to have private discussions with all the coaches and athletes in the program to let us know first so we could ask any pertinent questions, but he wasn't able to do this. This has got to be one of the strangest weeks in the history of University of Nebraska sports. I know this is one of the most emotional weeks for our coaches.

All of this has caused a lot of confusion on the team and has raised a lot of questions. Some guys don't know if they want to stay around here for the rest of their college careers. Other guys, who are almost done, have lost all remaining motivation. Also, Jeff Jamrog is the only defensive coach still on the team, so a lot of the defensive guys have lost their leadership and don't know what to do.

Coach Solich told us we will have new coaches for the bowl game, but that will be very tough for the team as well as those new coaches. They will have to come in with only about two weeks to learn our system, get to know our players, and then try to be effective.

All of this happening so close together really makes for an interesting theory. What if Coach Solich, knowing Bill Byrne would be leaving soon, decided to make these changes now instead of after the season just to show the new athletic director, whoever that may be, that he has full control of the team and he's willing to do anything to make it better, even fire coaches. Perhaps he's worried that a new AD will fire him, so he's trying to show that he's taking care of the problem himself. He also may want to show recruits the same thing, and bring in new coaches so recruits can meet them.

I really hope all of this doesn't affect recruiting. The past couple of years haven't been very stellar for recruiting, but we have some promising candidates for the coming year that could really give us a boost.

We have to lift four times this week with Wednesday as a rest day, but we also did a little running today. At 3:30, we met in the Cook and did an abbreviated running workout just to get us moving and keep up our conditioning. At the end Chris Kelsay spoke to all of us about coming together as a team right now and not letting anything tear us apart.

To symbolize this, we did our sit-up and push-up workout together as a team at the end of running.

Saturday, December 7, 2002

We practiced in full pads again this morning. It's never fun to get up early on a weekend, but it's magnified when you have to get up to go to a full-pads practice. One of the reasons we're practicing in full pads on a weekend is to show off for the recruits who are here. To make the situation more utterly ridiculous, there was only one recruit here today. We all hate days like these when we're supposed to show off for the recruits. The coaches make us go harder than usual in practice just to prove to the recruits that we mean business. In the meantime, we're all so tired that we don't even care. So, not to ruin it for any current recruits out there, but everything you see (at any school) has been meticulously staged just for you.

It was another good practice overall and Coach Solich spoke to us at the end again. Even with all the recent stresses, he managed to give a really good speech. He seems much more confident now and much more in control. He's not just telling us what we need to hear like he usually does, he's telling us the way it has to be if we want to be a good team. He's telling us that hard work will get us there. He's telling us that working together in these next couple of weeks will get us what we want and help us end the season in a manner that brings pride to our program. Overall, I think he raised his coaching effectiveness by about 50% in just under a week.

Sunday, December 8, 2002

We found out we're going to the Independence Bowl in Shreveport, Louisiana. This will be the first time Nebraska has ever been to that bowl and also will be the first time we've ever played Mississippi. Eli Manning and the rest of Ole Miss will give us a worthy challenge and we are looking forward to matching up with them on the 27th.

Friday, December 13, 2002

We practiced again today in full pads. So far this week, we practiced on Monday, Wednesday and today, and we will go again tomorrow in the morning. We've also had to lift four times this week. All combined, this is a pretty trying schedule when we go in full pads every practice, but add in the fact that finals are next week, and it makes it really tough.

I got a call from our academic watchdog Dennis LeBlanc last night and he said that if I don't raise my grade in my geography class, I won't go to the bowl game. It would be very embarrassing to miss my last bowl game because of academics, especially since I was just listed as First Team All-Academic Big 12. That's not the way I want to go out, so I'm going to study very hard these next few days. Trying to fit football into the equation really complicates things.

On Wednesday, as I was getting taped, one of the trainers came by with a form I had to fill out for the pro scouts. I laughed and said I wasn't going pro, but they said I had to fill it out anyway. I made some corrections, such as changing my weight from 300 to 280, and handed it in. It would be the ultimate joke if any pro team wanted me.

We picked up our gifts from Adidas before practice today. I thought that after going to the national championship game last year and presumably making Adidas a lot of money, they would give us some really good gifts this year. Instead, this is probably the worst assortment yet. The main thing is a leather suit/garment bag. It's very nice, but it's a very incongruous gift. Most of us don't own a suit and not many of us dress up too often, so this gift is lost on us. They said it's worth close to $300, so maybe I can pawn it or something. The other things we received were a new sweatshirt which isn't too bad, a blue Nebraska hat, and a new pair of shoes, only they didn't have shoes up to my size, so I just took a pair to give to someone as a gift. That was it. A pitiful pittance.

Scott Frost, quarterback of the 1997 national championship team and current professional defensive back, is in town taking some graduate courses and has volunteered to help coach the defense. He definitely has the qualifications. He knows our system and how we practice, and he also has learned how to play defense fairly recently, so turning around and passing on what he's learned should be very easy. Let's hope it works.

No offensive coordinator has been chosen yet and Coach Solich said he will probably call the plays during the bowl game. There also are a lot of rumors going around about other coaches and their job security. One is that Coach Dan Young will retire after the season is over and Dave Gillespie, the running backs coach, will step down as well. We have two weeks to see if this is true.

Monday, December 16, 2002

I found a nice surprise in my locker today—a framed picture of this year's Unity Council. I think it's funny because they rounded us up for the picture very quickly and all I'm wearing is the Unity Council t-shirt and a towel. Luckily I'm in the back row.

This week will be a little different from last week in that we will lift on Wednesday after practice and then have Thursday completely free. This will be a very nice break. Also, Thursday marks the start of the single-digit countdown of days until we're done. Joe Chrisman and I remember talking during two-a-days, when we were still in the 150s, how nice it will be to be in the single digits. One thing I can always depend on is that time will continue to tick by at the same rate, like it or not. Right now, I like it.

Wes Cody went down with a knee injury today. It appears to be an MCL injury, which is a lot better than an ACL. This is bad news either way for Wes, who was supposed to start in his final game as offensive guard. The trainers want to bring him back for the game, but there may not be enough time.

Thursday, December 19, 2002

I found out today that I got the C that I needed in my geography class, so I will go to the bowl game. All my studying paid off and I got a good grade on the final. I'm done with finals and am no longer a student athlete. Right now, I'm just an athlete, but that will also be over soon and I will return to just being a student. I'm looking forward to the life where I can do what I want in the afternoons, as well as actually have a good job and make some decent money.

Friday, December 20, 2002

We picked up money for the weekend today. We got $93 to cover meals, which is a little much, but I'm not one to turn down cash.

Saturday, December 21, 2002

After meetings, I picked up my travel reimbursement money of $252 since I will be driving back with my parents instead of taking the team charter. Once again, it's hard to not take free money.

Monday, December 23, 2002

On one of the coldest mornings we've had in a while, we met at the National Guard building by the airport at 7:00. As we entered the building we signed for our money and picked up $100, then picked up some fruit and rolls.

We then took a shuttle to the runway where the plane was waiting. We avoided going through the terminal because we wanted to avoid the security checkpoints to save time.

The flight to Shreveport was about two hours and we then loaded up a convoy of busses and went to our hotel, a Holiday Inn that seems to be in the middle of nowhere. We had a meeting with the officer who headed up the police escort and he told us what we need to know during our stay. He told us the names of some places to stay away from and landmarks to look for to know which part of the city we're in. Then he told us plainly that if we are not 21, there is nothing for us to do in this city. For those who are 21, there are some casinos on the Red River and some bars and clubs around the area that sound like good places to waste some time and money. Even if we want to just stay at the hotel, there isn't much to do. The players lounge is just a section of the lobby with some arcade games and a little snack bar set up. There are three games to choose from, along with a ping pong table, but the games are broken most of the time. I brought my PlayStation 2 to play in the room, but the television has some kind of protective thing on the cable line and I also don't have the right converter to play on this type of television. It doesn't feel like this trip will be much fun.

After lunch at the hotel we got taped and loaded up the busses for practice. We're practicing at the bowl-game site, which has a field surface very similar to Memorial Stadium. It was raining as we arrived and rained harder and harder as we prepared for practice. Coach Solich pushed back the start of practice a few minutes while we waited for the rain to clear up.

We practiced in full pads and it was pretty intense with a lot of good hitting. At the end Coach Solich told us that Bo Pelini from the Green Bay Packers had just been signed on as the defensive coordinator and will officially fill the position after our season is over.

After practice we had to lift, only we didn't have any of our equipment here. We borrowed an assortment of weights from a local high school. It looked pretty pathetic, but it reflects how we have one-third of the travel costs that we did for the Rose Bowl. I guess when you aren't poised to make a lot of money off the bowl game like we were for the Rose Bowl, we need to cut costs somewhere. We just had to do a bench workout today and then tomorrow we'll do a hang clean workout and that will be it for the rest of the trip.

Later in the day, we went to the welcome party at the Bossier Civic Center. We picked up our bowl watches before we left the hotel as well. The Independence Bowl watches are the same Fossil watches we got for the Alamo Bowl, only they have gold plating along the links and a gold face with the bowl logo.

We had a reception dinner for both teams tonight and it was probably one of the best we've ever had. We started off with a dinner of fried catfish and some other Cajun-style foods, all very rich and fried which seems to be the theme for our food so far on this trip. The coaches warned us before the trip began that we should watch what we eat, but all that's been available so far has been fried or fatty foods.

There was a big-screen television set up with the Playstation 2003 NCAA football game on it and a few players from each team were chosen beforehand to play a mock game between Nebraska and Ole Miss. Our guys were able to blow them away in the video game. After the meal and a short introduction by the bowl officials, a hypnotist took over and put on a very funny show. He used players from both teams as well as some girls from the audience. Some parts of the show were a little lewd, but the guy was quick to stop the hypnotized people before they did anything too embarrassing. One of the most hilarious parts was when Jemayel

Phillips and Mike MacLaughlin were told under hypnosis that they were friends. *Really* good friends. They looked at each other, smiled, hugged, and laid back on the floor of the stage. Jemayel threw his massive leg over the top of the much smaller Mike and we were all laughing hysterically when the hypnotist stopped them from going any further.

After we got back to the hotel, we had the rest of the night free until bed check at 2:00 in the morning. I'm rooming with Andy Wingender and we just decided to crash tonight instead of staying out late. Besides, the shuttle service for this bowl trip consists of the huge tour busses. This makes for very slow trips and a lot of waiting. Not exactly the best organizational scheme, especially since we're not within walking distance of anything.

Tuesday, December 24, 2002

After a late wake-up and an 11:00 lunch, we headed out for practice. We enjoyed a nice practice in sweats with slightly better weather. This means that I have no more padded practices ever. What a relief.

Andy and I went to the casinos tonight since they seem like the only thing to do in this city. I lost $25 pretty quickly and spent the rest of the time watching the other guys gamble. Josh Brown is the big winner so far, winning close to $1,000 playing roulette.

After Andy and I got back we met up with Scott Koethe who was determined to find the hospitality lounge. We eventually found it but we had to be careful. This lounge is just for the coaches, staff, and families, and is set up with TVs and a well-stocked bar with whatever you desire for free. There were a couple people in there, but lucky for us there were no coaches. We walked in like we had done this sort of thing before and helped ourselves to a few beers.

One of the guys in charge came over and we introduced

ourselves as graduate assistant coaches. Andy and I let Scott take over the conversation and he made up a great story about how he was working on his master's in physics. He was pretty believable, considering how much he'd already had to drink, and was talking about how much he detested certain branches of mathematics and once he found one he liked he followed it straight into his chosen path with physics. Andy and I were trying hard not to laugh, and managed to amuse ourselves with our own conversation so we didn't have to listen to Scott. Some of the video guys came by, as well as Art McWilliams, our team chef, and they all warned us not to get caught here. We just smiled and nodded, not really caring.

About 20 minutes later, running backs coach Dave Gillespie and his wife walked in and asked us what we were doing there. We casually said, "Just hanging out and enjoying some low-carb beers, you know, we gotta watch our figures!" Dave then replied, "You can't be drinking beer." We stood there awkwardly, waiting in anticipation for the punch-line as if he would just laugh it off. Instead, he continued, "Do you think I'm serious? You can't be drinking beer."

We were doubly stunned by his ability to be so terse. Nearly all of his position players constantly make fun of his perpetual stammering and seemingly miraculous ability to make even the shortest sentence live forever.

So, feeling very uncomfortable, we dropped our beers into the trash can and quickly left the lounge. We didn't know if we were in trouble, but we were laughing the whole way back to our rooms. Andy wasn't so jovial since he'd just gotten yelled at by his coach, but Scott and I didn't care at all because we knew that whatever punishment they gave us would only last three days at most.

Wednesday, December 25, 2002

Another Merry Christmas spent away from the family.

It's very rare that a person has the opportunity to enjoy a cold beer on a hot Christmas morning. Knowing that this is one of Homer Simpson's great loves, Andy and I made a special attempt to stash away some beer for this purpose. It was easily the highlight of our entire bowl trip.

Andy, Scott and I all expected Coach Solich to say something about the incident last night, but nothing was said. Either he didn't care or Gillespie didn't tell him; I'm not going to complain.

We picked up another $100 at lunch and then got taped and departed for practice. Today we had our little drill at the start where we catch passes from Coach Tenopir. This was the last time to do this fun little drill and I am proud to say that I caught all the balls that were thrown to me.

The team was invited to Harrah's Casino tonight and we enjoyed a nice buffet dinner. Nate Kolterman was Santa this year and he really had a hard time being funny, although it was obvious he was trying. Some of the kids were even scared of him, which made me laugh. We picked up a little gift from the casino at the end of the meal—an envelope with a 30-minute phone card, two Shreveport postcards, and a leftover pen from a pharmaceutical convention. They could have saved themselves a lot of trouble and just given us all a buck in chips for the casino. I joined a large group of our guys in the casino after the meal. I didn't want to gamble tonight because I didn't feel like losing any money, but that didn't stop Andy Wingender. He lost $300 in 10 minutes at the roulette table. He bet on red seven times in a row and the ball landed on black each time. It was a statistical anomaly. He then switched to blackjack where he recovered half of his lost money. I played a few hands eventually, was soon up $40 and gratefully walked away. I'm up $15 for the trip so far. It's not much, but not many guys will be able to say they actually won money at the casinos.

Thursday, December 26, 2002

Today we suffered through yet another boring luncheon. The speeches were as bland as the food, and time seemed to stand still as we waited for the torture to end. One of the things that helped us get through it was pointing out Coach Solich's verbal idiosyncrasies. He has developed a habit of saying various catch phrases, which he's probably unaware of, and says them so frequently that it has become an inside joke. In almost every speech, whether at a convention or just in a casual team meeting, he says, "In terms of…", "tremendous", and "…what we're all about."

When the luncheon was finally over we had our short walk-through and then were zipped back to the hotel. There was a dinner just for the guys suiting up and then later we headed to a theater to see *Catch Me If You Can.* This was by far the best movie we've seen all year long as a team.

A snack was waiting back at the hotel and bed check was an hour later at 11:00.

Friday, December 27, 2002

Ole Miss 27 – Nebraska 23

This morning was pretty interesting. After meetings, Coach Tenopir had Dan Waldrop and Nick Povendo stay so he could talk to them. Coach Tenopir said that because of Dan's weight, Nick will start the game at tackle. Dan was obviously very upset by this news. I've known Dan for a while now, and this was the most mad I have ever seen him. After a full season of starting as well as practicing the entire bowl preparation time like he was going to be the starter, it's no wonder he was talking about quitting or transferring.

Even with a 17-7 lead in this game, we couldn't pull off a win. I truly believe that all of our guys gave it their all, but something just wasn't there for us to win. If anything, I would blame it on the officials. There were many questionable calls and at one point even confusion among the refs as to what call to make. They didn't seem to notice all the holding and illegal blocking by the Mississippi offensive linemen. They had their hands on our guys' facemasks all game long.

There were a lot of things that went wrong in this game, but there were also a lot of things that were really good. For the most part, our kicking game was really good. Josh Brown connected on three field goals and two extra points, while Kyle Larson had three punts downed inside the 20-yard line, two of them inside the 3-yard line. There was one glaring error in the kicking game, however, but we had the right intention. On one of our punts, Ole Miss guys weren't covering our lone guy out to the left. Steve Kriewald, who usually is the personal protector (the guy a few yards behind one of the guards who calls the cadence), was filling in at guard for Scott Shanle who was too sick to play. This moved Judd Davies to the personal protector and Judd had never practiced the fake punt that we were perfectly set up for. He saw the opportunity for the fake and took it, but threw the ball short and gave Ole Miss good field possession and another score.

They had a much more consistent offense with Eli Manning at the helm. We were able to accumulate only minimal yardage and ended our season with three straight losses and a 7-7 record, the worst season in over 40 years.

I finished my five years with a record of 49-16. I finished my senior year taking every extra point and field goal snap. I finished my senior year by being perfect in my last game. I finished with no major injuries and no surgeries. I finished. I didn't quit.

End of the Year Summary

A disappointing year, but it was hard to avoid. The coaches seemed to have decreased power as there was no stern authority figure or even a revered workaholic among them. The players grew disenfranchised with a system that only played the top quarter of players while all the others were reduced to practicing away all of their time and energy. Very few people, athletes or staff, were overly optimistic throughout the season. All of the injuries, suspensions, desertions and expulsions had an affect on more than just the immediate players.

I'm very proud to have played in every game of my senior year. I'm very proud to have earned an athletic letter. I'm very proud that I had the perseverance to get through all the seemingly endless hard work and make it to this point. I can't wait to see what's next.

Sunday, January 12, 2003

Coaches Tenopir and Young announced their retirement today. Tenopir cited medical reasons and Young simply said he wanted to spend more time with his wife traveling and playing golf. The coaches told us linemen privately in their meeting room first, and then there was a media conference where it was obvious the reporters were either taken off guard by this or entirely expected it because they didn't ask very many questions.

Now, I hold a certain distinction of being the last group of players to be fully coached by Tenopir and the first group to be full head coached by Solich.

> Later on, directly from their own mouths, I learned that they were forced to retire by Solich. They were very gracious in this change, but obviously saddened, yet Solich had to do something to try to keep his job. Again, it was too little, too late.

Afterword

I compiled a nice list of accomplishments during my 5 years. I earned my letter for the playing time during my senior season. I'm officially listed as a letterman at the University of Nebraska for football and that's something nobody can take away from me. I'm also in a video game, *NCAA 2003,* by EA Sports®. I graduated in May 2004 with a degree in Social Sciences. I earned a Big XII Commissioner's Honor Roll award nearly every semester while in school. I was honored with being on the First Team Big XII All-Academic Team. I was named Mentor of the Year at the Middle School level for the TeamMates Mentoring Program. I was named to the Brook Berringer Citizenship Team and participated in several public engagements. I was an active member of the Unity Council. Most importantly, out of the 41 Walk-Ons that entered this program in 1998, only a quarter of them finished out their career at Nebraska and I can proudly say I am one of them.

There are many things I'll never forget. I'll never forget the thrill of running onto the field for a home game. I'll never forget the pride of doing my job well and helping win a major college game. Hopefully, someday I'll forget the fear of being late for lifting or practice, and waking up because of football-related nightmares.

My one main wish about my college years is that I would have dedicated more time and energy to searching for the best major for me. I hastily picked teaching as my degree field and eventually realized I didn't want to do that, but by then it was too late to change. I guess I could have partied less as well, but it was college.

I receive a lot of respect when people learn that I was a Husker and everyone wants to know what it was like. They always ask about the coaching changes. They ask what went wrong, how we could lose so many games, what certain guys are like, and so on. Hopefully this book does it all.

Since I left, Frank Solich and the rest of his staff were replaced, and Bill Callahan from the Oakland Raiders assumed the head-coaching role. In hindsight, I was able to capture the end of a very long and very exciting era of college football. The Nebraska teams that ruled the gridiron from the 1960's to the 1990's have faded into the past and now there are entirely new coaches, new plays, a constantly remodeled stadium, and a constantly rising level of expectations. The game was big when I was playing, but it's much bigger now, and the stakes keep rising.

I have a lot of great memories of my time at Nebraska. I made a lot of good friends, took great classes, and I had a lot of fun. I was also privileged to experience in great depth what it's like to be a Husker, something that thousands of people across this state would gladly sacrifice many things for. It was a fantastic experience, but I'm very glad it's over.

If this book seems too negative, I apologize and I mean no disrespect to the program, the coaches, the players, or the fans. But perhaps if I had reason to write a more positive reflection, then the overhaul of the program probably wouldn't have been necessary.

It's impossible to tell what exactly caused the deterioration of the program, but I think I'm qualified to offer some suggestions. For starters, I came in with one of the biggest freshman classes ever. Coach Solich probably overextended himself in his first year at the helm by grabbing all the talent that was interested in the program. This created a huge surplus of guys who would never see playing time, who were treated by the coaches like they were disposable, and were stuck on the scout team forever. There was a very high attrition rate, especially among the walk-ons. Only about one-fourth of the walk-ons I came in with finished their career on the field at Nebraska. Most of those who left did so to find a program in which they could get some playing time, and I have to respect that.

Still, with too many guys at each position, it created a division between the starters and those on the bottom of the totem pole. Some took it as a sign to work harder; others took it as a chance to trail along in the shadows of the program and still reap the rewards. I believe the latter attitude caused the program's ultimate downfall. There were too many guys who just wanted to slide through. They knew they had no chance of playing, but it was still better than not being on the team. Apathy is a poisonous attitude and it's hard to extinguish because even the starters get resentful and envious when they see the other guys not working hard. It's a lot easier to fit into the pack than to try to lead it.

The coaches also failed horribly at recruiting top prospects to come to Nebraska. In Osborne's era, there were some decent recruiting classes, but most of them were pretty average. Then those coaches would develop the young athletes along with all the walk-ons and build a great team by the time they were juniors and seniors. I guess the lack of high-level recruits never raised a red flag because of this legacy, but I think it's clear now that a strong program needs strong recruiting.

The coaches also failed at getting the most out of their players. In the later years, there was no coach who I could truly say was an inspirational figure for the whole team. Ron Brown and Turner Gill would have made terrific people to motivate the whole team; however, most of their influence was imparted just on their positional players since they had very little interaction with the team as a whole at any point.

On a similar note, there were several coaches who were unable to properly train their players. Some were so old that they couldn't demonstrate what they were looking for. Sadly, we even had a coach or two who were just filling in token spots who didn't have a clue what they were doing or how to do it.

Because of these failings among the coaches, many players had little or no motivation. We knew we had to play football, but we weren't really sure what we were playing for all the time. Our first listed goal for each season was "Win the National Championship." In my mind, that's not a goal that should have been placed first. When this goal is foremost on your mind, the moment you started showing any weakness in a game created a lot of fear and doubt, making you think that the whole season was shot and that you have nothing else to play for.

As for Frank Solich himself, I don't think it's appropriate to give him all the credit or the blame for his 6 years as head coach. For the first 4 years, he was playing the athletes that Osborne left behind. It wasn't until his fifth and sixth years that he was playing with a team that he built himself. The speculation of what he could have done to turn the program around will never end, but I think it was best to move on.

Leadership is one of those intangibles that is so important in football. A head coach needs to be the most visible person but also the most confident and assuring. Coach Solich had his title of head coach, but he looked like he was trying to steer a ship without a rudder. He seemed like he wasn't sure if what he was doing will work, but he was going to keep trying and make everyone else in the boat feel like everything was alright as they drifted further into the unknown.

The leadership of the players was a big part of the demise as well. We pick our own captains and they are always some of our best athletes. However, more often than not they were too quiet. They tried to lead by example and were not used to getting in someone's face to motivate them. Yet that was the kind of leader we needed.

Occasionally, we had a leader that would get in your face, but they didn't demonstrate the desired attitude or actions themselves so they were seen as hypocrites. The best example is our starting center for my last years. He was a good athlete and did well for us, but he was too much of a slacker to be taken seriously. Upon further review of his play, it was seen that he consistently made bad blocks and bad choices on the field, but the coaches were limited in their supply of game-ready centers. (Yes, I'm aware of the personal irony.)

There were even players whose abrasive and destructive demeanor crippled several attempts by others to take a leadership role. The best example of this is an offensive lineman to whom I refuse to give more press. He bullied his way around the team so much that very few people liked him but everyone knew to respect his wishes or face his wrath. More often than not he would just be mean for the fun of it. A young leader wishing to make his ability known would get made fun of by him until they gave up. I guess he wanted everyone to be as miserable as him.

The structure of the athletic department even contributed to the turmoil. The departure of the nutrition staff created a void in a crucial area that had been one of the key components of our training. I have no doubt that the health of the team slipped quite a bit when there was no nutrition staff to regulate our players' food intake. The strength and conditioning program also took a major hit during the later years. Much of the staff moved on to better jobs at around the same time. With decreased numbers and a few fresh faces, the leadership of the strength and conditioning staff was severely hampered, sometimes leaving the athletes personally accountable for their workouts. We worked hard all the time, but if we had a chance to save some time and energy we certainly took it, even at the expense of our training.

Internal strife between the strength coaches boiled over into their work with us. Differences of opinion between Coach Solich and our athletic director about the breadth of the nutrition program severely delayed its implementation. Everything from the top down eventually affected the players and their game-day attitudes.

I think the team is now back on track to being a dominating force because they're fixing the attitude of the team. They are now limiting the number of walk-ons and are shrinking the team to make practices more manageable, and so the starters don't have to practice against the less-than-qualified scout team all the time. The depth at positions is much less, giving more guys the chance for some playing time, so they should be ready.

In my first year out of football, I dropped my weight to 215 pounds and have since leveled off at 230. Most of the guys I played with hardly recognize me now. A lot of guys go the other direction with their weight because they eat the same and don't work out as much. I lost the weight mostly by dedicating myself to a rigorous and consistent cardiovascular exercise routine. Staying away from the training table certainly helped as well. Although, taking the weight off wasn't nearly as hard as putting it on in the first place. I can't describe how good it feels to not weigh 300 pounds anymore, but I have to admit I miss the intimidated looks most people gave me. Now I just stick out in a crowd because I'm tall, not massive.

After 11 years of playing full-contact football from middle school to the elite college ranks, I hung up my cleats. I was able to amass quite a collection of memorabilia—my helmet, most of my jerseys, my senior year's game pants with pads, game socks, and tons of gym bags, warm-ups, T-shirts, shorts, shoes, programs, ticket stubs, media guides, pictures, plaques and awards. It's a part of my life that I won't soon forget, but I'm glad it's over. Now I can strive for bigger and better things.

I think Lou Holtz said it best, "If what you did yesterday seems big, you haven't done anything today."

The following is from Andrew Wingender, my fullback friend and fellow walk-on whose senior year in 2003 was also Solich's last year as head coach before he was fired and a whole new set of coaches were brought in. I asked him to recap the last year of Solich and this is what he said:

> I get mad every time I hear that Frank was fired after a 9 win season. Sure, after his 9th win he was fired, but our season, his season, didn't end there. We were galvanized by what happened to Coach Solich, the coaches and players alike came together to do what was most important right then and there: win the Alamo Bowl! I won't deny that we threw a tantrum. The coaches held themselves well, but I know they were concerned. They moved their families, left jobs, and came to Nebraska for Frank Solich and his vision for our future. When

Frank was fired, they knew to get résumé's in order. But men of character don't abandon the thing's they believe in. I can safely say that the coaches believed in making the Huskers great, both the team and the players. We believed in them too. If you're wondering how that worked out: 17-3 victory over Michigan State in the Alamo Bowl. Not too shabby.

But let me start at the beginning. When the 2002 season ended at the University of Nebraska, we were faced with many changes. The defensive staff was completely changed and the offensive staff was reorganized to a great extent. What was asked of us as players was to take a leap of faith. We had to evolve to become a competitive team in a world of college football. What I'm most proud of is the way we bought in to the new systems presented to us. Defensively, the players responded greatly. Defensive Coordinator Bo Pelini's greatest strength was that he let everyone know their role. Each player had a job; sometimes that meant players had to sacrifice their own accomplishments so others could be in position to make the plays. It worked! We had the number 1 defense in the country for most of the year. Players like Barrett Ruud, Josh Bullocks, and others thrived under the system.

Offensively, we had to move from the option offensive. No other way to say it, not that it was a broken system, but we couldn't outrace defenses around the end, we couldn't shove the ball down defenses throats, and we couldn't pass well enough to get 8 people out of the box. Too many jersey's in too little space. That's the simple explanation. But we didn't abandon who we were. Nebraska was a running team, and we had recruited guys for that sole purpose. My friends Judd Davies, Josh Davis, Cory Ross, and Jamal Lord had been built for one reason, to run sprint options and isolation plays. How do you ask them to do something else? It's easy to criticize guys, and plenty of people were unfairly criticized, but what few people saw was how smart the coaches were. Offensive Coordinator Barney Cotton didn't ask us to reinvent the wheel, he wanted us to improve on our weaknesses. For the first time in my career, we had a passing coordinator, my position coach Tim Albin, and the same thing happened for our offensive as our defense; we understood the strategy.

Here is the greatest compliment I can give Coach Solich, he had to change what we did, not who we were. Football's as simple as blocking and tackling. I'm always amused when I see teams try to run the most complex schemes they can to confuse the offense or defense. I think that means they can't block or tackle well enough to win. Frank hired coaches with ties to the University, men who know why we care so much about football in this state. And a coach who took control of his staff and gave away control of his offense got fired. 10-win seasons are not common; they aren't Championship quality, but by no means are they mediocre.

Let me take a moment to admit that my role in these events is minor, I would never lie and say that I was a great football player. I was good enough to get in the door and good enough to never get kicked out, but my 2 carries for 4 yards will not be remembered by anyone, but myself and my family. The reason I put up with all the difficulties and constraints that football put on me was simple: I loved those guys. I am proud to call people like Dave Kolowski my friend. Each one of them is my brother in a very real sense and I will always love them. Thank you, to everyone who supported us through good and bad. I hope you all enjoyed the ride as much as I did.

Andrew Wingender
February, 2006

I'd also like to say thank you to the entire state of Nebraska. There are hundreds of thousands of fans that make this state and this team what it is. Thanks to the coaches and players that I worked with and all the behind the scenes people that keep everything together. I'd like to personally thank several people. A deep and sincere thank you goes to Joe Vojtech, Dan McLaughlin, Rick Hook, Mike Janis, all of my teachers in the Millard Public Schools and all the coaches that had the pleasure and/or pain of coaching me, all my fellow players and opponents, Chad Stanley, Nancy Evans, Bill Cornell, James Tansey, Andrew Wingender, Eric Crouch, Dennis LeBlanc, Keith Zimmer, Brian Nelson, Aaron Patch, Joel Hendrickson, Judy Kay, David Kay, Marshall Poole, Jeanie Poole, Helen Poole, Jocelyn Pierce, Brandon Pierce, Jason Kolowski, Stacy Markus, Rick Kolowski, Bonnie Kolowski, Edie Gunn, Craig Hollmann, Michael Callahan, Zac Beiting, Brent Reno, Brad Tirey, all of my family and friends whom I failed to mention, and, most importantly, thanks to my wife Lauren. This book is for you all.

Go Huskers!!!

-David Kolowski

The 1998 Nebraska Walk-on List:

Of all incoming walk-ons, roughly 25% were able to complete their eligibility playing at Nebraska (noted by *).

CHRIS BUTLER
I-back, 6-0, 190, Hoover, Alabama

JOE CHRISMAN *
Quarterback, 6-1, 200, Longmont, Colorado

DANNY CORK
Split End/Wing Back, 5-10, 200, Owasso, Oklahoma

WILL DABBERT *
Tight End, 6-4, 220, Lincoln East

CHAD DURYEA
Split End, 6-5, 200, Merna, Nebraska

MASON DUTTON
Linebacker, 6-0, 220, Plano, Texas

KYLE EISENHAUER
Offensive Lineman, 6-2, 250, Wausa, Nebraska

AUSTIN FORSTER
Wing Back, 5-9, 185, Gordon, Nebraska

JOE FREEMAN
Offensive Lineman, 6-4, 270, Millard North

GABE FRIES *
Linebacker, 6-2, 200, Benkelman, Nebraska
SAM GUTZ
Quarterback, 5-11, 170, Columbus, Nebraska
SETH GUTZ
Wing Back/Split End, 6-0, 185, Columbus, Nebraska (Junior-Transfer from Concordia)
ANDY GWENNAP
Offensive Lineman, 6-2, 285, Smith Center, Kansas
TROY HASSEBROEK *
Split End, 6-4, 220, Lincoln High
DAN HENNINGS
Wing Back/Split End, 6-0, 175, Omaha Westside
CASEY HUGHES
Fullback, 6-1, 210, Scotia, Nebraska
RICHARD HUGHES
Defensive Lineman, 6-5, 330, Winchester, Kentucky
PAUL KASTL *
Fullback, 5-10, 205, Lincoln Pius X
JOHN KLEM *
Split End, 6-3, 185, Lincoln East
SCOTT KOETHE *
Offensive Lineman, 6-5, 290, Central City, Nebraska
DAVID KOLOWSKI *
Offensive Lineman, 6-5, 265, Millard West
PAUL KOSCH
Defensive Back, 5-11, 180, Humphrey, Nebraska
ADAM LECHTENBURG
Defensive Back, 5-10, 175, Butte, Nebraska
JEREMY LYMAN
Rush End, 6-3, 200, Salt Lake City, Utah
JOSH LYMAN
Split End, 6-1, 185, Salt Lake City, Utah
STEPHEN MANNING
Defensive Lineman, 6-1, 270, Knoxville, Tennessee

CHRIS MORAN
Defensive Back, 5-10, 180, Walkersville, Maryland (Junior)
JEFF NELSON
Defensive Lineman, 6-7, 260, Superior, Nebraska
ANDREW OFFNER
Defensive Lineman, 6-4, 260, Red Cloud, Nebraska
TYLER RAUENZAHN
I-Back, 5-10, 190, Colorado Springs, Colorado
KYLE RINGENBURG *
Rush End, 6-4, 220, Elkhorn, Nebraska
SCOTT SHANLE *
Linebacker, 6-2, 220, St. Edward, Nebraska
LEIF SIDWELL
Offensive Lineman, 6-5, 270, Kearney, Nebraska
JEMOND SMITH
Linebacker, 6-0, 190, Kenner, Louisiana
LUKE SMITH
Linebacker, 6-1, 225, York, Nebraska
AARON TERPENING *
Defensive Back, 5-11, 175, North Salem, Oregon
TYRONE UHLIR
Fullback, 6-0, 210, Battle Creek, Nebraska
JUSTIN VALENCIA
Offensive Lineman, 6-5, 270, Lincoln Pius X
MIKE WILFORD
Offensive Lineman, 6-4, 270, Stevensville, Michigan
COLIN WILLS
Rush End, 6-2, 230, Omaha Burke
STEVE ZIEMBA
Offensive Lineman, 6-5, 300, Omaha Burke

For more information, pictures, documents and memorabilia, please visit the book's website at www.huskerstories.com

About the Author

David Kolowski was born and raised in Omaha, Nebraska. After helping the Millard West Wildcats reach the state playoffs in the second and third years of the school's existence, the University of Nebraska at Lincoln recruited him as a walk-on offensive lineman and long snapper.

Through good fortune, David was able to make it through five years on the team without serious injury or surgery (many others weren't so lucky). All the while, he kept this journal for the whole five years.

Since 2002, he has been editing and refining this journal, all while finishing his undergrad studies, working in sales for a year with 2nd Wind Exercise Equipment, and is now currently back in school at the Palmer College of Chiropractic.

David is married to the former Lauren Poole of Axtell, Nebraska. The couple lives in Davenport, IA where they both are attending classes at Palmer. David also works as a substitute teacher in the Davenport Community Schools.

Printed in the United States
68074LVS00001B/61-465

9 781425 962425